Books by
MILTON MAYER

IF MEN
WERE ANGELS

IF MEN
WERE ANGELS

Milton Mayer

New York

ATHENEUM

1972

To the memory of

JOSEF HROMÁDKA

A. J. MUSTE

NORMAN WHITNEY

"In heaven, methinks, there is laid up a pattern of such a city, which he who desires may behold and, beholding, take up his abode there. But whether such a city exists, or ever will, is no matter; for he will live after the manner of that city. . . ."

PLATO, *The Republic*

ACKNOWLEDGMENTS

BITS AND PIECES of these essays—in some cases large pieces —have been published in other form in *Christian Century, Harper's, The Progressive,* and *Saturday Review.* The sections on "Death" and "The New Man" are based on two essays published in *The Great Ideas Today,* edited by Robert M. Hutchins and Mortimer J. Adler, and are reprinted with permission of Encyclopaedia Britannica, Inc. "Man *v.* the State" was first published as an Occasional Paper of the Center for the Study of Democratic Institutions. Part of "The Young: Their Cause and Cure" was published in *Humanistic Education and Western Civilization: Essays for Robert M. Hutchins,* edited by A. A. Cohen (New York: Holt, Rinehart & Winston, 1964), and is reprinted here with the permission of the publisher.

I am greatly indebted to the many friends who have read parts of this book in manuscript, among them Mortimer J. Adler, Harry S. Ashmore, Ivan von Auw, Jr., Robert Barton, Simon Michael Bessie, Otto Bird, William Brandon, Catherine Carver, Clifton Fadiman, John Fischer, Ruth Hammen, John D. Harms, Bobbie Harms, Richard Haven, Francis Heisler, John H. Hicks, Robert M. Hutchins, John Jensen, Arthur L. H. Rubin, Morris H. Rubin, Isadore Silver, Leone Stein, Harlan Watkins, Peter Wolff, and the late Edward Reed. I have imposed on them all, but none so brutally as I have these twenty-five years on the companion of my bosom.

M. M.

Contents

III   THE THEORY AND PRACTICE OF DEATH

IV   THE YOUNG: THEIR CAUSE AND CURE

INTRODUCTION

Life Without Father

> Hooray, hooray,
> My father's gonna get hung.
> Hooray, hooray,
> The dirty son-of-a-gun.
> He was very mean to me
>   when I was very young;
> Now I'll get even with my father.
>
> *—Plain song to the tune of*
> *"Marching Through Georgia"*

"MORRIS," said Ma, "you have got to lay down the law to that boy," whereupon Pa said, "Boy, do I have to take the strap to you?" "No, sir," I said. "Then do as your mother tells you," said Pa.

Pa spake (or, as the New English Bible puts it, spoke) as one having authority, and not as the scribes like Old-Lady-Kelly-with-the-Cast-Iron-Belly-and-Eyes-in-the-Back-of-Her-Head, who occupied the highest seat in the Fifth Grade Temple of the Edmund Burke Elementary School on Calumet Avenue in Chicago. Old Lady Kelly was authoritarian, but she had no authority. All she ever taught me was the only thing that City Hall ever teaches anybody: disestablishmentarianism. Pa had authority, and if I should be willing and obedient I would eat the good of the land, but if I should refuse and rebel I would be devoured: for the mouth of my Old Man had spoken it. The Voice from the Whirlwind.

Before Pa was—the Voice from the Whirlwind—there was Ma. Ma knew, and knew why. Ma knew why I had to brush my teeth, keep my mackinaw buttoned up, and take my Castoria. Ma knew why, and I didn't. If she should ever be dead (Ma *dead?*) and Pa

(Pa *dead?*) was not there to lay down the law, I would lose my teeth, catch my death of cold, and cry out with the gripes. And when she died, I did.

Wear your rubbers.

Gosh, Ma.

Don't gosh me. Wear your rubbers.

Why do I have to wear my rubbers?

Because I say so, that's why.

(Or, to my big brother, *I want you to take care of your little brother this afternoon. Gosh, Ma, why do I always have to take care of* him? *Because I say so, that's why.*)

So the laying down of the law prepared me for the Laying Down of the Law.

The Laying Down of the Law was done one block east and three blocks north of the Edmund Burke School, at Sinai Temple. The Lawgiver sat in the foyer of Sinai Center, where we went to Sunday school. In His right hand He held the Law written in what the Micks and the Wops and the Jigaboos called Yiddish. He was big enough to be God—as big as George Washington at the entrance of Washington Park—and He sat on a throne like God and not on a bony old green horse like the Father of God's Country.

He was an old man with a long beard, and He failed and faltered not, neither did He sleep nor slumber. (I have heard since that He was a replica of Michelangelo's Moses, but I don't believe it.)

So grew I, and so grew you, our little spirits crushed, not by the authoritarianism of Old Lady Kelly or City Hall, but by the authority of Pa and Ma and God on His throne in Sinai Center. It was not that we loved the authority—or even abode it when it wasn't looking—but that we knew it for authority. (In Europe the peasants took off their hats when the Emperor's carriage went by *empty.*)

So grew we all, in ancient days; all of us, in ancient days, except for the little boy who stood in the puddle of icy water on a March morning of 1910 or so, his Pa beside him, and his Pa was Professor Dewey, and a man came along and said to Professor Dewey, "John, you'd better get that boy out of the puddle, or you'll have a sick boy," and Professor Dewey spake (or spoke, or Spock) and said, "I know. I'm trying to get him to *want* to get out."

To *want* to get out of the puddle.

And not *because I say so.*

So grew we up and old. And each night we left the world a little worse than we found it, and ourselves no better. And so did the prelates and the presidents and their packagers, the wisdom of our wise men hidden and our wise men as fools. So grew we old, and free, free to take our Castoria (or take care of our little brother), equally free not to; free to get out of the puddle if we wanted to, equally free to wallow in it.

Free because God is dead (and not just Pa and Ma and the Emperor).

He failed and faltered. He sleeps and slumbers, the God of Abraham, Isaac, and Jacob; the stone God in the foyer, stone dead.

Who cares, except for a few clerics (and they are busy kicking the clerical habit)? What had He ever done for us—especially lately? Omnipotent? Then why didn't He get us out of the puddle? Omniscient? Then why didn't He let us know what would happen to us if we didn't want to? Omnipresent? Then why did He let the wicked prosper and the righteous suffer? Omniprovident? Then why did He let the young ravens go unfed in Biafra, Bangla Desh, and where all else? (Even the Devil takes care of his own.)

Was He really the stethoscope at the secret heart, Who had every boudoir bugged and Who caught me in the act every time I liberated a penny from Ma's old purse for licorice, every time I foxed Old Lady Kelly with the answers gummed under my desk, every time I reported in sick and went to the ball game, every time I had a go at my neighbor's wife, every time I outsmarted City Hall? The things I got away with—still do—nobody will ever have me up for because they are so fast forgotten that they do not need to be forgiven. If He's dead now, and not just doggo, life is one perfect crime after another.

Take Me from Your Leader.

And watch me go.

Why not?

What had He ever done for us except take His Bible to us (like Pa's strap) and make authoritarian personalities out of us, and satisfy us with our lowly (or highly) lot, and forbid us the divine dissatisfaction that got us where we are today?

Where are we today?

Without a venerable God we look for a venerable man. Without Big Daddy we have got Big Brother. Free for a while, until our free world burst with freedom and Big Brother moved into the abhorred vacuum. And still in the puddle.

But at least God is dead. (Look who's talking.)

A little nervously, Nellie (for the fear of the Lord is the beginning of wisdom), we repair to the obituary notices to see if we can find out just Who or What He was and what He had on the ball, and how He lived, and lived so long and spooked so many. And how He died. And

how much He cut up at (as the London lawyers say), and Whom
He left by way of close relatives, and (hadn't He said that we were
the spitting image of Him?) whether He mentioned us in His will.
(If so, His will be done.)

But He has always been dead. Dead to Cain and the Pharaoh and
Antipas and Caligula. Always dead to the fabled few, dead now to the
fabled many in the fabled city of Demos. Dead wherever and whenever men marveled at their power and their pyramids and, marveling,
mistook their small part of His unaccountable freedom for the whole
of it and took to venerating their own beards.

Even under the false authority of despots the sorrows of this life
were still sometimes endurable and the agonies of society sometimes
manipulable. The mysteries were sometimes acceptable in the illusion
that in some Potsdam or Petersburg there was someone who knew
what he was doing, some *Little* Father of His People. But with God
dead died the despots whose fraudulent claim to authority was their
divine right to it; done down, along with the pork-chop popes with
whose shades they burned and froze in Dante's Hell. Then were men
free at last to wear no man's collar and no God's yoke and to install
their own government by ritualizing men like themselves (who sur-
prised them by turning out to be men like themselves). The false
authority of majoritarianism put Socrates to death and apotheosized
Hitler—and many a Socrates, and many a Hitler, before and since
and between.

"All Power to the People" is a tardy tocsin. The day of Demos
crescent, meridian, crepuscular, and Man still in the puddle, and the
puddle rises around him. But if Demos doesn't know, who does? If
the men of Demos disagree, who is there but the strongest man among
them to say, *Because I say so?* Instead of dissipating when its traditional sources were deposed, authority resettled itself in the hands
of men recognizing no superior above them or among them. But
Demos still had to have an apparatus—and a hand on its controls.
And from him whom Demos deputized there was no need of appeal:
Was he not one of our own, a mere man like ourselves?

But mere men (and we are all democratically mere) are uncertain
and their sentiments undependable. They do not have the detachment that gave a universal character to the old repositories. Their
apprehension of the truth is relative to their local situations, and
(there being no apprehension but men's) truth itself is seen to be
relative—ultimately in the moral order but immediately in the political. Irrepressible conflict is the necessary consequence of the confrontation of politicians having no authority over them all. They com-

mand unreliable followings; abroad (and among their enemies at home) they are detested and even despised. The fear of the Führer is not the same kind of fear as the fear of the Lord.

Thus has man, not truth, made man free, and thus has his liberation disappointed his hopes. The last of the pretenders to divine right in Russia and in Germany were spectacularly capricious absolutists; but they were models of stability and moderation, even of constitutionality, compared with the mere men who overturned their thrones. When the unanswerables must be answered (since men will not be put off by mere men's saying, *Because I say so*) and one mere man's answer is as good as another's, the validation of authority depends upon the number of votaries it can get and hold by magnetism and terror in combination; and magnetism soon or late loses its magnetic attraction.

Demos shucked his durable despotisms and got quixotic (and harder) despotisms in their place. Refusing to answer to the rudder, he answers at last to the rock. He is frightened now as he was never frightened when he knew the fear of his Lord or his lords. His bravado is reminiscent of Peter's—the other Peter. The other Peter was a European starling my friend Francis Heisler caught in Hungary long ago. The European starling (as who doesn't know?) can be made to talk if you slit his tongue. So Francis slit Peter's tongue and Peter learned to talk. What he learned to say, because Francis said it to him, was "Don't be afraid, Peter." One day Francis came home from school and saw that the cat had knocked Peter's cage down and broken it open and was swallowing Peter, and from the cat's throat came the words, "Don't be afraid, Peter."

Man's confidence in himself rose and fell with the Greeks and revived with the Renaissance. It seems to have ended with Auschwitz and Hiroshima and My Lai. (We know now what free men are free to do.) It probably ended a generation earlier, at Verdun, but it persisted (for another few years) in an America far from the ruins of Europe. Pessimism (or apathy, which is predigested pessimism) is pervasive now, and the characteristic hope (itself waning) is that things will get no worse; at best, that some part of the status quo can be held when it shouldn't be or recaptured when it can't be. We are wistful, in America now, about the "positive values" of the Great Depression as the midwife of an aborted new beginning, in Europe now about the stability (never mind the injustice) before and even between the Great Wars. Human progress is no longer axiomatic; it is no longer so much as an interesting hypothesis.

Authority discarded for freedom, and authoritarianism risen in its place; relativism triumphant over the old absolutism and the new absolutism triumphant over relativism—it is against this desponding background that these four essays raise the questions that man, on his own now, did not need to raise when he wasn't. (Or when, like Job, he raised them, was willing, like Job, to take *Because I say so* for an answer.) I think of two other issues (but only two) of the magnitude of the four examined here. One is Woman—a subject from which a strong man shrinks this season. The other is War. As the institutionalization of violence, war appears in all of the essays here; as the mystique of tribalism, in "Man v. the State" and "The New Man"; as the fulfillment of the "death wish," in "The New Man" and in "The Theory and Practice of Death"; as the milk of old men, in "The Young" (there, too, as the finest flower of science); and as the nature of the beast, in "The New Man" and in "Man v. the State."

In his horror of being taken for a tractarian, the essayist affects a dispassion with which neither he nor any other man is blessed. I know better than to tell myself that my being over sixty does not color (I do not say jaundice) my attitudes toward the young, toward death, toward the vision of the new man. And my treatment of the state, if it is not conditioned by my spavined condition, is certainly colored by my having been a ravening pacifist since I was thirty and a ravening socialist since I was twenty. But I have not mistaken man for God (or even for Pa). I have in my time carried, and I still carry, the fight sedately to City Hall in respect to military service, war taxes, and loyalty oaths: the man in the Brooks Brothers hair shirt.

To the extent that these essays are animate, they are animated by the issue of authority. My own position on that issue is something of an artful dodge (or what I have learned in the sere to call a cop-out); no more so, however, than Pascal's suggestion that a wager on God's existence is indicated by the wagerer's having nothing to lose. In the course of my hoofing I have performed as a pulpiteer on many an occasion and in many a land, and my friends, who tend to be scoffers, sometimes ask me if I *really* believe in God. My answer, now as ever, is "Who else?" *Faute de mieux.*

The nice thing about God as a man's last resort is that he is spared the storms of evangelism. He is in no more danger of Billy Graham than he is of being Billy Graham. I know enough about Billy Graham, and George Washington, yes, and Moses, to know that they all of them at their worst bear some perceptible resemblance to Milton Mayer. No man who resembles Milton Mayer is worthy of my veneration.

Men believe because they are reduced to believing, and they will take an unworkable faith (and have) if they will not take a workable. I know (and this is about all I need to know) that I would just as soon not encounter the stone God in the foyer of Sinai Center immediately before or after the perpetration of a dirty trick; but I have long since known (ever since my Fifth Year stretch at the Edmund Burke School) how to shake all my mortal pursuers. Aware that an apostolic penalty attaches to the diffident, I am none the less comfortable with my cop-out. I do not know if God is dead. But I know that He'd better not be.

Deerfield, Massachusetts
1971

I

The New Man

If we are going to fail because we believe
in man's ability to improve, then we will
fail.   *—Fidel Castro*

. . . and not breed one work that wakes.
Mine, O thou lord of life, send my roots
rain.   *—Gerard Manley Hopkins*

1: Operation Bootstraps

B i s h o p Professor K. H. Ting of Nanking Theological Seminary in Communist China was speaking of his country and I heard his words with (as my mother would say) my own ears: "Beggary, robbery, prostitution, gambling, and all other kinds of vices and evils have been done away with forever." * "This," I mumbled, with my own lips, "is the neatest trick of any week since the first."

And unlike the first, it had been achieved not by the Lord God Jehovah but by man, and by avowedly and ardently atheistic man at that.

To be sure, the president of the American Chemical Society had just suggested that science might find ways "to improve the breed of man himself." To be sure, too, the President of the United States had just appointed a National Commission to "banish crime." † But the Marxist-Leninists have always claimed the New Man for their own, with, however, the modest concession that his appearance awaited the supervention of the New Order in all its fullness. I had heard

---

* On the wall of a restaurant in the Chinese resort town of Peitaho, the correspondent of the Toronto *Globe and Mail* (August 23, 1969) read the following words: "People of the world, be courageous, dare to fight, defy difficulties and advance wave upon wave. Then the whole world will belong to the people. Monsters of all kinds shall be destroyed."

† The Commission was appointed in 1965. Five years later, with crime still unbanished, another President told the U.S. Congress that "the moment is at hand to put an end to hunger in America itself for all time." In his *Mao's Great Revolution* (New York, 1971), the Los Angeles *Times'* China correspondent Robert S. Elegant says that Mao came to power as "a total idealist, and his goal was Utopia. He would allow neither institutional nor humanitarian considerations to turn him aside from his mission—perfecting all humanity."

Academician Fyodor Konstantinov announce that human greed
would be eliminated by Communism. I had heard the Communist
Party of the Soviet Union assert that the New Man will combine
"spiritual wealth, moral purity, and a perfect physique." But I had
not heard that these wonders were already upon us; and to hear it
not from a Red protagonist but from a Christian prelate—I half expected him to add that where he came from it was no longer necessary
to marry or burn.

Still I could not believe Brother Ting. As a professor he would
know the truth, and as a priest he would say it. But neither could I
quite believe him.

Not because I knew better, though I *had* read that many Chinese,
resisting removal to the farms, had turned to urban thievery to support themselves; that the "capitalist black wind" of corruption had
been found blowing yuan into the pockets of some provincial Party
officials; and that a medical conference had been called in Canton to
discuss rising prostitution. No; the reason I could not quite believe
Brother Ting was his use of the word "forever."

Now "forever" used by secular personages is staggering enough;
used by an episcopal personage of the Anglican cloth, committed as
such to the Thirty-Nine Articles (especially Articles 9–18 on Sin and
Grace), it is more staggering still, suggesting, as it does, man's power
to regenerate his long-lost innocence when he has not, up to now,
been able to regenerate so much as his short intestine. Either Brother
Ting had come to the brink of blasphemy or the New Man promised
by the Communists (and by other fanaticists before them) was here.
And if the New Man was here, all shipshape and shriven, his arrival
would have the most serious eschatological consequences (apart from
its effect on the perquisites and emoluments of the episcopate).

I was peculiarly sensitive to the Bishop Professor's words, and to
an exact translation of them, because I have given over the better
part of the past twenty years to land-cruising ceaselessly, and inquir-
ing urgently, and watching persistently, at home and abroad, for signs
of a New Heaven and a New Earth. The last fifteen of these twenty
I have gone to and fro in the Communist countries where I had heard,
but never from a bishop, that the New Man was to be seen emerging.

And high time. As the post-atomic age approached, there seemed
to be arising a consciousness, if not a consensus, that the present
arrangement of things was unsatisfactory. There needed to be another
way for men to live, without so much anger, pride, and despair, and
for men to live together without perpetual disorder. There needed to
be a New World, and, it seemed, soon; but if a New World, first a

New Man. It would never do to commission the Old Man, y-clept the Old Adam, to do the fashioning; *ab nihilo nihil.*

Should my investigations uncover the unmistakable footprint of the New Man, I would have to confess, and candidly report, that the Old Man was done for. How would he, with his anger, pride, and despair, ever cope with the combination of spiritual wealth, moral purity, and a perfect physique? How, too, would the Old World, recurrently shredded and patched, and patched and shredded, compete, or even long coexist, with a New World fashioned of such invincible materials? If Communism were to produce the New Man—or so much as conduce, or even consent, to his production—it would conquer the West however and wherever the West tried to hold the line. But if not, it would be plain that the Communism jig was already up, its epitaph pronounced by the last of the Bonapartes when he heard of the Paris Commune: "So they're turning over the dungheap again." In replacing "mine" and "thine" with "ours," Communism presupposes the New Man and is unthinkable without him. Without him its cornerstone collapses and nothing but naked tyranny shores up the system in which, according to its philosopher, "the free development of each is the condition for the free development of all."

The notion—nostrum, if you will—of the New Man antedates Marx. It all but antedates Eden. It may have been the very cause of human history: "Ye shall be as gods," said the Serpent. It may have been the beginning, and it may be the end, of mankind: In the prehistoric Adam, Man became Old, and in the posthistoric Second Adam, the Christ of the Pentecost, the Old Man becomes New.

But the notion has never enjoyed any great respectability *within* history. New processes utilize new sources of energy to produce new marvels—but Goethe's apostrophe abides: *der Mensch bleibt Mensch:* Man remains Man. True, he has shown himself to be a sharp fellow and even, on occasion, a stout fellow—as the Devil discovered when he tried Job. But in *Faust* (some millennia after Job) the Devil was able to report that "earth's little god retains his same old stamp and ways"—an assessment generally confirmed from age to age by mundane observers (prior even to August 1, 1914, when the German Socialists voted war credits to the Emperor and their French comrades entered a government of "sacred union"). The face of the world—*sí.* The heart of the man—*no.*

Notion, nostrum, dream, or idyll, the New Man is somehow un-American. Your American glories (and with reason) in being practical. Oh, he dreams; but he dreams that he walked the moon and gets up and does it. For him the wild blue yonder is the shortest distance between two points. Vision is the corner grocer's nationwide chain of supermarkets. Philosophy is what consoles you when your wife elopes with the color-TV repairman, and poetry is both for, and by, the birds. The world sends him its theoretical physicists and he converts their theory into atomic power.

His politics is who gets what, how, when, and where. Compare the hippodrome of a national party convention in America with the national congress of the Communist Party of the Soviet Union and the latter's interminable documents published months in advance for public discussion and debate (if not for alteration). *Doctrine* affects the everyday life of every Russian, while the theme of the Great Debate between Presidential candidates Kennedy and Nixon is the defense of Matsu and Quemoy—which are never heard of again.

Let an American get off dead doctrinal center and America cries, "Extremist." Away with your vapors and your vaporings. The stuff that dreams are made of is *Sprengstoff*—explosive. Keep your feet on the ground and your eye on the ball. When an American enthusiast like Harry Hopkins promises to "make America over," the wholesome reaction of his compatriots is "Ah, come off it." One of the first Soviet books translated into English, *Red Russia's Primer,* began with the words "We have a plan. In America they have no plan"; a half century later U.S. Housing Secretary George Romney said, "The Communists have a plan. . . . They have the initiative in the contest between ideologies."

No word is more alien to the American than "ideology." His eighteenth-century forebears may have had one. He neither has one nor needs one, and as for his forebears, he is willing to let bygones be bygones. His ideological immunity may be dangerous; it leaves him peculiarly susceptible to ideological negations like *anti*-Communism. But dreams are dangerous, too, and none more dangerous than that of the New Man. What's wrong with the old one? Better take the tried for an answer—it works, doesn't it?—than the true for a question. Leave well enough alone; even if it isn't well enough, leave it alone.

Now and again the hungover American, even the Man Who Has Everything, has his longings. He cannot comfortably endure the self he knows at its worst (which even in America is at least some of the time). Reason and history tell him that he won't be better. But he would be. Soon. Soon—as Augustine says—but not yet. On the other hand, longing is the Russian's long suit—and for centuries the only suit he had. Every time was his time of trouble. His idea of the practical was a sigh. To ponder a poem, pray half the night, break his head on an algebra—this is your Russian. To stand transfixed in front of the local chess shop, where an end-game problem is set up in the window—this is your Russian. Not to build Sputnik or the Trans-Siberian Railroad but to ask, "What is man?"—this is your veriest Russian. And to proceed at once to the nature of the soul, above all, of the Russian soul, is the veriest distillation of your veriest Russian. Your Russian, Turgenev's Russian, his forgotten feet freezing at the end of the field at the end of a winter's day, asks himself the All-un-American question: "What am I?" *

This is the visionary, lettered or unlettered, drunk or sober, who responds to the vision. The visionary, no matter how mad the vision, is irrepressible by the nonvisionaries, who ought to have found out by now that the law of the race track is inviolable: You can't beat a horse with no horse. At the battle of Pleime in Vietnam, the American commandant said of the Vietcong, "I wish we knew what they are drugging them with to make them fight like that. They are highly motivated and highly dedicated. I wish we could recruit them." Just as he who suffers external oppression long enough and hard enough will one day rebel, whatever the odds, so he who suffers internal oppression will one day seize hold of the unlikeliest vision. The former may latch on to a profane messiah. The latter banks on the intervention of *Deus* (like a good Christian) or *machina* (like a good Marxist). In either case he will have a clean break—not a reformation or a reconstruction but a *re-creation*. He will lie down to sleep tonight as he is, to awaken tomorrow as he might (or even as he might not) be: reborn.

But even in Christian conversion man grows in grace infused little by little. The Apostles themselves came haltingly and waveringly to be New Men in Christ; and as long as they were men they could and did backslide. Before the age of universal fire the penalty was universal flood. Before Noah was the Deucalion of Greek legend, in which Zeus (Prometheus dissenting) engulfed the world to replace

* ". . . The Russian conversation, however, soon gropes toward fundamental attitudes, states of mind, the nature of the person rather than his occupation, and this is something we Americans do not know how to talk about; it verges on 'philosophy,' which to most normally educated Americans is what history was to Henry Ford—'bunk.' It is perhaps the basic reason why Chekhov, for example, is so hard to perform outside Russia, and especially difficult in the United States. To us the characters seem vague, disconnected from one another, strangely abstract rather than real. We are much more interested in what a thing is, how it works, and very little interested in what it means. We are the triumph of technology. The irony is that the Russian aspires to hard, materialist, dialectically sound explanations of process—the American style—when in fact he is extraordinarily quick to idealize and to reach for general principles. Nothing could be more alien to the American."—Arthur Miller, *In Russia, Harper's*, September 1969, p. 37.

the Old Man with a New. But Noah, like Deucalion, left Man as he was. Thus the good news of Christ at Christmas. Thus, too, the good news of Marx in October, for the bourgeois flood had left the property relationship as it always had been. In October (says the Communist Party of the Soviet Union, *officially*) "the creation of a new world began."

2: The Nature of the Beast, If Any

THE NEW MAN is the only issue between the totalitarian Communists and the parliamentary capitalists; what else? Is there anything that, in their season, the one have done that the other haven't, including, along with the godless Communists, the Christian capitalists who, in the name of the Holy Infant, have yielded to no Saracen in the fervor with which they have robbed, raped, burned, and butchered their kind? You may say that they have private enterprise to quarrel about, but if the issue on that head is not the New Man it is nothing; the capitalists invariably turn their deficit ventures (such as war and the mails) over to public enterprise, and the Communists are even now invoking the enterprising privateers of the market economy and proclaiming, in the words of Professor Liberman of Kharkov, that "the higher the profits, the greater the efficiency." *

* While investment, price, and wage structures are still centrally controlled in the Soviet Union, the emphasis on enterprise initiative (initiated by Khrushchev in 1965) by 1970 covered commercial outlets representing 72 percent of the consumer goods produced and 80 percent of the retail earnings. So well entrenched had the reforms become that Aleksandr M. Birman, a colleague of Professor Liberman, felt free to deliver a public attack on "the theoreticians divorced from practical economic work" who were worried about "preserving the purity of socialist society from the dangers of bourgeois sin." (New York Times, March 5, 1970.) The "bourgeois sin" of limited private enterprise, introduced by Yugoslavia after its break with the Comintern in 1948, has proceeded even faster in Hungary than it has in the U.S.S.R. In 1970, the third year of the Hungarian reform program, the prices of more than one-third of all retail items were uncontrolled, and prices of many other basic goods were partially determined by supply and demand. In 1969 Hungarian wage levels were made freely negotiable (ibid., October 14, 1969), and in Poland "most of agriculture is still in private hands" (ibid., December 15, 1969). But the Soviet-

Of course the Communist economists use the word "profit" equivo-
cally. The bonus principle, in both production and distribution, has
always been as much part and parcel of all the Communist economies
as the quota principle, and the new "capitalism without capitalists"
simply ties it (and pricing with it) closer to consumer demand and
therefore to managerial discretion. The current accentuation of pe-
cuniary incentive—which isn't *profit* at all—may be a sign that Communism is sacrificing the New Man to the hard Western reality of
original sin, but it may just as well mean that the New Man is so far
along in his development that he can be trusted with socially salubrious techniques which, in the Old Man, are animated by naked
cupidity. So, too, the current political and artistic liberation: Let the
burgeoning New Man travel from Budapest or Bucharest to Vienna
and see its depravity and reject it for himself, or hear its degenerate
tom-toms in his own cabarets, or read and see, or even write and
paint, the morbid existentialism of a world whose only appeal to him
has been its inaccessibility.

The current revisionism (as the Chinese call it) does not necessarily mean that the ex-prisoners of starvation have proved to be incorrigible gluttons, still less that Marxist-Leninism is going back to
the drawing board. We used to hear it said, prior to the late Mr.
Khrushchev's fall, that Communism was so unalterably monolithic
that it precluded a peaceable change-over of rule; so, too, the wish
that may be father to the thought that the Communists are surrendering now on their fundamental "anthropology," their idea of Man.
Temporizing, perhaps, and certainly improvising; but given their
axiom that all ideas but one, their own idea of Man, are the products

---

bloc country which had gone farthest—and fastest—in this direction was
Czechoslovakia between January and August 1968, and the Russian invasion
of August 20 is thought to have been motivated in part by the "extremist" economic program of the then Deputy Premier in the Dubček government, Dr.
Ota Šik. The Russians forced the economically distressed Czechs to abandon
their projected reforms and return to a rigidly centralized economy tied to
Soviet raw materials for heavy industry. Shortly before the invasion, the
Czechs, having got no reply from the Russians to their request for a half-
billion-dollar loan in "hard" currency, for the purchase of modern equipment
in the West, had threatened to borrow in the West. (The defiant Rumanians
were doing more than 50 percent of their business with Western countries, and
continued to increase it.)
  There is no discernible correspondence between economic liberalization and
political liberty, though the two did coincide in Czechoslovakia. The post-
Khrushchev "hard line" was, if anything, drawn harder as the economic reforms proceeded; in the U.S.S.R. the persecution of deviationist writers, scientists, and students was steadily intensified; Hungarian censorship, after several
years of relative relaxation, was reintensified in late 1969 (and no Western
correspondent was allowed to live in the country); and in spite of its economic
deviationism and its resistance to the Russians at the time of the Czech invasion, and thereafter, the Bucharest dictatorship did not in the least unbend
politically.

of objective conditions, there is, and always was, no orthodox reason why they should not shift ground with the shift of objective conditions (as witness the sudden "opening" of China to the United States in 1971).

A fairly full field investigation of Communist life does in fact turn up more than a few faint and wavering traces—nothing so much as a certain footprint—of the New Man's progress amid the unregenerate hankerings of the Old. There being no Jove in Marxist-Leninism, there is of course no Minerva; the New Man was never expected to appear full-panoplied except by some of the early enthusiasts. Several years ago Mr. Khrushchev prophesied that "the present generation of Soviet people will live in Communism"—a pronouncement almost as heady as Bishop Ting's. For a year or so his words were seen, if not looked at, on posters throughout the Red world, but the posters disappeared even before Mr. Khrushchev, who appears now to have been a late-blooming early enthusiast.

The dogma necessarily suffers from chicken-and-egg complaint. How will we know, until we have Communism, whether man is capable of being a Communist? And how will we have Communism until we have Communists? Like all dogmatists similarly afflicted, the Bolsheviks of October cut the knot by revolution and have gone on cutting it on the motto "Nothing ventured, everything lost." The most that could be expected was that the New Man would show himself little by little upon the stage set by the founding fathers, who could bring the drama so far forward, and no farther than would be congenial to his development. Until the goal should be reached—Communism, with all things common—the New Man could be expected to be seen only in fitful glimpses ever more pervasive and distinct; and nothing much more than that. The first, and perhaps even the second, generation would have to pass: "It will be a long time before we have Communism, and we'll have Communism for a long time before we have Communists."

The intrepid investigator thus has his hands full. He has to depend, on the one hand, upon haphazard encounters with both peoples and persons whose historical situations, traditions, and manners are neither his own *nor each other's* and, on the other, upon the necessary partiality of those he talks to. The longer the Westerner lives in the East, the surer he is that social science reflects what the social scientist had for breakfast. The same perspicacious friend in Warsaw whose opinion it is that the plastic lemons in the shops contain imitation juice assures me that the regime's foreign-travel restrictions are politically determined; and another equally perspicacious friend there, who ascribes the travel restrictions to the shortage of foreign currency, is of the opinion that the juice in the lemons is real; and, sure enough, the first friend predicts rain for tomorrow and the second sunshine.

So it is. So it is in Lidice, where we stand, a Czech pastor and I, at the mass grave, and he indicates the great gaunt Cross made of the embers of the murdered village and says, "I wonder how long they'll let it stay there"; and where I stand, a week later, with another Czech pastor, who says, "There it is—above our national monument, above our rulers, our people, and our land." So it is in Budapest, where a beauty, well enough dressed, but aggressively unshaven, says, "I have everything I need; just look at me," and a middle-aged woman, at least as well dressed, with two sisters long since in America, says, "We can't get anything here—nothing, nothing fit for a woman to wear," and a hardy old Communist, who had her vernacular Americanized in the California shipyards during the war, says, "I'm no chicken, of course, but I could use some of the frills I remember. Still, I'd look *decent,* even in California, don't you think?"

So it is in Budapest and in Peoria and in Peking.* To record the overt manifestations of attitudes and plot them and say "There" is comparatively easy. It is a bit harder to draw a bead on the motivation which explains them. My fellow passenger in the day coach to Peoria finishes washing and cleans out the bowl in one of those gents' rooms that does *not* have an inscription asking him to do so in consideration of the next user. I follow him intrepidly from the train and see him, in the public park, pick up another's gum wrapper from the path and, finding no depository for it, carry it home to his own wastebasket, which he himself has to empty. And a little farther on he lights his pipe and, rather than drop the burned match in the street, puts it back in the match box. At last, a man who is fit to be a Communist. And alas, his gabby psychiatrist informs me that he is a compulsive anal-erotic.

Petrov boards the bus in Leningrad or Zdenek the tram in Bratislava—the "honor system" on the Soviet buses and Czech trolleys operates without conductors or collectors—and drops his coin in the box. Hath any man greater love—or does something tell him that

* The American correspondents who were dispatched pell-mell to Peking after the great Ping-pong invitation were uniformly impressed by the apparent dedication of the Chinese people to Maoism, and one of them, Seymour Topping of the New York *Times,* who had been a reporter in Canton from 1946 to 1949, returned to that city to find "the face of society transformed. A new Canton man has emerged. His old verve and individuality seem to have yielded to passivity, but he also obviously lives better and carries himself with restored dignity. . . . The people look well-fed and content but strangely silent and ordered."—New York *Times,* May 24, 1971.

somebody may be looking; or is he a creature of unthinking habit; or is he a self-righteous prig? * Exactly why does the German, when he sees a Keep Off the Grass sign, keep off the grass? (Exactly why doesn't the American?) Why is the Switzer honest (if he is)? Why does the man turn monk or the occasional Quaker leave his door unlocked at night?

A hazardous, and haphazard, hunt, then, for signs that the New Man gestates within the gestating system while the Old Man shrivels like the leaves of a broken branch that still subsists in the tree. Of course, I should recognize the latter sooner than the former, for I know him like the back of my own hand; yea, knowing the back of my own hand, I know him in his every lineament. I recognize him instantly as he reaches for what is his—and for no more than what is his, unless, of course, what is his is threatened, and then he reaches for what adjoins his. I need only hear him say "That's the way the world is" to recognize him, with his reciprocity and his retaliation and his good intentions and his lifelong difficulty in distinguishing surplus and substance. Oh, I know the Old Man.

But I know the New Man too, though he may never yet have been. For the Old Man too has the impulse to do what the New Man does (or will do) and the still stronger impulse to be what the New Man is (or will be). He too obliterates "mine" and "thine" and wills the good of the other, and even of all the others, ahead of his own—and that not seldom. He too has disinterested motions of the brimming heart. But these motions, capricious and spasmodic in the Old Man, are (or will be) as steady as instinct in the New. The Old Man's heroics are the New Man's habit, unprompted by frenzy, unimpeded by prudence.

He will live in community and not in populous solitude around a shopping center. *Pro bono publico* will be neither boast nor bondage, but brotherhood. Of course the Marxists will have him perfect; but he won't be, not as his Father in Heaven is perfect, for he will still be fleshed. But neither will he be the good man we have sometimes seen in our bad societies here (so to say) below; no eccentric, but one like most, if not all, of the rest.† As it will be a matter of a shift in balance

---

* "A [Prague] newspaper noted that under the honor system 40 percent of the people did not pay."—New York *Times,* February 14, 1970.

† ". . . One man opened an artesian well and began giving the water away. Some of those who took his water hauled it a few blocks away and sold it for $1 a gallon."—United Press dispatch from Pass Christian, Mississippi, following the devastation of hurricane Camille in August 1969. Or: "It may not be possible to make the [UN] sanctions [against racist Rhodesia] more effective, since the repeated transfers of goods in normal commerce and the willingness of some foreign traders to evade sanctions for a profit has allowed Rhodesia to continue foreign trade."—New York *Times,* April 12, 1970.

in the society, so, too, in the individual: His otherness will have just
so far have subdued his ownness that the society may be securely
organized on its assumption.

The communist community has been established again and again
—by Christ's own disciples, among others. It piles up its goods, be
they few or many, in the public square, with none to check or reckon
while some come gladly to raise the pile higher and others unhesitant
to diminish it. That pile has been seen historically more than once
(in, for example, the Adamite community of Tábor in fifteenth-
century Bohemia). In symbol it identified the "Bible Communist"
communities of nineteenth-century America and the *Catholic Worker*
and Bruderhofer movements in America (and elsewhere) right now,
as well as the dropout utopias of the young, whose settlements sub-
sist for the most part (not all of them) for a summer season with an
occasional noncommunist handout from home.

The Old Man takes hardhearted heart from the fact that such
communist communities have never endured. He has "all" history
and psychology—and all theology, apart from the Pelagian heresy—
on his side. He sees no evidence that there has ever been a new kind
of man and no reason to suppose that there ever will be. And I can
document his cozy despair from the current annals of the New Man
apostolate: Prior to the Russian invasion of Prague in 1968, the
"Lysenkoist" nursery system, based on the inheritability of acquired
spiritual and intellectual characteristics, was being quietly (very
quietly) dismantled in Czechoslovakia, where, as in Poland, thorough
study disclosed uniformly that (a) the smallest child wants private
possession of the common property—i.e., toys—and (b) the teenage
products of the Lysenkoist nursery are not one whit less self-centered
than the privately reared child. (There have been no studies of this
decisive phenomenon in the U.S.S.R.—at least none that has ever
reached Warsaw.)

But there is that that asserts itself against the evidence that compels the reason. There is the dream, and who has not dreamed of
being new—of being, in a word, a communist? We Old Men know
another law than that in our members. Under that other law we have
lived, every one of us in our households; every one of us as church or
social or civic volunteers, many a Scoutmaster, many a Rotarian,
many a Legionnaire, yes, many a soldier under fire. We know the New
Man we dream of. We are all candidates for communism.

But there is no such communist *society* in Eastern Europe, nor any
indication that such a society is over the farthest horizon—and no
more talk of the state's withering away. The Party in Russia still says

that in the "transition to Communism" (presumably the present) "the sphere of action of the moral factor expands; the importance of the administrative control of human relations diminishes accordingly." Alas, the expansion is not spectacular, the diminution still less so. The investigator need not exert his intrepidity; he need only take a gander at the competitive avidity of all about him, masked or unmasked, for position, privilege, and favor, for New Year's Eve reservations, television sets, and, to be sure, turnips, to realize that he never left home.*

Muscovites clamoring to pay three dollars a pound for midwinter tomatoes (or $5.50 for a chicken) on the uncontrolled "peasant market"; three times as many paid orders for cars as the Czechs can produce; gray Communist Budapest a riot of non-necessities like whipped cream and espresso bars, cosmetics from Yugoslavia, scarves from Spain, and cameras from Japan; dun Communist Prague jumping with rock 'n' roll, while the largest electric sign (plugging children's books) in bullet-pocked Wenceslaus Square is dwarfed at last by an advertisement for Cinzano. There are, of course, things that money can't buy, there as here, and a few (remarkably few) things that enough money can buy here that it can't buy there. But pearls? Swine? Furs? Diamonds? Perfumes? The things that money, and money alone, has always bought everywhere, in every society and kind of society, can be bought with money, and only with money, in the Communist capitals.

It's the sime (so the Cockney jingle goes) the wide wurruld over. So never let it be thought that the luxury hotels in the New Order do not have "sanitized" drinking glasses, cellophane-wrapped, in the rooms; they do. Never let it be thought, either, that the clamor for the follies of bourgeois life fails to find a voice—and in high places— in the Soviet Union after three generations of rising young Communists who want to go to libraries, listen to lectures, or sit home with their parents. Says *Pravda:* "Is this boulevard"—Moscow's Broadway, Gorky Street—"hospitable? No— we have too few cafés, restaurants, and snack bars. . . . Young people don't want to go to libraries, or listen to lectures, or sit home with their mothers and fathers every evening. They want to be out among people. A street

* "The scene"—in a modern department store in Budapest—"might have been at Ohrbach's or Korvette's. . . . At a crowded new deluxe restaurant the band played American popular music almost exclusively . . . the cafés feature floor shows complete with striptease. . . . A Pole here on a semi-official visit remarked, 'One would not think he was in a socialist country.' "— Budapest dispatch in the New York *Times,* November 12, 1969. "The great fact in the Soviet Union today is the fact of getting and spending."—Joseph Kraft in the International *Herald Tribune,* September 17, 1971.

can be very pleasant if it is lively and well lighted with neon lights. . . ."

The report by that early investigator, Lincoln Steffens, that he had seen the future and it worked, was as necessarily premature as it was unnecessarily succinct. Is there a trace, in the Christian world, of the Christians of two thousand years ago who believed that the Kingdom of God was at hand? There is no trace, in the Communist world, of the Communist of fifty years ago who believed that the Kingdom of Man was at hand, that the Revolution would trigger such sociality that the timeless lusts, and the dreary institutions they drew in their train, the police, the prison, the poorhouse, and the palace, among others, would be gone in a day, or a month, or a year. The very memory of that October seems to have vanished.

But what an October it must have been! And what, even vanished, a memory! It was deluged with blood and brutality—as when had the world been otherwise?—but it was to be for the last time. Leon Trotsky was no millenary fanatic and no bishop. He was the Revolution's Chief of Staff. But as late as 1925, falling from power, he was still transported by the vision that "man will become immeasurably stronger, wiser, and subtler; his body will become more harmonized, his movements more rhythmic, his voice more musical. . . . The average human type will rise to the heights of an Aristotle, a Goethe, or a Marx." (In his transport he ignored the fact that Aristotle, Goethe, and Marx, having risen to those heights, themselves had no such vision.)

The early Communists would have called each other "brother" had not the Christians (and the bourgeois trade unions) pre-empted the term. They called each other "comrade." They still do. But they do it now with a formal, sometimes ironical intonation—even, on occasion, and certainly in Budapest since 1956 and in Prague since 1968, with bitter hostility (or so it is said; Party leadership sessions at all levels are as secret as the Pentagon's). The officials of the Communist countries do not live (or even look as though they lived) as comrades. They live, on the whole, as we do, in hierarchy (and in more old-world hierarchy than we Americans do); and their wives stand in line at the shops and stalls less frequently than their chauffeurs. And they regard one another as we do: as men about them, above them, or below them, to be watched, watched for, or watched out for. "Socialism," says the wisest old man I know in Sofia, "is for fools."

Still the intrepid investigator's impression abides that this poor report is not all that there is there—that something outside and entirely

2: *The Nature of the Beast, If Any*   17

apart from the Establishment may be trying to stir in the human depths, in spite of the fact that nothing there (or, for that matter, here) is as good as it was going to be (or is very good at all). I know no man in the East who, behind closed doors or on a woodland walk, sees so much as a glimmer of Trotsky's heavenly city. There are, nevertheless, those who, having lived open-eyed through every disenchantment, refuse to close the book for one and all and put the seal of whole hallucination upon it. But they, by almost their whole number, exceed the Westerners who have that much heart in the West. The investigator sometimes wonders whether the Communists have not, with their slogans, intensified the hunger of the human heart to the point where it is determined to appease itself in terms of those slogans—whether or not the slogans are any more honestly published or their present publishers comprehensive of them.

Of course the intrepid investigator is objective—observant, shrewd, but first of all objective. What makes him think so? What makes him think that he isn't misled by the hunger of *his* Old Man's heart? At the Tashkent airport a native anthropophagus in sweating shirt sleeves is elbowing his way into the Moscow plane, burdened, like the rest of the pasengers and crew, with a net bag of melons in each hand. (Midsummer, and no melons on the market in the capital.) The stewardess tries to persuade him to step aside for a pair of foreign visitors behind him. "These are guests," she says twice, and, when he persists, she says, "Comrade, these are *your* guests," and he steps aside. The New Man or the Old Russian hospitality? (One hears the word "guest," which sounds like the English, murmured all about him as he is pushed to the front in a crowded theater, lecture, or church.) On the street in Kharkov the visitor, finding no receptacle, thoughtfully goes to the curb to knock the dottle out of his pipe, and a man steps up to him and asks him to pick it up—and then takes it from him in a small paper box that he has in his pocket. A New Man —or an officious Ukrainian? In a Kazakstan village, a week after the first American space flight, a villager named his newborn triplets Gagarin, Titov, and Glenn. A New Man, or a space buff who didn't know that there was a Cold War on?

3: Everybody's Business Is Whose?

MAYBE the behavior of the Czechs is easier to interpret than that of the Russians. After all, the Czechs are the most "advanced"—i.e., bourgeois—of all the peoples under Communism, so bourgeois that Czechoslovakian Stalinism was, year in and year out, the toughest of them all and, in 1968, the first of them all to be overthrown (if only temporarily) by popular revolution. In the spring of 1967 there was a series, almost a continuum, of torrential rains in Prague. Everything leaked and the Praguer responded in fine communal—was it Communist?—spirit. Plasterers, plumbers, masons, and carpenters being in perpetual short supply, apartment dwellers banded together to make repairs evenings and weekends, and the city government released brigades of schoolboys to help. It was the kind of response that warms the Communist heart. It even wins grudging admiration from the non-Communists—who seem to have forgotten that it is frequently (perhaps just as frequently) found among capitalists in common calamity. And then one day as if on a signal, the way the vibration of a passing plane sends the "ripe" avalanche down, massive pieces of baroque masonry began falling from the rain-beaten brows of the heavily decorated old buildings in the center city. I don't know how many people were injured. I know that two were killed.

There was, of course, a kind of solemn panic as the gewgaws and gargoyles of centuries came crashing into the streets. But more solemn was the way in which people gathered for several days afterward outside the cordons. They didn't talk much. But they didn't disperse. Something uncommon had happened to the city, but something uncommoner still to the citizens whose lives do not ordinarily provide them much time to stand and stare. A delayed reaction.

I was told about it, still solemnly, by Communists and non-Communists, when I got there a few weeks later and found the whole center city skeletoned with scaffolding. The question had not needed voicing among the people who stood in the street looking up: Who was responsible? Communism's answer did not need voicing, either, and it would have been the same as yours and mine: the Owner. But who was the owner? Communism's answer this time would have been different from yours and mine: Everybody.

This was the answer that the Praguer could not and would not accept. If they were unfamiliar with Plato and Aristotle, they nevertheless delivered themselves of the latter's mordant rejoinder to the former's communist utopia: "Everybody's business is nobody's business." "How could it happen? How could nobody *ever* have inspected those buildings? Before 1948 there would have been somebody somehow responsible—and not just a state inspector, but the owner. He would have kept them in repair because they were valuable property. But now it seemed that nobody had enough reason to care. Nobody lived in them—"They were all shops and offices"—and nobody was making money out of them. Something was falling down—and people felt that it was not just the stone decorations of buildings.

Façade. Façade whose sudden fall pressed home the heart problem of Communism: "everybody's business." It is true that the Saturday-afternoon volunteers for civic cleanup are far more numerous in the East than they are in the West, if they are to be found in the West at all, and neither the pressure nor the recognition accounts wholly for the turnout. True, too, that factory workers, truck drivers, locomotive engineers, and airplane pilots seem to take better care of "their" tools and machines than they do in the West—motivated in part, presumably, by the machinist's pride and in part, to be sure, by self-interest: Equipment is short, and if it breaks down they are off the job until it is running again. Still these activities seem to have a modicum of ownership sense in them. But here, in the heart of Prague, was property which was indeed "everybody's."

There were those Praguer who, it appeared, were asking themselves for the first time if such catastrophes were inherent in the system because man is what he is and not what he is supposed to be or become. Are men capable of making everybody's business their own without just being busybodies, spies, or informers, or aren't they? There is no shortage of block wardens and other such corps of volunteer snoopers (as we would call them). But where are the *commu-*

nists who will take care of the commune without being one way or another paid to do so?

This is the question that is hidden behind the façade. It is never wholly hidden. In one area, at least, it is not hidden at all and can't be: farming. Nowhere in the Communist world is there any mistaking the communized peasant's private plot for the communal. Seen side by side, the contrast between the two pieces of land everywhere tells the eloquent story of "everybody's" business. The day they are mistakable, the one for the other, that day will the New Man have come into his own. But until that day . . .

The early Marxists despaired of what Trotsky called "the anti-collective skull" of the unconsciously proletarian peasant. He and his ancestors might have been 'croppers for centuries, but he would still wiggle his toes in the landlord's mud and talk about "my land." And with plausibility: Hadn't he done everything there was to be done with it except own it? (The industrial worker or white-collar clerk never spoke of "my factory" or "my business"; he knew what was his and, still better, what wasn't.) So many an anti-collective skull had to be broken—many a million, so the legend of the Stalinist 1930s has it—and even so the Communists had to allow the peasant his private plot for his own use. He could tend it only on his own time—after he had done his day's work at "everybody's business" in the collective garden, field, or orchard.

But even the city feller knows that crops don't grow by the clock. The vicissitudes of the weather determine whether, and when, and how big, and how good a crop will be made. A middle-of-the-night hailstorm or a snap frost may ruin a crop unless it is covered, cultivated, or even harvested then and there. The collectivized peasant is awakened by the storm and leaps from his bed—to save the communal crop or his own? Invariably his own. Doesn't it go without saying? Hadn't he finished his day's work in the collective at sundown?

The Communists have been able to do exactly nothing about it. A few years ago the U.S.S.R. tightened the regulations (and radically stepped up the penalties) governing, among other specified types of "parasite," those who "evade socially useful work." In this last catch-all category the decree asserted that "some persons have taken advantage of privileges allowed on collective farms." That was all. The allusion was clearly to farmers who neglected the collective's plot for their own. But there was no subsequent evidence of the decree's application to them, and a few years later the Soviet government liberalized its basic private-plot regulations by making concessions as regards the sale of private produce, the size of private plots, and the availability of seed and fertilizer, presumably (and quite probably) to ease the produce shortages in the cities.*

In the main, what ought to be the hottest kind of New Man "discussion"—that is, campaign in the press and the courts—seems long ago to have been abandoned altogether. Once in a while one stumbles on a halfhearted recital in the press of a Good Example: A Hungarian village priest "told the peasants they must not only work their private plots, something they do without exhortation, but that they must work equally hard on the communal land." A "remarkable patriot" writes a letter to *Pravda Ukrainy* urging that a specific piece of communal land be assigned each collective member instead of to an entire "brigade," and her letter is published throughout the U.S.S.R. Observing that the fields of a nearby collective are overgrown with weeds, she says: "Personally I do not think this is muddleheadedness. People in the Gorky Farm know how to do things. It's conscience that they lack. Just look at their private plots. They're like a picture." Her own farm (the remarkable patriot goes on) has adopted the new system of individual responsibility for an individual strip of the collective. She is proud to report the system's success: "Everyone completes his work on the assigned land as swiftly as possible to be able to devote time to his private plot." The sooner you finish with theirs—the doctrine calls it "ours"—the sooner you can get to what is yours, all yours.

* "Peking is attempting to make collective units in the countryside more self-sufficient as part of a new program of development of agricultural industries. But its renewed emphasis on the importance of the collective economy has run into resistance from peasants more concerned with accruing personal income. Chinese articles and broadcasts have complained about capitalist trends in the countryside. The reports have indicated that even Communist party officials have been affected by 'a capitalist black wind.'

"More than a year ago the Chinese press reported that many peasants were 'voluntarily' giving up their private plots—the tiny strips of poorer land on which individual families were permitted to grow produce for sale at free markets. Both the private plots and the free markets came under official fire during the Cultural Revolution and were linked to Liu Shaochi, the purged head of state. But recent reports from China indicate that some peasants have shown a reluctance to give up their private plots or contribute income from sideline occupations to the collective economy.

"A report from Hupeh Province by Hsinhua, the official press agency, accused 'class enemies' of inciting the peasants to dissolve the collective units and concentrate on private sideline production. The ruling Revolutionary Committee of the region called meetings to counter this development. After a period of 'class struggle' and 'mass criticism,' a new situation emerged of 'everyone hating the capitalist tendencies and loving the collective,' the agency reported."—Hong Kong dispatch to the New York *Times*, November 3, 1969. (On January 9, 1971, the American correspondent of the *Guardian Weekly* of Manchester reported that the peasantry were still hanging on to their private plots, and subsequent visits by American correspondents found the "free"—ostensibly of government-fixed prices—market cubicles flourishing in the cities.) (New York *Times*, May 23, 1971.)

But that wasn't the idea at all.

Not at all.

Professor Liberman says that "manufacturers should pay more to workers who produce more and fire workers who are inefficient," and the Chinese have raised the wages of workers getting less than forty dollars (100 yuan) a month, "not automatically, but according to the actual work done by each individual. Very exceptional work might bring a wage boost even if the wage was already high; very poor work might deny an increase, even if the bracket was low." * But that wasn't the idea of the New Man. The idea—lifted whole from the Christian Gospel—was from each according to his ability and to each according to his need.

* "Money remains at the core of the Chinese social program, even though its sights are set on equality, while the Russians deliberately encourage differences in income. We intend to get rid of the whole money myth. . . . We try to create the kind of social atmosphere in which no man works just for money, in which the very idea of personal enrichment has lost its appeal."—Fidel Castro to K. S. Karol, *Guerrillas in Power*, New York, Hill & Wang, 1970. The 1971 Five-Year Plan of the U.S.S.R., following hard upon the Polish workers' rebellion against the introduction of an "incentive plan"—a rebellion that toppled the Gomulka regime—was significantly silent on the issue of incentive. (New York *Times*, February 16, 1971.)

4: The Salivation Army

THE CREATION of a new world is no laughing matter. The *tierischer Ernst* that Schopenhauer ascribes to the Germans is the hallmark of the vision in all its standard and revised forms. Nowhere down the ages do we ever discover the least whimsy in its apprehension (except, of course, in the likes of Cervantes, Rabelais, and Voltaire, whose mockery of it we Old Men delight in). What will the New Man do for a lusty laugh? Apparently the laugh will be shed with the lust. Marx is exactly as jocular as Mark—or, *horribile dictu,* Manson.

But man is not only an animal and a rational animal. He is (being an animal) a laughable and (being rational) a risible animal.

The Communist dictatorships, whatever else they are, are unrelievedly sober and marvelously banal, ringing a kind of Pavlovian bell to which (as Peter Viereck put it) the Salivation Army can be relied upon to make the Pavlovian response. The strident slogans plastered on the walls and hoardings of the Communist countries may be effective subliminally. But I doubt even that: nobody looks at them, much less reads them.* At a student-faculty meeting at Moscow State University, a student's written question read: " 'The present

* What people do read, avidly, in the Communist world as in any other, is whatever is unofficial (all the more so where everything is official). It is in this area of the struggle against dictatorship that those who live by their wit, who could not go on living without it, reach their countrymen who are starved for a smile and are not to be heartened by anything else. The modern classics are, of course, the graffiti scrawled on the walls all over Czechoslovakia after the Soviet invasion of 1968: *Workers of the World, Unite or We'll Kill You; There Are Always Eskimos Who Can Tell Congolese What to Wear in Warm Weather; Silence!—Signed, Reichsprotektor.*

generation will live under Communism.' What exactly does this statement mean? If its meaning is vague, why bother saying it at all?" I
have seldom heard a Czech greet another with "Čest práci! Honor to
Labor!"—the counterpart of the Nazi "Heil Hitler!"—and I have
never known one to do so without a grimace.

Every variety—there aren't many—of communication produced
by a Communist government is simply deadly—and not just in "our"
terms. It may be true that the annual attendance at "educational
dramas" in Red China is two billion (and equally true that many of
the attenders have never seen a film before), but it isn't that way in
the cities, or even in the larger towns of Red Europe; during the
factory-and-fields documentary always inserted between Sophia
Loren and Victor Mature, the moviegoers buzz with chatter or drift
off to the buffet or the biffy.

Of course, the Prague (or the Leningrad, or the Bucharest) press
will misquote around-the-world pilgrimage of Western pacifists. That
goes without saying. The point is that it goes without saying that it
will concoct their having said that "all honest people must join together in the fight against Nazism and fascism . . . the struggle for
peace . . . the forces of reaction and war . . . international soli-
darity. . . ." Where the government cannot, in the nature of the
case, write the script, the cultural rebellion that is now endemic even
in the Soviet Union has always been in eruption in the arts. If man is
not grotesque, his posturing ridiculous, his capers contradictory, there
is nothing for any of the arts to discover in him. There are more
groans, of course, but more chuckles, too, in *Hamlet* than in all of
"Socialist realism" and more realism in the chin of Philip IV as
Velasquez saw it than in the tallest ten statues of Lenin. Man in transition from Socialism to Communism ought to be good for a giggle or
two; but no, he is already heroic, healthy, happy, and studded with
exclamation marks.

The arts are a continuing duel between the portraitists who can
only portray man as he is and the Communist "men turned Turk"
who will have man portrayed as he must be or, better, as he must
have been.* There is no question (and never was nor could be) who is

* "Granted that in the West the line between art and crassest commercialism
has almost vanished . . . one fact remains. It is interesting, and it changes
constantly. The streets of London, Paris, New York, Milan are in motion with
people going somewhere. In Moscow they are all on their way home.
"What can be so frightening about modern paintings that they must be kept
in the basement of the Tretyakov Gallery from which the public is barred?
Man and the world are still commanded to look as they did in 1875, and at the
same time the leaders who make and enforce these rules are perfectly at home
with the shapes of their space-ships, with space-time concepts. And it is known
that they get *their* London *Times* and *New York Times* every morning."—
Miller, *op. cit.,* p. 49.

winning the duel than why it is that the winner is winning it. However formidable the propaganda, however fearsome the police power, the genuine realist, whose worthless wight is more entertaining than the worthy New Man, plays to a full house; the "Turks," or their toadies, to an empty. Man as he is goes—willingly—to see and hear man as he is and no other. For several years (prior to 1968) a leading Czech comic sang a song in the cabarets about an obstreperous puppy which, when his master locked him up and fed him and exercised him, grew big enough to bite his master; the song wasn't published until its boot-leg popularity reached the point where there was nothing for the "Turks" to do but let it be recorded for public distribution.

This is the supremely hypocritical fact of Communism—and as positive proof of the Old Man's sovereignty as is Madison Avenue. The "Communists'" world-prize-winning achievements in music or the cinema are all masterpieces not of Marxist-Leninism but of art.* The official (or officially benisoned) output is so much mumbo-jumbo designed, like Hitler's Aryan physics, for contemptuous in-doctrination of the contemptible masses. This contempt exists, of course, in very high places in the "free world," too; it is easy to quote Western statesmen who merely substitute "revolutionaries" for "counter-revolutionaries" in echoing Mao Tse-tung's declaration that "counter-revolutionaries must be prohibited from exploiting freedom of speech for counter-revolutionary purposes." † And it is not just the courts that have to be relied upon to frustrate such statesmen; Ameri-can public opinion (far from being the world's most liberal) will not accept the condemnation of the New York *Times* by the country's Vice President. Novels of giant stature like Solzhenitsyn's *The First Circle* and *Cancer Ward* simply could not be suppressed outside the Soviet world with the explanation by a public official of much less than giant stature that "ideological militancy is an important quality under conditions of sharp ideological struggle in an atmosphere of sophisticated and persistent attacks by our enemy." ‡

Every society, as pedant or policeman, is just as continually duel-ing with artists and merchants of art whose renditions of reality, even if they are faithful, even if they are representative, are felt by Some-body Upstairs (or by enough Somebodies Down Here) to be un-wholesome, unholy, or unpatriotic. Every society determines the

* "Isn't it absurd that many Communists are enthusiastic about promoting feudal and capitalist art, but not socialist art?"—Mao Tse-tung, quoted by Anna Louise Strong in her *China Letter* from Peking, June 1969.

† Strong, *ibid.*

‡ Georgi Markov, secretary of the National Writers' Union of the U.S.S.R., in announcing the author's expulsion from the organization. (New York *Times,* December 11, 1969.) In 1970 Solzhenitsyn was awarded the Nobel Prize for Literature.

canons of art by popular hubbub—or by political or papal proscription, or by agonizing, continuous, and endless reappraisal by judges whose wisdom may or may not be as Solomon's. *Or tries to.* There are not many respectable defenders of the steady diet of violence dished out on American television. But there is good reason for the critics' not knowing what ought to be done about it: the danger that the counterpart of "Socialist realism" will replace it if the Frankenstein's monster of government is got after it. Only take the "El" between the two Berlins and see, at the crowded kiosks on the western side, the bawdy publications that everybody wants to look at and, at the uncrowded kiosks on the eastern side, the disembawdied publications that nobody wants to read.

What will you have, then—decadence or dictatorship? Well, neither, but, rather, decadence (and the Old Man leers). The alternative is the rehabilitation of a Prokofieff when the official musicologists decide that his *Alexander Nevsky* successfully presents "the antagonism of the two intonational spheres, that the aggressors [blunt, mechanically crude rhythms, harsh polytonal harmonies, the use of unmelodic instruments, emotionally inexpressive choruses] and the sphere of Russian music [melodies akin to the Russian folk song, euphonious instruments, strings, female voice, emotionally colored choruses] . . . an interesting continuation of the ideological tradition in Russian music. . . ." *Imprimatur.* In Prague a largely Western audience settles in its seats to enjoy a performance of the Ninth by the magnificent Czech Philharmonic and is handed, in elegant format, and in five languages, the Program Notes: ". . . Beethoven proves to be a typical representative of the progressive intelligence inflamed by revolutionary ideas. . . . One day the time will come, and the people of the whole world will shake hands. . . . All who fight for progress, happiness, and peace will keep Beethoven as a shield." *Imprimatur.* And so to Leipzig, to tiptoe into the Thomaskirche and hear an East German professor elegize *Bach* as "pre-Marxist."

5: The Fallen Angel and the Risen Ape

UP UNTIL the Enlightenment—a mere two centuries ago—human nature had been taken to be a static entity and (on balance) a seamy one. Supermen there might be, like Homer's Agent 007, with a friend at Divine Court, but entertainments like the *Odyssey* did not presuppose either mankind's progress or man's. Nor did the first astronomers quarrel with the first poets, the historians with the astronomers, or the philosophers with the historians. As the world rolled first forward and then backward in "infinite cycles of years," and (according to Herodotus) "those cities which are now great were once nothing, while those that are now nothing were once great," so the forms of social organization and government went from the worst to the best to the worst again. The raptures rose and subsided, and mankind remained unchanged—like man.

The very best that could be done for St. Bernard's "sack of dung" was the ascription to him of an unsteady standoff between reasoned and irrational desire: the two steeds of the soul pulling in opposite directions. Plato said it; Aristotle parsed it; Paul versified it in Romans 7, and John Stuart Mill won the argument with the pig—as to whether it was better to be Socrates dissatisfied than a pig satisfied—by observing that his four-footed friend had been only a pig while he, Mill, had been both Socrates *and* a pig. But man had always been moved (and always moved to his ruin) to put the pig behind him and soar with Socrates. Whence the delirious impulse, we know not. But when, we "know": when Adam and Eve went for broke in the Garden. Like the Lord, the gods had been jealous gods, and like His,

their vengeance on the impudence had been pointed. Two or three
thousand—or a million—years after Icarus sought the sun on his
wax-pinioned wings, Pascal decided that "he who would act the angel
acts the brute." If there was no quarrel with the Plotinus who asked,
"What could be more fitting than that we, living in this world, should
become like to its Ruler?" neither was there any quarrel with this
same Plotinus when he said, "Humanity is poised midway between
gods and beasts."

It took Christianity to cut man to size without cutting him down
altogether. Man's *first* nature was not man's at all, but God's, limited
only by the innocence of good and evil and the debarment of eternal
life. The nature imposed upon him at the Fall, his "wounded" nature, is human nature as we have always known it and always will.
The restitution of his innocence is outside his power and outside his
history, the free and unmerited gift of God made possible by Christ's
ransom. Paul's "new man in Christ" is neither a better nor a different
man but another creation. During this Gospel Age he may be seen
emerging as an "earnest" of the New Man to be—but he has to have
active grace operating upon him to strengthen him in the struggle in
his inward parts, a struggle that will end only at the end of the Gospel
Age.

Thus Christian theology, like pagan philosophy, accepted the im-
mutability of human nature; but it accounted for, and even fed, the
longing for mutation which was perpetually clamant in that nature.
The primitive Christians were the marvel of the perspicacious pagan,
and the Roman nobleman said of them, "See how they love one
another"—"an observation," says Mill dryly, "that would scarcely be
made nowadays." The marvel passed and passed soon, with the rapid
advancement of Christian civilization—i.e., of ecclesiastical power.
The medieval Christian view of man (man here and now) was not too
different from the pagan—if anything, a little darker, for the prevalent difference between doctrine and day-to-day life was greater in the
Christian case than it was in the pagan. By the time of the Renaissance there were few to argue with Machiavelli's laconic first principle that "men are bad."

It was only in the eighteenth century that the vision of the New
Man—or, in the phrase of the day, the perfectibility of man—reap-
peared significantly, in concurrence with the revolutionary rise of the
democratic (or, more accurately, the republican or constitutional)
nation-state and the no less revolutionary onset of the scientific and
industrial age.

In 1793 the Marquis de Condorcet, mathematician, encyclopedist, philosopher of history, statesman, and republican, was condemned to death by the Revolution of "Liberty, Equality, Fraternity" which he had helped inspire. In hiding—he was ultimately caught—he wrote the great statement of the eighteenth-century Enlightenment, *Sketch for an Historical Tableau of the Progress of the Human Spirit*. In the most optimistic picture of man ever painted, this most indomitable of optimists maintained that "no bounds have been fixed to the improvement of the human faculties; the perfectibility of man is absolutely indefinite; the progress of this perfection, henceforth above the control of every power that would impede it, has no other limit than the duration of the globe upon which nature has placed us."

Fifty years after Condorcet, Alexis de Tocqueville, in his analysis of American democracy, called the idea of perfectibility "one of the principal notions that the intellect can conceive . . . a great philosophical theory." It wasn't new, but the new faith in human equality had given it a new dimension. The image of "an ideal but fugitive perfection" now affected the behavior even of men who had never thought about it, dominating the common character of life in the new American society. With progress on every front (or on every front but one) before their eyes, men could not help but believe that *man himself* was either making progress or would. Who in early nineteenth-century America could say what "things" might be like in twenty years' time—and if things, why not man? The miracle was within man's competence after all—not, to be sure, by instantaneous transformation, but by what was much the same thing, an evolution so precipitate that the world was changed within an ordinary lifetime: The issue need not be argued on the basis of history. Every man's observation was sufficient to support the meliorist conceit.

Men saw, and saw rightly, that the new machinery and the new discoveries, generally transmitted by the new rights of man, could be used to speed up the amelioration of the human condition to a tempo never before imagined. In the splendor of the new day all history receded. No one seemed to remember that the Greeks (and the early Jews and Christians, too) had seen that the human condition in *their* time had improved radically over the more ancient antiquity. Homeric life was on every count benighted—as was that of the contemporary "barbarians"—in comparison with that of Periclean Athens and Augustinian Rome. But their attention to the past saved the ancients from the euphoric inference drawn by the egalitarian moderns from the new conditions.

Only a nit-picker would deny that man with the wheel (or with liberty) was better off than man without. But (the nit-pickers wanted to know) was he *better*—and if so, how, and how durably? The nit-pickers insisted that man's improvement of his environment was neither the necessary consequence of his own improvement nor its cause—nor a sign of his improvability. What he had achieved (they insisted) was wholly within the capabilities described by the Greeks. If his nature was actually changing (as the nit-pickers insisted it wasn't), the changes had to be inheritable and irreversible; otherwise (the nit-pickers insisted) the improved conditions flowing from those changes would be in perpetual jeopardy.

But the new view of man the perfectible swept everything before it. The perfectibilists and the progressivists and the optimists and the liberals brushed the nit-pickers aside, as they still do—with, however, less of a whoop and a holler since Verdun and Auschwitz and Hiroshima and My Lai. There was weighty evidence (as there still is) that refining conditions refined some (if not all) of the sensibilities of some (if not all) men. Chattel slavery and some of the less onerous forms of economic cruelty were waning. Crime, insanity, sexual deviation, alcoholism, even poverty, were seen with clearer and more compassionate eyes than they had ever been before. The burning of witches became a scandal and even the beating of demons out of madmen. The niceties of the few—bodily care, dietary considerations, medicine, and even preventive medicine—were becoming the niceties of the several if not yet of the many. The compulsory education of children was advocated and, little by little, accepted.

War itself seemed to be losing some of its sharp edges with restraint in the treatment of prisoners and especially of civilians. Private violence, the duel, the feud, and the lynching, were transferred gradually to the public prerogative. The principle of revenge was, if not eliminated, palliated by the notions of deterrence and even correction. The prohibition of torture in theory led to its reduction in practice, to the restriction of execution to high crimes, to the removal of execution from the titillated sight of the mob, and finally to the elimination of capital punishment for civil offenses in country after country.* The bestialities of sport—the prize fight, the cock fight, the bull fight— were marvelously polite compared with the gladiatorial combat of the Roman arena. And "everywhere"—nowhere so spectacularly as

---

* Since Portugal took the initiative in 1867, more than seventy countries have abolished the death penalty. With its final elimination by Great Britain in 1969, after a trial period in which the homicide rate remained remarkably stable, only France and the United States, among Western nations, still retain it. (But there was no execution in France in 1968 or 1970 and only one in 1969; and none in the United States in 1968, 1969, or 1970, and only one in 1967. Fourteen of the fifty states had outlawed the practice by 1970.)

in America—the arbitrary position of political rulers yielded to the rights of universal citizenship.

The seventeenth-century Baconian dictum that knowledge is power was at once the seal of the Renaissance and the signal of the Enlightenment. It was an incontrovertible dictum—still is—if its second term was left undefined or was defined as man's manipulation of the external world. Knowledge meant better techniques and better instruments, whose application evoked and enabled the rise of better social conditions and political institutions. Those conditions and institutions had always been dreamed of—but only dreamed of. Now they came to be, to an ever increasing extent, and for something like two centuries, certainly up until 1914, it was next to impossible to believe that their actuality did not mean more sensitivity in the attitudes of men. That sensitivity, too, was as old as the world; a few men had displayed it memorably in every age, and many more, doubtless, whose sentiments were not recorded. But now it seemed possible to man, and not just to this stoic or that saint.

So spectacular and cumulative was the evidence that something wonderful was happening—or was sure to happen—to man that the traditional view was as good as abandoned (outside of theology) in the nineteenth century. A dichotomy was driven between environment and heredity, the one thundered ever more aggressively from the podium and the press, the other ever more defensively and unpersuasively from the pulpit. After all, the world at the end of the eighteenth century—still more so at the end of the nineteenth—was nothing at all like the world at the end of the eighth. Who had so changed it in a thousand years—in a hundred—but man? What inference was possible but that man himself had changed in a thousand, yes, in a hundred years? He who had, so suddenly after so many ages, shaped nature to his purposes—why shouldn't he shape his purposes—in effect, create himself anew?

What, now, was human nature, the perdurable obstacle to human improvement? Avast; the new slogan was "nurture, not nature." Man's soul was apprehended, like the void on the eve of Creation, as a formless bundle (even an imaginary bundle) of purest plastic potentialities. The fallen angel gave way to the risen ape—or to a more protean entity (or nonentity) as the bygone "behaviorism" of the late psychologist John B. Watson resurfaced in the person of Harvard's "behavioral technologist" B. F. Skinner. Calling for the complete control (*by whom?*) over man, his conduct, and his culture to save the, yes, *human* race from extinction, Prof. Skinner dismissed "autonomous man", as a mythological device to explain the hitherto

inexplicable. Man is nothing but the interaction of the environment
(*whose* environment?) and the individual (*what* individual?) and
"traditional concepts of freedom and dignity have made an immeasurable contribution, but they've served their purpose."—New
York *Times,* September 6, 1971. (If the professor was bedeviled by
what the Germans call the *Teufelskreis,* or vicious circle, of his reasoning, his bedevilment did not appear to trouble him.)

Could there possibly be trouble ahead? Clay might be awesome
in the hands of the Lord God Jehovah and bearing His image; but
it might be less awesome, and some day not awesome at all, if it was
man of clay who was doing the shaping according to his clayey lights.
Whose would be the Word in the New Beginning? Who would shape
—or undertake to shape—whom? There was a paradox here of
stupendous proportions. Was it possible that the unlimited dignity of
man on his own would end in the loss of the limited dignity he had
from God and leave him utterly undignified? (But the trouble was
still far off.) The despotism of man over man was the world's oldest
political story and its most recurrent. There had been an occasional
despot who had tried to be of use to his subjects, but none who had
thought to change their very nature or to assert the totalitarian power
commensurate with the undertaking; none (always excluding the Holy
Office) with *a science of man* so certainly held as to justify the extremes of tyranny for the redemption of the tyrannized. Some day
there would be such sciences of man—some far-off day—in Nazism
with its eugenic engineering and in Marxist-Leninism with its
economic.

Someday—some far-off day, when the term "brainwashing" would
be a commonplace—there might even be physicochemical procedures
to apply such sciences. Some far-off day—twenty years after Hiroshima—the American Association for the Advancement of Science
would be being informed by Professor David Krech of the University
of California of the "beginnings of genuine breakthroughs into the
understanding of the mind. If not today, then tomorrow—or the day
thereafter, or the year thereafter. I need not spell out for you what
such understanding of the mind may mean in terms of control of the
mind." Two years thereafter Dr. Arthur Kornberg and his colleagues
at Stanford University produced the first biologically viable DNA, the
master chemical which determines the form and function of every
living entity. And two years after that, biophysicist Humberto
Fernandez-Moran of the University of Chicago said that with the
completion of high-voltage electron microscopes "it may become
possible not only to predict, but also to design life at the molecular

level," and a world meeting of eminent biologists at the Center for the Study of Democratic Institutions agreed that one of the biological advances of our time—"present and prospective"—was "control, through genetic engineering, of human instincts, drives, and emotions, indeed all physical and psychological characteristics." The 1970s had begun, and they were not very far along when one eminent psychologist predicted a "knowledge pill," and another a "peace pill" to be administered (*by whom?*) to aggressive national leaders; and the futuristic cyborg, or combination man and machine, would, according to British geneticist J. B. S. Haldane, include (as the result of the induction of regressive mutations) legless astronauts who (or which) would take up less room in space capsules and require less food and oxygen.*

* *Time,* April 19, 1971; New York *Times,* September 6, 1971.

6: Old Men—
New Hats

THE ENLIGHTENMENT and its heirs of the next century (the Communists included) discovered wonderful new forces: environmentalism (as if Plato had not noticed that "the city educates the man"), conditioning (as if Circe hadn't changed men into swine), and, finally and triumphantly, determinism (as if Socrates in his death cell hadn't challenged his legs to pick him up and carry him away to freedom). And environmentalism, conditioning, and determinism gave rise to what would come to be called the *social* sciences of the infinitely manipulable man turned mass. Gloomy Goethe stood pat: *Der Mensch bleibt Mensch.* Old hat. Still older hat he who (oddly enough) had first spoken of perfectibility: Rousseau, who wondered whether the forces of civilization "may have improved the human understanding while depraving the species, and made man wicked while making him sociable."

New hat was the greatest historian of the age. Who better than Edward Gibbon had the right to adduce from all history—up to 1787 —"the pleasing conclusion that every age of the world has increased and still increases the real wealth, the happiness, the knowledge, and perhaps the virtue of the human race"? Still newer, by a few decades, was George William Frederick Hegel. Man's freedom ("however limited or conditioned") to *will* change (the emphasis is Hegel's) conspired with his spirit (or mind) to produce "a *real* capacity for change, and that for the better, an impulse of perfectibility." (The emphasis is still Hegel's.)

Under this enraptured attack the Christian view of human nature appeared ever darker. The Reformation spread of the Bible had democratized the darkness without dispelling it. (And Luther was no gladder a voice than Calvin.) The Church was now isolated. The new knowledge conspired with the new faith in knowledge to provide the evidence of things seen in such weight as to tip the scales. The philosopher, like the theologian and the churchman, was rooted in the prescientific past. He, too, gave way to the man of the present and the future, whose advent was certified by Darwin himself: What man now was, was godly compared with what "man"—i.e., the lowest zoological primate—had been in his prebeginnings; why shouldn't he be godlier still, world without end?

Darwin the biologist was carried away to a judgment which, if it lay anywhere, lay somewhere outside biology: "Looking to future generations, there is no cause to fear that the social instincts will grow weaker, and we may expect that virtuous habits will grow stronger, becoming *perhaps* [emphasis added] fixed by inheritance. In this case the struggle between our higher and lower impulses will be less severe, and virtue will be triumphant. Man," he goes on, "has risen by slow and interrupted steps, from a lowly condition to the highest standard as yet attained by him in knowledge, morals and religion." And yet—yes, and yet?—"with all his noble qualities, with sympathy which he feels for the most debased, with benevolence which extends not only to other men but to the humblest living creatures, with his godlike intellect which has penetrated into the movements and constitution of the solar system—with all these exalted powers—man still bears in his bodily frame the indelible stamp of his lowly origin."

What difference did the "bodily frame" make to the spirit (or mind) in which Hegel's man consisted? Could it be that the "indelible stamp" signified more than biological evolution? Could it be that there was a naked ape to contest the triumph of virtue? Could it be that the strengthening of the "social instincts" would not *necessarily* strengthen virtuous habits—or even virtuous social habits? Could it be that instincts were something which did not grow stronger or weaker but remained the same in the whole life of the species? Could it be that the biologist was trying to say that *der Mensch bleibt Mensch?*

There was a certain Sir Charles Galton Darwin a century later who would seem to be taking issue with his grandfather: Arguing that man is a "wild" animal, to whom the eugenic breeding of domestic animals is inapplicable, and that the noninheritance of acquired characteristics (a principle familiar in animal biology) is "all too seldom invoked in connection with human beings," the twentieth-century biologist supposes that "it will take a million years before anything notably different will arise in [man's] nature." * And there was a certain Sir Julian Huxley, a century after the other great theorist of evolution, who took issue with *his* grandfather: "We all know the disillusionment that has set in within the brief space of half a hundred years. How the orderly mechanisms of nineteenth-century physics gave way to strange and sometimes non-rational concepts that no one but mathematicians could grasp; how the idea of relativity, and its somewhat illegitimate extension into human affairs, destroyed faith in the absolute, whether absolute truth or absolute morality or absolute beauty; how our belief in the essential rationality and goodness of man was undermined by psychology and sent crashing in ruins by the organized cruelty of Belsen and the mass folly of two world wars; and how our idealistic notions of progress as the inevitable result of science and education were shattered by events. In brief, man's first evolutionary picture of nature and his own place in it proved false in its design and had to be scrapped." †

The argument that man's nature is changeable, and has in fact changed, is a weak (or worse than weak) one—and is in any case growing weaker in the face of current history. But the argument on the other side is not ironclad and never will be. The traditional view of unchangeability has never been able to explain the sudden surge that led to the Enlightenment after ages (or eons) of relative stability in the human situation. True, there had always been a kind of steady, almost paced, advance from stone to metal and to the refinement of metal, from skins to textiles, and from the pack animal to the wheeled cart and the wagon. But it was modest as well as gradual. Man the tool maker appeared on the earth without tools and figured things out as he went along. He *was* different from the rest of creation. But the explosion that was heralded in the optics and navigational mechanics of the fourteenth, fifteenth, and sixteenth centuries—this was, and remains, something wonderful.

The traditionalists explain it as nothing more than a sharp *increase* —much of it fortuitous—in intellectual combination and recombination. So be it; but why did it happen when it happened? Why hadn't it happened before? It did not coincide with the first meetings of previously separated tribes of men who, on such occasion, might have brought its ingredients together. It did not come into being as the

* *The Next Million Years,* Doubleday, Garden City, New York, 1963, pp. 79–207.
† *New Bottles for New Wine,* Harper & Row, New York, 1957, p. 42.

result of the chance discovery of previously unknown materials. It was not a breakthrough in some one area of inquiry or by some one or half dozen geniuses. It was down-the-line and across-the-board. It could not be explained away, nor can it now. It was as if—to put the matter cautiously—a change had taken place in man.

What is more, the change, if there was one, seemed to satisfy the two classic requirements of mutation: hereditariness and irreversibility. Man as a whole and men individually comprehended and assimilated the new wonders, carried them purposively forward, and spread them everywhere. The first words spoken over the transcontinental telephone—"What hath God wrought?"—were understood to mean "What hath man wrought?" These were not Jove's thunderbolts (or lightning), but man's, in unsurprising profusion. Why did Louis Pasteur appear in the nineteenth century after Christ instead of the nineteenth century before? Why, because the New Man had been born, and Pasteurs were and would be everywhere. It was the first Age of Reason. Its wonders went forward faster and faster. They still do, without reverse or reversion. If the modern mind was not qualitatively different from the ancient, the ancient mind must have been slumbering for thousands, and not just hundreds, of years—a thesis without credibility.

Man certainly seemed to have a New Mind and, in so far as that, a new nature. He seemed even to have a New Body, outwardly and organically unchanged, but bigger by anthropometric and even historical evidence. Bigger, stronger, and more durable. The New Body was, of course, itself the product of the New Mind's production of a more salubrious environment. But where men might suddenly expect to live half again as long, or even twice as long, as the generality of men had always lived, the environmental prospect contributed mightily to the liberal doctrine: Here, too, appeared to be illimitable perfection. Was the fruit of the tree of eternal life, guarded by angels with flaming swords, really outside man's remorseless reach? There seemed to be no reason now why it should be—why man should not escape the death sentence of the Garden and be as a god at last.

The new conditions of life seemed to soften human behavior. Living more "human" lives as regards access to food and shelter and medicine, men seemed to be learning to restrain their aggressions in their relations with one another—unless those aggressions were only being given new and more mannerly forms. (The term "sublimated" was still to be heard.) However civilization was defined, men seemed to be becoming more civilized. Societies and society became stabler. There was a whole century, from 1814 to 1914, of general peace in the Western world, again for the first time in history. (True, there were the Crimean, Franco-Prussian, Boer, and Russo-Japanese wars and a few other such modest conflicts, and, of course, the American Civil War, in some respects the most bitter ever fought; but hadn't the latter been fought on the clear moral issue of slavery, as such itself a spectacular testimony to perfectibility?)

There was only one little hitch. The Gibbon of the "pleasing conclusion" that the wealth, the happiness, the knowledge, and perhaps the virtue of the race was increasing from age to age was constrained to observe of the son of the illustrious and virtuous Marcus Aurelius of Rome that "every sentiment of virtue and humanity was extinct in the mind of Commodus. . . . The influence of a polite age, and the labour of an attentive education, had never been able to infuse into his rude and brutish mind the least tincture of learning; and he was the first of the Roman emperors totally devoid of taste for the pleasures of the understanding." So, too, Socrates in Plato's *Meno,* arguing that virtue could not be taught, had cited the sons of the greatest of the Greeks in evidence. Men like Pericles, Themistocles, Aristides, and Thucydides had had the unlimited conditions to improve their offspring. The best tutors had been able to teach them gymnastics and horsemanship. But the best tutors had not been able to teach them virtue.

This was the little hitch. The traditionalist view of man's nature was a moral view. Man, by virtue of his rational desire and his freedom, was a moral animal. There was no other in all creation. The bestiality of the brutes was neither good nor bad, much less changeable. But the moral creature's bestiality was bad, and the same powers that, rightly directed by virtue, raised him so far above them, wrongly directed by vice, sank him at least that far below them. Give him a better intelligence than he had and a better body besides, and leave his desire unchanged, and his *human* nature would be unchanged. His improved intelligence and his improved body would only serve to make him more effectively good—or bad. They would not make a New Man of him. They would not make his behavior better or worse except in some superficial manifestations. The New Man would be a morally New Man or he would be the Old Man.

Prudence, instinct, or their acquaintance of men led the apostles of the Enlightenment all to hedge their bets on man, from Gibbon's pleasing conclusion that the wealth, happiness, knowledge, and *perhaps* the virtue of the race was increasing to Darwin's equally pleasing, and equally guarded, conclusion that the virtuous habits would *perhaps* become fixed by inheritance. Hegel saved himself by recogniz-

ing that the impulse of perfectibility was "however limited or conditioned." It was not too early to be amazed that man had overnight
perfected smokeless powder, popular schools, the penny press, poor
laws, and parliaments; it was too early to say how he would use them.

Among statesmen none had greater reason—or faith—to represent
the spirit of the Enlightenment than Jefferson, the American democrat whose eighteenth-century career extended through the first quarter of the nineteenth. And represent it he did—but he, too, with a
precautionary foreword: "Although I do not, with some enthusiasts,
believe that the human condition will ever advance to such a state of
perfection as that there shall no longer be pain or vice in the world,
yet I believe it susceptible of much improvement, and most of all, in
matters of government and religion; and that the diffusion of knowledge among the people is to be the instrument by which it is to be
effected."

By the middle of the nineteenth century, John Stuart Mill, himself
an ardent exponent of "the diffusion of knowledge among the people,"
betrayed a deep-seated ambivalence as to the efficacy of education
alone. He did not doubt that "most of the great positive evils of the
world are in themselves removable, and will, if human affairs continue
to improve, be in the end reduced within narrow limits." The world,
he thought, might easily be made an almost painless place "if will and
knowledge were not wanting." The knowledge was growing at a great
rate; but there remained the will, and "we ought not to forget that
there is an incessant and ever-flowing current of human affairs towards
the worse, consisting of all the follies, all the vices, all the negligences,
indolences, and supinenesses of mankind; which is only controlled,
and kept from sweeping all before it, by the exertions which some
persons constantly, and others by fits, put forth in the direction of
good and worthy objects. . . . A very small diminution of those
exertions would not only put a stop to improvement, but would turn
the general tendency of things towards deterioration. . . ."

To say that these wise men all hedged their conclusions and predictions—as if in wisdom they might have come down flat-footed on
the issue—is not to do them justice. It was remarkable, in their time,
that they displayed the resistance that they did to the general euphoria.
Perhaps they saved themselves by referring, consciously or not, to the
old-hat tradition which they inherited, in which the mind itself, like
the body, was only a tool in the hand of a creature who was more
than mind and body. These pre-computer, pre-thinking-machine
thinkers were all familiar with the medieval (and pre-medieval)
Golem and Sorcerer's Apprentice legends. They were all familiar

with the mythological young Greek who would soar to the sun. They were all initimately familiar with the word of the prophet through whom Jehovah said that his people were "wise to do evil, but to do good they have no knowledge"; with the Psalmist's answer to the question "Who shall ascend into the hill of the Lord? Who shall stand in his holy place?" "He that hath clean hands and a pure heart"; with the Samuel who said, "I am this day fourscore years old: and can I discern between good and evil?"; with the Christ who taught his disciples to "put off the old man, which is corrupt according to the deceitful lusts . . . and put on the new man, which after God is created in righteousness."

They were all familiar, in a word, with the only change that would change man's nature, and they had heard it said that no man by taking thought could add a cubit to his stature. So, while some of them were so dazzled that they failed to make a sharp distinction between condition and nature, and others beguiled into taking new modes of behavior for new kinds of behavior, they all hedged. Hedging must have taken more foresight then than now.

7: With a Red
Ribbon on It

I N T H E midst of the enthusiasts—at the very height of their nine-teenth-century enthusiasm—there appeared—with a red ribbon on it —the newest hat of all. Karl Marx disagreed with the men of the Enlightenment on one point: He was convinced that the human condition was becoming not better but worse. And on another: Where they dwelt in the utopian conviction that the race would *find* a way out of its cyclical experience, he proclaimed the inevitability of social (if not personal) perfection on the basis of inviolable historical law. But on another point he agreed with them: The techniques of pro-duction and distribution which had come cascading from the mind of man in the past century or two carried with them the promise of man's liberation from his woes. And on another he went the whole hog in rejecting the traditional view of man. "Human nature," he said, "has no reality."

Since human nature had no reality, there was no natural obstacle to the development of the New Man. The only two things that stood in the way were religious and "philosophical"—Marx liked to put the word in quotation marks—superstitions as to man's nature and the economic system which those bodies of superstition supported. The whole history of the human race had been a struggle for the owner-ship of the means of production. Until the eighteenth century the dispossessed masses had been misled by heavenly ecstasies and blinded to their dispossession. But industralization had opened their eyes: The tools they used now were bolted down to the floor of an-other man's factory. They were stripped of their age-old delusions.

They saw themselves at last as they were—propertyless—and the system at last as it was, naked expropriation (in the form of profit) of the wealth that labor, and labor alone, created.

To quote Marx as saying that "human nature has no reality" is, in a large sense, to quote him inaccurately. He never decided—at least in print—whether there was something in man that endured all change and what that something might be. To have decided that there was would have been to take the nonprogressive, nonevolutionary position which his revolutionary social doctrine could not abide. In his earlier writings he did refer to "the human essence" (an expression that does not occur in his later work), but even then he insisted that this essence was "no abstraction inherent in each separate individual. In its reality"—note here that it *does* have a reality—"it is the ensemble of the social relations." His general materialism required his repeated assertion that "man is a part of nature," but the issue seems to have had no real interest for him.

The consequences of his having really believed that man is indeed a *part* of *nature*—that is, of the physical universe—would have been equally fatal to his doctrine. He was as aware as the Greeks that nature in this sense repeated its patterns incessantly except for the eonian process of mutation. As long as a species persisted, its whole history recapitulated the history of each of its members. It mattered not whether they willed, or what they willed; their lives and the lives of their generations were all determined with such unfailing rigidity (barring accidents) that man could "plan" his own in perfect confidence of that rigidity. A man of sound disposition does not argue with necessity, and nature is necessitated. (Who would urge the oak trees of the world to unite and fight?) But Marx's *part* of nature was to argue with the rest of it and conquer it; and to do so by changing itself by convulsion; and by changing itself change the whole of which it was a part. When Marx described the production and distribution of a bolt of cloth, his acuity never failed him, but he was satisfied, when he spoke of nature, to do so with as much imprecision as if he were writing an ode or an anathema.

His recklessness flowed from his strong distaste for metaphysical, moral, and political abstractions. They were—"justice" above all— auxiliary devices, verbal weapons, of the exploiting class. Having demolished them, he always resurrected them: *Real* justice was possible only under Communism. When he says that "he that would criticize all human acts, movements, relations, etc., by the principle of utility, must first deal with human nature in general, and then with human nature as modified by each historical epoch," or, again, that "men are products of circumstances and upbringing and . . . there-fore changed men are products of other circumstances and changed upbringing," or, again, that "by [thus] acting on the eternal world and changing it, he at the same time changes his own nature," Marx came as close to the question as he ever would, or perhaps cared to.

What he was saying—and he said it in so many words—was that circumstances change men, but "circumstances are changed precisely by men." This circularity was the Achilles' heel of his doctrine, as it remains the Achilles' heel of his doctrinaires in the ruling places of the Communist empire today: The new institutions are easy enough to blueprint and declare operative. Their end product will be New Men worthy of them. But how is the Old Man to be got to operate the new institutions that require the New Man to operate them? The Marxian man was, and is, of course, at the mercy of fundamental circularity of the "behavioral technologists" in psychology.*

Marx would neither accept the idea of human nature—of a some-thing-or-other that endured through circumstances—nor altogether reject it. If he accepted it, he had no basis for his revolutionary faith that the sharpest (indeed, the first sharp) turn in human history was possible. If he rejected it, he had no basis for the man who would consciously and willfully take that turn. His only alternative was to posit an undefined interaction, to *call* men to the consciousness and willfulness that slumbered in their natures, so that they would once and for all change the circumstances that would thereafter produce the New Man. A hundred years later the Marxist-Leninist doctrinaires were still balanced on the horns of his dilemma: "The moulding of the new man is effected through his own active participation in com-munist construction and the development of communist principles in the economic and social spheres. . . . As communist forms of social organization are created, communist ideas will become more firmly rooted in life and work and in human relations, and people will de-velop the ability to enjoy the benefits of communism in a rational way." (Program of the Communist Party of the U.S.S.R., 1961.)

Marx, who, as far as I know, never used the expression "New Man," never really claimed that the New Man would be in essence—i.e., in irreversible and inheritable essence—of a different nature from the old. But Engels did. Maybe. Engels insisted that industrialism had made of the peasants and handicrafters a "quite different people" and that Communism would require "an entirely different kind of human material"; but he goes right on to say that men under Com-munism will "no longer develop one of their faculties at the expense

* *Vide supra,* pp. 31–32.

of all others," but will be "well-rounded human beings," freed from
"the one-sided character which the present-day division of labor im-
presses upon every individual." Nothing qualitatively or categorically
new there. The character of the Communist change would be the
emancipation—one of Marx's favorite terms—of man. No new creature would be created; rather, the original creature would be restored.
This creature had been reduced by private property to "a crippled
monstrosity." Communism would not alter him but heal him so that
he would be "a fully developed human being"; nothing new there
either.

Private property was Marx's original sin—but his refusal to face
the dilemma did not permit him to ask how private property came to
be. He did not deny self-interest as one of the two abiding facts of
(nonexistent?) human nature, but called upon the other—namely,
reason—to recognize that self-interest was served by assigning
primacy to the social interest. Personal advantage remained the ultimate consideration, just as it did in Christian salvation hereafter and
in Christian commitment here. Had it not been said, "Seek ye first
the Kingdom of God and his righteousness and all these things shall
be added unto you"?

After all, Marx was addressing himself not to ecstatics, or to comfortable intellectuals and esthetes, who might be moved from their
comfort by utopian fancy, but to the masses of men to whom "all
these things" were of desperate necessity, men who lived uncom-
fortable physical lives and saw themselves and the world in uncom-
fortable physical terms. He was addressing himself to the poor, above
all to the new poor of the machine age whose labor was cruelly un-
related to their own lives and their own interests. The man who could
shut down a shoe factory for any reason, or for no reason at all, could
bring starvation upon thousands of men and women (and children)
who, even when they had work, could not afford to buy the shoes
their labor produced. Ripe as they were for revolution—for a New
World—they had to be addressed according to their condition. They
were self-interested first of all, and with reason enough.

Marx was no less optimistic than the Enlightenment about the
future of the race. He had no quarrel with Gibbon's "pleasing conclusion" or with Hegel's "impulse toward perfectibility." Human
nature might or might not have any reality, but man, who did or didn't
have that real or unreal nature, was good. He was so good that the
curse of private property had only to be lifted from his shoulders
and he would stand forth in aboriginal splendor and resume the
aboriginal habit of brotherhood which capitalism had suppressed.

Marx was, if anything, more optimistic than any man, even Condorcet, had been before him.

Was he a mad romantic—just another Icarus—or had he discovered something new under the human sun after all the woebegone millennia? Whatever the original human society may have been when man emerged from the hypothetical state of nature,* it was true that the whole record of history supported the Marxist assertion of class struggle between what Plato called "the city of the rich and the city of the poor." Every city was two such cities, and the rich were the few and the poor the many, and they were always at declared or undeclared war with each other. Both the Mosaic Law and its Christian fulfillment damned the rich and pleaded for the poor—"my people"—whose faces were ground in the dust. But there was never a suggestion that the structure of society would be changed by the Lord in the present dispensation—and if not by the Lord, not by a German theorist.

The trouble with the theory of the class struggle was the exclusiveness of its implication. The struggles of men are not of one kind but of many. There are incessant struggles between classes, incessant struggles within classes, incessant struggles between strangers in pride of place (and without regard to economic consequences), and incessant struggles between brothers in anger over a stick or a stone or a woman or a corpse. There are, more incessant than any of these, incessant struggles between conflicting desires and terrors within a rich man and within a poor man without any reference whatever to his riches or his poverty. (Said Chesterton, "I am a walking civil war.")

Marx let it be supposed that the new mode of material production would eliminate sorrow—as well as the superstition of sin—from the life of classless man. What it (or the assembly line, whatever the mode) eliminated (or tried to eliminate, and succeeded in deracinating) from the life of the classless mass was purposive, personal, passionate man. Marx was obsessed with the "objective conditions" of human life; but man is desperately subjective about those conditions and desperately (if unclinically) conscious of his subjectiveness. Even

* More romantic than Marx, perhaps, but no more mad, Petr Kropotkin made, in his *Mutual Aid* (London, 1914), what is still the classic case for voluntary communism as the natural condition of man and beast. His scientific study of animal and human sociality convinced him, not that Darwinian (more properly, Huxleyan) competition for survival was nonexistent, but that "in the ethical progress of man, mutual support—not mutual struggle—has had the leading part." Subsequent anthropological and archaeological findings have left Kropotkin's conclusion substantially untouched: "Unbridled individualism is a modern growth; it is not characteristic of primitive man."

Communists have their troubles. After ten years of Communism in Czechoslovakia, Prague's leading actress ended an unhappy love affair by committing suicide. In a public discussion shortly afterward, President Antonín Zápotocký said: "We are starting the new society with sinful people, not with heroes. Everyone has many good qualities, but everyone has failings too. In February [1948, the date of the Communist takeover] we did not create the Socialist New Man. . . . Even in the Communist society, we must prepare our children to know how to meet the troubles and difficulties of life. How, for instance, can anyone protect you from falling in unhappy love? If you yourself are not strong enough, you will meet the same end as Rybářová did."

8: Sigmund's Serpent

MARX dreamed neither of breeding a new species genetically nor of producing (by whatever means) a superman or a tribe of supermen to rule the rest of mankind. Whatever their nature—if they had any—men were all of one paste. What was more, no inferiority, real or ostensible, was ineradicable. Neither the Kluxer's Negro nor the Nazi's Jew existed, *nor,* indeed, the Kluxer or the Nazi: The capitalist of *Das Kapital* was, like the proletarian, a victim of the system; as the old "mode of production" had made him what he was, so the new one would remake him. The pogrom (in contrast with the purge) is nowhere in Marx or in Marxist doctrine.

As there is no irremediably inferior individual in Marx, neither is the inherently superior individual (or the class or race of such individuals) to be found in the catechism. As a class the proletarians are distinguished by their economic situation and destined to lose it when, because of their distinction, they have completed the revolution that their distinctive awareness of their condition requires them to lead. Their dictatorship is transitory, their assumption of it a "mere" historical necessity. Not proletarian man, but man, once the revolution is completed, will (according to Trotsky) "make it his purpose . . . to create a higher social biologic type, or if you please, a superman."

Many, perhaps most, of the ancient and modern appliers of plant and animal breeding to man abandon (if they ever held it) the possibility of changing the nature of man—the substitution of a differently endowed being for the entire human race—for the more manageable production of a new kind of being in limited quantity to lead the otherwise hopeless mass of mankind. "I teach you Super-man," says Nietzsche. "Man is something that is to be surpassed. All beings hitherto have created something beyond themselves. . . . What is the ape to man? A laughing-stock, a thing of shame. And just the same shall man be to the Superman. . . ." This sort of hocus-pocus, in which apes create men, is so far from being confined to German romantics that it crops up again and again among evolu-tionists. Crudely as it comes from a Nietzsche, it is the old stumbling block of all New-Manism, no matter how sophisticated. It is the stumbling block of all utopians, all liberals, all progressivists, all revolutionaries: By combining and recombining characteristics A, B, and C, we shall get not some end product of the order of ABC, but X, or Y, or Z. Out of nothing comes something.

Marx didn't bother to distinguish eugenics, Nietzsche's or any other, from utopian rubbish in general. His fixation has no place for particularist prejudice or test-tube miracles. The only miracle he required was revolution, the only man he foresaw was every man unchained. As it was in the power of all men to live in a new social form, so it was in the power of all men to be as new as men needed to be. His faith in revolution was a conservative faith. It required no angel's brew, no divine or superhuman intervention or leadership. It followed inexorably from the pattern he saw in the whole of human history. The pattern had only to be broken, Prometheus unbound, and man would be what he was meant to be. What he was meant to be was good. Capitalist bondage had deformed him. Ah, but how had he got himself bonded in the first place? How had the Serpent ever got into the good man's Garden?

How, in fine, had private property and private profit come into existence? "Self-interest," said Adam Smith before Marx was born; and if he said it with something like a yawn, why, so had Homer. Smith's analysis of the new industrial capitalism might have been agreeable to the Communists—certainly as regards the relation of labor to rent and profit—if only he had not contradicted their first assumption: He did not believe that man was good. But he did not trouble himself to assert that man was bad. Man was—well, what we have always known him to be. His motivation is self-interest, and nothing but self-interest, and that social system is best which turns that motivation to the best account.

Marx, too, was to allow self-interest as the ultimate justification of the cooperative commonwealth; each would be better off because all were. But Smith had no time for such involutions. Each was right now, and always would be, as well off as his own immediate interest could make him.* As for all: "People of the same trade seldom meet together, even for merriment or diversion, but the conversation ends in a conspiracy against the public. . . ." † The public had, and could expect, no protection except the hidden hand of self-interest, which sooner or later would strike at the monopolist and compel him to re-enter the arena and war against his own kind to the inexorable, but unintended, advantage of the consumer.

Was Smith right about man? Was man neither good, as Marx supposed, nor bad, as Machiavelli said, but simply and brutally (not bestially; brutally) propelled by self-love without the moralist or immoralist embroidery of selfishness or altruism? Industrial-commercial capitalism had broken the bonds—including the benevolent bonds—of feudalism and landed property, converted rich and poor alike into free enterprisers, and thrown the arena of self-interest wide open to unrestrained competition. It pitted every man against every other and each against all in the dawning new day of the shopkeeper. Did we expect the shopkeeper to weep when his competitor's shop burned down? If we did, we expected men to be angels. Did we expect the factory hand to be elevated by his new occupation? If we did, we expected machines to angelicize men: "The man," said Smith, "whose whole life is spent in performing a few simple operations generally becomes as stupid and ignorant as it is possible for a human creature to become." ‡ ("What can be expected," said Tocqueville a half century later, "of a man who has spent twenty years of his life in making heads for pins?") §

If Smith was right, there would not be a New Man. There would be nothing new. Man's ingenuity would merely have adjusted him better to his jungle environment, while it stultified the new masses and polished the manners of the new masters. As long as the counting-house sublimation satisfied his belligerent propensities, he would survive more comfortably than his predecessors who knew no other way than the cumbersome and two-edged sword. Men would be sharp instead of weapons—at least those men who got into the counting-

---

* ". . . But man has almost constant occasion for the help of his brethren, and it is in vain for him to expect it from their benevolence only. He will be more likely to prevail if he can interest their self-love in his favor, and show them that it is for their own advantage to do for him what he requires of them. . . . It is not from the benevolence of the butcher, the brewer, or the baker, that we expect our dinner, but from their regard to their own interest. We address ourselves, not to their humanity but to their self-love, and never talk to them of our own necessities but of their advantages."—*An Inquiry into the Nature and Causes of the Wealth of Nations,* Book I, Chapter 2.

† *Ibid.,* Book I, Chapter 10. ‡ *Ibid.,* Book V, Chapter 1.

§ *Democracy in America,* Book II, Chapter 20.

house instead of the factory. Ingenuity and cunning would be worth
more than muscle and agility. Like any environment—like the jungle
and the desert—the social order would strengthen one propensity
rather than another. Man's external condition would improve—even
the workman's (Marx to the subsequent contrary notwithstanding).
The *appearance* of his behavior, in the countinghouse or in the
factory, would improve. But he would be the same man.

Was Smith right? Two hundred years later, with capitalism (even
modified, "humanized" capitalism) challenged by the Marxists
swarming into the world's marketplace with a competing system *plus*
swords, there were modern non-Marxist and anti-Marxist—yes, and
even Marxist—observers who seemed to be saying that Smith *had* to
be wrong and some sort of enthusiast *had* to be right if man was to live
even as comfortably as his most primitive forebear—or, indeed, live
at all.

Communist enthusiasm had not produced the Communist man any
more than Christian enthusiasm had produced the Christian man.
Dean Josef L. Hromádka of Prague's Protestant theological faculty
had inspired the "Christian-Marxist dialogue" of the 1960s by proclaiming the social failure of the Church Temporal as the root cause
of Communism and, at the same time, proclaiming the insufficiency
of Communism to lift the spirit of man to the exaltation under which
alone it would be possible for the Communist life to endure and be
endured. The agony went beyond economics and beyond determinism
and beyond social Darwinism. After half a century of hot and cold
running war all over the world, a threnody of halfheartedness, halfheartedness shading off to hopelessness, was heard beneath the bombs
bursting in air. The second half of the twentieth century found man
miserable in precisely those areas of the earth where the adoration of
human progress was the state religion. As more and more men came
to feel, vaguely or sharply, that man, howl how he might, was not
going to be a howling success, another new hat made its appearance
at the onset of the bloody aftermath of the Enlightenment. And this
new hat was black unto ebon.

The hat was worn spectacularly askew, and for a long time its
wearer was barred from the respectable salons of the late Victorian
sunburst. But the angle at which it was worn was misleading: The
hat itself went straight back to the conservative Aristotelian mode of
observation and classification and description, the mode that ran
through Galileo and Harvey and Fourier and Pasteur and Linnaeus
and through Adam Smith—and absolutely counter to the dervish
dance of all the enthusiasts who preceded, followed, and included

Marx and prated of science while they propagated science fiction. Sigmund Freud was a clinician. Freud was unimpressed by the Enlightenment. He was unimpressed by human progress. He was unimpressed by man. Unlike Marx, he lived to see Verdun and to see man mowing man down with the most sophisticated of his wonderful machines (those machines of wholesale slaughter that seem so polite, as well as primitive, fifty years later). The Marxists took Verdun as the last agony of the old order and the signal for the new. For Freud it was the same old antic in which the same old man was engaging in the same old sport of self-destruction. Other observers had argued that the way man was was good or bad; Freud (like Smith) thought that it simply was.

Was, and ever would be, because man was as much a creature of changeless instinct as the beasts of the field. His instincts—or drives, or urges—were not to be denied. A great mechanism of repression, sublimation, substitution-formation, and reaction-formation produced conscious civilization and its conscious values, and between that mechanism and the body of instinct man tried to maintain a tension that broke under duress and let the instinctual man take over. These instincts were unconscious, and in the unconscious lay the only psychic source of their recognition. Through psychiatry—specifically, through psychoanalysis—man could come to know himself for what he was. But what he was wasn't beautiful. The man who succeeded in digging down through the layers of his consciousness would be "healthier" or, more accurately, more capable of achieving health and less likely to break under the tensions and pretensions of civilization; but what he found when he got to the bottom of his digging would not be the makings of a New Man. Very far from it. Remove the polite inhibitions—which function in easy circumstances—and you have man revealed as (the characterization is Freud's) a savage beast.

The clinician concludes that man's basic drives are self-preservation on the one hand and death or self-destruction on the other—neither of them in the least heartening to the nineteenth century (or the eighteenth, or the twentieth). Both self-preservation and the "death wish" express themselves in that "ineffaceable feature of human nature"—aggressiveness. "Men are not gentle, friendly creatures wishing for love. . . . Their neighbor is to them . . . a temptation to gratify their aggressiveness on him, to exploit his capacity for work without recompense, to use him sexually without his consent, to seize his possessions, to cause him pain, to torture and kill him. *Homo hominis lupus* [Man is to man a wolf]; who has the courage to dispute it in the face of all the evidence in his own life and in history?"

Freud replies to his own question: The Communists have not the courage but the blind folly to dispute it: "Man is wholeheartedly good and friendly to his neighbor, they say, but the system of private property has corrupted his nature. . . . If private property were abolished, all valuables held in common and all allowed to share in the enjoyment of them, ill-will and enmity would disappear from among men." This view is founded on an egregious illusion: "By abolishing private property one deprives the human love of aggression of one of its instruments, a strong one undoubtedly, but assuredly not the strongest. It in no way alters the individual differences in power and influence"—differences for which nature itself lays the foundatión in its unequal endowment of men—"which are turned by aggressiveness to its own use, nor does it change the nature of the instinct in any way. This instinct did not arise as the result of property; it reigned almost supreme in primitive times when possessions were still extremely scanty; it shows itself already in the nursery when possessions have hardly grown out of their original anal shape; it is at the bottom of all the relations of affection and love between human beings—possibly with the single exception of that of a mother to her male child."

Hard words, the clinician's; none harder, condemning every man not to death but to murderous and suicidal assault upon every other. And in perpetuity. The Freudian instincts are not flexible or "educable." There is nothing "plastic" about human nature. Rousseau's naturally good man, "everywhere born free and everywhere in chains," was crushed by society, Marx's by the form of society, Freud's by the fact of his being man. Not a man's, but Man's, heredity imposed an everlasting determinism on him, which would force its way through any and every environment or alteration of environment.

Some—not all—of the post-Freudians and the neo-Freudians (Marxist or no) have found themselves constrained to abandon the master's iron concept of instinct. The "games theory" psychologists put great store by the sublimation of aggressiveness, which they think can work itself out in a variety of kinds of ceremonial tournament; many of them point to the Soviet-American race to the moon, with its stupendous consumption of wealth and energies, as an inexpensive and civilized substitute for the still more stupendous consumption of wealth and energies (and of life and property) by overt war. A Freudian "utopian," like Erich Fromm, examines the contemporary social situation with unanswerable psychological insight, but with hopeful insistence upon the continuous evolution of human consciousness and its protean response to "healthier" social and economic possibilities. With an almost plaintive assertion of faith he says, "Man, in spite of all his intellectual and technical progress, is *still* caught by the idol worship of blood ties, property and institutions. His reason is *still* governed by irrational passions. He has *still* not experienced what it is to be fully human."

The very title of the book in which these words appear—*May Man Prevail*—sounds like a wing and a prayer and nothing more. The grim physician of Vienna lived to see his disciples' "eager denial of the bit of truth" that man is to man a wolf. *Homo hominis lupus;* let the buyer, and the seller, and every man beware of every other and fend for himself, and no nonsense about his social responsibility and the common weal. Strip him of his pious pretensions, his guilty philanthropy, his labored dignities, and his self-serving and chauvinistic superstitions; see what it is to be "fully human," at Verdun, and at all the Verduns gone before and to come. See the oldest of the Old Men, the Hun turned Nazi, as he methodically machines his millions into the crematorium, or the Communist New Man of the Red Army as he careens through the flaming streets of Berlin crying "*Uri! Uri!* Watches! Watches!"—or the New Man of the New World as he "lets 'em have it" in the village of My Lai.

Of course, said Freud, men could persuade themselves to join with one another in common purpose, but what common purpose? "It is always possible to unite considerable numbers of men in love towards one another, so long as there are still some remaining as objects for aggressive manifestations." Observing that "once the apostle Paul had laid down universal love between all men as the foundation of his Christian community, the inevitable consequence in Christianity was the utmost intolerance of those who remained outside it," he reaches the unpleasing conclusion that nothing is "so completely at variance with original human nature as culture's command to love one's neighbor as oneself."

This in-group, out-group caricature of universal love is nowhere more stridently manifested than in the newest New World of Communism. There the adversary motif is perhaps the only staple of the national diet that is never in short supply. On the most sacerdotal of Marxist-Leninist occasions, the "enemies of peace" are excoriated and the "fighters for peace" summoned to the barricades. (There are organizations actually denominated Fighters for Peace.) Depressed by his own culture's surrender to anti-Communist rabidity (and to such slogans as that of the U.S. Air Force, "Our Profession Is Peace"), the Westerner proceeds in vain to the far corners of the Communist empire to find freedom from the vocabulary of neighborly hatred. Mount Ararat in Turkey is plainly to be seen from Jerewan, the capital of Soviet Armenia, but a well-educated Jerewanian refuses to talk to me about it. I finally ask him if it isn't true that the Marxist workers "have no country"; he says it is, "but you forget what they"— the Turks—"have done to us in the past." The non-Marxists in Russia tell of a pious Russian who went to see a holy man and asked him to find out from God if there was going to be a war. The next day the holy man, having consulted God, reported that "there will be no war, but the struggle for peace will be so furious that not one stone will be left standing upon another."

From the vantage point of Verdun, Sigmund Freud (in a single paragraph in *Beyond the Pleasure Principle*) made none too gentle mockery of Gibbon's "pleasing conclusion" as to human progress (Freud called it "a pleasing illusion") and Hegel's "impulse to perfection," along with Nietzsche's Superman. "The development of man up to now," the father of psychoanalysis wrote, "does not seem to me to need any explanation differing from that of animal development, and the restless striving towards further perfection which may be observed in a minority of human beings is easily explicable as a result of that repression of instinct upon which repression of what is most valuable in human culture is built." Ten years later—and ten years before the onset of World War II—he confessed his uneasiness as to the continued efficacy of repression: "The fateful question of the human species," he wrote in *Civilization and Its Discontents*, "seems to me to be whether and to what extent the cultural process developed in it will succeed in mastering the derangements of communal life caused by the human instinct of aggression and self-destruction. In this connection, perhaps the phase through which we are at this moment passing deserves special interest. Men have brought their powers of subduing the forces of nature to such a pitch that by using them they could now very easily exterminate one another to the last man."

Those words were written in 1929. In 1932 the phase through which we were passing was even more interesting, and Freud told Einstein that he saw "no likelihood of our being able to suppress humanity's aggressive tendencies." * On September 1, 1939—one can imagine Freud's saying, "He might at least have had the decency to wait another three weeks and I'd be dead"—Hitler attacked Poland. Six years later, on August 6, 1945, President Truman gave the signal for the grand opening of the Atomic Age. Another twenty-five years have passed, and men have not exterminated one another to the last man yet.

* *Sigmund Freud: Collected Papers*, Hogarth, London, 1950, Volume 5, p. 283.

9: Down to Hard Cases

THE MARXIST genesis of "the Socialist New Man" or "the New Soviet Man" is no less obscure than the usage of the expression. Lenin refers to the notion only peripherally and (so far as I know) like Marx does not use the expression itself. In his *The State and Revolution,* he says in passing (but, for purposes of our inquiry, significantly) that "it has never entered the head of any Socialist to 'promise' that the higher phase of communism will arrive; and the great Socialists, in *foreseeing* its arrival, presupposed both a productivity of labour unlike the present and a person *unlike the present man.*"

The emphasis on *foreseeing* and *unlike the present man* is Lenin's, and his insistence that Communism presupposes a person unlike the present man on its face runs counter to the doctrinaire canon that human nature is the product of the form of social organization. At least Lenin refuses to say that Socialism (in contrast to Communism) will produce the New Man; and at least he refuses to say what will. His assertion might well be taken to square with the Scriptural miraculous, and, at least at this point, he might be putting his imprimatur on the classic Christian epigram of Jacques Maritain that "the social revolution will be a moral revolution or it won't be at all."

He makes a more (but not much more) elaborate statement in his essay *A Great Beginning,* dealing with the "subbotniks"—that is, "Saturdayers"—who on their day off volunteered to repair railway cars, etc. (The term soon came to mean all volunteer workers.) "It is the beginning," he wrote, "of a revolution that is much more difficult, more material, more radical, and more decisive than the overthrow of the bourgeoisie, for it is a victory over personal conservativeness,

indiscipline, petty-bourgeois egoism, a victory over the habits that
accursed capitalism left as a heritage to the worker and peasant. Only
when *this* victory is consolidated will the new social discipline, Socialist discipline, be created. . . . Communism begins when the
rank-and-file workers begin to display self-sacrificing concern that
overcomes all obstacles for increasing the productivity of labour, for
husbanding *every pood of grain, coal, iron,* and other products, which
do not accrue to the workers personally, or to their 'close kith and
kin,' but to their 'remote' kith and kin, i.e., to society as a whole."

It is harder, here, to put a finger on the chicken-and-the-egg dilemma than it is in the first brief statement in *The State and Revolution;* and I know of no others in Lenin. But here, again, one senses a
reserve that is missing from Trotsky's flamboyant "higher social
biologic type." In Nikolai Ivanovich Bukharin—whom Lenin called
"the greatest theorist of the party" and whom Stalin, who later had
him killed, called a "Himalaya"—the fuzziness reaches its peak: The
great theorist always puts the expression "human nature" in quotation marks and follows Marx in his rejection of its determination (indeed, of its existence) outside historical circumstances. It is wholly
indeterminate and, of course, "a change in 'human nature' (either a
corporeal one or its spiritual correlation) is derived from social development. The law of its development is determined by the law of
the development of society as a whole, at the basis of which lies the
law of the development of productive forces, that is, a specifically
social law."

For several years the Soviet New Man appeared in "Marxist-
Leninist" ballyhoo, but invariably cloaked in imprecision. In the
bombast of the "Bukharin period," before the purges, he is sometimes
the living Russian, already transformed, sometimes the Russian of
the invariably near future, and sometimes the character which the
"building of socialism" requires at once of those who are still stuck
fast in the mud of bourgeois selfishness and bourgeois superstition.
Then—as may have been expected—he disappears suddenly and
completely in the nationalist fury of World War II, when what was
wanted (in the U.S.S.R. as elsewhere) were men and women to kill
and die for their country and themselves. He reappears in the early
Fifties, perhaps to rouse the war-fagged from their torpor and their
hunger for the amenities (and perhaps to cover Stalin's rampant ter-
rorism), only to lose vogue (along with so many many-splendored
postures) with Stalin's departure, and to reappear in the late Fifties
and early Sixties (coupled now with "Communist morality") as a
counterweight to the pervasive cynicism that followed Khrushchev's

denunciation of Stalin, fading again with dekhrushchevization.

With the current *embourgeoisement* of the whole Soviet world, in which the cry from top to bottom (or from bottom to top) for consumer goods is dominant along with an irrepressible liberalization in industry, agriculture, trade, and the arts, and even in ideology, the New Man is nowhere trumpeted at all—not so much as a whisper or a whimper. Instead, the hard-rockers sound an ever more plaintive call for a return to the fading ideals of the fathers, a call almost indistinguishable from those recorded on the Monday-morning church page of the Western press. Even in People's China the recital of the new nation's achievements and pretensions on the whole is considerably more restrained than the Soviet pronunciamentos at the same stage of historical development, and the "self-criticism" rhapsody of Maoism is increasingly interlarded with the complaint of backsliding, the admission that bourgeois vices (not just errors) persist, and the threat of the big stick.*

The bombast and the trumpeting are not to be dismissed out of hand as Fourth of July—or Seventeenth of October—oratory produced by servitor hacks for delivery by party panjandrums. In 1957 Boris Pasternak addressed himself "to friends in East and West" in a New Year's greeting published for the first time in 1965 (five years after his death) in *Literaturnaya Rossiya:* "Our revolution . . . filled this century with sense and meaning. Not only we, and our younger generation—even your banker's son is not the same as his father and grandfather were before him. . . . He enters life unencumbered, as a man should: he comes as a guest to the feast of existence, and knows that what matters is not how much he inherits but how he behaves at the feast, and what people remember and love him for.

"Thank us then for this new man, even in your old society; thank

---

* On August 24, 1969, the United Press in Hong Kong monitored the following editorial on Radio Peking (and from the authoritative Chinese press): "There are always some people, namely unreformed landlords, rich peasants, counter-revolutionaries, bad elements and rightists, reactionary bourgeois elements and a handful of hidden counter-revolutionaries who are not reconciled to their defeat.

"They seize every opportunity to stir up trouble and to attack the proletariat at what they consider to be weak spots. They try to sabotage the socialist ownership, use various methods to corrupt our old and new cadres and youth, whip up the evil wind of counter-revolutionary economism to disrupt the socialist productions . . . engage in speculation to sabotage the state economic plan and try to use feudal religious superstitions to undermine unity among the various nationalities." The editorial concluded with the kind of animadversion which could not help but dishearten the true believer in the Soviet New Man (unless, of course, he accepted the Maoist view of recent history): "We must do more to eradicate the poison spread in the past by the Soviet modern revisionist in the cultural, ideological and scientific spheres in China."

us that he is livelier, finer-witted, and more gifted than his heavy and pompous predecessors; for this child of the century was delivered in the maternity home called Russia."

The Pasternaks will not surrender the New Man in the face of every imaginable manifestation that the Old is simply adorned with new (and transparent) trimmings. It is the poet's political function to see the New Man coming and to see him here. And it is the poet's political triumph that the prosist fails, and fails, and fails again to shoot his way into a New World without a New Man. But the maternity home called Russia has had more than fifty years—into the third generation now—to deliver the New Man, and elsewhere in Eastern Europe more than twenty. Grant the extraordinary historical obstacles under which the Communists labored. They began with every imaginable disadvantage except ardor for something new and disenchantment with everything old. They were poor and unskilled and unequipped, and shackled to a classism no longer extant anywhere in the West (except in American racism). They have had to proceed in the face of intense internal hostility, external attack, "counter-revolutions" within their buffer zones, and the grand schism with China; the rigors of "war Communism" have gone on unabated decade after decade. Grant, above all, that fifty years is no time at all for the kind of revolution they proclaim; it is taking more than a hundred, without the disadvantages, to do much more than proclaim the modest goal of the emancipation of the Negro in America.

All these conditions granted, the intrepid observer cannot dismiss certain attitudes (and less certain practices) as mere appearances of new behavior patterns engendered in part by fiat and enforcement and in part by the original vision which, like all visions, tends to run out of gas as the generation that responded to it disappears. In the more backward countries of yesteryear, the Soviet Union, Bulgaria, Rumania, hamlets whose prerevolutionary inhabitants had never so much as seen a book now have bookstores offering not only the party authors (and the Western critics of capitalism) but Shakespeare at a nickel or a dime; and it is in these countries where bellboys, elevator operators, countermen, clerks, and bus drivers at the end of the line may be seen quite commonly reading on the job. (We learned from Nazi Germany that there is nothing necessarily new about the literate Old Man, but a people newly come to literacy may be forgiven for supposing that there is.)*

* ". . . He was reading a book while he waited. I came closer and saw that it was a dialogue, a play. The idea of a truck driver reading a play was, to say the least, amazing. Ehrenburg had traveled the world and knew why foreigners made so much of this, and he said, "Yes, that is one thing we did do—we made readers of them."—Miller, *op. cit.*, p. 38.

Begging is outlawed as it was by Mussolini and Hitler, and (in their cases, too, certainly in Hitler's) not entirely for showcase purposes. The absolute necessity for begging is, as it was in Hitler's, if not Mussolini's, case, nearly eliminated by the social program—nearly, not entirely, when an old-age pension is inadequate for coffee, tobacco, and beer. Mendicancy is condemned as an indignity to man and society and a vice to be suppressed from earliest childhood. In Budapest, Sofia, Belgrade, Warsaw the little beggars for ballpoints come arunning when they identify a Western pedestrian or motorist— but with some circumspection lest they be shagged by one of their elders. But every visitor who has strayed from the Intourist beat in the U.S.S.R. has had the repeated experience of, on the one hand, the eagerness of children to trade anything for anything and, on the other, their refusal to accept anything for nothing. (I have known even the supposedly magic *"Napamyet,"* "For remembrance," to fail to move the prospective recipient.)

So passes, in the Communist world as in ours, the lady or gentleman bountiful and the Christmas basket; passes (along with the high motivation of *caritas*) to the cold consideration of rights. Passes, too, begging's kissing cousin, tipping, the ultimate indignity of the Old Man, whose "mine" is not only his money but his whim in disposing of it a penny at a time to the wheedling waiter whose supper depends upon flattery and the size of whose supper depends upon the degree to which the tipper is celebrant. Tipping isn't outlawed in the Communist countries and it is still *de rigueur* in the tourist joints of the big cities, but the visitor who has traveled on his own, even in the neighborhood streets of the cities, has not gone very far, if he makes any contact at all, without being told, "Thank you, no; I am paid for my work."

If tipping is still the rule rather than the exception, shame has been successfully inculcated into the practice. It is this small flickering shame that may be real and, if it is real, may be new. Who is there in the West who won't accept a tip in one form or another? The Supreme Court Justice serving as consultant to a foundation? Or the Senator to whose law firm corporate clients gravitate? Or the headwaiter—or the railroad-station "redcap" who explains that the fixed charge for carrying a bag "goes to the company"? The notion of shamefulness, apart from compulsion, certainly adheres in the Communist world to the responsibility to work and the extirpation—even by the criminal treatment of "social parasites"—of idleness among the able-bodied, though this is a triumph that has its rapidly growing parallel in the whole West without formal penalty except for the high taxation on unearned income. The American (or the Englishman, the Frenchman,

or the German) who does not work is stigmatized in the egalitarian
society, and they are all egalitarian societies now; it is as unthinkable
for a Rockefeller not to work as it is for Joe Palooka. I am assured
that in the ubiquitous monuments of the Worker and Peasant in the
Soviet Union, the workers and peasants see themselves and their
social role glorified; but I can assure my assurer that the American
sees himself at least equally glorified by his possession of a Mustang.

It is my profoundly studied conviction that the Worker/Peasant,
East or West, is disposed to settle for the bucket seat and let the
granite go. Between unionization and governmental controls (and
supports) the Westerner doubtless finds himself (like the Easterner)
harder to identify as an individual. But his farm or labor association
(even the United Mine Workers or the National Association of Letter
Carriers) is not a mere front, as it is (and as he knows it is) in the
Communist world. I have watched the shift changes in Communist
and capitalist mills and factories, and the long, slow, premature
preparation for the quitting whistle is far longer, slower, and more
premature in the Communist. I have heard repeatedly and credibly of
the dispersion by Communist police vans of knots of workers and
peasants grumbling *outside* the gates about injustices and the prospect
not of strike but of mere protest. And when I read that the brewery
workers of Pilsen vote *unanimously* to give up their traditional four
free liters a day of beer as "unworthy" of a free worker, I do not need
to be told (though I am) that a secret ballot would produce something close to a contrary unanimity.

Still, the blue-shirted comrade does not step aside in the queues for
the white-shirted, or take off his hat to him, or call him "sir," as he
always did in the old Europe (which is not the old America); this,
too, may be genuinely meaningful and not just a New Insolence or a
New Dungheap. And the man in the miner's cap will as often as not
slam his door on the neighborhood functionary (that "dread" informant) who comes around on a special collection campaign for the
Party. Of course, there is a ruling caste under Communism, throughout the whole order, and not just in the first-, second-, and third-class
distinction in hotels, restaurants, theaters, and railroad trains ("hard"
and "soft" in the U.S.S.R.), a caste, moreover, whose mark of its rule
is the same as the Old Man's: house, car, clothes, and, above all,
privilege.*

---

* "Virtually all Soviet city-dwellers are part peasant at heart and those who
can afford it have country dachas of one kind or another. A dacha can be anything from a shed or corner in a peasant hut to a villa. . . .
"The Vilnius correspondent of the newspaper *Selskaya Zhizn* (*Country
Life*) described a dacha building boom around the Lithuanian capital. The

It's the sime the wide wurruld over: When you want something, and the waiting list is as long as it invariably is in a Communist country, the man who gets to the head of the list is the man who "knows somebody"—or who knows somebody who knows somebody. In the lush wurruld of free enterprise, it is likeliest to be money; in the hard wurruld of Eastern Europe, it is goods and services at any price: an apartment (or a bigger one), a half ton of coal (or a scuttleful), a pair of shoes soled, a railroad, theater, or restaurant reservation, a come-right-in appointment with the doctor or the dentist. If you are a highly placed comrade you get it; if you're a lowly comrade you can still holler for it and maybe get it; if you're a non-Communist non-comrade, you may get it some day or never. The boiler broke down in a seminary where my wife and I were living as guests in Prague. It was April, and still chilly, but an auxiliary hot-water heater did (or didn't quite do) for cooking and washing. The building engineer (no Christian) advised waiting until July to ask for repairs, and the request was duly made in July. In mid-December the repairman arrived—and the auxiliary heater, too, had to be shut down for two weeks. On the other hand, an atheist (or at least a professing atheist) of my acquaintance in Krakow who was told that his wife would have to wait her turn to equip her new kitchen endeared himself (with his wife's gloomy consent) to the wife of a middle official of a ministry unconnected with kitchen equipment, and the truck backed up to his door in a jiffy.

Not just to be privileged but to look privileged, not just to ride in a Cadillac but to be seen riding in it is the hallmark of the Old Man. Many a Soviet New Man goes defiantly to the Bolshoi in his shirt and sweater still—something that wouldn't happen in "Western" Warsaw, Prague, or Budapest—but never a Man of Distinction. But Nikolai Lenin didn't need a status symbol, not even a new suit, not even a

---

correspondent dwelt particularly on the dacha of Jozas Shimaliunas, deputy director of the district distribution center of the Lithuanian Consumers Union. The two-story structure is perched on concrete pillars beside a picturesque waterfall. From the second-floor balcony, it is possible to dive directly into the pool beneath, or sit and fish while watching television. . . .

"When the correspondent put some pointed questions to another dachnik, Izaak Kibarkis, manager of a farm machinery depot, he said Mr. Kibarkis replied: 'Why do you pick on us poor dachniks? Wouldn't you rather have a nice new car? Don't you write anything about how I got building materials for my cottage and I won't mention providing you with the car.'

"Instead of accepting the offer, the correspondent reported the episode to Ionas Smilgavicius, the first deputy mayor of Vilnius. But Mr. Smilgavicius was in no mood to take action against a fellow dachnik. The deputy mayor has moved his own spacious country residence from one public recreation zone to another. . . . Other city officials followed the deputy mayor's example, and, according to the correspondent, the public recreation zones around Vilnius were 'melting like snow in the spring' as a result of these encroachments."—London *Times,* November 28, 1970.

new cap. The Stalins, the Hitlers, the Maos, and the Castros who came after the Founding Father all made as much of a status symbol of their corporal's jackets as the American hippie of his tattered blue jeans. Stalin's restoration of military rank before World War II in effect left the dictator the only man in the country without chevrons, epaulettes, and medals. In the Communist world, China and Albania alone cling to the symbolic rejection of official insignia. But it's the wage differential, and not the rosette in the coat lapel, that makes the ultimate point; as it does in the world that is building capitalism, so, too, in the world that is building Communism. The gap between the lowest and highest paid worker's take-home—the latter a minister of state, with, to be sure, his perquisites and privileges—is something on the order of a modest ten: if fifty crowns (or whatever) a month at the bottom, five hundred at the top. "I would calculate," says Prague's leading non-Communist economist, "that probably eighty-five percent of the Czechs are living on substantially the same level. Taking the countries of the bloc all together, I'd guess that Communism has improved the economic condition of eighty percent, worsened it for fifteen, and left five unchanged."

Many the marching Doughface who has sung, "You'll never get rich, you son of a bitch, you're in the Army now," but few who thought they'd never get out of the Army and make a killing. The people who live under Communism know that they won't. Where there are no riches—and no rags—there are no rags-to-riches sagas. Most of the East Europeans seem to have learned to temper (not subdue, but temper) the acquisitive spirit to a pretty much settled situation. There is no less talk of bodily goods and, of course, no less scramble for them; but the possibilities are so modest that there is not much sense in panting—and none at all in reading the ads. Half the professional men of my acquaintance, everywhere in the Communist world, get along well enough without a car. Women work—and work with pick and shovel and street broom and not because of their espousal of Women's Liberation.* A revolution of falling expectations *has* occurred among the old bourgeois and among the natural candidates for bourgeois status.

The proletarians, with their new purchasing power, crowd the shops, and there is occasional open criticism of official boasts of the rising standard of living and of governmental stimulation of the lust

* *Cf.* "the *Cosmopolitan* girl" advertisement for an American magazine in 1970: "[She] babies a man but expects to be babied in return . . . a girl who wants to do it herself, doesn't want to live through her husband and children, probably has a job, because it's more fun to work than not. . . ."

for goods. Old (and an increasing number of young) idealists who want to believe that Communism means brotherhood, when Premier Kosygin tells the XXIII Congress of the CPUSSR that "Communism means the raising of living standards," ask one another (and an occasional trusted visitor) how, if that is what it means, Communism differs from capitalism.* When André Malraux quoted Kosygin's assertion to Mao Tse-tung, the Chinese leader said, "And swimming is a way of putting on bathing trunks."

But there's a built-in ceiling on stimulation when, instead of fifty-seven varieties, there are two or three or one—no bargains, close-outs, midsummer clearances, or January white sales. Take the titillation out of the *caveat emptor,* take the charm out of shopping around, and you've taken away a good deal of temptation (and, I suppose, a good deal of virtue in resisting it). When I asked a Christian pastor in Rumania what he could say *for* Communism in his country, he replied, "One thing: We still lie, of course, *but we don't lie as much for money as we used to."*

All these people have lived and died in the wars, the occupations, and the revolutions of our time, in their cities and villages, their streets and their houses. Doing without may make big spenders of people when they no longer have to, but it may be good training for having to go on doing without. And when everybody (the Joneses included) has had to do without long enough, and with some immaterial end in view, a fair, if deceptive, imitation of the New Man seems to take shape in at least this one respect. As the present profligate American (or West German) is the most undignified man I have ever seen, so the most dignified was my old history professor, William E. Dodd, reading examination papers on a Chicago streetcar a couple of months after he had resigned the U.S. Ambassadorship to Nazi Germany.

Call the East European a slave and his Western counterpart free— "the difference," said my friend in Budapest, "is that we *know* we are brainwashed"—the Easterner is free from the kind of bottomless terror of poverty, relative or absolute, that either makes a money-making machine of a man or gives him the pretext for being one. There are other terrors in the Communist society, but on this one head the society has a comforting commitment to its every member. Its first premise is that its labor force is its treasure. The reduction of that

* What strikes diplomats as significant is the apparent willingness of the Kremlin leaders—not least those in the majority—to disregard the warnings of many conservatives that stress on consumer goods turns people away from revolutionary ideals, and encourages bourgeois thinking."—Moscow report in the New York *Times,* February 16, 1971.

force—through poor training or none, through joblessness, or through illness or dietary insufficiency—is the squandering of that treasure. The individual's "right," then, to medical care, to the essentials of a healthful diet, and to the development and employment of his capacities coincides with the society's first need and becomes the government's first obligation. The obligation imposed by reality coincides happily with the dream of eliminating the acquisitiveness which, in the Marxist view, is imposed on man by his lifelong dread of unemployment, by the necessity to provide for his children, by the prospect of catastrophic illness, and by the economic unsupportability of old age.

10: How Like
an Angel

IF THESE are signs or symptoms of something new—if they signify anything more than compulsion and habituation to compulsion—there are surer signs that the Old Man is more than holding his own. The New Man was (and still is) to be as honest, constant, and continent as the Old was (and still is) corrupt. In the first raptures of the Russian Revolution, the New Puritan, if not the New Man, was certainly to be seen in the leadership. But the rapture, along with the leaders, is long gone.

The assessment of "Communist morality" is hard to make. The statistics on social behavior are notoriously unreliable and still more notoriously sketchy. The vast category of "economic crimes against public property" tends to raise the Communist crime rate *vis-à-vis* ours, as does our generally higher age allowed for the designation of delinquency. In the United States the official reports show a spectacular year-to-year rise in crime as against the U.S.S.R.'s unverifiable and unbelievable claim of a year-to-year decline. Drunkenness, drug addiction, divorce, and sexual laxity (including prostitution, which was supposed to disappear with the "disappearance of its economic base") are clearly on the increase everywhere in the East, probably as phenomenally as in the West. The Leningrad police chief recently asserted that the city's vodka consumption has increased by 15 percent in the past five years and population by 5 percent, and the 1970 edition of the Great Soviet Encyclopedia eliminated its earlier statement that "the social roots of alcoholism have been destroyed" and that "conditions for its full liquidation have been created," and said simply that the state is trying to overcome "the so-called alcoholic tradition" in Russia.*

Over the decades the Communist penal codes have been progressively ameliorated—except for the reintroduction of the death penalty in the Soviet Union. At the height of the de-Stalinization jag an unnamed "senior Government official" in Moscow said that "Stalin thought that everything could be cured by official decrees and tough police methods. This was nonsense. People must be taken into consideration, with all their weaknesses and temptations. . . . The cure is to be found through the education of each and every citizen from childhood," etc. ("The force of habit of millions and tens of millions," said Lenin in his *Left-Wing Communism,* "is a most terrible force.")

Though star-chamber procedures are still a Communist staple, the confessions (never followed by absolution) of Stalin's capricious show trials are rare nowadays, and much less bizarre (even in the process of re-Stalinizing Czechoslovakia).† But hte 1956 shootouts in Poznan and Budapest, the 1968 put-down in Prague, and the 1970 labor riots in Poland, like those of the Stalinist Thirties, all had the same depressing spinoff of denunciation and counter-denunciation,

---

* The New York *Times,* March 24, 1970. Calculations of actual social conditions in the Communist world are almost all inferential, usually from editorialized articles or the publication of letters in the central press. In 1969 the Soviet papers said that a survey showed that alcohol was the cause of 85 percent of the country's murders, 50 percent of the traffic accidents, 40 percent of the divorces, and 68 percent of the drownings. (New York *Times,* May 19, 1969.) A year later a newspaper campaign against vodka began, with letters suggesting everything from its outright prohibition to the payment of "the drunkard's" wages directly to his wife, and Politburo member A. N. Shalapin called upon the trade unions to "strengthen the struggle" against "absenteeism, loafing, and drunkenness." (*Ibid.,* January 13, 29, 1970.) The Prague journal *Kvety* (December 27, 1969) said, "The time has come to talk about drug addiction. For a long time we also doubted the existence of prostitution"—visibly rampant not only in Prague but in Warsaw, Budapest, and Bucharest. "Reality found us unprepared. To hush up drug addiction would be equally myopic." At the same time, the Czechoslovak Assembly increased the penalty for car theft from three months to two years, and Hungary lowered from sixteen to fourteen the age at which an identity card has to be carried. (New York *Times,* December 28, 1969.) Meanwhile, back at the home ranch, *Izvestia* published an article which, the London *Times* reported (November 15, 1968), "caused some surprise in a country that consistently proclaims that it has created a new man, superior in all respects to the old." The writer wondered whether Soviet society had perhaps gone too far in rejecting "the narrow-mindedness introduced by religion and private school teaching." In relations between the sexes "some young people understand the abolition of harmful prohibition as an abolition of all prohibition," with mothers allowing their children to "proceed directly from childhood to the dirt of corruption without the purity of first kisses."

† A letter reportedly sent by the Party Central Committee to all Czech diplomats abroad charged "that with few exceptions, a spirit of 'self-criticism' had not appeared [among them] despite the proceedings in sessions of the Central Committee in May and September 1969."—New York *Times,* March 14, 1970.

leaving the observer with the same depressing pair of questions: Were these New Villains, too, New Men once? Are those who denounce them New Men now?

With the widest latitude allowed for unreliability and genuine variables (such as the designation of "crime"), all of the European Communist countries have much less criminality, in all categories, than nearly all of the West (and compared with the U.S.A. a minuscule amount). The comparison is all the more impressive in the light of the pervasive presence (or possible presence) of plainclothes authority throughout East European society; the Westerner wonders that there is any crime at all. But violent crime has always been low in Europe (except in libertarian England); violence, like tobacco, tea, and coffee, has always been a state monopoly. "Peace" means the hope that the government remains at peace. (Since it never does, there is no real doctrinaire nonviolence in the Anglo-American sense. Pacifism has the dissenting churches at its roots, and there have never been dissenting churches of consequence on the Continent. West *and* East Germany give conscientious objection to war full recognition, unlike the rest of Eastern *or* Western Europe.) The dark streets of the Continent—even of Paris, on the whole—have always been safe at night. Small arms are next to impossible to come by, and, in the Communist world, where everything is registered, closer than that to impossible. Sneak thievery is common enough, especially as one proceeds southward, but mugging, rolling, robbery, burglary, and rape are, as they always were, rare. Like sex, violence is not to be seen on TV or in the comic books. But the American Westerns are ever more popular, the picture postcards of Soviet actresses are somewhat friskier than they were ten years ago, and if you know where to go in Warsaw or Budapest, even in Prague, you don't have to go to Vienna for the skin shows or the *Exotische-Sex-Attraktionen.*

But these goodies—vulgate murder included—are not indigenous to most areas of what is now Communist Europe. What is certainly prevalent under Communism—*noblesse oblige* disappears with the disappearance of nobility great and small—is petty corruption of the traditionally incorruptible civil servant in societies all of whose members are now civil servants. Rampant are short-weighting, short-changing, corner-cutting, quality-upgrading, quota-faking, smuggling, bad or stale produce at the bottom of the basket, and, above all, small-time bribery and commercial favoritism and chiseling.* (The

---

* In Sofia "there is a surprising number of new Western autos with Bulgarian plates on the roads. It is hard to get an official explanation. A Sofia-born Macedonian said with a chuckle: "Our new class! A smart Bulgarian plant

corner grocery may have no eggs and only half-soured milk—except under the counter.) The black market in currency is so plainly irrepressible that, except for an occasional burst of police activity reminiscent of the speakeasy raids of Prohibition, no serious effort is made to repress it. On one occasion in 1971 I was offered an illegal exchange rate by a Czech official whose basis for trusting my confidence was so slight that the conclusion is irresistible. A Polish wag says in public that an American worker makes $400 a month and saves $100, while a Polish worker makes 2,500 zloty a month and saves 5,000.

The people of the Communist countries are short, none of them of the necessities, almost all of them of the amenities. We always suppose that the urge to transgress is proportionate to the need, but we don't always bother to decide what we mean by need. Far fewer Americans have absolute needs than East Europeans, but relative need appears to be more urgent. The American does not even have the onetime reputation of the much poorer German for honesty. Estimates of shoplifting in the United States range from two to two and a half billion dollars a year and of employee thievery from one to three billion (as against strong-arm's five hundred million).*

In one especially interesting (to Westerners) area of social conduct the suspicion that it's the sime the wide wurruld over is again confirmed. At precisely the time when American young people were beginning to kick up the dust a few years ago, the then Czechoslovakian Minister of Justice noted (on the introduction of relaxed penal laws) that all categories of crime *except one* had shown a steady decrease since 1956: "Juvenile delinquency increased from 7.9% of the total number of crimes committed in 1963 to 8.9% in 1964." And a year later the respected Soviet journal *State and Society* found that juvenile delinquency was highest in the middle-income group (and confessed the most un-Marxist conclusion that "mental, rather than economic and material, factors are decisive in moulding criminals"). And Afanasi F. Yeshtokin, Party Leader of the Kuznetsk coal-basin

---

manager knows how to convert his productivity bonus into a shiny Mercedes, and some foreign firms show their appreciation for the collaboration they find here. . . ." (New York *Times*, March 4, 1970.) It is almost as hard to get a newspaper report of corruption as it is to get an official explanation. But an occasional item is suggestive, such as a Moscow newspaper's statement that four telephone installers had been imprisoned—there were no other details—for charging tenants $550 to $2,200 to lay telephone lines to their buildings and an extra $55 to provide an individual phone. (*Ibid.*, December 24, 1969.)

* "One in Ten Shoppers Is a Shoplifter"—headline in New York *Times Magazine*, March 15, 1970. (The report quotes an FBI finding that U.S. shoplifting increased more than 150 percent between 1960 and 1970, with retailer estimates that it accounts for 15 percent of the price level of consumer goods.)

region of Siberia, started a large discussion in *Sovetskaya Rossiya* with his report that the school dropout rate prior to the eighth grade was 60 percent.

Heigh-ho.* It used to be a Communist axiom that the hard line had to be held until the last of the bourgeois generation had passed—and the new generation come of age without nostalgia. The new generation is come of age—the third such in the Soviet Union—and the axiom is no longer heard. It didn't happen, and it isn't happening, not even, apparently, in China, where Mao complained to André Malraux that "the youth do not show true revolutionary spirit. . . . They are not interested in Communism or political education. They are materialistic and indifferent to the national struggle."

The rebellion of the Marxist young in Europe breaks out in hippieism or in poetry (or in what the wide wurruld over the Russians call hooliganism) on a limited scale in the cities; but throughout the land it takes the characteristic form of deepest-dyed apathy, an apathy underlined by the sudden surge of animation among the young Czechs under Dubček and their reversion after the Soviet invasion of Prague in 1968. The "system" is something that has to be lived with, and lived in, and that is all. The young, on their own, resist it by simply blocking it out. Like military conscription, it may have everything to do with their living conditions or (on the India-Pakistan or Egypt-Israel border) with their deaths; it has nothing to do with their lives. Apart from the fringe extremes—the red-hots of the Communist Youth on the right, the poets and protesters on the left—the attitude of the twenty-year-old in every Communist country I know is exemplified by the answer in Bucharest to the question "How much influence has religion with people your age?" "About the same as Communism—not much."

The heart of the resistance, of the "youth problem," seems to be at bottom identical in Bielostok and in Berkeley—and in Berlin and Buffalo and Tokyo and Nanterre. The depersonalization of life, by commissar or computer, or both, is alienating the young from the Establishment without regard to ideology, racism, poverty, pollution, Vietnam, or even (in England) conscription. This was the case in ur-

* "Circumstantial evidence that can be gleaned from Eastern European newspapers and random observation points to bored and politically frustrated children of a relatively affluent new class of officials, technocrats and plant managers as a major source of the present teen-age trouble. . . . Investigation of the social background of the members of youth gangs showed, the Hungarian newspaper *Nepszava* said, 'that half of them came from families with above-average incomes and 10 percent from families owning a house or a cooperative apartment.'" (New York *Times,* December 27, 1969.) Heigh-ho again.

ban, industrialized Bohemia before Communism; it is now the case everywhere. The floating resentment of the card-indexed drives them, before they reach the age of quiet despair, to assert their I-am-ness against *whatever* the Establishment represents. In Communist society the Establishment represents enthusiasm and participation; the form of the adolescent rejection is according. The West is the official Enemy; and whatever comes from the West, whether or not it has any native appeal, is therefore the object of clamor. No instrument is less indigenous to musical Czechoslovakia than the guitar; but there it is, selling as fast as it goes on the market, along with the beard and the sandals and the hair—defiance of the Establishment *whosever it is*.

Any system, in so far as it is antithetical to the new, must be anti-thetical to the New Man. The unrelenting pressure of Communism in practice pushes depersonalization as relentlessly as does advertising (or supermarkets or conscription) in the West. Masses are easier to deal with than men. The massification of life under Communism, like that of the assembly line, puts a premium on the interchangeability of individuals. They are appendages to the machine. I find myself in a great square-filled demonstration (it was the Anniversary of October) with academic associates of advanced years who, in the West, or in the East before Communism, would never stand for two or three hours in the rain to be doubly drenched with the platitudes that cas-caded from the platform. Now they are "expected" to attend such gatherings, and there *may* be a neighbor, yes, or a colleague, to take note of absenteeism; and lo! it is 1970, the American universities are struck by their students, and I find myself in a great square-filled demonstration with academic associates of advanced years . . . drenched with platitudes . . . "expected" to attend such gatherings.

This pervasive invasion of privacy—apart from the spying and in-forming—seems to be inherent in the "continuing revolution" in the East, with a positive purpose that still differentiates it sharply from its counterpart in the Western societies: The citizen has to be taught to understand Marxism and its problems. In the West the man of the Silent Majority has only to keep his silence and fasten his decal to his windshield; in the East he has got to demonstrate his fidelity like a camp-meeting convert. He is not allowed to *non*participate, and who-ever does, or is laggard, or intermittent, is suspect; and the "re-education" of the highly educated bourgeois, like my academic asso-ciates, is more earnestly undertaken than the education of the prole-tariat. True, there is less compulsion of this kind than there was (and a little more in the West); but it is still the pattern (rigorously re-stored in Prague since the Soviet occupation of 1968). There is no indication that it is erasable; and the Hungarian friend who told me "One wishes that he could be your famous 'forgotten man' " was not speaking for himself alone.

In so far as human dignity is externally affected or determined, nothing indignifies a man more thoroughly than his being watched like a child, scolded like a child, coerced like a child, and cajoled like a child. Maturation means social no less than individual responsibility. The New Man will never be the ward of a government, nor will his goings and comings, above all, his life in his home and his personal contact with others, be the subject of surreptitious surveillance. Whatever small signs there may be in the Communist world that something genuinely new may be emerging are nullified by the persistence of a network of humiliating controls extending to, and into, his private life. "I can accept every indignity but one," a Polish architect told me. "I cannot accept the decision of my uneducated inferiors as to what I may and may not read. So I am an anti-Communist. I am an anti-Communist because I am a man."

This congeries of controls—symbolized by the invariable practice of arranging conversations on a park bench or a country walk rather than a public or private room—is now intensified, now reduced a little, depending on both domestic conditions and the world situation. But the over-all sense of over-all repression remains (after more than a half century in the Soviet Union), with its train of caution, circumspection, and named and nameless fears, and the clam-up among the "political" few—five percent? ten? fifteen?—of the people who in any society have a doctrinal concern with social issues. How can this steamrollered soil be the seedbed of anything new?

11: All the Armageddons

YOU NAME IT—he's tried it.

He's tried (*inter alia*):

Steak, whiskey, wine, women, song, *and* the grapefruit diet, and starving 'em out in Troy and the Alamo.

Push-ups, put-downs, sundowners, sun lamps (and sunspots)—he's tried them.

He's tried sit-ins and shootouts.

Carnival and *carne vale* (*inter alia*).

Burma Shave, Cambodia Coup.

The Falls in a barrel, the bottom of the barrel, and the decline and fall of the (*inter alia*) Roman empire.

Inter alia:

Marriage and divorce (and marriage) (and divorce).

Coupling and uncoupling.

And homo-, hetero-, mono-, auto-, and polyunsaturated sexuality.

Family counseling, group dynamics, group therapy, T-groups, and tea leaves. (*"He used to be the most miserable son of a bitch in town, and then he got psychoanalyzed and now he's the happiest son of a bitch in town; same son of a bitch."*)

And that isn't all.

He's tried gargling, and, after gargling:

Hindsight, foresight, prophecy, profit-sharing, futurology, pastology, presentology, and professors of Business Administration. (And Billy Graham and Buffalo Bill and Moody & Sankey and Sanka.)

Inter alia:

Alienists, alienation, fenestration, defenestration, devaluation, *and* Couéism, table-tilting, ouija boards, mah-jongg, macro- (and anti-) biotics (and anti-toxins and tocsins) and prophylaxis, not to mention, except in passing, extrasensory perception, logical positivism, variable lags, the Uncertainty Principle, conditioned reflexes, parapsychology, black and white magic, "Black & White" Scotch, Scotch (and Irish) oatmeal, astrology, *and* anatomy. He's tried metaphysics and astrophysics and tarot cards, smoke signals, Satan worship, *Walpurgisnacht, Walden, Weltschmerz, élan vital, Vital Speeches, Vichy water.*

He's tried the Living God and the Dead God. ("Why not try God?" said Mary Pickford.)

He's tried Mary Pickford, Fatty Arbuckle, Colonel Lindbergh, dianetics, Spam, deflation, afflatus, and folkless folk dancing.

You name it.

He's tried it.

Jogging, for instance, and, *inter alia:*

Peace and plenty, war and plenty, education and re-education and training and retraining, Upward Bound, Outward Bound, Inward Bound, and Prometheus Unbound (the bounder), and (as an Oak Park, Illinois, preacher said) a gnashing and wailing of teeth.

The carrot and the stick, the honor system and the Pinkertons, Sominex and No-Doz, Cascara, mascara, Ankara, Palm Springs, inner springs, and Outer Space.

Getting away from it all and taking it (after death and taxes) with him. He's tried it where the action is, killed in action at Russian roulette, in the Russian Revolution, on Russian Hill in San Francisco, and shooting the rapids of the Russian River (or one too many *oeufs à la Russe* may have done it).

Oeuf.

Cooking on the front burner and burning, baby, burning, and burning babies.

He—who else?—has tried pesticides, genocides, suicides, and a house by the side of the road where he mixed his drinks and then went big-game hunting, little-game hunting, witch-hunting, Communist-hunting, anti-Communist hunting, no hunting, no fishing, no nothing (except search and destroy).

(House-hunting, too, for a house by the side of the freeway.)

A bigger bang for a buck, or, alternatively, no bang at all for no buck at all: karma, sitar, Upanishads, Krishnamurti, Hare Krishna. Shazam. (But you cannot avoid your Karma-corn, and you know it and I know it and the Greek chorus knows it.)

You name it.

French fries, hash browns, hashish, dropping in for a minute, out for a minute, off for a minute, and acid (for a minute that seems like eternity with second cup free), and a second cup of acidophilus milk.

Acidosis.

Electrostatics, electrolysis, electrocution, electric heating, levitation, and (this, too) participatory democracy.

Inter alia (among other things):

Vaccination.

Prayer shawls.

Electric sox/ guitars/ toothbrushes/ can openers/ submarines/ broilers/ belts/ blankets.

And the Bill of Rights *and* Aristotle's six kinds of good and bad government sixty times, and Mrs. Aristotle Onassis, and onanism.

Don't forget cruising, boozing, snoozing, bruising, losing—even, in the Nursing Home, musing. He's tried it.

He's tried it by candlelight and stroboscope and stethoscope, he's tried it by lynching and by inching and he's tried it by busing and he's tried it by bussing.

He's tried—you wouldn't believe it, but he's tried it—frontal lobotomy. He's tried raising lobelias and swallowing loblolly, fire, sword, people, pride, penitence, goldfish, phonograph records, and bubble gum when the teacher called on him.

Pop culture, subculture, and organic farming in the spring.

You name it: Summer? Winter? Spring? He's tried it.

No go (*same son of a bitch*).

Speculation, accumulation, and grinding the faces of the poor and the faces of the rich. (If it wasn't Confucius it was Buddha who said, "He who says, 'Rich men are fools, but when I am rich I will not be a fool,' is already a fool." If it wasn't Buddha it was Confucius who said, "If I am a fool when I leave Peking, I shall be a fool when I reach Nanking.") (Or was it the Bishop of Nanking who said it?)

No go.

Gimmickry, with spinoffs. *With solid stuff so close together, they had to come up with a better insulator. And they did: teflon. This not only made the integrated circuit possible (and a landing on the moon), but a nonstick frying pan and scores of other items.*—President Gordon L. Ness of Ness Industries of Palo Alto, California, quoted in the San Francisco *Chronicle*, August 20, 1969.

The Old Man's tried it, and he's down in the dumps, and nobody says he's mad any more when, instead of saying, "India? I think I'll go there," he says, "Mars? I think I'll go there." But neither does anybody think he's mad when he says (as does Professor Paul R. Ehrlich of the Center for the Study of Democratic Institutions), "It is possible that the rapid growth of technology will lead to that common end of runaway evolutionary trends—extinction. The signs now point that way." *

The signs point that way—not forward to Superman, not backward to Subman, but to Man where he is and to Man what he is: the Old Man, chained by the marvels of his mind to progressive self-enslavement, the dream of freedom slipping from him. How long ago the dream—five years or so?—of Martin Luther King. How long ago Whitman's American "solitary, singing in the West," how long ago Whitman's letter to the 333rd anniversary of the founding of Santa Fe, New Mexico:

> The seething, materialistic and business vortices of the United States, in their present devouring relations, controlling and belittling everything else, are, in my opinion, but a vast and indispensable stage in the New World's development, and are certainly to be followed by something different—at least by immense modifications. Character, literature, a society worthy of the name, are yet to be established, through a Nationality of noblest spiritual, heroic and democratic attributes—not one of which at present definitely exists—entirely different from the past, though unerringly founded on it and to justify it.

That was 1883, the poet sober and modest in his assessment of things to be and sober and prosaic in his assessment of the things out of which the things to be would emanate. Men spoke still of the New World and the New Man, and in 1883 Karl Marx died in London and Georgi Valentonovich Plekhanov arrived in Moscow bringing Marxism to Russia; and a religious boy named Vladimir Ilyich Ulyanov, the son of the superintendent of schools of Simbirsk on the Volga, won a gold medal at school.

A century after Vladimir Ilyich Ulyanov (called Lenin) was born the world is spending $56 per person per year to produce the weapons of war—more than it spends on health and education combined—an expenditure requiring the labor of half of all the people in the world to produce an equivalent amount of all the world's goods and services, and in the "poor man's arms race" the military expenditures of the underdeveloped countries are rising faster than their gross na-

* *The Center Magazine*, II, 6, November 1969.

tional product.* But the People's Republic of China produces books, too. In one year it produced eight hundred million copies of the various works of Chairman Mao (compared with five hundred million books in the United States, where people have the right to read all kinds of books by all kinds of authors). With six years to go, the Washington columnist of the New York *Times* expressed the dry hope that the American people would keep their Constitution's Bill of Rights "at least until the 200th anniversary of the Declaration in 1976."

Character, literature, a society worthy of the name . . . and the New Man is no longer singing and no longer sung, not in the West or the East or the Earth or the Moon. A twenty-four-billion-dollar flagpole there now, complete with plastic flag, and the hope of men everywhere is that things will not get worse . . . or get worse any faster than they are getting worse now. On the roads of wretched Albania, "the land of eagles," there are red-and-white posters with slogans signed, simply, "Enver," Enver Hoxha being the name of the tyrant, and one of the slogans reads, "I will turn Albania into a flourishing garden of socialism." A flourishing garden of innocence when Man was New and, in the almost image of God, almost perfect; and for a long time thereafter when, "seated under the baobab, the heads of the various families discussed how to bring in the harvest, how to build the houses they needed, how to help Samba or Demba. They drew up plans together. Oh, they weren't very complicated plans. There weren't many people to consider, and the resources at their disposal were only enough to ensure the future life of their own little community." This from the wistful depths of Senegal's President Senghor announcing his country's second "four-year plan." Or this from the wistful report of Danilo Dolci on the U.S.S.R.: "Certain moral principles the 'new' man cannot but adopt. He must admit, for example, that life belongs to everyone. . . . I do not believe it will be long before mankind has taken these principles for granted. . . ."

That life belongs to everyone: "The people didn't know what they were dying for," said the soldier at My Lai in Vietnam, "and the guys didn't know why they were shooting them. . . . Gooks were gooks, and you killed them. That's what they were really for."

A flourishing garden: but first the gardener. Who can doubt Chair-

* Among merchants of death the names of the United States and the Soviet Union, in that order, lead all the rest, but the Defense Ministry of one underdeveloped country recently sent a mimeographed advertisement to a handful of private arms dealers offering to sell them 202,887 "small arms, ranging from perfect to battlefield salvage." The seller: South Vietnam.—New York *Times,* August 20, 1969.

man Mao—eight hundred million copies—when he says that power comes out of the mouth of a gun? But the New Man is no more likely to come out of the mouth of a gun than he is to emerge en masse from the eight hundred million books of Chairman Mao or from the up-ended desks with pigeonholes for people that constitute urban renewal in Buffalo or Bucharest or Birmingham or from the long lines of shanties restored to the one place on earth where they would certainly never be built again: Hiroshima. A flourishing garden, in which life belongs to everyone: The signs, says Professor Ehrlich, do not point that way, except on red-and-white posters signed, simply, "Enver."

Was Marxist Communism the last best hope of demonstrating that man as he was was, or ever would be, fit to be a Communist? We have a pretty good idea now of the date that the hope ended for Vladimir Ilyich Ulyanov, called Lenin: March 15, 1921, when the Bolshevik terror collapsed against the bourgeois resistance on the land, in the cities, and, of course, at the Kronstadt naval base, where the perpetual revolutionaries rebelled for the last time. The New Economic Plan of 1921 was the great retreat of *all things common* and the readmission of private trade (and the substitution of state trusts for the mass management of factories). The New Class of Old Men—the "NEPmen" —was born in 1921, born not to die in the doublement and redoublement of purges and still more purges. It was, rather, Lenin who died, "died struggling vainly," says Harrison E. Salisbury, "for some new formula to cope with ignorance, superstition, prejudice, chauvinism, slothfulness, narrowness, and bureaucracy, which he felt would choke and smother the Bolshevik dream of creating a new man and a new way of life." * Character, literature, a society worthy of the name . . . a Nationality of noblest spiritual, heroic, and democratic attributes. A flourishing garden.

Not, at least, from the mouth of *that* gun, nor yet from the mouth of the gun of the U.S. Navy F-4 Phantom fighter-interceptor which on March 28, 1970, shot down a North Vietnamese jet fighter 210 miles north of the demilitarized zone between North and South Vietnam: "This protective reaction to an enemy threat," said the American briefing officer, "is an inherent right of self-defense," and a reporter who asked if the MIG had fired on the Phantom was told that the question fell under the "rules of engagement" which are "classified and cannot be discussed." † Not from the mouth of a gun the New Man, nor from the mouth of a briefing officer, nor yet from

* New York *Times*, April 23, 1970.   † *Ibid.*, April 1, 1970.

the mouth of Vladimir Ilyich Ulyanov, called Lenin, called Stalin, called Khrushchev, called Brezhnev, called even, in eight hundred million copies, Our Savior Mao Tse-tung.

A hundred years after Ulyanov, called Lenin, was born, the Soviet dictatorship stood at his tomb and denounced his betrayal by the Chinese dictatorship, and every drop of vodka in Moscow had been sold a week before the celebration, right down to the little sample bottles put up for Western tourists; and Chairman Mao celebrated the centenary by telling the readers of his eight hundred million books that the celebrants at the Kremlin were "a handful of oligarchs of Soviet revisionist social-imperialism, arch-criminals preparing to start a world war." "All the demons that Communism believed it had banished from the forthcoming, as well as the real world have crept into the soul of Communism and become part of its being." This is Milovan Djilas, once the heir apparent of the Yugoslav Communist dictator Tito. "Communism, once a popular movement that inspired toiling and oppressed people of the world with the hope of creating the Kingdom of Heaven on earth . . . has become transformed into national political bureaucracies and states squabbling among themselves for prestige and influence. . . ." *

After the night of August 20–21, 1968, the recriminations were all superfluous. For eight months the civilized Czechs—if the Old Man is civilized anywhere—had been making a civilized try at demonstrating that the Old Man was new enough to create a New World. Bloodlessly overthrowing a regime that had, year in and year out, been brutally subservient to the Stalinist tyranny, the regime of Alexander Dubček proclaimed as its cornerstone the abandoned dream: "socialism" (as Dubček put it) "with a human countenance." (*"No liberty without bread, no bread without liberty"—but that was Fidel Castro ten years before.*)

The Czech people, socialistic in spirit centuries before Marx, and sufficiently humane to have erected in Prague "the Paris of the East," had risen to the proclamation and the promise that the land in which Christian Communism had been attempted by the Hussites of Tábor in 1420, with "all things common" *and* "no man subject to any man," would be the land which would try it again and perhaps (the Czechs are strong for "perhaps") prove against the most inauspicious of odds that man was fit to be a Communist. For eight months the demonstration proceeded, uncertainly, but unrelentingly, its hallmark equal justice under promulgated law, its spectacular (and, in the event, fatal)

* *The Unperfect Society,* New York, Harcourt, Brace & World, 1969, p. 16.

rejection of vengeance upon its fallen enemies.

Halfway around the world from Prague, in Peking, may have been the only people left alive who were not astonished by the atheist adoption of the Christian Scripture universally rejected by the Christians: "Vengeance, saith the Lord, is mine"—and its corollary of regeneration of the most unregenerate offender. The Scripture and the corollary were surely the surest evidence of the New Man in Christ, Who came to save all men while all were yet sinners, and before Christ the promise of the Israelites' Redeemer: "though your sins be as scarlet, they shall be as white as snow." But before Christ, and before Marx (who rejected incorrigibility), and before the Israelites, the Chinese had accepted confession, penitence, restoration, and restitution, and still do. Unlike the Stalinists and the anti-Stalinists, the Maoists have neither preached nor practiced genocide or liquidated their domestic enemies with abandon. Like the leaders (including the President of the People's Republic) anathematized in the more recent Cultural Revolution, the counter-revolutionary figures of the Long March days, such as Vice Premier Chen Yun (still a Vice Premier), old Marshal Chu Teh, and Foreign Minister Chen Yi, all survive, all of them under constant verbal attack. "Even Chiang Kai-shek is not lost," the Los Angeles Times–Washington Post News Service reported (November 11, 1969). "When an aide criticized Chiang in his presence not long ago, Mao is reported to have snapped: 'Don't speak that way about a man who once ruled China.' "

In the Mysterious East sinfulness against the system is overcome by the marvel of self-criticism and subjection to the kind of "out front" confrontation that is coming into vogue in the sensitivity training (or "T-group") cults in the West, in which people let each other "have it," openly attacking ("cutting through") each other's shortcomings, to reach a real, instead of a superficial, camaraderie. In *Jin Jen Pao,* the official Peking daily, we read of two Kwangtung peasants who had "concerned themselves with income from subsidiary occupations" and were made to see the error of their ways through "revolutionary mass criticism." Shortly before her death in 1970 Anna Louise Strong, the old American Communist living in Peking, reported in her adulatory *Letter from China* that in the Kwangtung village of East Flower two of twenty-two former landlords and "bad elements" wound up the self-criticism trip "fully reunited with the masses," and the other twenty were judged "law-abiding in varying degrees or 'still doing bad deeds' and needing to be watched." Just how the masses watch those who are still doing bad deeds she didn't say, but if their redemption involved some very close watching by people with very big sticks, the strictest probation is not as pessimistic about human nature as the gallows is; besides, the ancient rehabilitation of those whose sins, though they had been as scarlet, would be as white as snow, involved a modicum of watchfulness, too, in its magnanimity: "If ye be willing and obedient, ye shall eat the good of the land, but if ye refuse and rebel, ye shall be devoured with the sword: for the mouth of the Lord hath spoken it."

For eight months in 1968 the enemies of the new Czech regime were free—free to live and work and organize against the men who declined to destroy them—and Dubček resisted the passionate demand for their heads made by those who had suffered at their hands and survived. And then, the midnight of August 20–21, the demonstration ended with the Soviet tanks in Prague. Men who had watched and wondered if the Czechs would make it and, making it, revive the try at Tábor saw the curtain fall on the dream of Socialism with a human countenance. But the Czechs, who, besides being Socialistic and somewhat humane, are also intelligent, abjured the futile gesture of violence, and, even as they were swept back into the Soviet net, left the world with a vestigial hope, the very shadow of a hope, of what might (or, of course, might not) have been. They made fools of their conquerors—no great task for the heirs of the Good Soldier Schweik. And two months after the invasion the country's university students went on a three-day "strike"—locking themselves in their classrooms while the Soviet Kommandatura (which had forbidden street demonstrations) bit its fingernails; and at the Prague theological faculty, whose students had emerged as pillars of the resistance, there appeared this handwriting on the wall:

> *Nonviolent resistance against injustice and despotism is the only
>   way of carrying forward the truth.*
> *The use of violence is madness.*
> *Returning evil for evil leads to hatred and war which employs
>   any and every means of vanquishing the adversary.*
> *The issue is not the conquest of the adversary.*
> *The issue is the victory of truth. . . .*

Two months afterward—the curtain was not yet all the way down—five hundred thousand people, the entire mobile population of the Czech capital, stood in stony silence, under the Soviet guns, as the body of a student, who had burned himself alive at the monument of Good King Wenceslaus, was carried through the streets.

The Russians had been right to attack: The proclamation of Socialism with a human countenance itself said that this which would be was that which had not been. In its deadpan way it damned the Communism of the Kremlin, the Communism to which Lenin retreated in 1921 when he saw that the Russians as they were were not fit to be Communists. Socialism with a human countenance was the New Man's battle cry against the Old; we shall not know now, certainly not for a while, whether it could have been. It has never been yet.

If, as the Congress of the Communist Party of the Soviet Union promised in 1961, "Communism accomplishes the historic mission of delivering all men from social inequality and exploitation, from the horrors of war, and proclaims *Peace, Labor, Freedom, Equality, Fraternity* and *Happiness* for all peoples of the earth," it would seem to imply man's natural virtue; but the rejection of both nature and virtue as mere products of the social, and ultimately the economic, order is not readily reconciled with the promise of all these nonmaterialistic splendors. But this is where we came in, two thousand years ago. Man outside the Garden was bad, having forfeited God's goodness. But he was still God's handiwork and still redeemable by God's grace; and Christ was his ransom (or his pretense).

Peter Chelčický, one of the spiritual fathers of the Bohemian Reformation, said of "the crested gentry" in the fifteenth century: "If they were but outside of the faith like true heathens and did not hide behind the wounded body of Christ, there would be nothing surprising about their wicked practices. . . . Like the ignorant heathen, they consider only their earthly and temporal life of value." Without Christ, man would try to live by bread alone—"the religion of economics" both capitalist and Communist. And trying so to live, he would go on killing and dying in the struggle for bread (or more bread). His good intentions would continue to pave and repave the road to hell. "They aim at justice," Dostoevsky's Father Zossima says, "but, denying Christ, they will end by flooding the earth with blood."

As between capitalism's Old Man and Communism's New, the Christian concept settles for the Old every time: Man is a sinner. But it does not settle for man, not even in its view of man. Man is more than man. He is more than the creation of God; he is the creature of God. In terms of utility, both capitalism and Communism may "work" for the short run, or may not work, depending on immediate historical conditions, but not for the long, while Christianity makes no claim to "work" for the short run but only for the long. On the Christian view, the capitalist and the Communist are both of them right, and both of them wrong, about man. The capitalists are right

about his being bad, and wrong in settling for his badness and erect-
ing a social system upon it, for in Christ he *can* be good enough to be
a Communist. The First Adam is corrigible in the Second. And the
Communists are right about his being corrigible (and therefore good)
and as right on this point as the capitalists (and Freud) are wrong,
but mortally wrong in supposing that he can correct himself and make
himself good by his own powers. The capitalist and the Communist
doctrines, contending with each other, both of them contend with the
Christian. The Christian—on the run since the Enlightenment—remains irrepressible. It even revives, and not only in the West; in the
past five years the dialogue between Marxists and Christians has
grown phenomenally in all of the Communist countries (except in
the papo-caesarist U.S.S.R., where theology, now as always, is ceremonial), as more and more Marxist thinkers (and believers) proclaim openly the indispensability of some sort of "spiritual strength"
to the construction of the social order that continues to disappoint its
constructors.

Tocqueville says—he said it in 1835—that "the idea of perfectibility is as old as the world." He proceeds at once, as others have
before him and since, to identify the idea of perfectibility with the
idea that man is "endowed with an infinite faculty for improvement;
man improves, [the brutes] are incapable of improvement." But
improvement (even infinite improvement) is not the same as perfectibility. What is more, our rationalist Frenchman has put himself in
the undistributed middle when he says "man" instead of "men." Men
improve (and degenerate, and improve and degenerate again);
the weight of the evidence is still on the side of Mephistopheles that
der Mensch bleibt Mensch.

It wasn't Tocqueville's business, in *Democracy in America,* to
analyze perfectibility (or indefinite improvement); he was concerned
to trace the American faith in progress to its American root, which he
decided was the love of equality in the rich new wilderness that
beckoned to the descendant of a hundred generations of serfs and
said, "Make what you want of this" (providing his skin was white).
Tocqueville was not the first European to be fascinated by the
spectacle of American optimism. A half century earlier his country-
man, Hector St. J. de Crèvecoeur, in the last years of the French
Revolution, penned his *Letters from an American Farmer,* in which
he asked, "What, then, is the American, this new man?" His question was answered by Tocqueville, Bryce, Keyserling, and a hundred
other New World watchers: an *amazing* man, yes—but not a *new*
one. Taking Crèvecoeur's question for his presidential theme, Profes-

sor Arthur Schlesinger of Harvard, addressing the American Historical Association in 1942, described the "American new man":

. . . The composite portrait that emerges deserves our thoughtful consideration. The attributes most frequently noted are a belief in the universal obligation to work; faith in progress; the eternal pursuit of material gain; an absence of permanent class barriers; the neglect of abstract thinking and of the aesthetic side of life; boastfulness; a deference for women; the blight of spoiled children; the general restlessness and hurry of life, always illustrated by the practice of fast eating; and certain miscellaneous traits such as overheated houses, the habit of spitting, and the passion for rocking chairs and ice water.

"Probably none of these traits is peculiar to the American people"—indeed, the historian was able to trace them all, with the single exception of the passion for ice water—"and some of them we may regard with more humility than pride; but the sum total represents a way of life unlike that of any other nation." * The historian, like the philosopher, has his difficulties; a combination of traits found in various societies and embodied in one produces a way of life different from that of any other, but a way of national life does not validate Crèvecoeur's casual characterization of the American as "this new man." It may be fairly assumed that the New Man, when he does appear, in America or anywhere else, will be possessed of other, and more marvelous, traits than a unique passion for ice water.

Fly in the face of common knowledge and grant the "infinite improvement" of man *qua* man—as long as *der Mensch* remains *Mensch* his infinite improvement will leave him what he is until he undergoes a species mutation. Let him do what he will, he can only do what he can; he will only be, at best, better and better (and better); he will not be perfect unless the potentiality of perfection is demonstrated to be in his nature and until it is demonstrated to be dominant in his nature. Let him be better and always better—an hypothesis unlikely to be advanced any more, even in America—and he will still be man and not something else.

The Christian awaits the Second Coming, the Last Judgment, and the Second Death in the millenary confidence that Djilas' Kingdom of Heaven on Earth will come to be and men will be angels and men no more—and *then* they will not be perfect, not as their Father in Heaven is perfect. Next only to the Eucharist among the Christian mysteries

* *American Historical Review,* XLVIII, No. 2 (1943), 225 ff.

that the theologian confronts as philosopher is the counsel of perfection: "Be ye perfect." If perfection, and not improvement, is what it will take to be the New Man, the non-Christian confidence (if there is any left) is certainly misplaced, and the Christian so pious as to defy attack. The Christian says that we are all sinners. If there has been so many as one man who was not, and if that man was man and not God, there is nothing to prohibit, however much to dishearten, our being sinless one and all. We watch and wait for that one man; we have not seen him yet.

The primitive Christians undertook to have nothing to do with Rome. Like the Jews before them, they failed, and the same Gibbon who reached the pleasing conclusion that every age of the world has increased "the happiness, the knowledge, and perhaps the virtue of the human race," discountenanced that conclusion in his mordant view of the Church of his own time; and failed, like Plato before him and all men (including Freud) after him, to discover the genesis of the vision of the heavenly city that no man had seen. Whence the pattern—of the New Jerusalem *or* the New Jerusalemite? *Ab nihilo nihil:* The Old Man groaning in the earth's travail beholds the New in persistent vision. Always *ab nihilo nihil:* The New Man *must* be in him somewhere, or he could not be envisioned.

If he is there somewhere, the roughhouse of revolution will never end until he is seen; and if he is never seen, it will never end. "Men," says Shaw, "will die for human perfection," and, if die for it, of course kill for it. They will *transgress*—step over—every bound that is set them and every bound that they set themselves. They will expend themselves zealously in order to clear the ground, seeing Armageddon in their every sacrifice of themselves and others. "It is enough," cries Hertzen in nineteenth-century Russia, "that there will perish the world which oppresses the new men of the new time. . . . Long live chaos, therefore. Long live destruction! *Vive la mort!* . . . We are the executioners of the past!" * And the executees of the future. Selfless seekers of something that is not his own—except to *clear the ground* so that the New Man may grow from it—the Nihilist is in fact the Omniumist. His is the unassailable justification for violence *if* only in his transgression he is able to step over the gap between man and God. But this is where we went out—of the Garden.

And yet—there was that summer evening in storied Bokhara in Central Asia, at the far end of Soviet Uzbekistan, where I saw a

* Alan Moorehead, *The Russian Revolution,* New York, Perennial Library, 1965, p. 31.

perfectly terrible piece of "Socialist realism" performed in the amphi-theater of the Park of Culture and Rest. When it ended, the cast and the director took seats on the stage and all Bokhara discussed the play across the footlights. It was roundly condemned as primitive— and much less roundly defended. Some wanted Shakespeare instead; one wanted Shaw; and many wanted something "critical," "more like real life." This wasn't Boston, mind you; this was Bokhara, whose far-from-oldest inhabitants remember the total illiteracy, the open sewers, and the Emir and his four hundred women. Who am I to say that the Bokharan is the same old Bokharan? Who am I to say that the New Man will not be next season's fruit of all the Armaged-dons?

Literacy, sewers, a passion for ice water, and tomorrow a flag on the farthest planet. Eighty-five (or 95) percent of the Bokharans (and of every city, and of every country, and of every age) are prepon-derantly preoccupied with bacon and beans (and at last with color TV). The worker is still *alienated* from his labor; the bosses are still *they,* in Bokhara and everywhere else; and neither Marx nor anti-Marx, DeQuincey nor DeSoto, Faust nor Leary has yet found the potion that assuages the craving or satisfies it. "Peter no longer has to say, 'Silver and gold have I none,' but neither can he any longer say, 'Arise and walk.'" We tell ourselves that time is running out. The Old Man is sharper aware every day that something must somehow be done beyond the rearrangement of things by men like himself. To say that the New Man has never been—even to say that he can never be—is not to say that we can do without him.

I I

Man *v.* the State

I think that we all have moral obligations to obey just laws. On the other hand, I think that we have moral obligations to disobey unjust laws because non-cooperation with evil is as much a moral obligation as co-operation with good.

—*The late Martin Luther King, Jr., winner of the Nobel Prize for Peace*

An ordered society cannot exist if every man may determine which laws he will obey . . . that only "just" laws need be obeyed and that every man is free to determine for himself the question of "justness."

—*Justice Lewis F. Powell, Jr., of the United States Supreme Court*

1: More Trial, More Error

THE REVOLUTIONS that shook the Western world in the middle of the nineteenth century were nothing more than a good shake-up. But they tumbled the royalists from their privileged perch and compelled them to accept the rule of law. For a hundred years thereafter law as the rampart of liberty—no man above it, beneath it, outside it—sustained the great expectations of Europe and America and the hopes of the rest of mankind. But in the middle of the twentieth century, revolution struck again—this time *against* the rule of law as the *enemy* of liberty.

It struck in the "open" societies and the "closed"; to the distress of all patriots everywhere, its votaries disdained the distinction of "good" and "bad" states. It struck in Italy, India, Germany, Spain, and Chicago against what was lawful right there—and in Japan and Russia against lawful racism in America, in France against the lawful prosecution of Russia's poets, in London against the police of Paris. It struck all over the world against the lawful repression of "anarchy" in Berkeley and the lawful (even fraternal) rescue of Czechoslovakia from "counter-revolution." On the walls of the Sorbonne in May of 1968 was inscribed its universal slogan, *A bas l'état*—not this state or that one, but the state itself.

Most of its votaries were young, articulate, well educated. Not all of them. Mrs. Rosa Parks was none of these things when, on December 1, 1955, at the end of her day's low labor, she boarded the bus for home in Montgomery, Alabama, and, instead of going to the rear, as the law required of Negroes, sat at the front and was duly arrested,

charged, and convicted by due process of law. Mrs. Parks overturned the state she happened to inhabit; old, inarticulate, and uneducated, she may not have thought, as she fell to her knees to pray,
that what she was doing was overturning the rule of law itself. She
said later that she decided to do what she did because her feet hurt.

The rule of law has disappointed its expectations. It has not
mitigated the agonies of political association. Its full force applied on
"the devil's warrant" of public necessity has been seen to be monstrous in the most benign societies. The mounting tension between
man and the state cries for principled consideration in the light of the
political experience unavailable to those who considered it in ages past.

Couch it how you will, in terms of liberty and authority, or rights
and duties, or security and dissent, Man v. the State is what all the
boiling issues all boil down (or up) to—democracy and dictatorship,
public and private enterprise, self-reliance and social welfare, civil
rights and individual determination, civil order and civil disobedience,
national security and public protest, national defense and draft refusal, public service and the right to strike, public sensibility and
four-letter words (or pictures, or public performance), prosecution
and the protection of the accused, criminal investigation and the right
of privacy, "crime in the streets" and the police power, and the invasion of private and public property by break-in, sit-down, or
blow-up against every vexation from dormitory hours to the war in
Vietnam.

The most acute (if not the most vivid) illustration of the eyeball-to-
eyeball confrontation is the sharp and persistent division in the United
States Supreme Court, be it the "Warren" Court or the "Burger"
Court, where crucial decisions are commonly made, and then un-
made, with a shift of one Justice to one side or the other, by a "four-
and-a-half to four-and-a-half" vote.* If after all these millennia of

---

* The hyperbole may be read literally in the case of at least one of the
eminent voters. "I am," former Justice Abe Fortas wrote, "a man of the law. I
have dedicated myself to uphold the law and to enforce its commands. I fully
accept the principle that each of us is subject to the law . . . bound to obey.
. . . But if I had lived in Germany [under Hitler] or had been a Negro living
in Birmingham . . . I hope I would have refused to wear an armband, to
Heil Hitler, to submit to genocide. . . . I hope I would have disobeyed the
state law that said I might not enter the waiting room reserved for
'whites.' . . .

"How can I reconcile my profound belief in obedience to law and my
equally basic need to disobey *these* laws? Is there a principle, a code, a theory
to which a man, with honor and integrity, may subscribe? Or is it all a matter
of individual judgment? . . ."

The Justice then proceeds to wrestle with the dilemma—and, it would appear, to be thrown by it.

He disallows "efforts to overthrow the government or to seize control of an political experience the nine most highly elevated judges in a highly advanced society cannot discover the balance between the conflicting claims of the individual and organized society, we would seem to be doomed to live on in unrelieved twilight as a prelude to ineluctable darkness.

In this twilight one tendency is clear: the state's power waxes and the individual's wanes. Even in the traditionally libertarian societies (and apart from social pressures) we are forbidden or compelled in a hundred ways unimaginable to our grandfathers—from compulsory vaccination and medical certification for a marriage license to building inspection and zoning regulations, from government standards for motorcar manufacture to income and social-security taxes. Peacetime conscription, restriction of travel, and self-exculpation of disloyalty are required of large sections of the American people, as are compulsory trade-union membership and growing limitations upon the individual's liberty to hire employees, to choose his customers, or to sell or rent his home as he wishes.

"Defense" and "welfare" legislation cascades from every parliament in the world, regardless of the form of government. Under Communism, said Engels a century ago, the state would wither away at last; and a century later (after more than a half century of Communist rule in Russia) the state power, for good or ill, is more pervasive and prolific under Communism than any ancient despot could have dreamed of, and the state apparatus more ponderous. *Collective* man

---

area or parts of it by force, or by the use of violence to compel the government to grant a measure of autonomy to part of the population. These are programs of revolution. They are not in the same category as the program of reformers who—like Martin Luther King—seek changes within the established order." But he does not explain why, for example, the mass entrance into a waiting room reserved for "whites" is not an effort to seize control of an area by force or how he would have refused to submit to genocide without using violence to compel the government to grant a measure of autonomy to part of its population. He would (it appears) have "spurned revolution in favor of seeking changes," but he doesn't tell us how this could have been managed "within the established order" of National Socialism.

"[The deliberate violation of law] is never justified in our nation where the law being violated is not itself the focus or target of the protest." The corollary would seem to be that such focus or target *does* justify deliberate violation of the law. But isn't each of us "subject to the law . . . bound to obey"? Apparently not. The justification is moral, not legal: the justified violator should . . . "admit the correctness of the state's action" and submit willingly to prosecution and punishment "if he is wrong or unsuccessful." (Hitler's Germany comes to mind again.) In any case the laws violated by the reformer King were not the focus or target of his protest; his entrance into waiting rooms, etc., was strictly symbolic. Apparently the reformer was a revolutionary.

And so on.

may be freer from economic insecurity or hardship, but the individual who bothers to look beyond his own outstretched hand knows that he is paying a steadily increasing price in terms of his own independence of government controls.

Since the great age of national insecurity began some forty or fifty years ago, the "balancing" doctrine has grown increasingly popular in Congress, the courts, and the law schools, insensibly replacing both the view that the state might not on any grounds circumscribe certain individual prerogatives and the Holmesian criterion of "a clear and present danger" as the warrant for circumscription. In substance the current doctrine asserts that the ascription of absolute supremacy to one of the two contending goods, liberty or authority, or freedom or security, annihilates the other; common sense, then, requires us to balance the two in the light of prevailing conditions to see how much of each we can preserve. But there is ringing dissent from Constitutionalists of the stature of the late Justice Hugo L. Black, who maintained that "the balancing approach assumes to legislators and judges more power than either the framers [of the Constitution] or I myself believe should be entrusted, without limitation, to any man or any group of men."

The sticking point is the ambiguity of *prevailing conditions.* Under the ordinary conditions of ordinary life nearly all men live and die without coming into square conflict with the state. You and I are not Socrates on trial for his life, or Antigone facing death for having defied the unholy edict of the king, or even draft-card burners, or student militants, or segregationist governors standing in the doorway of a university in Alabama. We pay our taxes, and otherwise conform to the laws, and that's the end of it. We grumble, of course, but the weight of the state is not onerous. What's it to you and me, *law-abiding citizens,* that a suspected murderer be uninformed of his right to be silent; or that a professional gambler have his telephone tapped or his boudoir "bugged"; or that a radical agitator be compelled to disclose his associations; or that the publisher of a raunchy book be punished unless he can prove its "social value"; or that an arrested person with a criminal record be held in what the Attorney General of the United States calls "preventive detention" (and what the Third Reich called "protective custody")? What's it to you and me? *We* are not murderers or gamblers or agitators or publishers or ex-convicts.

You and I are "little men," as such men call themselves in Germany. After World War II, I was arguing with one such there, who had been (and still was) a good Nazi; and I pointed out that the

National Socialist dictatorship had deprived him and his fellow Germans of their freedom of speech. His reply was as significant as it was ingenuous: "Who wants to make a speech?" Who wants to make a speech? Not many of us. The tenor of our lives under ordinary conditions does not require us to note (much less examine) the tension between man and the state. You and I do not have to make Patrick Henry's choice, and the few who feel that they do—well, they are the few. They are those over whom the Supreme Court splits. They are not, ordinarily, you and I.

It is the few who choose one or the other of the black-and-white extremes and, in doing so, point up the issues that escape the rest of us under ordinary conditions. They are not heroes; they may, indeed, be common criminals held for questioning. Or they may be "nonpolitical" individuals, like the softhearted farmer in southern Ohio who let a runaway slave into his house and found himself aiding and abetting the theft of another man's property under the Dred Scott decision before the American Civil War. Many were the nonpolitical farmers—or townsmen—then who came under the whole weight of the state. But that was long ago . . . or was it?

The issues that convulse the courts—and the world—are, in the last analysis, the issue that confronted the Ohio farmer. The man who says, "Better dead than Red"—if he really means it—is speaking the same language as Patrick Henry. The criminal who *takes the law into his own hands* is raising the same question as the priest who defies the Southern sheriff in a civil-rights demonstration, or, for that matter, the Southern governor who defies the U.S. marshal in the second stage of the same demonstration: Does the law set the limits of liberty? What is there to keep the law from setting the limit at no liberty at all? Does the individual have rights that the law invades at *its* peril and not his? And if not, is not every state totalitarian in nature, however limited the actualization of its totalitarian nature under *prevailing conditions?*

The farmer who hid the runaway slave certainly found the state totalitarian. Of a sudden he no longer lived, as do most of us, in a world of comfortable grays: He either handed over the slave to his master or faced a terrible penalty. He had no time—and no impulse— to obey the law while he campaigned for its repeal ("within," as former Justice Fortas would say, "the established order"). He had to choose then and there, with the runaway slave on his doorstep. And his choice, like that of the common criminal, was the destruction of the state in so far as he set himself above it. If (in addition to being humane) he was philosophical, he was aware that his humane decision was nothing less than anarchy.

A few years ago a religious pacifist, who refused to pay taxes for military purposes, sued the United States to recover the tax which the Internal Revenue Service had seized under a warrant of distraint. His lawyer was arguing the case before the United States Court of Appeals and the presiding judge interrupted to say, "Counsel, is your client aware that if this court holds for him, and permits him not to pay taxes because he objects to one of the purposes for which they are used, the court itself will be laying the ax to the root of all established government?" The lawyer said that he supposed that his client was so aware; and the court dismissed the suit.

The question, at bottom, is not whether there is more liberty now than formerly, or here than there; the question at bottom is the basis, if there is one to be found, upon which the citizen may be protected against the state, or the individual against society, without the danger of anarchy and the ruin of the community. The 18th Amendment— "Prohibition"—was adopted in the interest of the general welfare of the American people as the legislatures of three-fourths of the states conceived the general welfare. It was overturned by lawbreakers (scofflaws in the then vernacular) in such number—raising the cry of liberty against tyranny—that the legislatures yielded to anarchy and repealed the amendment. Had Prohibition impermissibly invaded a human right, and, if so, what right? What kind of right is it that validates the subversion of representative government? The duly constituted bodies that enacted and sustained the 18th Amendment located no such right; but the subsequent history of Prohibition indicated that there is no guidepost but trial and error, and more trial, and more error.

What is wanting is a line of demarcation between the conflicting claims of liberty and authority. Not, to be sure, a line so clear that every imaginable case will fall untroubled on one side or the other— that would be too much to expect in human affairs. What is wanting, rather, is a line that may be drawn with sufficient precision to indicate, when a given policy or practice of government is drawn across it, that the dosage of law may be too much for man or too little for the state. The UN Declaration of Human Rights makes (or should we say "made"?) a stab at some such demarcation, but some states (the U.S.A. among them) refused to ratify it and others ratified it without any visible disposition to abide by it. Without some such demarcation we are hard put to say what civil society is—much less the good society—and harder put to keep from swinging forward and back to the end of time, in the seesaw turmoil as the recent Supreme Court decisions symptomize.*

The problem may be insoluble—which is not to say that it is a dead horse that will bear no beating. True, men, if they were angels, could live without government or be content with it (since it would be an angelic government); but they are not, and they cannot. But to say that the central problem of political life—the problem that *is* politics—is insoluble is to accept the counsel of despair. The problem deliquesces in academic limbo. At the very least, we ought to be bold enough to live with the anguish of its public discussion, recognizing that the division of courts, parliaments, and peoples is a hard one that is not to be disposed of by slogans like "Love It or Leave It" or "Impeach Nixon." The dead horse, for all its beating, is kicking up a fearful pandemonium in the modern world.

* The Court was just as dramatically divided after the first Nixon appointments were made, overturning by one vote the "Warren" Court's landmark decision in *Miranda* that a suspect had to be informed of his rights to silence and counsel before he could be questioned. Man *v.* the State likewise split the National Commission on the Causes and Prevention of Violence, which in 1969, after eighteen months of deliberation, split 7 to 6 on the issue of civil disobedience, the majority condemning it as the prelude to anarchy, the minority (including Chairman Milton S. Eisenhower) holding that it might at times be the only means of overturning unjust laws or government policies.—New York *Times,* December 9, 1969.

2: Roll Call of the Wise Men

TO FACE the problem is to face the uniform failure of political philosophy to solve it—or even to confront it. At the very beginning of recorded Western thought stands Plato's Socrates on trial for treason: "Men of Athens, I honor and love you, but I shall obey God rather than you. . . . Either acquit me or not; but whichever you do, understand that I shall never alter my ways, not even if I have to die many times." After two thousand years the Athenian's defiance of the state remains the most eloquent of all testimonies to human liberty. But hear the same Socrates a month later, in the death cell, rejecting his friends' arrangement for his escape: "A man must do what his city and his country order him; or he must change their views of what is just. . . . He who disobeys [the laws] is thrice wrong; first because in disobeying [them] he is disobeying his parents; secondly because [they] are the authors of his education; thirdly because he has made an agreement with [them] that he will duly obey [their] commands."

Remember—these conflicting sentiments are not a tired old man's, but the formal handiwork of his disciple Plato, who uses Socrates as his dramatic mouthpiece. How shall we square the libertarianism of the *Apology* with the authoritarianism of the *Crito?* We shall not. The attempt has often been made, with the citation of Socrates' last speech in the *Crito* that he is " a victim, not of the laws but of men"—a vain attempt when we but consider that the laws are necessarily made and applied by men. Nor does Plato's pupil Aristotle serve us better maintaining, as he does, on the one hand that "the state comes into existence [in order to furnish men with] the bare needs of life, and continues in existence for the sake of a good life," and, on the other, then asserting that "all belong to the state."

Nor have any of the heirs of the Greeks succeeded in making themselves any clearer.* The pantheon of post-Hellenic libertarianism—Milton, Locke, and Mill—all hang up on the horns of the dilemma. He whose *Areopagitica* rings with the cry "Let [Truth] and falsehood grapple . . . in a free and open encounter" is quick to seize the despised weapon of suppression when it comes to "popery, and open superstition, which, as it extirpates all religions and civil supremacies, so itself should be extirpate" (an argument which latter-day papists, antipapists, and Communopapists direct against Communism or capitalism). Milton denies liberty not only to Catholicism but to "that also which is impious or evil absolutely either against faith or manners no law can possibly permit, that intends not to unlaw itself." Off, then, to the death cell with Socrates on the finding of his judges that he is impious—or at least evil absolutely against prevailing faith or manners. Off, too, a bit later, with the advocate of Russian capitalism or American Communism, whose offenses, whatever he has done, or whether he has *done* anything, so self-evidently come under the "faith or manners" proscription.

John Locke, that ancestor direct of the American Declaration of Independence, would appear to exempt the generality of heretics and boors from the hemlock, but he is no less enthusiastic than Milton to extirpate the superstition of "popery": "These . . . who attribute unto the faithful, religious, and orthodox, that is, in plain terms, unto themselves, any peculiar privilege or power above other mortals, in civil concernments; or who upon pretence of religion do challenge any manner of authority over such as are not associated with them in their ecclesiastical communion, I say these have no right to be tolerated by the magistrate; as neither those that will not own and teach the duty of tolerating all men in matters of mere religion. . . . That Church can have no right to be tolerated by the magistrate which is constituted upon such a bottom that all those who enter into it do thereby *ipso facto* deliver themselves up to the protection and service

---

* Aquinas' argument that the state is both an end in itself (as the common good) and a means to man's happiness (as a constitutive condition of that happiness) is a representative exercise. It leads to the cheerful conclusion that, given the perfectly just man and the perfectly just state, the conflict is only apparent, "the issue between individualism and totalitarianism false." (M. J. Adler, "The Theory of Democracy," in *The Thomist*, IV, 1942, 313–28.) Less cheerfully, "Unfortunately, neither men nor States are perfectly just." (*Ibid.*) *Cf.* Aristotle: "It is evident that the good citizen need not of necessity possess the virtue which makes a good man." (*Politics*, Book I.)

of another prince." Out of the shades of the not too remote past of
Al Smith and even of John F. Kennedy emerges the specter of "the
Pope in the White House."

In his classic *Letter Concerning Toleration* Locke turns out to be
no more tolerant than Milton of those whom the pious find impious:
He strips toleration from "those who deny the being of a God," on the
ground that "promises, covenants, and oaths, which are the bonds of
human society, can have no hold upon an atheist." (So to the stocks
or the stake, apparently, even those who reject oath-taking on the
view that a person must always be truthful and cite Christ's injunction
to "swear not at all.") Thinking itself comes under the state's control,
though just how the control is to be administered Locke does not explain: "The taking away of God, though but even in thought, dis-
solves all." Religion, oddly, is *the* justification for intolerance: The
atheist "can have no pretense of religion whereupon to challenge the
principle of toleration." *

We are looking for liberty unfettered, and we find it cribbed, cab-
ined, and confined by Plato and Aristotle in ancient days and by
Milton and Locke between ancient days and our own. Pretty badly
bemused by this time, we proceed to the paladin of nineteenth-
century liberty, John Stuart Mill, who speaks to us in our own post-
monarchical idiom. Mill sets the limit upon the state in terms so
plain and so strong as to preserve his position almost unchallenged as
the darling of the twentieth-century libertarian:

> . . . the sole end for which mankind are warranted, individually
> or collectively, in interfering with the liberty of action of any of
> their number, is self-protection . . . the only purpose for which
> power can be rightfully exercised over any member of a civilized
> community, against his will, is to prevent harm to others. His
> own good, either physical or moral, is not a sufficient warrant.
> He cannot rightfully be compelled to do or forbear because it
> will make him happier, because, in the opinion of others, to do so
> would be wise, or even right. These are good reasons for remon-

---

* We are not concerned here with those prelacies, episcopacies, and puritan-
isms which by "liberty of conscience" mean their own; rather, with the hapless
self-contradiction of those men and governments which mean to espouse universal liberty. Thus William Penn, in the Pennsylvania Charter of Privileges
(1701), *both* repudiates the abridgment of freedom of conscience "as to Religious Profession and Worship" *and* protects whoever "shall confess and acknowledge One almighty God, the Creator, Upholder and Ruler of the World"
against such abridgment; so the humble Quaker, like the Catholic Inquisitor
and the Protestant Reformer, places the atheist, and even the agnostic, in outer
darkness, and along with them those true believers who deny the state the right
to require confession and acknowledgment of belief.

strating with him, or reasoning with him, or persuading him, or entreating him, but not for compelling him, or visiting him with any evil in case he do otherwise.

Reading Mill (up to this point) we are satisfied that at last, after a few thousand years of beetle-browed bumbling, a political philosopher has appeared who is able to lay down a line of demarcation to which the lover of liberty may repair. A short-lived satisfaction, for we have only to turn the page, a single page in the same essay, *On Liberty,* to find that the watertight doctrine is the same old sieve:

> There are also many positive acts for the benefit of others, which he may rightfully be compelled to perform; such as to give evidence in a court of justice; to bear his fair share in the common defense, or in any other joint work necessary to the interest of the society of which he enjoys the protection; and to perform certain acts of individual beneficence, such as saving a fellow-creature's life, or interposing to protect the defenceless against ill-usage, things which whenever it is obviously a man's duty to do, he may rightfully be made responsible to society for not doing. A person may cause evil to others not only by his actions but by his inaction, and in either case he is justly accountable to them for the injury.

We are looking for liberty unfettered, and here we are, back with Plato, Aristotle, Locke, and Milton—or further back still. On one page the state may prevent my doing harm to others—that much and no more; on the next there are "certain acts of individual beneficence" which the state may compel me to perform. A woman screams on the street in the night—and I rush (unarmed as I am) to her aid or suffer the state's penalty for remaining in my room. A lynch mob passing my house . . . A man crying for help in a flaming building or on a storm-swept sea . . . A bully (bigger than I) ill-using a defenseless man (of my own small size). I must plunge in, wade in, dive in—at the peril of my own life—or "rightfully be made responsible to society." My benevolence is not mine at all; the law drives me to it. I am a conscript hero. A marvelous doctrine, this, which I have seen applied (though mildly) under a Communist or fascist tyranny, but never in a society that was even fairly free.

And that dreadful limitation of liberty is not the last of Mill's. He urges nothing less than despotism (the very term is his) as "a legitimate mode of government in dealing with barbarians, provided the end be their improvement, and the means justified by actually effecting that end. Liberty, as a principle, has no application to any state of things anterior to the time when mankind have become capable of being improved by free and equal discussion. Until then, there is nothing for them but implicit obedience to an Akbar or a Charlemagne, if they are so fortunate to find one." Of whom are we speaking here? Over whom are we licensed to practice despotism? Why, "barbarians." But who are the barbarians? Clearly, the subjects of European imperialism, Kipling's "lesser breeds without the law"—to be enslaved first, then to be improved, and then, but only then, liberated when the imperial power decides that they are civilized. But one man's civilization is another man's barbarism. Gandhi was a barbarian ("a half-naked fakir," Winston Churchill called him). So were the Irish, and the Indonesians, the Algerians, and, come to think of it, the American colonists (and in Lord North's words). The whites of Southern Rhodesia presently regard the blacks as barbarians—but the United Nations found the whites barbaric and imposed economic sanctions on them to starve them out. And which are the barbarians in Mississippi who are not yet "capable of being improved by free and equal discussion"? Only stamp a man, or a people, or a nation, or a party, or a person a barbarian and you have legitimized his enslavement.

Abraham Lincoln hated slavery with his whole heart, excoriated it, and asserted that, rather than accept the view that all men are created equal except Negroes, he would "prefer emigrating to some country where they make no pretense of loving liberty—to Russia, for instance, where despotism can be taken pure, and without the base alloy of hypocrisy." Here, if ever, was the lover of human liberty above all other goods. But as late as the summer of 1862, resisting Greeley's demand for emancipation of the slaves, he wrote, "If there be those who would not save the Union unless they could at the same time *destroy* slavery, I do not agree with them. . . . If I could save the Union without freeing *any* slave, I would do it; and if I could save it by freeing *all* the slaves, I would do it; and if I could save it by freeing some and leaving others alone, I would also do that. What I do about slavery, and the colored race, I do because it helps to save the Union. . . ." This was (as he proved to be) "the great emancipator," *balancing* liberty and authority, freedom and security, man and the state, and coming down for "the Union."

The Union was, in the military event, the majority. The slaveholders were an important minority, whose strong opposition was overcome not by the genius of the American system but by the big battalions. But the runaway slave—the supplicant at the Ohio farmer's door—was neither an important minority nor a strong opposition. Who pleads *his* liberty, and on what rationale? He stands there still, done down by the wisdom that runs all the way from ancient Athens to the nineteenth-century White House. He stands there still, and he fares no better today than he ever did. "The genius of the American system," says Walter Lippmann, "is that it limits all power—including the power of the minority. . . . The American idea of a democratic decision has always been that important minorities must not be coerced. When there is strong opposition, it is neither wise nor practical to force a decision." If only the runaway hadn't been unimportant and weak—or if only he had been patient enough to wait a century until he had accumulated Black Power and become an important minority and a strong opposition—the democratic genius might have stayed its hand in the face of his importance and his strength instead of dragging him away from the farmer's door and returning him to his master.

We search for an unassailable rationale for the unfetterable rights of man, and the wisdom of the wise fails us from age to age. We turn perforce to the eternal wisdom of the Scriptures. Christ's reply to the Pharisee's question, Whose was the tribute money? has always been cited (and always will be, no doubt) on both sides of the case. But He seems to have made it with the precise intent to frustrate those who meant to entrap him and compel him to say either "Caesar" or "God," for we read that he made it *perceiving their wickedness* in asking it. True, His kingdom, He said, was not of this world; but His apostles formed a congregation of men who (though their kingdom was elsewhere) were men, and, as men, men of this world and members of one of its states. To the Book, then, we resort, and, sure enough, Peter tells us how the dilemma is to be resolved: "We must obey God rather than men" (and the other apostles all said so with him). But we proceed from Acts to Romans—again a passage of a few pages—and find Paul saying, "Let every soul be subject unto the higher powers. For there is no power but of God: the powers that be are ordained of God. . . . For rulers are not a terror to good works, but to the evil." Lackaday. If we would pay Paul the respect due him, we must rob Peter. But we shall not get off as easily as that, if we but proceed to I Peter 2:13, where *Peter* robs Peter and says, "Submit yourselves to every ordinance of men for the Lord's sake: whether it be to the king, as supreme; Or unto governors, as unto them that are sent by him for the punishment of evildoers and for the praise of them that do well."

Little wonder that modern philosophers and politicians are tempted to avoid the question altogether. Their difficulty, and ours, is that they do not avoid the answer but, like heaven and earth before them, go on answering both ways. If there is one contemporary American platitude that pleases us more than another it is that *there* man exists for the state while *here* the state exists for man. Breathes there an American with soul so dead who ever to himself has said otherwise? And was not John F. Kennedy a great American patriot? Who was it, then, who said so imperishably, "Ask not what your country can do for you; ask, rather, what you can do for your country"? And what people was it that responded, and still responds, so fervently to the words which on second thought (or first) say something very like the contradiction of the received American platitude that the state exists for man? Mr. Kennedy's hagiographic utterance could have been just as hagiographically uttered by Adolf Hitler or Joseph Stalin.

Are we, then, demanding an absolute where none is possible and no reasonable man will ever find one? No, there is one possible, and reasonable men have found it. The absolute is autocracy, the whole denial of liberty, and it has been advanced again and again, in modern times as in ancient (and not always by madmen). Hobbes will do for the rest. "The commands of them that have the right to command," says the author of the seventeenth-century *Leviathan,* "are not by their subjects to be censured nor disputed." If this is where the quest for certainty leads us—to absolute monarchy and the divine right of kings to make the law and live above it—we say we will every man-jack of us choose uncertainty and go on playing it by ear. A thousand times rather the pitfall than the pit. Are we sure?

3: Sweeney Discovers Russia

THERE ARE social scientists, no less than rulers and philosophers of rule, who look upon the state (or the society) as a "social organism" and study it as such and on it postulate a politics. The philology of the expression is itself suggestive: "Organism" is not a collective noun and has no way of denoting an aggregation of *individuals*. But it has a kind of historical sanction in the most (as well as the least) reputable historical contexts. Libertarianism no less than despotism invokes the authority of a people—the Declaration's "one people," Hitlerism's *"das Volk,"* the UN Charter's "self-determination of peoples"—as if the whole number of persons dwelling in a given geographical area had an organic integrity and no other.

But a true organism is a self-subsistent entity, its "members" wholly dependent upon its function, devoted to its maintenance, and dispensable (when necessary) to its survival. The sociological usage of the term at once conjures up the totalitarian state, the "ant heap" whose members, though they are physically individuated, act like subservient parts of a whole. We libertarians reject the analogue and insist that the state is an association of organisms and not itself one. The social-organism school has, however, a long line of weighty forebears and aftbears from Aristotle to Spiro Agnew.* Says Aristotle: "The whole is necessarily prior to the part; for example, if the body be destroyed, there will be no foot or hand, except in an equivocal

---

* Says Agnew: "[The liberal community] are presently so blinded by total dedication to individual freedom that they cannot see the steady erosion of collective freedom."—Washington *Post*, May 2, 1970.

sense, as we might speak of a stone hand. . . . The proof that the State is a creation of nature and prior to the individual is that the individual, when isolated, is not self-sufficing; and therefore he is like a part in relation to the whole." *

If we agree that the state is a creation of nature and that man is therefore born a political animal, we seem to be accepting the Aristotelian priority which holds that the individual needs organized society as the part needs the whole, but that organized society does not need the individual. But our troubles have only begun, for the same philosopher who calls the state natural (and man by nature political) praises him "who first founded the state" as "the greatest of benefactors"—as if to say that the state is an artifact and that men, however well or badly they may have lived, once lived without the "whole" of which they are "parts."

If man is *by nature* political, it is plain that he cannot realize his nature—i.e., fully be a man—without the state; without it, says Aristotle, he is not a man but "a beast or a god." (Score one for the social organism.) The case is classically argued in political philosophy on the hypothesis of a state of nature chronologically antecedent to the state of society. The supposition that man in the state of nature was free—or freer than he is in society—is traditionally dismissed as romantic. For the legendary noble savage, life (according to Hobbes) was "nasty, brutish, and short," with (as Locke put it) every man's hand raised against every other. To escape these inconveniences, men abandoned the state of nature, and society came into being. Men might be less free—less free to take and to kill, but less free to be taken from and be killed. Freedom with absolute insecurity of life and property is illusory. Score again for the social organism . . . and abandon altogether the liberty of the "part" against the "whole"?

Hung up on the concept of the state of nature—a state for which there is no evidence archaeological or historical—lovers of liberty no less than its enemies have contributed their mite to its reduction. Jean Jacques Rousseau searched out an imaginary "original" of society in the absolute but fatal freedom of presocial conditions. He decided that there must have been one occasion—the celebrated and mythical moment at which free men in the state of nature assembled to form a social compact and freely voted, every one of them, to "[alienate] all his rights to the whole community," putting "his person and all his

---

* In 1967 the Prime Minister of Greece, Colonel George Papadopoulos, informed an interviewer that his military dictatorship *emulated Aristotle's theory* that "the State can intervene in regulating the individual."

power in common under the supreme direction of the general will" in which "each member [is] an indivisible part of the whole."

Here again, of course, we have the part-and-whole doctrine of Aristotle, just as we have the Aristotelian analogy of the hand and the body in a statement of Abraham Lincoln's at the height of the Civil War: "By general law life and limb must be protected, yet often a limb must be amputated to save a life; but a life is never wisely given to save a limb." So, too, the Genevan friend of liberty lays the foundations for universal slavery in the surrender of every man's "person and all his power" to the general will of that artificial whole, the people.

Rousseau's "one occasion," on which that surrender was made, is no more than a gloss on the argument of Socrates in the *Crito:* He must not disobey the law of Athens, under which he is sentenced to die, because when he came of age he had been free to emigrate and take his goods with him, and having had the experience of Athens' laws, he "chose" to remain an Athenian and thereby "entered into an implied contract that he will do as [the laws of Athens] command him." Here the sovereign individual has exercised his sovereign choice to abandon his sovereign liberty—in theory. The actuality is something else altogether. Habit conspires with necessity to keep almost all men where they are; neither are they conscious of Rousseau's "one occasion" or of any Socratic commitment (though they may approve of the present laws generally) to obey whatever laws may be enacted in the future.

In and of itself majority rule—which is all Rousseau's "general will" comes to—does not in the least protect the liberty of the minority. The "tyranny of the majority" is as old in political theory as majority rule itself, and as familiar in practice. Common sense and common experience reject the doctrine that the common good is *ipso facto my* good, the general welfare *ipso facto* the particular; we want to know more about *my* participation in it before we accept it; still less are we enthusiastic about "the greatest good of the greatest number." What about the smaller number? The Negroes of the United States are 11 percent of that country's number, the Jews of Nazi Germany were 1 percent. What about the smallest number? What about one man? Mill argues that if all the members of the state are on one side, and Socrates alone on the other, the state still needs to hear Socrates. But the prospect is poor that it will—as poor as the prospect that the Russians will hear the single anti-Communist in their midst or the Americans the single Communist.

"There is," the fourth President of the United States wrote to the fifth, "no maxim, in my opinion, which is more liable to be misapplied, and which, therefore, more needs elucidation, than the current one, that the interest of the majority is the political standard of right and wrong. Taking the word *'interest'* as synonymous with *'ultimate happiness,'* in which sense it is qualified with every necessary moral ingredient, the proposition is no doubt true. But taking it in the popular sense, as referring to immediate augmentation of property and wealth, nothing could be more false. In the latter sense, it would be the interest of the majority in every community to despoil and enslave the minority of individuals."

Maxim Gorky drags the skeleton from the democratic closet when he says, "The people is the enemy of man." Consider, if you will, that I am the only Druid in the state, whose whole population, numbering one hundred, consists of fifty Methodists, forty-nine Baptists, and me. My religious faith and practice are a scandal of horrendous proportions, and there are a dozen charges on which I can be had up; disturbing the peace is one of them. Whether I have disturbed the peace is determined by a jury whose peace is disturbed by my very existence. They convict me on Milton's permissible grounds as "evil absolutely against faith and manners," or on Locke's complaint that I am an atheist ("though but even in thought"), or on Mill's that I do not perform "certain acts of individual beneficence"; and I have had my day in court and the services of the greatest of all solicitors of liberty. The jury then vote the penalty, as was the case in ancient Athens and in the hypothetical state I speak of. The Methodists propose hanging, the Baptists electrocution, and the campaign between them is carried on in the best two-party tradition of democracy with a public fully informed. The vote, however, is along strict party lines; the fifty Methodists prevail; and democratic justice is done the one Druid.

The hyperbole may be suggestive. Arguing for the adoption of the Constitution, the authors of *The Federalist* reported that "complaints are everywhere heard from our most considerate and virtuous citizens, equally the friends of public and private faith, and of public and personal liberty, that our governments are too unstable, that the public good is disregarded in the conflict of rival parties, and that measures are too often decided, not according to the rules of justice and the rights of the minor party, but by the superior force of an interested and overbearing majority. However anxiously we may wish that these complaints had no foundation, the evidence of known facts will not permit us to deny that they are in some degree true." The founding fathers thought that the remedy lay in the selectivity and restraint inherent in the representative (or republican) government the new Constitution envisaged, and in the great variety of parties (or factions, or interests) in the larger Union in contrast with the individual states. But the trend of succeeding times, impelled by technological advances in communication, and especially in public-opinion polling, has been away from variety and, concomitantly, in the effective direction of direct (or, perhaps, "instant") democracy. The Federalists, now perhaps more than then, are helpless to guarantee *my* liberty against "an interested and overbearing majority."

Nor does representative government serve me any better. So far from being a guarantee, it is itself a denial of my liberty: It does not represent *me*—it represents *us*. If I am one of the 49.99 percent who voted against "my" representative, and he wins by 50.01 percent of the vote, I may be unrepresented. And if the minority to which I belong shrinks to 1 percent or less, my prospect of representation is remote indeed. I am supposed to have given my consent to a government whose sole legitimization is the Declaration's "consent of the governed." But here I am governed without my consent by laws enacted by a legislator I opposed; and I am to subside in the cold comfort of the proposition that what I consented to was not this law or that but representative government. But it is precisely this law, or that, that limits or destroys my liberty.

We shall be reminded that the basic charter of a representative government provides explicit safeguards of the person against "the people." But these safeguards, even when they are enshrined in a constitution, have been known to be meaningless, while the best-protected person in the world is probably the Englishman, who has no constitution in which to enshrine them. Civil law is not a substitute for civilization. The Bill of Rights was amended into the United States Constitution. It can be amended out by the same process. Or it can be interpreted out by the courts.* Or it can effectively be suspended by the executive and its suspension validated by the courts on the ground of national emergency even without martial law.† Or it can be overridden by a government which has managed to render legislature and judiciary supine, as in Nazi Germany or the Soviet Union or Franco Spain. Or it can be nullified by popular pas-

---

* "The meaning of due process and the content of terms like liberty are not revealed in the Constitution," Justice Felix Frankfurter wrote. "It is the justices who make the meaning. They read into the neutral language of the Constitution their own economic and social views. . . . Let us face the fact that five justices of the [United States] Supreme Court are molders of policy."

† See, for example, the case of the Nisei of the United States West Coast, p. 122 *et seq.*

sion which the state power itself (above all in a democracy) may be hesitant to resist or incapable of resisting.*

We shall be told that these are hollow terrors all.—That we do not look to Communist Russia or Nazi Germany to discover where liberty is or whether it can be guaranteed against the tyranny of the many or the one.—That we are splitting hairs (the hairs of the dead horse we are beating) with our medieval excursions into the metaphysics of whole and part and the mythology of the state of nature.—That government is sufficiently responsive and liberty sufficiently secure in the good society and we have got to get down to cases closer home than the Druids if we would persuade the reader otherwise.† Closer home, then.

It is Saturday evening and, being a good, clean American, or, at least, a clean one, I am running the water for my weekly bath. While it runs, I sit in the sitting room of my home. (Who but the most egregious of despots would deny that a man's home is his castle?) Being an artistic as well as a clean American, I am strumming on my electric guitar; the melody, naturally, is "Home on the Range." There is a hard knock at the door, as of wood on wood. I unlock the lock of my castle, and Officer Sweeney walks in without so much as a by-my-leave.

Now, Officer Sweeney and I are old friends, but his demeanor tonight is such that I ask myself whether he might not have broken down the door had I declined to unlock it.

* A popular passion like anti-Communism can starve a man by refusing him a job, as it did in the blacklist cases of the McCarthy period of the 1950s. In the same period the popular passion of anti-Nazism silenced the late George Lincoln Rockwell in New York City by refusing him a public platform, and in the 1968 Presidential election the popular passion of anti-segregation deprived the third-party candidate, George Wallace, of the use of that same city's only arena large enough to accommodate his audience. In 1969 the popular passion of law and order deprived the radical Students for a Democratic Society of a campus for their summer convention. (They were refused by thirty-seven colleges and universities—including Harvard.) In 1970 the constitutional convention of the Black Panthers could not find an adequate meeting place in Washington, D.C.

† A little closer home than the Druids is the *liberté, égalité, fraternité* of France: "Right now, two-thirds of the men and women held in Paris jails have not been legally convicted of any crime. . . . '*Garde à vue*' permits police to hold and question any man for 24 hours without even notifying his family, friends, or lawyer. This period can be extended another 24 hours with approval from a judge. If the crime is political, the first period is ten days, and the extention is another ten days. . . . After '*garde à vue*,' the suspect is delivered to court, where the judge finally tells him that he has the privilege of answering or not and that he may see his lawyer. But once accused, he can be held in jail indefinitely. The magistrate imposes 'preventive detention' when the charges are made and renews the sentence every four months, or until the trial takes place."—Paris dispatch in the San Francisco *Chronicle,* August 21, 1969.

"Turn off that water," says Officer Sweeney, "and get your boots on and report for duty at the corner of Pleasant and Prospect at once. The town is on fire, and the fire is out of control, and we've got to save water and have help."

"Now, see here, Sweeney, old boy," I say, still strumming my guitar, "are you telling me, an American citizen, that I cannot sit in my own house, disturbing nobody, *and take a bath* on Saturday night?"

"That's what I'm telling you," says Sweeney, reaching for his club.

"And," I go on, laying my guitar aside and reaching for my copy of the United States Constitution, "are you telling me that this is America—or are you telling me that this is Russia?"

"I'm telling you," says Sweeney, "that the mayor has proclaimed martial law."

"And *I'm* telling *you,* martial law, smartial law, the Constitution is the supreme law of the land and it says something here about search and seizure and the privacy of my home and—"

"And I'm telling you," says Sweeney, advancing upon me and brandishing his club, "to turn off the water and get going to Pleasant and Prospect—or else."

" 'Or else' what?" I say, brandishing my Constitution, but Officer Sweeney has retired, and not in confusion, either, and is heard banging at the portal of the castle next door.

The fire is extinguished, the city is saved, and the citizens, including me, are told by mayoral proclamation that they have done their duty, except for a few laggards who refused to cooperate and will be punished to the full extent of the law (martial), which is "repealed" in the same way it was "enacted"—namely, by mayoral fiat, or tyranny. My electric guitar gathers dust for a week as I meditate my Constitutional rights (apparently dissolved at the whim of the mayor, against whom I voted at the last election and who got in by gerrymandering three wards) and my un-Constitutional duty to save the city in which (to put it plainly) I have no interest and away from which my castle lies at a sufficient distance so as to be unendangered by fire.

It is Saturday night again, and I am running the water and, for the first time since the fire, trying "Home on the Range" on my guitar. There is a gentle rap on the door, as of knuckle on wood, and I unlock my castle, and there stands Officer Sweeney, ununiformed and unarmed. "May I come in?" he says. "Of course," say I. He comes in and says, "Professor, I told the boys down at the precin't house that you have a copy of the Constitution and they want to know if there is anything we can do about wages and hours and working conditions."

"Well," I say, "it does say that involuntary servitude is prohibited. Are you serving involuntarily?"

"To be perfectly frank and tell you the honest truth," he says, "we are. We were going to go on strike, that's how bad it is, and the Governor sent a telegram saying he'd have us in jail—imagine! loyal and honest policemen—if we struck for better hours and wages and working conditions. Can they do that to us? Can they *make* us work if we don't want to? It's slavery, that's what it is."

"Call it what you want," I say, "and be it what it may, policemen can't strike."

"Why," says Sweeney, "it sounds like—"

"Russia," I say. "And," I go on, "you may remember when you dropped in last Saturday night—"

"I'm sorry about that," said Sweeney, "but the city was on fire and it had to be saved."

"And tonight," I say, "the city is crawling with criminals and you, as a policeman, are its only hope of salvation."

Sweeney has become pensive. I strum softly.

"Say, Professor," he says, "you know my boy Martin."

"Since he was—" I say.

"Well," says Sweeney, "they put him into the Army and he doesn't like it. He says they are going to ship him off to Vietnam, and he might get shot. He's going to resign."

"Oh, no, he isn't," I say.

"He'll just quit," says Sweeney. "He won't go."

"And if he quits," I say, "he will certainly be shot, or otherwise punished."

"By the Russians?" says Sweeney.

"No," I say, "by the Americans. Soldiers can't quit any more than policemen can strike."

"But that," says Sweeney, reaching for my copy of the Constitution, "is involuntary servitude."

"Just as mine was last Saturday night."

"I never thought of that," says Sweeney. "What about those Constitutional rights you were talking about? Are they all suspended? It sounds like Russia."

"It sounds," I explain, "like Russia and every other country that ever was or ever will be, including the Scandinavian, the Medes, and the Persians. The rights are not actually suspended—they're simply, well, put on ice until the emergency blows over. You know—the safety of the state, or the city—the national security—a clear and present danger—that sort of thing."

"And who decides that there's an emergency?" says Sweeney.

"The government," I say.

"But," says Sweeney, "it's the government that we're up against in the first place, and now it's the government that decides there's an emergency that won't let us argue with the government. Do you call that fair?"

"You don't call it fair or unfair. You call it emergency."

"And how long does the emergency last?"

"As long as the government says it lasts. In Nazi Germany it lasted as long as the Nazi government lasted—twelve years. In Communist Russia Lenin's five years of 'war Communism' goes on and on. We're nothing like Nazi Germany or Communist Russia, of course, but some of the national-emergency powers the President asked—and Congress granted—in 1917 are still in effect, and so are some others from the Nazi emergency of 1940 and the Korean emergency of 1950."

"So," says Sweeney, "we have to wait for our rights until—"

"—until the state decides that their exercise does not jeopardize the safety and security of the state," I say, strumming softly, "and that, old friend, is exactly what I had to do last Saturday night when all I wanted to do was take a bath." And *that* stops Officer Sweeney at last.

Had I not been a week late for my bath already, I'd have told Sweeney about Milligan, whose first name, as every law student knows, is Ex Parte. Milligan, a civilian, was arrested in Indiana by order of the military commandant on October 5, 1864. A military court (established by authority of President Lincoln) sentenced him to be hanged by a military commission for inciting insurrection. A year later the United States Supreme Court freed him in one of the great cases of American legal history. "No doctrine ever involving more pernicious consequences," said the Court, "was ever invented by the wit of man than that any of [the Constitution's] provisions can be suspended during any of the great exigencies of government. Such a doctrine leads directly to anarchy or despotism. . . ."

If, the Court went on, the commander of an armed force in time of war has the power to suspend all civil rights and subject citizens to the rule of *his will* (italics the Court's) and cannot be restrained except by his superior officer or the President as Commander-in-Chief, then "republican government is a failure, and there is an end of liberty regulated by law. Martial law, established on such a basis, destroys every guarantee of the Constitution and effectually renders the 'military independent of and superior to the civil power'—the attempt to do which by the king of Great Britain was deemed by our fathers such an offense that they assigned it to the world as one of the causes which impelled them to declare their independence. Civil liberty and this kind of martial law cannot endure together; the antagonism is irreconcilable; and in the conflict one or the other must perish."

4: Alienable Rights

P L A I N L Y , what one man calls justice, another calls expropriation; and one man's security is another man's slavery; and one man's liberty is another's anarchy. And it is just as plain that there is no great point in moving at all if we do not know where we want to go. In practical matters the objective is necessarily the ruling principle. If our inexorable objective, or ideal, is the maximization of the state's security *or* the maximization of the individual's liberty, we shall never know how to make our public or private decisions as legislators, judges, or citizens unless we approach the problem in the best dialectic tradition by projecting it to its two contradictory extremes and seeing what happens to us.

We have already seen that the one extreme, of security through the maximization of authority, has its earnest advocates and its equally earnest practitioners. The absolute monarchy of Hobbes has a long history in theory and in action under the benevolent despot exercising the divine right of kings and the naked violence of the ancient or modern tyrant. The libertarian philosopher (who thinks of himself as Hobbes's antithesis) concedes the absolutism of the state under certain conditions or with reference to certain classes of citizens (such as the criminally insane). So does the libertarian politician: We shudder with horror when Sophocles' Creon, condemning Antigone to death, says, "Whomsoever the city may appoint, that man must be obeyed, in little things and great, in just things and unjust. . . . Disobedience is the worst of evils. This it is that ruins cities"; but we accord our approbation to America's Lyndon Johnson when, as President, he summons his countrymen to an all-out war on crime and says, "Public order is the first business of government. When public order breaks down . . . when contempt and mistrust too often characterize public attitudes toward lawful authority, all . . . suffer the consequences. Lawlessness is like a plague."

We suppose that no responsible member of society would argue that only individual liberty exists, with no sovereignty whatever inhering in the state. Nor has any society ever *evolved* on that principle. The record of social enterprise is strewn with the wreckage of "intentional communities" or (as they are significantly known, even to themselves) utopias established on the basis of absolute liberty of their adult members and entered into not by accident of birth but by personal choice. Some such communities have endured a few months, some a few years, a very few some very few decades—all of them within the boundaries of the ordinary state, under its laws, and at more or less continual odds with it, but all of them composed of like-minded individuals of a character and purpose so radically different from the generality of their time and place that no lesson could be drawn even from their successful operation and their capacity (which none of them has ever displayed) to endure much beyond the lives of their founders.

It would seem, then, that the libertarian extreme, in contrast with the totalitarian, is without example in theory or history and insusceptible of dialectical confrontation except as a straw man. But its very nonexistence is an argument that the state is by nature totalitarian. That it is *and must be*. The assertion of individual liberty as absolute (be it only to take a Saturday-night bath) is nothing more nor less than the assertion that an omelet can be made without breaking eggs. We hear that men are not eggs and are not to be broken, but the point is unaffected. Define liberty as nothing more than deviation from the norm; let the deviation, as to compulsory vaccination, compulsory public schooling, or compulsory military service, spread unchecked and you find the house divided against itself and falling. Deviation extrapolated is random behavior; in society, chaos. In mechanics the second law of thermodynamics denies equilibrium to a dynamically balanced tension; without external energy input (i.e., authority, in our argument) the maximization of entropy (or disorder, or, in our argument, liberty) is unexceptionable in dynamic systems and the unexceptionable end is disintegration. So, too, the condition of a biological organism's survival is the coordination of its parts and their incoordinate behavior fatal. The analogy of politics with mechanics and biology is dangerous, but who, on the face of the matter, would quarrel with Plato's contention that the best-unified state, with each man in his proper place, doing his proper work, is the most just, that there can be "no greater evil than discord and distraction and plurality where unity ought to reign, or any greater good than the bond of unity"?

The opposite threat of the random is, of course, the rigid. Opposite, yes—but equal? Given that the community is indispensable to the very survival of the social animal, and his survival the first condition of his having any liberty at all, is it not easier contended (indeed, self-evident) that the community's (and therefore its members') chance of survival is better under totalitarianism than it is under that unrestrained liberty which goes by the name of anarchy, and to opt, when opt we must, for the former as, at least, the lesser evil? If our reasoning is agreeable to this point, does it not follow that the insistence that any liberty whatever beyond the reach of the law is the sanction of "the ruin of cities"? The straw pours forth from a thousand wounds in our straw man, and our argument proves to be the *absurdum* our auditors suspected from the first. But not quite.

We have to dispose of him (should such a *rara* be found) who dares to maintain that there are liberties protected by reason from the state power (and therefore to be protected by statute) on one of two grounds: *Either* they do not threaten the existence of the state—but where shall we find such liberties, if my Saturday-night bath is excluded?—*or* they are so proper to human life that it is not worth living without them (as those latter-day Patrick Henrys seem to be saying when they cry, "Better dead than Red") and the proper justification for the state's existence, its service to man, is lost with their suppression. And there are such men—not merely patriotic orators or religious or irreligious fanatics, but men of comparable intellectual weight to Hobbes and his autocracy. At least there would seem to be, and if they will step forward now the issue may yet be joined.

Who will come to the support of the humane farmer who sheltered the runaway slave—or, in the same era and on the same issue, that John Brown who took up arms and attacked the United States of America, and was hanged for it, and of whom millions of men defending that same United States of America were singing, a few years later, "His soul goes marching on"? Who speaks for liberty untouchable by authority, let the laws, yes, and the state itself, fall where they will?

Why, the founding fathers themselves on the first Fourth of July, appending their signatures to the document that was, and still is, heard 'round the world. The words written by Jefferson in collaboration with Adams and Franklin, proclaiming that all men, created equal, are endowed by their Creator with certain inalienable rights. "Inalienable," in one authoritative dictionary, means "not transfera-

ble; that cannot rightfully be taken away." The state cannot touch
them rightfully, but only wrongfully. And if it touches them wrongfully? The founders would not allow it to touch them at all: "Congress
shall make no law abridging . . . "

Another dictionary of the highest repute defines "inalienable" as
"incapable of being alienated, surrendered, or transferred to another,"
and explicates: "That is inalienable which one cannot give away or
dispose of even if one wishes." These rights are more than inherent
(Jefferson's first draft referred to them as "inherent and inalienable");
they cannot be got rid of. They are more properly mine than my
possessions or my person; they are more properly mine than my life,
which I can give up, if I wish, to my family, my friend, or my country.
I cannot surrender my rights if I want to.

Let us look at the matter in such a way that the professors of fine
print cannot fudge it: Does "inalienable" mean "inalienable" or
doesn't it? And if it does, does the state fall as the man stands, or
doesn't it? This, and nothing else, is the issue here, and Jefferson's
as good a way as any other of encapsulating it. Or is the Declaration
to be dismissed as so much Fourth-of-July euphoria?

Along with the contemporaneous Virginia Bill of Rights (which
used the term "inherent," and which held that as men cannot divest
themselves of their rights, neither can they "by any compact deprive
or divest their posterity"), the Declaration, in proclaiming inaliena-
bility, seems to make a modest innovation on the doctrine of Locke
(to whom Jefferson acknowledged the founders' obvious indebted-
ness). Locke held, indeed, that "freedom from absolute, arbitrary
power is so necessary to, and closely joined with, a man's preservation, that he cannot part with it but by what forfeits his preservation
and life together." No man, then, has a right to give or sell himself
into *absolute* slavery, according to Locke, for a man, having no
power over his own life, has no power to give another that power; but
"having by his fault forfeited his own life by some act that deserves
death, he to whom he has forfeited it may, when he has him in his
power, delay to take it, and make use of him to his own service; and
he does him no injury by it. For whenever he finds the hardship of his
slavery outweighs the value of his life, it is in his power, by resisting
the will of his master, to draw on himself the death he desires. . . . "

However irresistible Locke's delineation, there is something sar-
donic in the logic that guarantees liberty to the slave by granting him
the liberty to bring his own death upon him at the hands of his
master; if this isn't suicide, which our logician forbids, what (except
technically) is it? To be sure, Locke's deprivation of liberty rested

upon wrongdoing of a capital character in which the wrongdoer has forfeited his life, and the American founders forbade neither imprisonment nor capital punishment of duly convicted criminals. But slavery is something else—involuntary servitude without wrongdoing, without conviction, and without even the color of merited punishment.

The great contradiction in theory, between liberty and authority, also was the great contradiction in practice on that first Fourth of July. The majority of the Southern signers of the Declaration were the owners of slaves, including Jefferson and the author of the Virginia Bill of Rights, George Mason of Virginia (who had five hundred "blacks"). But Jefferson was at least willing to live with the contradiction. The Declaration as he wrote it contained twenty-eight charges against the British Crown. In the course of three days of continuous debate in the Continental Congress—here is a tale told out of school more often than in—the twenty-eighth charge was struck out "in complaisance," Jefferson wrote in his notes, "to South Carolina and Georgia," adding, "Our Northern brethren also I believe felt a little tender under those censures; for tho' their people had very few slaves themselves yet they had been pretty considerable carriers of them to others."

This was the deletion:

> He [George III] has waged cruel war against human nature itself, violating its most sacred rights of life and liberty in the persons of a distant people who never offended him, captivating and carrying them into slavery in another hemisphere, or to incur miserable death in their transportation thither. This piratical warfare, the opprobrium of *infidel* powers, is the warfare of the *Christian* king of Great Britain. Determined to keep open market where MEN [are] bought and sold, he has prostituted his negative for suppressing every legislative attempt to prohibit or restrain this execrable commerce. . . .

Trapped by the dilemma, like all the philosophers and politicians and apostles before him and since; trapped like the Ohio farmer who might have written the twenty-eighth charge and (had his humaneness not overcome him) still obeyed the law that mocked the charge, Thomas Jefferson knew, as did everyone else, that the slave trade, in which the English engaged, depended upon slavery itself, in which the English did not engage and their American colonists did. He knew that "our Northern brethren" were hot competitors of the English slave traders. He knew that a "market where MEN should be bought and sold" was carried on not by George III but by Philadelphians around the corner (so to say) from Independence Hall.

The British Cabinet called the Declaration "frivolous," and a slave-state governor of later time explained that "our forefathers, when they proclaimed this truth to be self-evident, were not in the best mood to become philosophers. . . . They were much excited." A slavery preacher called "every word of it . . . the liberty and equality claimed by infidelity." And John C. Calhoun maintained to the end that "it is a great and dangerous error to suppose that all people are equally entitled to liberty." That all men are created equal had been asserted—and in those words by Aquinas in the thirteenth century—again and again throughout history. That *as men* they had certain rights, inherent, inalienable rights that no government might ever invade was palpable nonsense in the world of hardheaded realism. But that "nonsense" was the real revolution made by men who created a form of government that astonished the world and a system of government that still astonishes it.

Between 1861 and 1865 the American people paid a terrible price for the contradiction between the theoretical "nonsense" and the practical problem posed by its application. They are still paying it, in Harlem and Watts and Detroit and Newark, in Arkansas, Mississippi, Alabama, and Chicago. The scales are tipped from day to day, now this way, now that, one crying "Law and order," another "Freedom *now.*" There is not much theorizing. Each sets his own limit of liberty—or authority—in the heat of the moment. When the state power grows in the direction of liberty, it grows at the expense of the liberty of the individual states within the Union, or of the restaurateur who cherishes the liberty to serve whom he will; when it grows in the direction of authority, it provides no compensating liberty, as in the Supreme Court's *Ginzburg* decision of 1967, when a publisher found himself in prison because the advertising for a book he published (not the book itself) was salaciously "titillating"—a nice point, as the lawyers call it, for Nine Old Men.

But the oldest of the Nine Old Men of our time stood pat for liberty unlimited—*almost.* "In the history of the Supreme Court there has been no more zealous, no more single-minded advocate of individual liberty than Justice Black," the assessment by the New York *Times,* is not widely challenged. Hugo Black believed, he said, that "there *are* 'absolutes' in our Bill of Rights, and they were put there on purpose by men who knew what words meant, and meant their prohibitions to be 'absolutes.' . . . I understand that it is rather old-fashioned and shows a slight naïveté to say that 'no law' means no law, but what it says is, 'Congress shall make no law.' " *

This is plain, and lonely, speaking. It rejects the balancing of freedom and security, even to the point of passionate dissent from the conviction of Communist leaders for conspiring to advocate the overthrow of the government. It excludes libel and slander, even obscenity, from punishment; and Justice Black often said so and held so. No American may be made to answer for his speech, his writing, his belief, or his association. The senior member of the Court remained its most peppery until he died. A few years earlier, his great colleague and close friend Justice Frankfurter, in a majority opinion, made a passing reference to "the so-called Bill of Rights," and Hugo Black's voice rang with something like rage when, in reading his dissent, he said, "This case concerns the Bill of Rights, not the so-called Bill of Rights."

His most eminent supporter was a nonlawyer and his senior by many years, Alexander Meiklejohn, onetime president of Amherst College, who died a while back at ninety-two. "The First Amendment," said Meiklejohn, "seems to me to be a very uncompromising statement. It admits of no exceptions. It tells us that the Congress and, by implication, all other agencies of the Government are denied any authority whatever to limit the political freedom of the citizens of the United States. . . . [It] might have been written, not as it is, but as the Courts of the United States have re-written it in the war-maddened years since 1919. The Amendment might have said, 'Except in times and situations involving Clear and Present Danger to the national security, Congress shall make no law abridging Freedom of Speech.' Or it might have read, 'Only when, in the judgment of the Legislature, the interests of order and security render such action advisable shall Congress abridge the Freedom of Speech.' But the writers of the Amendment did not adopt these phrasings or anything like them. . . . "

Meiklejohn hammered the argument home: Individual liberty is not derived from the state or from any of its organs—or from society. It is not bestowed or conferred. It is not revocable by any man or institution under any conditions. It is inherent and inalienable, and it cannot be touched in the name of security. Meiklejohn pointed out again and again that "a general legislative power to act for the security

---

* *Cf.* the French Declaration of the Rights of Man and of the Citizen (1789), Article XI of which reads, "The unrestrained communication of thoughts and opinions being one of the most precious Rights of Man, every citizen may speak, write, and publish freely, *provided he is responsible for the abuse of this liberty in cases determined by law.*" (Emphasis added.)

and welfare of the nation was denied by the Constitutional Convention
on the ground that it would destroy the basic postulate of popular
Self-Government on which the Constitution rests." It is the *Preamble*
of the Constitution that contains the celebrated "general welfare"
clause, and the Preamble is written in the name not of Congress or
the government but of "We, the people." Meiklejohn: "We Americans have, together, decided to be politically free."

But the great "absolutists" are not *absolute* absolutists. When
Meiklejohn says that "the experimental faith by which we Americans
have undertaken to live is that suppression is always foolish, freedom
is always wise," he, no more than Black, allows action a free rein. But
the *advocacy* of action against the state *is* protected by the Bill of
Rights "where it falls short of incitement," as the late Justice
Brandeis said in the *Whitney* case, "and there is nothing to indicate
that the advocacy would be immediately acted upon." "Tendency"
to incite is not enough; the state has the burden of proving that immediate action would in all probability follow.*

There are exceptions, then, in the doctrine of the absolutists of
liberty. Justice Black, though he quarrels with the ambiguity of the
doctrine, would agree with Holmes that "the First Amendment, while
prohibiting legislation against free speech as such, cannot have been,

---

* The *proof* that action would *in all probability* follow speech turns, of
course, on the state of mind of the judge and/or jury before which the case is
tried. Given the necessary imprecision of the matter, the court's state of mind
might well be responsive to strong sentiments held in high places. ". . .
on the question of where does free speech move toward public disturbance,
my answer would be 'pretty soon'. . . . I'd call something a riot sooner than
maybe other people might. Don't you think that's the attitude generally of this
Nixon Administration?"—Assistant U.S. Attorney General Will Wilson
(1969).

In 1969 the "criminal syndicalism" statutes of the Red scare that followed
World War I were still on the books of many states, among them California,
which appealed to the U.S. Supreme Court for a ruling which would enable it
to proceed against the Black Panthers, in whose newspaper there appeared this
advertisement: WANTED DEAD FOR MURDER—S.F. [San Francisco] PIG [police-
man] MICHAEL O'BRIEN, followed by O'Brien's home address. (California submitted, among other items, an alleged Panther explosives manual: "Now, to
make an actual grenade, a weapon that kills, the following can be done. . . .")
Like the federal Smith Act after World War II, the criminal-syndicalist
statutes forbade the teaching or advocacy of violent overthrow, but in the
Dennis (1951) and *Yates* (1957) cases the Supreme Court, bitterly divided, as
usual, limited the applicability of the act to occasions "when the group is of
sufficient size and cohesiveness, is sufficiently oriented towards action, and
other circumstances are such as reasonably to justify apprehension that action
will occur." The "apprehension," as well as the determination of size, cohesiveness, orientation, and "other circumstances," is, of course, the state's; and in
any subsequent adjudication a defense would have to be attempted against the
justifiability of the apprehension of the state's expert representatives on the
scene at the time—and against their determination of size, cohesion, orientation, and "other circumstances."

and obviously was not, intended to give immunity to every form of language." I am not free, in Holmes's classic expression, falsely to cry fire in a crowded theater—or to counsel murder, or to hand a small child what I know is a strychnine pill and tell him that it is candy. To say that speech may be controlled, to say that I may not sing at the top of my voice outside my neighbor's open window in the middle of the night, is not the same thing as to say that speech may be forbidden.

"There *are* absolutes in our Bill of Rights." *Hélas!*—other times, other opinions. As mass public protests grew in the United States at the end of the 1960s, the decisions of the liberal "Warren Court," prior to the retirement of the Chief Justice, swung more and more frequently to a new 5-to-4 alignment, with the decisive vote for the limitation of rights cast by Justice Black. Writing the majority opinion in *Adderly* v. *Florida,* Black upheld the arrests of Negro demonstrators who were standing peaceably on public property in Tallahassee. "If that is not allowed," said the respected Tom Wicker in the New York *Times,* "what is? Justice Black's views would appear to a layman to prohibit all but the most pallid means of public protest." The venerable jurist sharply distinguished speech, writing, and assembly from "conduct," although the Court had previously held that the burning of draft cards was "symbolic speech." In a television interview, he elaborated: "I've never said that freedom of speech gives people the right to tramp up and down the streets by the thousands, either saying things that threaten others, with real literal language, or that threatened them because of the circumstances under which they do it. . . . [The First Amendment] doesn't have anything that protects a man's right to walk around and around and around my house, if he wants to, fasten my family up into the house, make them afraid to go out of doors." It is not true, he added, that "the only way to protest anything is to go out and do it in the streets," and he cited elections, church gatherings, and meetings as acceptable means of protest and dissent. "But," said Wicker, "if Southern Negroes had restricted themselves to those means, rather than resorting to boycotts, demonstrations, marches, and sit-ins, even such meager gains as they have would have been a long time—if ever—in coming."

When we look for the absolute antithesis to absolute autocracy, we nowhere find it in jurisprudence. To permit the state to move against my liberty is to circumscribe my liberty, whether I am "controlled" or "forbidden." To permit it to do so in the name of national security is to circumscribe my liberty. To permit it to do so because I am injuring or have injured another—though no one would defend the contrary position—is to circumscribe my liberty, and to permit it to do so because I am thought to be injuring another, or because I *might* injure another, is to circumscribe my liberty still further—my liberty, that is, to do as I please. My liberty to walk down Main Street naked is circumscribed as disorderly conduct. *At some point* I belong to the state—as I discovered when Officer Sweeney would not let me run my bath.

And in one of the most disconsoling cases ever brought to bar in America, the authority of the state to seize a citizen who had not been charged with a crime, strip him of his property, deport him without a hearing, and imprison him indefinitely, was upheld by the United States Supreme Court in an opinion written by none other than "that single-minded advocate of individual liberty," Justice Black. Korematsu was an American of Japanese descent, one of 112,000 rounded up and, on two weeks' notice, shipped from the West Coast to abandoned stables (one family to a stall) in the interior of the country in April of 1942 on order of the Western Command of the United States Army. Although the commanding general, in his official report of the action, referred to all of them as "subversive," as belonging to "an enemy race" whose "racial strains are undiluted," and as constituting "over 112,000 potential enemies at large," not one of the 112,000 was then, or ever thereafter, accused of an act of disloyalty. But Justice Black held, for the majority, that "we cannot reject as unfounded the judgment of the military authorities and of Congress that there were disloyal members of that population, whose number and strength could not be precisely and quickly ascertained. . . . We uphold the exclusion order as of the time it was made. . . . Korematsu was not excluded from the Military Area because of hostility to him or his race. He *was* excluded because we were at war with the Japanese Empire, because the properly constituted military authorities feared an invasion of our West Coast and felt constrained to take proper security measures, because they decided that the military urgency of the situation demanded that all citizens of Japanese ancestry be segregated from the West Coast temporarily, and finally, because Congress, reposing its confidence in this time of war in our military leaders—as inevitably it must—determined that they should have the power to do this. . . ."

The Korematsu decision evoked some of the most furious dissents ever heard from the highest bench. Justice Roberts condemned the conviction of a citizen "as a punishment for not submitting to imprisonment in a concentration camp"—Korematsu had not reported for deportation—"solely because of his ancestry." Justice Murphy, pointing out that martial law had not been declared, called the decision a "legalization of racism" and a denial that "under our system of law individual guilt is the sole basis of deprivation of rights." And Justice Jackson acidly protested that Korematsu's crime "consists merely of being present in the state whereof he is a citizen, near the place where he was born, and where all his life he has lived"; Korematsu was a criminal because "he belonged to a race from which there is no way to resign."

"I believe," said Justice Black, ten or fifteen years after Korematsu and in connection with another case entirely, "that it is time enough for government to step in to regulate people when they do something, not when they say something"—the same Justice Black who wrote the Court's opinion that Korematsu was properly "regulated" not for something he did, not for something he said, but for being where he had always been. Korematsu's "absolute freedom" was struck down as handily as mine to sit in my rocker strumming my electric guitar the night that Officer Sweeney rapped at my door. "Nothing," said Chief Justice Vinson in the celebrated *Dennis* case, "is more certain in modern society than the principle that there are no absolutes." Either Black is dead wrong—and was wrong by his own lights in Korematsu—or Vinson is wrong. And until we know which, how are we to establish a society whose first principle is liberty?

5: The Criminality of Conscience

F R O M Antigone through Martin Luther to Martin Luther King the issue of liberty has turned on the existence of a higher law than that of the state. When the authors of the American Declaration of Independence bottomed their case on "the laws of nature and of nature's God," they were not being prolix. They were Deists who found the limitation of governmental power in divine revelation; but they were also political philosophers who harked back to the *ius naturale* of Roman jurisprudence which derived from pagan as well as religious sources among the Chinese, the Hebrews, and the Greeks. The natural law doctrine is in limbo nowadays, maintained largely (though not exclusively) by Catholic philosophers against the modern materialist position that, as all political power emanates from man, so all human law is made by man fully enfranchised in a fully representative government.*

Natural law—if it exists—is not made by man but discovered by him in his own nature: Thus, and only thus, are his rights indeed inalienable. They are not, said Alexander Hamilton, "to be rummaged for among old parchments or musty records. They are written as with a sunbeam, in the whole volume of human nature, by the hand of di-

---

* The "modern" position isn't all that modern. An historical (and historic) instance of it is the revolutionary French Declaration of the Rights of Man and of the Citizen of 1789, which asserts that "the nation is essentially the source of all sovereignty; nor can any INDIVIDUAL, or ANY BODY OF MEN, be entitled to any authority which is not expressly derived from it." Nor is constitutional confusion in the matter modern: The article preceding this one in the French Declaration asserts that "the end of all political associations is the preservation of *the natural and imprescriptible rights of man*." (Emphasis added.) Rights are, apparently, natural to man—*and* derived from the state.

vinity itself and can never be erased or obscured by mortal power."
To be a man is to possess those "sacred rights," antecedent to and
superior to the *ius civile,* which stands or falls by virtue of its conformity to the *ius naturale.* Cicero asserted that a statute contravening
the natural law is no statute at all, any more than "the regulations of
a band of robbers." But a thoroughly secular society in a secular age
is not to be governed by the "hand of divinity itself"; nor is a pragmatic society in a pragmatic age likely to look for sacred rights in a
sunbeam. Most modern jurists dismiss the concept of natural law—
and Jefferson and Hamilton with it—as superstition or, perhaps,
fideism disguised as philosophy.

But those who still maintain the doctrine, and who maintain that it
is confirmed by what Darwin called "the natural light of reason," without regard to faith, argue that there is no defense of liberty against the
state unless men are under a law which is higher than the state's. The
only answer to the absolutist state is an absolute standard by which
human law is tested, a Constitution which measures all constitutions.
Failing such objective standard, there is no way to justify noncom-
pliance with a bad law or resistance to a bad state. The "naturalists"
point to the indictment of the Nazi leaders at Nuremberg charging
them with "crimes against humanity." Their alleged offenses were
legal under German law, illegal only if there should be a kind of law
transcending that of the sovereign German state and making universally criminal those acts which offended human nature itself.

Law, including natural law, would seem to require a lawmaker or
lawgiver. In Judeo-Christian doctrine this is God Who stamps His
ineradicable plan—Eternal Law—upon the soul of His human creatures. This stamp is the natural law. Man is given reason with which
to discern it and free will with which to follow it in the pursuit of a
destiny beyond this life and, therefore, beyond the state. It is the business of the state to "secure"—i.e., make secure—the natural rights
man has from God; thus far, and no further, may organized society go.
Christian doctrine on the issue was enunciated in the thirteenth century by St. Thomas Aquinas: "Human law does not bind a man in
conscience . . . [and if it conflicts with man's participation in the
Eternal Law] human law should not be obeyed."

In the realm of faith the natural law is in part explicated, in part
indicated, in the commandments of God in Holy Writ. But how are
we to understand the commandments of God, including, for hard
example, "Thou shalt not kill," when God Himself has commanded
to kill? Does "kill" mean what we call murder, and not war? And if
murder, is it murder for a husband to kill his wife's lover under the

"unwritten law," or for the Nazis, under the law of their own country, to exterminate the Jews?

The Church arrogates to itself the interpretation of God's commandments, but the history of the Church is the history of schism and war between churchmen and churches over irreconcilable interpretations. Some denominations accept war as the will of God and some as the ineluctable consequence of the Pauline doctrine that "the powers that be are ordained of God"; others maintain that the "just war" alone warrants the state's conscription of its citizens to kill. (But who is to determine that *this* war is just, and who is to tell the members of the denomination who find themselves on the "unjust" side that they are to refuse to fight on the pain of death for desertion or treason?) Still others, the historic "peace churches," like the primitive Christendom of the first century, reject war altogether and advise their communicants to do likewise. In the War of 1812 the American Shakers, who had been mobbed, reviled, and imprisoned by their countrymen during the Revolution, proclaimed that "God has required of us to abstain from all acts of violence against the lives of our fellow-creatures." It followed that they had to obey this requirement "even at the expense of our lives," their duty to God being "paramount over all other duties." (By the time of the Civil War, President Lincoln granted them military exemption.)

The concept of the *person*—the human individual—was transmitted from Greek Stoicism to Christian theology through Hellenistic Judaism and Roman jurisprudence. As an individual, man may be required to surrender his goods and services to meet the needs of his fellow men and the human community; but not to the point that jeopardizes his (or another's) person. His person is more than his life, but his life is sacred as the vessel (here below, at least) of his person. So is his liberty. His person may not be used as a means to any end whatever; it may not be sacrificed to the common good; it may not be discarded (or eliminated) as useless. His person is his own, under God—unanswerable to any man or aggregation of men. It has individual duties to itself and others; it may be appealed to, reasoned with, prayed for, persuaded; but it may not be compelled. To require a man to kill another—for whatever reason—is as much a violation of the *persona* as to require him to kill himself.

The despised Shakers were few, like those of the other "peace churches," Quakers, Mennonites, Brethren, Jehovah's Witnesses, and (as regards actual combat) Seventh-day Adventists. Their exemption from war constituted, as it still constitutes, no "clear and present danger" to their country. *But what if they should be many?* In that case, with a million or ten million men refusing to fight, the few countries that now exempt conscientious objectors from military service would indeed be confronted with a clear and present danger; and, on the doctrine those countries themselves have recognized, they would have to accept what no sovereign society has ever yet accepted: the probability, if not the certainty, of their own uncontested destruction. The fact that the United States Congress grants such exemption as a "privilege," not as a "right," would be a legal sanction for the withdrawal of the privilege. But the fact that the Shakers and their kind would not fight would be unaffected. I discussed this point twenty-five years ago with a man much interested in it, the son (if I recall correctly) of a Mennonite mother. "That," said General (then Lieutenant Colonel) Lewis B. Hershey, long-time Director of Selective Service, "would be a hard one, for this or any other country. I can't imagine a solution to it."

I can: Should the number of war resisters ever reach the point where the country's military security appeared to be in danger, the liberty would fall (as mine fell before Officer Sweeney's nightstick) and the absolute power of the state, even the best of states, would emerge from the shadows in which it dozes peacefully under ordinary conditions. Article XIII, Section 1 of the United States Constitution forbids involuntary servitude except as a punishment for crime, but conscription for military *or* civilian service (such as fire-fighting at the command of Officer Sweeney) is, whatever else it may be, involuntary servitude. The courts of the United States (and of all other countries) have never let Article XIII, Section 1 stand in the way of conscription. How could they—and still perform their Constitutional duty of "provid[ing] for the common defense"?

When the churches disagree (as they always have) as to what is Caesar's, or I disagree with one or all of them, my only guide is my conscience. The otherwise law-abiding man, when he breaks the law, pleads the necessity of conscience and always has; the term is as often as not used for the command of God or the voice within us with which that command is issued. "The rights of conscience," says Jefferson in his *Notes on the State of Virginia*, "we never submitted, we could not submit [to government]. We are answerable for them to our God." We have only, then, to discover what conscience is, and what it compels, and our troubles are over; we have discovered the limit of the state's power and, so, the scope of individual liberty. The discovery has not been made, nor does it seem likely that it will be.* For my conscience

* The volubility of statesmen on the sovereignty of conscience has generally failed them when they got down to the business of writing state papers (includ-

tells me X and yours tells you not-X, and the state's only hope of allowing me the liberty of what I call conscience is its undependable decision that I appear to be, and generally have been, a "conscientious" man. And it is the state—equipped with no true instrument for the purpose—that will do the deciding. How can it help but overrule my claim to acquittal on the ground that it was my conscience that compelled me to blow up the Brooklyn Bridge?

The lawyers talk of "an order of values" in the claim of conscience; but if conscience is beyond the reach of the state, how can the state or its lawyers, or its laws, presume to discriminate among acts of conscience? As a Mormon, I am constrained in conscience to advocate polygamy; as a Jehovah's Witness, I am constrained to play anti-Catholic phonograph records over a loudspeaker in a street whose residents are 90 percent Catholic; as an atheist, I am constrained in conscience to refuse to pledge my allegiance to the American flag "under God"; as a churchman, I am constrained to refuse to swear an oath of loyalty to the state. In the courts the law upholds my right of conscience in every one of these acts; I am told that the state cannot touch me, even though I offend others and even assault public morality or (in wartime, when I refuse to pledge allegiance) sow dissent in a beleaguered community. How, then, can it touch me when my conscience requires me to discard my clothing in public or, indeed, to blow up the bridge? How can *it* determine "an order of values"; how can *it* decide what conscience is and still leave conscience free?

It can't. So it does what it can't do either: It decides what conscience is, and in its own worldly terms it would be derelict (as no state ever has been) if it didn't. It decides, in the case before it, by submitting me to its investigation and interrogation, as if conscience were susceptible (as the philosopher Sidney Hook says it is) of "rational analysis" (by, of course, the state, which is assumed to be the competent custodian of rationality). What, then, has become of Jef-

---

ing constitutions). A cursory survey yields only two outright affirmations in public documents—both of them in the context of denominational liberty in religion. In 1647 the *Agreement of the People of England,* presented by the Levellers to the Army Council, and by the Council to the Commons, asserted that, in matters of religion, "we cannot remit a tittle of what our consciences dictate to be the mind of God without wilful sin"; and the Virginia Bill of Rights (preceding the Declaration of Independence by three weeks) found all men "equally entitled to the free exercise of religion, according to the dictates of conscience." Confronted with the claim of conscience, the United States Supreme Court said that "the Bill of Rights recognized that in the domain of conscience there is a moral power higher than the State"; confronted with the same claim in another case, it said that "civil government cannot let any group ride roughshod over others simply because their 'consciences' tell them to do so."

ferson's insistence that we are answerable to God alone, and not to government, for our rights of conscience? What has become not only of Aquinas in the thirteenth century but of Chief Justice Hughes in the twentieth? "The essence of religion is a belief in a relation to a God involving duties superior to those arising from any human relation." What has become of the Supreme Court's classic finding in *Girouard* that "throughout the ages, men have suffered death rather than subordinate their allegiance to God to the authority of the state. Freedom of religion guaranteed by the First Amendment is the product of that struggle"? What has become of my "most fundamental personal values," on whose basis the Solicitor General of the United States (a former dean of the Harvard Law School) validates my *moral,* if not my *legal,* right to disobey? The state, when I ask it these questions, shakes its head sadly. God is not dead; he's alive and well in the Department of Justice.

I sympathize with the state in its dilemma, but I cannot help it. I dare not help it without putting all liberty on the block. Today my conscience compels me to spit on the sidewalk; the state (though my sputum is uninfected) arrests me on its "clear and present danger" doctrine and calls my claim to conscience self-evidently false. I yield my conscience to the state—and tomorrow it arrests me for refusing to pay my war tax. In yielding today, in the matter of expectoration, I have yielded the principle that would alone protect liberty tomorrow.

I say I sympathize with the state. The good state—such as mine—writhes in its agony to protect my liberty and assures me, in earnestness, on its highest judicial authority, that the "working principle" that "finally emerges from 'clear and present danger' cases" is "that the substantive evil must be *extremely serious* and the degree of imminence *extremely high* before utterances can be punished." It writhes —but I cannot acquiesce in a doctrine so arrant and so deadly. The state that is permitted to determine the extreme has been permitted to determine the mean. I have let it become the arbiter of conscience— liberty's only security against it.

If conscience resists definition in many respects, it has general acceptance in at least one: It is not a people's or a majority's, but a man's—one man's. *My* conscience is not, and cannot be, the property of a pastor, a premier, or a parliament. It is no more the property of the whole community together than it is a majority's. It reprobates democracy as readily as it does tyranny. Though it may listen more sympathetically to the former than to the latter, it answers them both with identical assumption: "Men of Athens"—or "Man of Athens," it matters not which—"I love and honor you, but—" What his conscience demands of the conscientious individual, this he does. And at that moment he is an anarchist, as much so the Muslim who faces west to pray (when the rest all face east) as the American who blows up the bridge or sets forth with his gun to liberate the slaves in Bloody Kansas (or runs the bathwater when the mayor has forbidden it under martial law). There is exactly as much political theory in the tea spilled in Boston Harbor as there is in the blood spilled at Lexington and Concord.

Whoever breaks the law for whatever reason—call it what he will—is a common criminal, however uncommon a man with however uncommon a motivation. What jurisprudence calls equity may suspend the sentence of the starving man who filched a loaf of bread or the Jehovah's Witness who would not let his dying child have a blood transfusion; legend may acquit Robin Hood for the use he made of the money he stole; and history may acquit Gandhi for having taken salt from the sea without paying the British salt tax—but they are criminals all, along with every first and last signer of the Declaration of Independence—lawbreakers "laying the ax to the root of all established government." In equity we try to distinguish between the conscientious and the unconscionable criminal. If he transgresses openly and not furtively, and freely accepts the consequences of his crime and "turns himself in" to pay the penalty, he seems to be conscientious; thus Gandhi, pleading guilty of "evading" the salt tax, asked for "the highest penalty that can be inflicted upon me for what in law is a deliberate crime and what appears to me to be the highest duty of a citizen." But John Brown is thought to have been conscientious, too, and he neither surrendered himself nor invited the penalty he paid. So, too, he who means to commit the crime in the interest of others and not in his own, or (though he, too, may be a beneficiary) means to attack a social injustice, seems to be conscientious; but it may be that the conscientious or unconscionable Negro who refuses to move to the back of the bus may in fact mean neither; and it is possible, even probable, that some of the white and black militants "liberating" university buildings on behalf of Negro rights (or "student rights") are not so much interested in rights as they are in promoting what is sometimes called a rumble. Men's motives are marvelously mixed and just as marvelously inaccessible to definitive determination by courts of law, which are not required to decide whether my heart is in the right place or the wrong one. In any case, motivation is peripheral to the problem here.

The problem here is the individual's obedience and disobedience to the state in the person of its laws, not the purity of his motivation or the consequences of his act. He says he means to change a bad law and has no other objective. He is wrong, though his course of action may (like that of Martin Luther King or the rioters of the ghetto or the campus) actually have that effect. There is only one way for a citizen to change the law and that way is prescribed by his country's Constitution. The law-breaking claimant of conscience is not so much a political man performing a political act; a political man changes the law by the rule of law, which provides the means for effecting change. To set about changing the law by breaking it—if this be the purpose of civil disobedience—is to perform a political act in a manner impermissible to a political man.*

There are two immediate difficulties here, both of them suggestive that the state in fact brooks no claim whatever to a "higher law." The first is the *insignificance* of conscience *vis-à-vis* the state: What is a conscience for, and how can the "rights of conscience" be argued, if the superior right of the state is acknowledged to slap down a man every time he exercises it? Here is an empty "right" if ever there was one; and all that there is to be said for its practical significance is its expression of God's will to be punished on earth and rewarded in heaven. But in that case it is only on a religious view that conscience has any effective liberty, while here below its liberty exists at the pleasure of the state and the pain of the libertarian.

The second difficulty is as troublesome. I am told that the way to change the law is to campaign for its amendment or repeal by a better law—and meanwhile to go on obeying it. I am told (by the Washington *Post*) that "those who disagree with the policies of the government have available to them a whole arsenal of orderly and lawful devices for changing those policies. Those who dislike an administration in power have a whole assortment of democratic processes by which the administration can be changed. The proper place for opposition is on the forum, the hustings and at the ballot box. The proper means is orderly debate and argument." Good enough, if the obedience required of me does not violate my conscience until such time

---

* Acts of civil disobedience are, however, not uncommonly performed for the purpose of testing the validity of a statute. Under these circumstances the nonpolitical act has a clearly political character. There is no way for a citizen to challenge the constitutionality of a law except by breaking it. This paradoxical procedure is not only recognized by the juridical process; it is actually encouraged. In acquitting a member of the German-American Bund who, just prior to Pearl Harbor, counseled refusal of military service on the ground that the Selective Service Act unconstitutionally excluded Bund members from "sensitive" posts, the U.S. Supreme Court held that "one with innocent motives, who honestly believes that a law is unconstitutional and, therefore, not obligatory, may well counsel that the law shall not be obeyed; that its command shall be resisted until a court shall have held it valid. . . ." Even after a court (including the highest court) has sustained a law, disobedience is an accepted way of challenging it and has reversed innumerable decisions which otherwise would have stood.

as, by orderly debate and argument, I have persuaded a majority of my countrymen to change the administration or its policies. I can endure a twenty-five-mile-per-hour speed limit until such time as I can get it changed to thirty, or a Saturday garbage collection until I can get it changed to Monday. I can endure no end of *prohibitory* laws—all the more lightly if they forbid me things I don't much want to do, such as sell narcotics or shoot my tiresome neighbor. But there are mandatory laws which command me to perform. The runaway slave is at my door in Ohio; a Negro enters my restaurant in Atlanta; the truant officer comes to my home to order me to take my child to the "worldly" school forbidden by my Amish religion.* What then? Am I to do the wrong—according to my conscience—and go on doing it until such time as the legislature permits (or commands) me to do right? The state's answer is, and must be, "Yes—or put yourself at war with the state." I may do the required wrong with "mental reservations," with uncomplacent, even tortured, conscience; the state has no way to subdue my reservations and no interest in doing so. The state commands the act; I perform the act. It has got what it wants of me. If it has my compliance, it will survive without my enthusiasm.

Or perhaps I am not required to do, but only to abide (at no inconvenience, except to conscience) the wrong commanded others by the state or, just as likely, unforbidden by the state and commanded by convention. I am to stand by, distressed, to be sure, and see the wrong perpetrated and proliferated and raise no overt voice, no overt finger—and thus serve as an accomplice in the wrongdoing of others. In October 1968 nine Roman Catholic priests, missionaries, and laymen were convicted in Baltimore, Maryland, of burning military-conscription files (an act they admitted). In the course of their trial the prosecutor stated that in the view of the federal government a reasonable man could hold the view (as the defendants did) that the American war in Vietnam was illegal; and the government conceded that the defendants were reasonable men. None of them was eligible for conscription, and they had acted to disengage themselves from complicity in a war they considered illegal—and which the state thought they might reasonably consider so.†

---

* In 1967 the United States Supreme Court—by a one-man majority—refused to review the conviction of an Amish farmer in Kansas who would not send his daughter to school on the ground of the Biblical injunction "Be not conformed to this world" (Rom. 12:2). Because the Amish declined to litigate, the defense was conducted by the National Committee for Amish Religious Freedom, composed of leaders of other faiths.

† "By God," said that reasonable man Ralph Waldo Emerson of the Fugitive Slave Law of 1850, "I will not obey this filthy enactment." Other reasonable

If a man cannot confer his conscience upon the state, and the state cannot permit him to do whatever his conscience dictates, the two can abide together only by happy accident, like a Hatfield and a McCoy who do not happen to meet on the street. Fortunately, a few men are so sure of the dictates of conscience as to move to bring down the state on this occasion or that. Most come, in sufficient time, to recognize the dictate as nothing but the still, small voice of private interest; or they hesitate to set one man's dictate (be it even their own) above the contrary dictate of the men of conscience around them and in their government; or they lose heart at the prospect of the unpleasant consequence of heeding the dictate; or they value society, and the state into which it is organized, so highly that, rather than dismember it, they will suffer in conscience yet a while longer or until such time as a more painful violation of it is required. So good men go on living quietly, for one or another of these reasons, in bad states; so, too, men of great goodness remain in office under bad governments they hope to restrain from becoming still worse. Tragic they may be, and tragic their fate, as was that of Baron Ernst von Weizsäcker, who accepted the post of State Secretary of the Nazi Foreign Ministry and was convicted at Nuremberg by his signature on document after document ordering the deportation of Jews to their death, in spite of the uncontradicted testimony of high Allied statesmen and churchmen that he had held on to his dreadful post in the hope (which proved futile) that he might meliorate the Hitler policy by doing so.

So conscience is constrained by the countervailing consideration of its exercise. When the American colonists finally rebelled, they said, "Prudence, indeed, will dictate that governments long established should not be changed for light and transient causes; and accordingly all experience hath shown that mankind are more disposed to suffer, while evils are sufferable, than to right themselves by abolishing the forms to which they are accustomed. But when a long train of abuses and usurpations, pursuing invariably the same object, evinces a design to reduce them under absolute despotism, it is their right, it is their duty, to throw off such government, and to provide new guards for their future security. Such has been the patient suffering of these col-

"anarchists" did not disengage themselves so easily from complicity: "In consequence of helping some 2700 slaves to freedom, Thomas Garrett, Quaker merchant of Wilmington, Delaware, met prosecution after prosecution, fine after fine, that finally reduced his comfortable means to bankruptcy. After the sheriff's sale that took his last asset, a pompous official said that he hoped this would cure him of lawbreaking. Said Thomas: 'Friend, I haven't a dollar in the world, but if thee knows a fugitive who needs a breakfast, send him to me.' "—J. C. Furnas, *Goodbye to Uncle Tom,* New York, Sloane, 1956, p. 210.

onies; and such is now the necessity which constrains them to alter their former systems of government. . . ."

The "patient suffering" of the Declaration is required by the law, and the "right and duty" forbidden. And the law is right, grounded as it is on the Aristotelian dictum that "no man is a judge in his own cause." You may say that my objectivity is demonstrated by the suffering I bring upon myself as a violater—but how do you know that I have not undertaken the violation for the purpose of exploiting its penalty to my political or economic—or emotional—advantage? How do *I* know that I am not a compulsive sufferer, the victim of a martyr complex? (I have heard Socrates so dismissed.) Am I to sit in judgment on the limit of my own patience, on the length of the train of abuses and usurpations and the clarity with which those abuses and usurpations evince a design to reduce me under absolute despotism? The law as psychologist says No: I am not competent to take it into my own hands in my own case; I have a stake in the outcome.

We are all lawbreakers. When a spectator was killed by deputy sheriffs during the student convulsions in Berkeley, California, in 1969, the ineffable governor of the state said, "He was killed by the first college administrator who said some time ago it was all right to break laws in the name of dissent." But it is not only college administrators—or the founding fathers of the American Republic—who believe in breaking laws. Breathes there a man with soul so subdued that he has never practiced civil disobedience and done his bit for anarchy by violating closing hours or traffic regulations or fireworks ordinances or wartime rationing or the nontransferability of a commutation ticket (or a streetcar transfer)? The state itself sets the happy-go-lucky example on state occasions. It will not arrest you for obstructing traffic or disorderly conduct or public drunkenness on V-E Day or V-J Day. It will not prosecute you too relentlessly for minor—or, if you're a good party man, major—infractions of the municipal building code. It will use its discretionary powers (nowhere delineated in law) to settle an income-tax case or forgo a criminal prosecution "in the public interest." And it will go further than closing its eye to this celebrant or that miscreant; it will commit civil disobedience in its own right—in the South by resisting racial integration ordered by the Court, in the North by conducting classroom prayer forbidden by the Court, in a century of peace by denying or abridging the right of citizens to vote on account of color, in a decade of warmaking in both hemispheres without the declaration required by the Constitution.

The state's excuses, like ours, are good: "I'm on my way to the hospital, Officer. My wife just had a baby boy. Have a cigar." Like us, its needs are unforeseen, its situations suddenly altered. Like us, it is carried away. And like us, the state has a little larceny in its heart and another law in its members. "If," says Shakespeare's Orlando, "I had my liberty, I would do my liking." Give you or me our sovereign liberty—or the state its—and we are conscientious objectors all.

Legislative intent—and often its extent—is unclear and necessarily so; no law can cover every contingency. Contradictory statutes, and contradictory rulings under the same statute, bedevil me. I have got to find my way through the murk, acting uncertainly and finding more leeway in my uncertainty than a man or a state can be trusted with. If only I had a standing rule to go by—if only I knew the *ius naturale* with absolute precision and the *ius civile* with equal precision—I should know what moved me to do what. I once met such a man in California, at the time the churches of that state were trying to decide whether to obey a new law requiring them to take a loyalty oath on pain of losing their tax exemption. Meeting him in town one day, I said, "And what are you Jehovah's Witnesses going to do about the loyalty oath?" "Oh," he said brightly, "we 'swear not at all.' Matthew Five, Thirty-four."

Theologians have always cried up lawbreaking in the name of God's dictate to conscience. As Augustine in the fifth century: "When God commands a thing to be done against the customs or compact of any people, though it were never by them done heretofore, it is to be done. . . . For, as among the powers in man's society the greater authority is obeyed in preference to the lesser, so must God above all"; so the twentieth-century American hierarch Eugene Carson Blake, General Secretary of the World Council of Churches: "We must be entirely clear that law is not God. It has always been a basic Christian conviction that there are times when a Christian ought to break the law." When, where, and how a believer should implement Christian doctrine on this point has always been a sticky matter. No end of "Allied" churchmen joined political personages in urging rebellion against the Communist, the Fascist, and especially the Nazi regimes of Europe and recognized religiously motivated rebels as heroes and martyrs. But these same churchmen, and their heirs, found it more painful to urge lawlessness in their own lands under freer regimes. It was only when the national fabric in the United States was rent with massive dissent from the war in Vietnam that clergymen of all faiths—among them the Protestant Chaplain of Yale University—rose in increasing numbers to the support of young men resisting military service and of fellow citizens refusing to pay their taxes or (in violation of the Trading with the Enemy Act, but in obedience to the Scripture, "If thine enemy hunger, feed him") contributing medical aid to all parts of Vietnam.

Open rebellion on the part of clergymen poses so difficult a problem for the government of a country that considers itself pious that their prosecution was notably slow to be undertaken. But in the late 1960s they began to be indicted and convicted under federal law just as their brethren in the civil-rights struggle, white and black, Protestants, Catholics, and Jews, had always been (and continued to be) jailed under the criminal statutes of some of the Southern states. They could quote Holy Writ and the Church Fathers, ancient and modern, in defense of their revolutionary activity, and, in addition, the greatest names in their country's political history. "God forbid, we should ever be twenty years without such a rebellion," said Jefferson in 1787. "What country can preserve its liberties, if its rulers are not warned from time to time that this people preserve the spirit of resistance? Let them take arms. . . . What signify a few lives lost in a century or two? . . . The tree of liberty must be refreshed from time to time, with the blood of patriots and tyrants." And Lincoln in his First Inaugural proclaimed "the revolutionary right to dismember or overthrow [the existing government] whenever the people shall grow weary of it" a sacred right "which we hope and believe is to liberate the world."

Let Augustine and Blake assert the primacy of God's dominion over conscience; no matter. Let Jefferson and Lincoln asseverate the right of violent revolution; no matter. In the 1960s (and into the 1970s) the single practitioners of nonviolent revolution in the name of God were packed off to jail under statutes held Constitutional in either the provincial or federal jurisdictions. Among them was Martin Luther King—at whose unrepentant death a year later the President would proclaim a day of national mourning. (The United States Supreme Court found that the Alabama law which King had broken in the name of conscience was untouchable by the United States Constitution. Let Augustine and Blake hold otherwise, and Jefferson and Lincoln; they are not sitting in this court—or in any other.)

6: One Obnoxious Man

THE POLITICAL philosophers, like the judges, either disagree flatly with the theologians (and the statesmen they quote) or retreat to crude equivocation or honest ambivalence. "Seditious," "false," "repugnant to civil society," says Hobbes (of course) of the notion "that every man is judge of good and evil actions"; the law "is the public conscience by which he hath already undertaken to be guided." Locke finds it "an inconvenience, I confess, that attends all governments whatsoever, when the governors have brought it to this pass, to be generally suspected of their people. . . . When [a majority or all of] the people are persuaded in their consciences that their laws, and with them, their estates, liberties, and lives are in danger, and perhaps their religion too, how they will be hindered from resisting illegal force used against them I cannot tell"—a masterpiece of shoulder-shrugging which, in addition, identifies law with liberty and bypasses the issue. Kant would seem to be foggier still: God is "the power over all" and conscience is "the subjective principle of a responsibility for one's deeds before God"; plainly "the power over all" is the supreme power commanding loyalty—but we have only to read on a half-hundred pages to learn that the supreme power is something else entirely: "Resistance on the part of the people to the supreme legislative power of the state is in no case legitimate; for it is only by submission to the universal legislative will, that a condition of law and order is possible. . . . It is the duty of the people to bear any abuse of the supreme power, even then though it should be considered to be unbearable. And the reason is that any resistance of the highest legislative authority can never but be contrary to the law, and must even be regarded as tending to destroy the whole legal constitution. In order to be entitled to offer such resistance, a public law would be required to permit it. But the supreme legislation would by such a law cease to be supreme, and the people as subjects would be made sovereign over that to which they are subject. . . ."

The philosophers, like the statesmen, do not come to grips with the issue of liberty at all—not as it ordinarily arises in all societies. The liberty of a minority (including a minority of one) is what is at issue, not the liberty of "the people." To speak of "the people" and *their* rights—not a fraction of them and *its* rights—enables political philosophy to present itself with a manipulable simplification. The collective "people" either reserve or delegate their individual liberties to the state, and the state, by invading them, puts itself at war with the people and (at least in Locke's view, and in Jefferson's and Lincoln's) loses its authority. "The people" then assert or recapture their rights by revolution.

This is the "right of revolution" by Locke's *majority or all*—a revolution which, in a democracy, is possible by ballot and is ordinarily an overthrow of the party in power, not of the form of government or of government itself. This is no insurrection; heads roll, but they roll on their shoulders. Still less is it a confrontation of man with the state or the anarchy of a majority (or a minority) rejecting the law or the system of law. It is not in the least criminal, any more than was the accession to power of the Nazis in 1933, the Czechoslovak Communists in 1948, or the Chilean Communists in 1970; they all came to power legally under the parliamentary system. We may witness the most outrageous devices to pervert the legal process in Berlin or in Prague—or in Jackson, Mississippi—but the color of legitimacy has prevailed. "The people" have judged, by constitutional majority or plurality, and they have judged that "the people's" liberties are safe.

That this judgment is an impious fraud—that the "democratic process" as such does nothing for human liberty—was at last brought home to what the majority of its citizens were pleased to call the land of liberty when the United States was convulsed by its Negro minority at the end of the 1960s. A concatenation of events and processes produced rebellions, proceeding from prayerful nonviolence to "burn, baby, burn" among a people reduced, after three hundred years, to absolute despair of legal redress in a nation which had achieved the *summum bonum* of King John's Magna Carta: ". . . nor will we condemn him . . . excepting by the legal judgment of his peers, or by the laws of the land." Neither the first ten amendments to the

American Constitution, nor the Thirteenth, Fourteenth, and Fifteenth had provided liberty to the American blacks; and the blacks knew it, and the whites knew it, and the world knew it. White "Establishment" spokesmen sonorously proclaimed that "the United States is a society where [the] essential conditions [of liberty] prevail—certain inalienable individual rights are secure, the lawmakers represent the community, the courts and juries are free to interpret the laws without coercion, there are political means available to revise laws that are repressive or unjust."* True, true—and black men, weary of crying out against the pretensions that underlay these truths, were at last in the streets exercising Locke's "right of revolution."

Politically the right of revolution is a contradiction in terms. No sovereign state, no "people," writes a Constitution purposively providing for its own dismemberment or dissolution, nor has any philosopher or statesman that I know of suggested that one be written. Lincoln's assertion of the "revolutionary right" of overthrow—contrasted, in the First Inaugural, with the *"constitutional* right" of amendment—may be supportable, but what appears to be the counterassertion, in the same address, does not need support: "It is safe to assert that no government proper ever had a provision in its organic law for its own termination." (He was wrong historically, as we shall see later; but the Polish exception was cataclysmic enough to prove the rule.) The United States Constitution is law, the Declaration of Independence is not; and it is the Declaration, not the Constitution, that "legalizes" the overthrow of the government. Many of the former colonies, carried away by the July 4 fervor of the Fathers, actually embodied the right of revolution in their constitutions, either in the preamble or in a Bill of Rights like New Hampshire's, which proclaims that "whenever the ends of government are perverted . . . the people may, and of right ought to, reform the old, or establish a new government. The doctrine of non-resistance against arbitrary power and oppression is absurd, slavish, and destructive of the good and happiness of mankind." But neither New Hampshire nor any other right-of-revolution state has yet turned a lawbreaker loose.

A nice distinction may be made in terms of the objective of illegal action: Is its intent the overthrow of the existing government in the name of revolution? Or of government (i.e., the state as distinguished from society) itself in the name of anarchy? Or of a single "unjust" law (or set of laws such as those that protected slavery)? This last, too, may come to revolution, though it is usually denominated insur-

* New York *Times,* editorial, May 7, 1967.

rection, up to the point where it involves the whole society. The principle we are closest concerned with here bridges the distinction: Who breaks *any* law, with *whatever* intent, overturns the state in principle and, whatever his objective, may do so in fact.

The parliamentary state does provide for its own legal overthrow by "the people," who are also empowered to eradicate every individual liberty. When the United States Supreme Court in *Ex Parte Milligan* asserted that "the principles of constitutional liberty would be in peril, unless established by irrepealable law," it was speaking of a law that never was and never will be; the whole of the U.S. Constitution can be repealed as, of course, parts of it have been.

The right of "the people" to rebel, by ballot or bullet, presupposes that the citizen will rebel in behalf of his own liberties or, still more nobly, in conscientious behalf of another man's. But what if conditions should obtain in which most of the people have been transformed into Hamilton's beast? Transported by fright—and the hatred of the frightful—great majorities have suppressed all liberty (including their own) in their panic. They have called for Caesars—and got them. They have denominated every deviation treason and made the denomination stick. And not only in distant times or places, and not necessarily by means of government except as an ancillary, and sometimes reluctant, ally. Dwight Eisenhower was as far from being a Caesar as a chief of state could be, but it was during the American terror of the 1950s that Claude Bourdet, the distinguished French editor, asked for his single sharpest impression of an extended visit to the United States, replied, "An American can say or do anything as long as he begins by saying, 'I hate Communism,'" and an American trade-union official caught with his hand in the till said, "I was using the money to fight Communism." Liberty is at the mercy of a much more formidable force even than the state power. Custom (as every social philosopher has observed) is weightier, speedier, and more durable than law. If we define liberty no more narrowly than deviation from the behavior of the community in general, we know how effectively the outraged community may smother dissent under the great wet blanket of its hostility. Let it be carried away by fear and anger, and state and local statutes and ordinances will almost invariably outrun repressive federal law in their fervor to curtail and suppress; and even without benefit of statute or ordinance, it will come down on the deviationist like a wolf pack on a one-sheep fold. Jefferson defended the exclusion of government action in the area of religion on the ground that religious extremists would be "laughed out of doors"; but the nineteenth-century Mormons, assaulted and murdered wherever they went, hounded westward from town to town and state to state, and finally subjected in Utah by the U.S. Army, did not feel that they were "laughed out of doors."

The cardinal offense of government is that it wants to govern; and the cardinal folly of men is that they want to govern not only themselves but others. The record of American "frontier justice," of vigilanteism and lynch law, is the historical scandal—and televised delight—of the world. In the past, as in the present, the state's power was often (if it arrived in time) invoked against the illegal exercise of social power with the individual haplessly dependent for his rights, or even his life, on the preponderance of the massed violence of the government over the massed violence of the mob. Indeed, such is the melancholy history of mass fury that the case can be made that the power of the state alone, even though it be totalitarian *in posse,* is the individual's only protection against society turned (so to say) posse. We speak of Hitler's and Stalin's tyranny, of their destruction of the liberties of the people, but hear Hannah Arendt in *The Origins of Totalitarianism:*

> In view of the unparalleled misery which totalitarian regimes have meant to their people—horror to many and unhappiness to all—it is painful to realize that they are always preceded by mass movements and that they command and rest upon mass support up to the end. Hitler's rise to power was legal in terms of majority rule and neither he nor Stalin could have maintained the leadership of large populations, survived many interior and exterior crises, and braved numerous dangers of the relentless intra-party struggles if they had not had the confidence of the masses. . . . Nor can their popularity be attributed to the victory of masterful and lying propaganda over ignorance and stupidity. For the propaganda of totalitarian movements which precede and accompany totalitarian regimes is invariably as frank as it is mendacious, and would-be totalitarian rulers usually start their careers by boasting of their past crimes and carefully outlining their future ones.

The mendacious propaganda of totalitarian movements, bringing totalitarian regimes to power, is dramatic. Much less dramatic, much more commonplace, and much more durably ruinous of liberty is the settled custom of the society. No law and no government—and, indeed, no propaganda—are involved in the Negro's making way for the white man on the sidewalk (or anywhere else) in the American South, in the inadmissibility of a Jew to a medical school or a suburb, in the inability of a professing Communist (in the United States) to obtain a hearing or a hall in which he might make himself heard. It is not likely that the disadvantaged Negro or Jew, given his liberty, would use it to incite revolution; or that the Communist, if he so used it, would constitute a clear and present danger to the state. The persistent and pervasive enemy of liberty is the Way of Life acceptable to the culture generally, and it needs no statute, decree, proclamation, or indoctrination to effect its instinctive ends.*

Liberty is the liberty of one man or it is not liberty at all, and I do not see how the issue will ever emerge from its welter of contradictions and self-contradictions until we talk about *the person* instead of *the people*. *The people* may lose their liberties by usurpation or incursion (or by abdicating them, as President Truman thought the Americans were doing when he vetoed the Internal Security Act of 1950). But they are less likely to lose theirs (or we ours) by usurpation or incursion than I mine. For they (or we) have recourses, legal and illegal, which are denied me when I stand alone. Standing alone, I am obnoxious. Liberty is the liberty of one obnoxious man.†

Almost all societies are almost always sufficiently libertarian for the orthodox. It is not the Young Man of the Year who is, or is likely to be, in trouble. Liberty's first and last test is its application to those we suspect, to those we dislike, to those we dread, to those we detest— to those, as Justice Holmes said, whose thought (or act, or appearance) we hate. Thus the rising hubbub against the "Warren" Court's decisions "coddling" suspected criminals and protecting the rights of the "lawless" few against the lawful powers of the police and the prosecutors; thus the Nixon administration's replacement of the coddling Justices with "strict constructionists" and its Attorney General's fulminations against "legalisms" and "proceduralisms." Ordinarily directed against the common criminal, the outrage of the community is most fervently directed against the social or ideological noncon-

---

* The American Bar Association's Committee on Protection of Civil Liberties and Civil Rights, reporting on "the present [1971] climate of repression," which, it said, constituted the greatest threat to civil liberties in the country's history, noted that "public opinion polls show increasing intolerance on the part of the American people."—New York *Times,* July 9, 1971.

† The sensational case of the New York *Times'* publication of the "Pentagon Papers" in 1971 was, said the *Times* on June 21, "the purest possible conflict between individual freedom and national security . . . between the rights of the citizen and the rights of society." True, the *Times* was obnoxious to the federal government in the matter; true, too, this "individual," this "citizen," standing heroically alone, with no other support than that of the entire press and nearly the entire American people, was the country's most important and powerful newspaper, its most respected, and one of its richest—rich enough to fight and win in the Supreme Court.

formist, the Negro or student militant with his nonnegotiable demands and his threat to "close it down" (or burn it down); above all, the Communist.

In the United States suppression of the rights of the Communist— or the alleged Communist—is the clearest example of the inability of the law (even of the courts) to withstand the power of public opinion. The "McCarthy period" of the early 1950s saw many Americans silenced, and even stifled, by one United States Senator on behalf of a frenzied society, and the government itself impotent against the fantastic charge (for instance) that there were 205 Communists in the State Department. It ended with the downfall of the Senator *when he attacked the Army*—an attack which turned public opinion against him. But Joe McCarthy's soul went marching on, in the persons of other politicians using the Congressional powers of investigation to "expose" the Red Menace and lay the foundations for repressive legislation.

A decade or so later Presidential candidate Richard M. Nixon explained his own conspicuous association with McCarthyism by saying, "I was very young then." But the evil that very young men do lives after them. In 1963 the American Institute of Public Opinion and the National Opinion Research Center found that 68 percent of the American people would not allow a Communist to make a speech; 66 percent would take his books out of the library; 90 percent would fire him from a defense-plant job; 91 percent would fire him from a high-school teaching post; 89 percent would fire him from a college professorship; 68 percent would fire him from a clerk's job in a store; 77 percent would take away his American citizenship; 61 percent would put him in jail; and 64 percent would give the government the right to listen in on his, or anybody else's, telephone conversations in order to get evidence against Communists.*

On June 5, 1961, the Supreme Court handed down two decisions, by that tremulous 5-to-4 margin, upholding the McCarran and Smith Acts, which, between them, required the Communist Party of the U.S.A. to register as a foreign-controlled agency of international Communism and punished membership in any organization which the member "knows" advocates the overthrow of the government by force

---

* By mid-1971 the Red Menace was worn so thin that President Nixon, on the heels of the "Ping-pong diplomacy" opening by the People's Republic of China, announced his intention to visit Peking—and even called the host nation by its right name (instead of "Red China"). But the mystique of anti-Communism had enough vitality still to extract a record appropriation from the American Congress for the Red-hunting House Internal Security Committee (the infamous Un-American Activities Committee renamed).

and violence. Protesting, on behalf of the four dissenters, that the majority was, for the first time in American history, "banning an association because it advocates hated ideas," Justice Black called the date "a fateful moment in the history of a free country." (Congress had already, in 1950, passed the McCarran Act over President Truman's veto.) In subsequent split decisions, the Court, with an altered personnel, reversed itself on some of the powers it had upheld, notably registration. It would seem that the fate of a free country—as Justice Black looked upon it—depends upon one vote by one man appointed to his post by the executive of the state power, the President.

The libertarian philosophers and statesmen will not take me standing alone and (because I stand alone) obnoxious; only the libertarian theologian and an odd bird like Tolstoy or Thoreau. Among secular personages, it is they and their like who without much philosophical respectability address themselves to the predicament of the solitary, they alone who confront the dilemma of one man and the state.* *They* are the true antithesis of Hobbes's absolutism; they hem and haw not; and they exclude themselves from the serious consideration of political theory by coming down on the side of purest anarchy.

Thoreau refused to pay his tax for the support of the Mexican War and slavery, spent a night in Concord jail, and was sprung by his friend Emerson, who paid his tax. (The legend is that when Emerson peered at him through the bars and said, "What ever are you doing in *there?*" Thoreau replied, "What ever are you doing out *there?*") "Unjust laws exist," Thoreau wrote in his *Civil Disobedience.* "Shall we be content to obey them, or shall we endeavor to amend them, and obey them until we have succeeded, or shall we transgress them at once? Men generally, under such a government as this, think that they ought to wait until they have persuaded the majority to alter them. They think that, if they should resist, the remedy would be worse than the evil. But it is the fault of the government itself that the remedy is worse than the evil. *It* makes it worse."

If an injustice (he goes on) is part of "the necessary friction of the machine of government . . . then you may consider whether the remedy will not be worse than the evil; but if it is of such a nature that it requires you to be the agent of injustice to another, then, I say, break the law. . . . It is not my business to be petitioning the governor or the legislature any more than it is theirs to petition me; and,

---

* "All government," says the still stately, and once rock-ribbed, London *Times,* "is based on the illusion that the individual is powerless against the Government." Do our eyes deceive us? They do. The next sentence reads: "When *enough individuals* [italics added] protest together, the strongest Government bends."—London *Times,* May 20, 1968.

if they should not hear my petition, what should I do then? But in this case the state has provided no way; its very constitution is the evil. . . . I do not hesitate to say that those who call themselves abolitionists should at once effectively withdraw their support, both in person and property, from the government of Massachusetts and not wait till they constitute a majority of one before they suffer the right to prevail through them. Moreover, any man more right than his neighbors constitutes a majority of one already. . . ."

So our majority of one "quietly declares war with the state, after my fashion," assured as to the eventuation: "A minority is powerless while it conforms to the majority; it is not even a minority then; but it is irresistible when it clogs by its whole weight. . . ." But he isn't all that confident, and in the end he wonders whether "democracy, such as we know it, [is] the last improvement possible in government. Is it not possible to take a step further toward recognizing and organizing the rights of man? There will never be a really free and enlightened state, until the state comes to recognize the individual as a higher and independent power, from which all its own power and authority are derived, and treats him accordingly. . . ."

And when will that state be? Never. On this point "liberal" political theory is one with "conservative," the reformer with the standpat contemporary journalist William F. Buckley: "That which is anarchic within me (which is very strong) tunes in strongly on the idea of a society in which people decide for themselves what taxes to pay, what rules to obey, when to cooperate and when not to with the civil authorities. But that which is reasonable within me, which I am glad to say most often prevails, recognizes that societies so structured do not exist, and cannot exist." Agreed, says that most liberal of American Attorneys General, Ramsey Clark (in 1968): "If the test of the law is the conscience of the individual, then we have chaos and anarchy."

Henry David Thoreau's polemics have affected the course of history—certainly in the liberation of India. But they have not changed the nature of the state and its relationship to man, and the government of liberated India is no more the state Thoreau dreamed of than any other.* The widespread application of his dreamy doctrine to the civil-rights campaign (and the dropout commune movement) in the United States has had a profound effect on American law and American culture. But it has had none whatever on *the supremacy of law;*

---

* "The prisons are crowded with people arrested under emergency laws, with no charges given—the implication being that they are mixed up in some kind of pro-Pakistan subversion."—dispatch from Indian Kashmir, New York *Times,* October 4, 1969.

although state and local statutes have been struck down at the federal level as unconstitutional, no judge and no court has upheld civil disobedience *to the Constitution*. The state which Thoreau pleased himself (as he said) to imagine is no more visible than it was a hundred years ago, or a thousand.

7: E Pluribus Einheit

S T A T E S differ, and differ radically, in regard to their forms of government and the extent to which the liberty of the individual is protected by law and by government's adherence to the law. But in the rock-bottom respect of the ultimate power of the state there is no difference at all. The gulf is immense between Western democracy and the overt tyranny of, say, the most liberal Communist regime. But it is not an absolute gulf. A difference in degree, however immense, does not constitute a difference of kind. I know of no penalty imposed upon deviation by one modern state or society, legally or customarily, that is not imposed by another to some extent upon some segment of its citizens, with an inexorable tendency toward closer resemblance as "prevailing conditions" approach identity. On April 27, 1970, the New York *Times* said editorially: "Less than a generation ago the tapped wire, the bugged room, the secret informer evoked contempt and ridicule in the minds of most Americans. These were the marks of police states in a jaded Old World. It could not happen here. It is happening here now." (Twenty-five years earlier, Dr. Joseph Goebbels said, "Even if we lose, we will still win, for our ideals will have penetrated the hearts of our enemies.")

In America (or in Russia) the indignant cry is at once raised: "Do you mean to say that *we* are no different from *them?*" Only in this one respect, only in the last analysis (which we are trying to make here). Think of the Americans' national slogans and their univocal applicability to the most tyrannical of states: "E Pluribus Unum," "United We Stand," "In Union There Is Strength"; and think of Hitler's *Einheit.* Whatever *any* state has to do—or in its less than infinite wisdom believes (or says it believes) it has to do—will be done and has been done. The deportation of the Nisei from the American West Coast was done. The British government's exclusion of its own citizens of Asian origin was done. The West German government's seizure of a respected oppositionist periodical—in the name of protecting the morals of the young—was done. And no one doubts the earnestness of segregationist former governor Wallace of Alabama when he says in his campaign for the American Presidency, "I would keep the peace if I had to keep 30,000 troops standing in the streets, two feet apart and with two-foot-long bayonets." "The peace" has been kept this way, the way of liberty's denial, in "free countries" everywhere—as the always regrettable alternative to anarchy.*

Anarchy as a doctrine is at least as old as the Stoics of the third century B.C. Though it has independent roots in the England of Godwin, the France of Proudhon, and the Italy of Malatesta, its most powerful advocacy emanated (understandably enough) from the ferociously repressive conditions of Czarist Russia. Tolstoy was its theologian, its Thoreau; the gentle, optimistic Kropotkin and the wild Bakunin its philosophers. They held that government's ultimate function was the maintenance of an unjust order that crushed individuality; take government away, and injustice would disappear. It would not follow that men would be unorganized, but they would organize themselves voluntarily, in local communities and industries, with every man's consent, and on this voluntary basis maintain a truly associative society. Some anarchists were terrorists, and the political assassins of the end of nineteenth century all claimed the terrifying designation; it was the black flag of anarchy, not the red flag of Communism, that represented the End of Everything to the Victorian rich and their bourgeois royalty. But most anarchists were pacifists, and all of them Socialist exponents of mutual aid. And one of the first acts of the "dictatorship of the proletariat" in Russia was to use artillery to destroy the anarchist headquarters in Moscow and suppress the anarchist movement (which had been sympathetic to the Russian revolution). American law, without anywhere saying what an anarchist is, still forbids the immigration of foreign anarchists and provides for the deportation of anarchist aliens.

The classic advocates of anarchy as a system—a self-contradictory concept—are all romantics. Their no-state has no more substance, no more operability, no more *imaginability,* than Thoreau's; nor is it likely that it will have until men are angels. Its romanticism is evidenced in the divergence of its witting or unwitting adherents. They include not only the Martin Luther Kings, resting their case on the

* The triumphant Gaullist slogan in the French elections of 1968, following the student uprising in Paris, was, CONTRE L'ANARCHIE—DIVISION-IMPUISSANCE.

supremacy of God, but the most violent atheists; not only the revolutionary students of Paris (and elsewhere), but the man who for thirty years symbolized the state's most far-reaching abridgment of the liberty (even the lives) of its law-abiding citizens, the same General Hershey who (on another occasion) said he knew of no solution for the problem of conscientious objection in any large proportion of the men of military age. Faced (at the Yale Law School in 1966) with the question, What would he do if he were of draft age and found it morally impossible to support a war? the General replied: "I'd rather go to jail."

So amorphous is anarchy that it has room not only for terrorists, pacifists, Negro Christians, and generals, but also the deepest-dyed Tory. In the sunny groves of Orange County, California, probably the most politically conservative diocese in America, the Santa Ana *Register* was published for thirty years by the aged Raymond Cyrus Holles, who called himself "a radical for freedom." Mr. Holles opposed taxation as "just plain stealing." "The government," he said, "ought to be supported on a strictly voluntary basis." Did that go for parks, post offices, police, and the schools? Absolutely. *And* for conscription and immigration laws and the outlawry of Communists. He had, says columnist Arthur Hoppe, carried conservatism to its logical extreme, and "the more you talk to him, the more he sounds like an anarchist."

To say that no state has ever supported the right of revolution—or of anarchy—is not literally accurate. Four great states—the U.S.A., the U.S.S.R., Great Britain, and France—not only supported it but demanded it, and demanded it, *ex post facto,* of every soldier, in the Nuremberg Judgment of 1946 that the Nazi leaders were to be hanged. The New York *Times* hailed the decision of the four-power tribunal as historic, "proclaiming new legal rules and standards which now become integral parts of international law. . . . National sovereignty has been superseded by the superior sovereignty of international law and international organization, which takes jurisdiction not only over states and nations but also over individuals responsible for their Governments and policies. And every kind of crime connected with . . . aggressive war is subject to the same authority, which accepts no excuse of either 'superior orders' or the peril of disobedience." The high Nazi officials had all pleaded "superior orders" from Hitler, the head of state, who was dead, as their defense. The plea was rejected in advance; the Four-Power Agreement establishing the tribunal asserted criminality "whether or not [the acts were] in violation of the domestic law of the country where perpetrated."

If the Nuremberg Judgment meant anything, it meant that the soldier (not to say the civilian) has to decide for himself whether or not he can obey an officer's (or an official's) legal order and be held responsible, even on pain of the death penalty if he does obey the order and in doing so commits what may be subsequently held to have been a war crime, a crime against peace, or a crime against humanity. Here is prescribed the right—indeed, the duty—not merely of civil but of *military* disobedience. It may be impossible to imagine an army operating under such conditions—but it is easy to imagine what would happen if it tried. Nuremberg was, of course, a sham. None of the four great states which imposed the doctrine on the defeated Germans has adopted it for its own soldiery (and the new German *Wehrmacht* has also ignored it). When four American soldiers refused transfer to combat duty in Vietnam, on the ground that the war was "unjust, immoral, and illegal," Counsel for the Department of Defense announced that they might be sentenced to death by a court-martial— for doing what the Nuremberg Tribunal required a soldier to do under threat of death if he did not.*

Besides the members of the Nuremberg Tribunal, the publisher of the Santa Ana *Register,* and the Director of Selective Service, anarchy may claim one other eminent advocate: the government of every existing state, whose independence (or anarchy) is the pride of its patriot citizens. The recognition that all sovereigns live in the fabled state of nature *vis-à-vis* one another is as old as the state itself. Every Mus-

---

* In 1970 the ghost of Nuremberg arose in Washington when, following a newspaper "leak," several U.S. soldiers and officers (one of them a general) were charged in connection with the mass murder of South Vietnamese civilians in the village of My Lai two years earlier. Facing trial by court-martial —and the possible penalty of death—those directly accused of murder said that they had only been obeying orders. Aligned against them were the Nuremberg Judgment, the Geneva convention of 1949 concerning treatment of prisoners of war and civilians, and a unique finding by a U.S. Military Board of Review, in a 1953 court-martial case, that the fact that an enlisted man was ordered by his lieutenant to shoot a Korean POW was no defense against murder: "The obedience of an automaton. A soldier is a reasoning agent. He does not respond, and is not expected to respond, like a piece of machinery. It is a fallacy of widespread consumption that a soldier is required to do everything a superior officer orders him to do." One of the soldiers court-martialed after My Lai, Lieutenant William L. Calley, Jr., was convicted of murdering twenty-three persons there. On appeal, after President Nixon promised to review the verdict, his sentence was reduced to twenty years. Meanwhile, James Reston, Jr., in a letter to the New York *Times* (October 26, 1970), protested the Army's dismissal of General William C. Westmoreland's "command responsibility" for My Lai. The Secretary of the Army had asserted that General Westmoreland had had no knowledge of the My Lai "incident." Reston pointed out that an American military tribunal had executed the Japanese General Yamashita in 1946 because of his soldiers' atrocities in the Philippines—even though it was admitted by the tribunal that he had no knowledge of them.

covite, every New Yorker is under the city's ordinances; every city is under the statutes of the province or state; and every province or state is under the law of the land. But the land itself is under no law; if it accepts the "decisions" of the United Nations, it does so uncoerced and (in the case of a great power) uncoercible. And so deeply inbred is nationalism that the unilateral (i.e., anarchic) actions of nations are supported by nearly all of their people. In 1969 the anarchy of the world was extended to the solar system when the Congress of the United States memorialized the United States Space Administration to plant the American flag and no other—the United Nations flag had been suggested—on the moon. (Ten years earlier the Russians had dropped the Red flag of the U.S.S.R. on that defenseless satellite.)

The determination of individual liberty is, and must be, the prerogative of the state because of the state's paramount function: to preserve itself—i.e., its sovereignty. In 1931 the United States Supreme Court, in a case involving a divinity-school professor who was denied citizenship because he refused to bear arms, held that though "we are a Christian people . . . we are a Nation with the duty to survive." We must, therefore, "go forward upon the assumption, and safely can proceed on no other, that unqualified allegiance to the Nation and submission and obedience to the laws of the land, as well those made for war as those made for peace, are not inconsistent with the will of God." One is reminded of the genuine astonishment of the British soldiers of World War I who first saw the buttons on a German uniform bearing the inscription *Gott mit uns,* since they themselves had been called to the colors for God and Country. What the Supreme Court said of the American nation could be said (and has been) on behalf of every nation that has ever existed: It has "the duty" to survive.

Only once, so far as I know, has this "duty" been called into juridical question; and the question was not pursued, on or off the bench. In 1967 the Supreme Court struck down a provision of the Subversive Activities Control Act of 1950 that made it a crime for Communist Party members to work in a defense plant. It was held that the provision violated the freedom of association guaranteed by the First Amendment. Speaking for the Court, Chief Justice Warren said that "the phrase 'war power' cannot be invoked as a talismanic incantation to support any exercise of Congressional power which can be brought into its ambit." He went on: *"This concept of 'national defense' cannot be deemed an end in itself, justifying any exercise of legislative power designed to promote such a goal. Implicit in the term 'national defense' is the notion of defending those values and ideals which set this nation apart.* For almost two centuries, our country has taken singular pride in the democratic ideals enshrined in its Constitution, and the most cherished of those ideals have found expression in the First Amendment. It would indeed be ironic if, in the name of national defense, we would sanction the subversion of one of *those liberties*—the freedom of association—*which make the defense of the nation worthwhile."* (Emphasis added.) Neither of the two dissenting members of the Court touched on the doctrine that "the national defense cannot be deemed an end in itself." Nor has any learned comment that has come to my attention. Perhaps the most spectacular lapse of all was the failure of the chauvinist advocates of Mr. Justice Warren's impeachment to rise to the occasion on which their *bête noire* appears flatly to have rejected the dictum "My country, right or wrong."

Liberty, then, is what the state allows in fulfilling its "duty" to survive. The omelet *does* take precedence over the egg. The answer to the question How much power over the individual is the property of the state? is, As much as the state deems necessary to preserve itself, including all. To talk about *responsible* or *limited* government is to talk about government hamstrung.*

But the preservation of the state is all things to all men. I do not endanger the state's very existence by throwing a rock through my neighbor's window or snatching his purse. The state is not dissolved so easily. What I endanger is its preservation in a certain condition generally characterized as order (or, platitudinously *and* more ominously, law and order). But order—in human affairs—is a chimerical thing, no easier to define than it is to achieve. Life is a tumult of accidents, frenzies, exaltations, and desperations. Men are not orderly. States—least of all in their relations with one another—are no more orderly than men.

What is social order? In one society it is chattel slavery or concentration camps. (President Thieu's South Vietnam suppressed newspapers convicted of carrying reports "likely to cause confusion among the masses." Like the Soviet Union's, the government of Spain provides imprisonment for publication of anything "detrimental to the government, the state, the armed forces, and the interests of the country." "Maybe we will be permitted to publish the weather report," said a Spanish journalist.) In another society social order may mean legalized prostitution, wide-open gambling, free access to firearms, racial or religious persecution, or trial by lynch mob.

---

* In *The Spirit of Liberty* Judge Learned Hand, universally recognized as one of the greatest of contemporary jurists, said wryly (but unequivocally) that "liberty is so much latitude as the powerful choose to accord the weak."

The military junta on the right, the Revolutionary Committee on the left, when they suspend civil liberties, do so in the name of preserving or restoring order. In the center, the President of the United States summons the governors of the states to "a crusade for public order, in every sense of that phrase," to eliminate "crime in the streets." "No society," he says, "can tolerate attacks upon itself"— true, and the invariable dictum of every democrat and of every dictator.

What is "an attack upon society"? My wartime dissent which gives "aid and comfort to the enemy"? My insistence upon taking my Saturday-night bath in my own home? My letting my hair grow as long as Andrew Jackson's (in contravention of an anti-hippie ordinance of the city of New Orleans, where General Jackson won his most famous battle)? We do not agree on a definition, my neighbor and I; neither do the Supreme Court Justice and his neighbor on the bench. Consider the Thirteenth Amendment's prohibition of involuntary servitude. It is a dead letter as regards military conscription. But its protection of strikers—of the right not to work—was cemented into public law by the National Labor Relations Act. The civilian employer *must* bargain with his collective employees. Fair enough, if the Thirteenth Amendment is to mean what it says. But the President "finds" that the striking longshoremen have brought about a national transportation emergency, and he threatens to seize the facilities and compel their continued operation; and collective bargaining ends with the state's power to knock the contending parties' heads together.

Labor Relations Act or no Labor Relations Act, civilian (no less than military) public employees are forbidden to strike by national, state, and local legislation. But by the 1970s the United States (and many other countries) had to put up with such unthinkable stoppages, not only by public employees from garbage collectors to teachers, firemen, *and policemen,** but by private employees in such vital services as air and surface transport and even hospital and medical care; with, in the mounting outrage of the affected communities, an ever increasing, and ever less effective, spate of prohibitory legislation.†

---

* On October 7, 1969, Canada's largest city, Montreal, was "struck" by its 3,700 policemen, with (according to the New York *Times*) "near-anarchy as a result." After a day and a night of widespread looting, robbery, riot, and arson, and with one man killed and four wounded, the Provincial Government broke the strike by emergency legislation providing imprisonment and fines of up to $50,000 for continued absence from duty.

† When it became apparent that the mail cannot be sorted with bayonets, the U.S. government yielded to its illegally striking postal workers in March 1970. President Nixon bravely proclaimed the issue "the survival of a government based upon law," but the mailmen returned to work only after they got an effective guarantee of Congressional action on their wage grievances.

Do I likewise jeopardize the survival of the state by standing on a soap box before a small audience and actually crying up revolution? The commonest of Sunday-afternoon diversions of my boyhood was to accompany my father to Washington Park to hear the wild men in "bug-house corner" off the ball field. A single policeman, Big Tom by name, was the entire representation of the state, swinging his club ferociously at the small children on the edge of the crowd when they made so much noise playing that their fathers could not hear the revolutionaries rant. My father listened attentively every Sunday afternoon—and went right on voting the straight Republican ticket. These days the meeting of man with the state appears in clearer outline, with the disappearance of the solitary bug-houser and his replacement by the massed mob wielding brickbats in confrontation with the massed nightsticks, tear gas, buckshot, and bayonets of Big Tom's successors—a progression that demonstrates how "public order" and "public necessity" may be (and more often than not are) stretched to cover every great public and private passion against every last human liberty.

Zechariah Chafee, Jr., perhaps the foremost legal scholar in the First Amendment field, holds that no one "should be allowed to say whatever he wants anywhere and at any time. We can all agree from the very start that there must be some point where the government may step in. . . ." Such points *seem* clear—and simple. The state may let me cry "Fire!" in an empty theater, but prohibits my doing so in a crowded one. (Or at least prohibits my doing so falsely; but I shall be sure to insist that I smelled smoke or thought I did.) I agree that the prohibition is proper. But as soon as I agree that freedom of speech is unprotected by the First Amendment in this one "extreme" circumstance, I have accepted the principle under which all liberty may be suppressed. A distinction is made (by Meiklejohn, among others) between *suppression* and *control*—a distinction which may or may not comfort the man who is told that his speech is simply being controlled. "The First Amendment," said Justice Holmes, ". . . cannot have been, and obviously was not, intended to give immunity to every form of language. . . . We venture to believe that neither Hamilton nor Madison, nor any other competent person, ever supposed that to make criminal the counselling of a murder would be an unconstitutional interference with free speech."

Good enough—but have we not, then, taken our position with the absolute power of the state? The First Amendment, with its guarantees of freedom of speech, press, assembly, and petition, begins, "Congress shall make no law respecting an establishment of religion, or prohibiting the free exercise thereof . . ." The separation of church and state in the United States is the first of all absolutes. Congress shall make no law *having anything to do with religion.* Pious humbug, but humbug; and it takes the Army to call it by its right name. Presiding over the court-martial trial (and conviction) of a Negro soldier who refused to cut his "Afro"-style hair, Judge Advocate Lieutenant Colonel Edward L. McHugh ruled that the offender's motivation " 'has no greater status than a religious belief' and that religious beliefs are not a proper cause for willfully disobeying an order." *

True, the Supreme Court held, in 1961, that the requirement of "a belief in the existence of God" as a qualification for public office "unconstitutionally invades . . . freedom of belief and religion and therefore cannot be enforced." But it is also true that this same Supreme Court, whose Chief Justice uses a Bible to administer the oath of office to the President, continues to open its sessions with the words "God save the United States and this honorable court." In 1969 the President established what theologian Reinhold Niebuhr called a "modern version of the king's chapel" by inaugurating divine services in the state-owned Executive Mansion. Every American coin is inscribed, "In God We Trust." Every public officeholder swears his allegiance on the Bible (as does every juror and witness in a lawsuit). Congress opens with an invocation to God (delivered by the Chaplain of Congress) and the Pledge of Allegiance to the American flag puts the nation "under God." Convicted under a Maryland blasphemy statute, an American was imprisoned in 1968 on the charge that he "did unlawfully use profanity by taking the Lord's name in vain." (The 245-year-old statute originally called for the offender to be bored through the tongue for the first offense, branded with the letter B on the forehead for the second, and put to death without benefit of clergy for the third.) Churches and parochial schools receive government aid in the form of tax exemption and always have—and public schools may release students for prayer and must release students for Christmas. Congress provides state-employed chaplains to the armed forces—and, until 1970, prescribed exemption from military training and service only on the ground of "religious belief." †

* New York *Times,* December 11, 1969.
† In order to grant the exemption, Congress had to decide that the applicant's belief was in fact religious; it had therefore to distinguish between religion and nonreligion, which is precisely what the First Amendment forbids it to do. On June 15, 1970, the Supreme Court—Justice Black wrote this opinion, too—in a 5-to-3 decision extended conscientious objection to those whose beliefs are "purely ethical or moral in source and content."—New York *Times,* June 16, 1970.

So much for the first clause of the First Amendment, *"Congress shall make no law . . ."* But what if the free exercise of my religion involves human sacrifice and the victim is willing? Congress says No. What if it involves my handling a poisonous snake? Congress says No. What if it involves polygamy? Congress says No. What if it forbids my being vaccinated or my drinking fluoridated water? Congress says No. What if it forbids my sending my child to school? Congress says No. What if it forbids me (or my children) access to information about contraception? Congress says No. What if it requires me to love my enemy and provide medical supplies to the civilians of North Vietnam? Congress says No. Every one of these cases (except the first) is real and contemporary; and every one of these infringements on religious liberty has been upheld by the courts. Congress has made no end of laws respecting religion, and the courts have sustained them. (The Supreme Court refused to stay an order that a sick woman be given a blood transfusion even though she *and her husband* refused it on the ground that it violated the Biblical injunction against "drinking blood." This is the same Supreme Court that said, "If there is any fixed star in our constitutional constellation, it is that no official, high or petty, can prescribe what shall be orthodox in politics, nationalism, religion, or other matters of opinion or force citizens to confess by word or act their faith therein.")

By word *or act*—there is the sticking point. I may believe—but I may not act upon my belief or do the things my belief requires of me. I am condemned *unless* I stand with the Pharisees condemned by Christ because *"they say—and do not."* Let the law permit me to act on my religion and, as Jeremy Bentham put it long ago, you "arm every fanatic against all governments"; for "in the immense variety of ideas respecting natural and Divine law, cannot some reason be found for resisting all human laws?" Very probably; and so one of the two, divine law or human law, must fall. One does, and that one is not the human law, which (in the United States Constitution) specifically protects not only religion but *the free exercise thereof.*

So, too, with reference to every other "absolute" right. Under the United States Uniform Code of Military Justice, Army counsel in the celebrated court-martial of Captain Howard B. Levy in 1967 argued successfully that a citizen under arms has the right to *think* as he will but not to act upon his thinking *or* utter it. The U.S. Post Office invades my privacy (if I am a suspect person) by putting a "mail cover" on me—i.e., making a record of the sender's name and address, and place and date of postmark, of every letter I receive; and the Postmaster General of the United States says, "There's no question in my mind that mail covers do, to some degree, invade individual rights. . . . [However] I'm not ready, at this point, to talk about abolishing them." The same Post Office defends the interception of mail addressed to delinquent taxpayers—a "sneaky, un-American, undemocratic Gestapo tactic," former Senator Ralph Yarborough of Texas called it on the floor of the Senate—on the ground that an order of the Internal Revenue Service "has the same authority as a search warrant." For several years (until the Supreme Court restrained it) the Post Office itself opened printed matter addressed to Americans from Communist countries—and in 1970, with a reconstructed Supreme Court sitting, the Postmaster General announced that "suspicious mail" from abroad would be "scrutinized." My *truthful* statement about another man (unless he's a public figure) may be held criminal as slander or libel. The limitation of my right to label such products as foods and drugs—fought long and hard in the courts a generation or two ago—is now accepted as a proper state control. As every homeowner knows who has come up against urban renewal or the construction of a freeway, my Fourth Amendment right to be secure "against unreasonable . . . seizure" is at the mercy of the supersedent right of eminent domain under which the state does the seizing and also determines the reasonableness of the seizure; and my concomitant security in my "effects" is at the mercy of the state's unlimited power to destroy me by taxation.

Nor is it possible to justify all these whips and scourges on the ground that the exercise of my liberty would injure another. The "unnatural"—that is, unpopular—"practice" of Mormon polygamy was religious, and it outraged the sensibilities of the monogamists who constituted almost the whole of American society; but it is hard to see how it injured them. The Christian Scientist was held to have injured others by his rejection of vaccination against epidemic disease; but it is hard to see how his rejection of medical care, say, for cancer, was an injury to others—unless the state is to decide that his family is injured when his family denies it. What if a bachelor orphan of what the law calls consenting age forms a homosexual attachment with another bachelor orphan of consenting age? What if a heterosexual bachelor who doesn't drive a car is a drunkard? Whom does he injure by his drinking? Himself? Is the state (through the Volstead Act) to determine what constitutes injury to oneself? If so, may it not determine what I shall eat (and when, and how much) and drink (as it once did under Volstead) and read and hear, and whether I shall be permitted to go out of my house in the rain without an umbrella, and how hard a mattress I shall sleep on?

A reduction to absurdity, you say. But the absurdity is established in the principle that I am not free to do as I like (to use narcotics, for instance) when my doing so does not injure another. And if I may be restricted on the ground that what I do *might* injure another, then there is no possible limit at all to the state power. I *might* do anything. I might kill a man with the gun which the Second Amendment guarantees my right to possess. If I carry a baseball bat, I might use it to club a passer-by as I go down the street en route to the baseball field; and if I study chemistry I might use my knowledge to concoct poisons or blow safes. So baseball and chemistry fall under the ban.

8: Who Says There's a Fire?

W H A T is marvelous is not that Congress has made laws in violation of the First Amendment freedoms, or that some of them have or have not been struck down by the courts, but that the doctrine on which they are made and upheld or struck down continues to be disputed with unabated heat. The most learned men of the law continue to accuse one another, from the highest bench, of being the enemies of freedom or security. When the Supreme Court voted 5 to 4 that the Fifth Amendment protection against self-incrimination permitted the police to take a blood sample from a driver suspected of being drunk, Justice Black said it was "a strange hierarchy of values that allows the State to extract a human being's blood. . . ." "What happens under this law is typical of what happens in a police state," said Justices Black and Douglas in dissenting from the opinion upholding New York's "Feinberg Act" requiring the dismissal of teachers belonging to subversive organizations. "The hallmark of a totalitarian regime," dissenting Justice Potter Stewart called the 5-to-4 conviction of the publisher of erotic books in 1966. Speaking in 1971 for the 5-to-4 majority which held that the press could continue publication of the "Pentagon Papers" while the Court was deliberating the issue, Justice Black, still going strong at eighty-five, said that his four dissenting brethren "would make a shambles of the First Amendment."

The ambiguity of freedom is epitomized, in the United States just now, by the lurid confusion attending "snooping," electronic and otherwise, by government agencies. Federal statutes regarding the invasion of privacy are in utter conflict with one another and with state statutes. But what are statutes between friends? Former Senator Gruening of Alaska says (without refutation from any quarter) that the Internal Revenue Service, in order to install telephone "taps" in taxpayers' homes, disguises its agents as Bell Telephone workers and uses fake telephone-company trucks. Senator Fong of Hawaii said several years ago that the Department of Justice was "bugging" suspected criminals as a matter of course, in spite of Congressional refusal to legalize its doing so. Senator Long of Missouri, having produced an admission by the Internal Revenue Service that it maintains a special school in snooping, conducted the following dialogue, in Congressional committee, with the IRS representative:

> LONG: Is there a special course in that school on teaching the use of burglar tools?
> OWEN B. YUNG (Intelligence Division, IRS): There is, or was, up until this year a course in lock-picking.
> LONG: What would you use the art of lock-picking for?
> YUNG: For surreptitious entry.
> LONG: Well, that would still be breaking and entering, wouldn't it?
> YUNG: Technically, I guess so, sir.
> LONG: Violation of the law?
> YUNG: I wouldn't know, sir. I am not a lawyer.

But while statesmen and bureaucrats argue the secret surveillance of suspected criminals and tax-dodgers, there is no argument whatever on the snooping activities of one branch of the government. This is the so-called "security community," the FBI, the CIA, and the intelligence divisions of the Departments of State and Defense. So wholeheartedly is power conceded to these agencies that "the indispensability of the Central Intelligence Agency to the security of the State" strips men of their protection against defamation, and even against murder. The courts dismissed the suit of an Estonian émigré leader against a CIA operative who called him a Soviet secret agent. The judge, though he found the function of the CIA "an esoteric subject," held that its activities should not be hampered "by a too strict application of legal principles, including the principles of libel and slander." In 1969 the U.S. Army dropped murder charges against a group of officers of the "Green Berets" in Vietnam on the ground that the CIA refused to let its agents testify in the case.

The revelations of government (and private) prying, especially by highly sophisticated electronic devices, became so sensational in the

1960s that former President Johnson addressed himself to the matter in his 1967 State of the Union message. "We should," he said, "protect what Justice Brandeis called 'the right most valued by civilized men'—the right to privacy. We should outlaw all wiretapping, public and private, wherever and whenever it occurs, except when the security of the Nation itself is at stake—and only then with the strictest safeguards. We should exercise the full reach of our constitutional powers to outlaw electronic 'bugging' and 'snooping.' "

". . . *Except when the security of the Nation itself is at stake.*" The echo of the words had hardly subsided when the Congress of the United States, with a whoop and a holler, and a handful of dismayed dissenters, passed the Omnibus Crime Control Act of 1968. Here for the first time in American history legal sanction was provided for telephone wiretapping and "bugging" by federal, state, and local law-enforcement officers investigating murder, robbery, "organized crime," "drug abuse," and "other offenses" involving danger to "life, limb, and property." A court order was required, and the subject had to be informed of its issuance—but only after the tap or the bug had been removed. Libertarian protests in both Houses were brushed aside by the argument (of the House Republican leader) that "there can be no further quibbling about the urgent need for tougher law-enforcement legislation."

It all had a familiar ring: "There is no time to waste on hair-splitting over infringement of liberty," said the Washington *Post* on the occasion of Attorney General A. Mitchell Palmer's "Red raids" in 1919. Exactly fifty years later another Attorney General, John Mitchell, revealed that the FBI had ignored the Congressional requirement of a court order to listen in on the conversation of the "Chicago Seven" indicted (and subsequently convicted) for crossing a state line with the intention to incite riot at the Democratic National Convention of 1968—*and would go on doing so.* "While it may be appropriate," said Mr. Mitchell, "for Congress to establish rules limiting the investigative techniques which the Executive may employ in enforcing the laws that Congress has enacted, a serious question exists as to the power to restrict the President's power to gather information which he deems necessary to the proper exercise of powers which the Constitution confers on him alone. If the Congress cannot tell the President whom he should employ to direct the Army, there is a strong basis to argue that Congress cannot tell the President what means he may employ to obtain information which he needs to determine the proper deployment of his forces. . . . The President . . . has the constitutional power to authorize electronic surveillance to gather intelligence information concerning domestic organizations which seek to attack and subvert the Government by unlawful means." "For the first time in American history," said an attorney for the men upon whom the FBI had snooped, "a member of the President's Cabinet has publicly, and proudly, stated that he has, in open violation of his oath of office, taken the law into his own hands."

"*. . . Except when the security of the Nation itself is at stake.*" "The security of the country takes precedence over all First Amendment freedoms," Maximilian W. Kempner writes in *The Supreme Court and the Establishment and Free Exercise of Religion*—a doctrine which sweeps away every liberty and is nowhere seriously challenged. And it makes no difference whether the state is a "good" one or a "bad" one, the principle of self-preservation abides intact and inviolable. The absolute-rights men—the Blacks and the Meiklejohns —concede that overthrow might, or (under conditions of extreme tyranny) would and should occur. But their argument for liberty unconfined is invariably based on the postulate that that liberty is the very means of preserving the state—at least the free state. And it is certainly true historically that a nation like England or the United States, with its Magna Carta or its Bill of Rights, has proved itself surer against revolution than a thoroughly repressive tyranny like Czarist Russia's.

That the cure of the ills of the free society is more freedom is a concept from which the inference is irresistible that there are states or governments worthy of preservation, and others unworthy, and that those that are overthrown by the most desperate exercise of freedom (namely, revolution) ought to be. But no government has yet been found that considered itself unworthy and, as a consequence, took no measures for its security. Thus it is, as Officer Sweeney lamented, that the very government against which my rights are guaranteed by the Constitution itself determines the conditions under which it may circumscribe my rights. "Who," Hamilton asks in *The Federalist,* "is to be the judge of the *necessity* and *propriety* of the laws to be passed? . . . I answer . . . that the national government . . . must judge, in the first instance, of the proper exercise of its"—that is, its own— "powers, and its constitutents in the last." And if it passes tyrannical laws? Why, "there is then no resource left but in the exertion of that original right of self-defense which is paramount to all positive forms of government." But it is here, as everywhere, "the people" who will defend themselves; and this is not the issue. The issue is one man— one Nisei deported by the U.S. Army because of his (or his father's, or his grandfather's) national origin, or I myself, all alone confronted by the community's whole power in the person of Officer Sweeney the night the town was on fire.

The town is on fire—and that is enough for Officer Sweeney. But is it in fact? And if it is, is the fire so widespread and so far out of control as to jeopardize the town's existence? Who says so? Before I surrender my sacred liberties, I have to be convinced. If Officer Sweeney has the time—*if* he has the time, in so terrible an emergency —he will describe the extent of the fire to me in convincing detail, and I (as a reasonable man) will be convinced and at once forgo my bath and report for fire duty.

But the emergency most commonly affecting my liberty is not local, but national, and the security in jeopardy is the national security. Officer Sweeney is then President Sweeney of the United States, elected by me (or perhaps over my opposition) to minister to my sovereign needs. Unfortunately (as he himself says *), he alone understands the extent of the emergency, which is beyond my inexpert and uninformed comprehension. (And even beyond that of the courts. Attorney General Mitchell, in his assertion of the absolute right of the President to use electronic surveillance, said that it "should not be subject to judicial review.") Still more unfortunately (as President Sweeney has his deputy tell me), the interest of national security prevents his informing me. "Look," said Assistant Secretary of Defense Arthur Sylvester to American reporters in Saigon, "if you think any American official is going to tell you the truth, then you're stupid." Mr. Sylvester went on to explain that it is the inherent right of government "to lie to save itself," and that the nation's leaders are justified in lying to its people when the national security is threatened.

So, in the interest of security, I am first of all denied the right to know that there is a fire or how formidable it is—and then denied the rest of my rights because there's a formidable fire. So complex, recondite, and delicate are the matters affecting security that my *ministers* must be my *masters;* and if there's a war on and I criticize their war policies, even on the basis of the expert information available to, say, the chairman of the Senate Foreign Relations Committee, they invoke the nation's wrath against me (*and* against the Senator)

---

* After President Nixon invaded Cambodia in 1970 without so much as informing Congress (*or* the Cambodian government) in advance, Congressmen received an unsigned memorandum from the White House: "Only the President has all the facts on this situation." A year later, during the secret SALT talks with the Russians, Senator Hubert Humphrey, the titular head of the opposition party, told his colleagues, "The President, as Commander-in-Chief, is primarily responsible for our security. He, alone, must make the final decision. . . ."

by accusing us of giving aid and comfort to the enemy. At some point dissent must become treason: "The more divided we are at home," said President Nixon to the American people, "the less likely the enemy is to negotiate in Paris."

"An idle man who wants his politics done for him, will have them done for him," said the British historian Bagehot. In the age of kings, soldiers said, "We know enough if we know that we are the king's subjects." Only *he* knew what was right and wrong and what should be done, and *our* only responsibility was to do as he said. "When our country is in a position of crisis," said former President Eisenhower, "there is only one thing a good American can do, and that is support the President." In the fifth year of the Vietnam war, Secretary of State Rusk lost his cool at a press conference and told the correspondents: "There gets to be a point where the question is, Whose side are you on. . . . I'm on our side. None of your newspapers or broadcasting apparatuses are worth a damn unless the United States succeeds. . . ." But a free government is founded upon the people's consent; if consent is to be uninformed or deceived, is it consent? Not in the common criminal law. And if consent consists of nothing but supporting the President, what is the difference between a government with consent and a government without it?

The citizen of the great superpower in the last third of the twentieth century is not uninformed or deceived simply because he is idle; to be informed and undeceivable he would have to spend his whole time informing himself, and have a highly trained research staff besides. It is not just technology that has diminished him; the world in which "his" superpower is hyperactive is too hopelessly wide for him. He cannot be expected to know who's who in Laos, or the relative locations of Guinea, Ghana, and Guiana. He has no competence and could not have if he would. He makes a manful effort to "keep up" on television news for a few minutes each evening, but in fact he has long since surrendered his judgment to an unidentified "Administration spokesman," who tells him what to think and what unknown bourne to think it about.

Thus the "Presidential war" replaces the "King's war." In 1966 Chairman J. W. Fulbright of the Senate Foreign Relations Committee said that the Senators of the United States "have only ourselves to blame" for signing "a blank check" on President Johnson's Vietnam policy. The check was signed, he said, on August 7, 1964, when the so-called Tonkin Gulf resolution authorized the President to take "all necessary steps to repel any armed attack against the forces of the United States and to prevent further aggression." (The resolution served as "the functional equivalent of a declaration of war," in the State Department's view.) Mr. Fulbright said he had supported the resolution "because I was confident that President Johnson would use our endorsement with wisdom and restraint"—but he added that his support was "a source of neither pleasure nor pride to me today." Five years—and thirty thousand dead men—later, leading Senators charged the Administration with having provoked the North Vietnamese attack (on two U.S. destroyers) which gave rise to the resolution.*

How can men suppose that unlimited power can be relied upon to limit itself? John Stuart Mill thinks that dictatorship, freely given such power for a strictly limited time period, "can only be excused, if, like Solon or Pittacus, the dictator employs the whole power he assumes in removing the obstacles which debar the nation from the enjoyment of freedom." This is the same great libertarian who thought that barbarians were properly governed by a despot, a good despot, he hoped, like Akbar or Charlemagne; now he hopes that civilized men will have the good fortune to have a dictator like Solon or Pittacus.

But the alternative to "the blank check" is the preservation of the people's (if not the person's) liberty at the risk of the nation's destruction from without or within. The first of the two evils is generally the more terrifying. "Safety from external danger," Hamilton wrote in the great debate over the adoption of the Constitution, "is the most powerful director of national conduct. Even the ardent love of liberty will, after a time, give way to its dictates. The violent destruction of life and property incident to war, the continual effort and alarm attendant on a state of continual danger, will compel nations the most attached to liberty to resort for repose and security to institutions which have a tendency to destroy their civil and political rights. To be more safe, they at length become willing to run the risk of being less free."

Should nations, then, weigh these grim considerations in the decision to go to war? But nations no longer "go to war"; they find themselves in what President Truman at the time called a "United Nations police action," which, after the fact, is recorded as the Korean War. *Governments* go to war now (as they did when citizens were subjects) and the people in whose name they *govern* have no voice, direct or indirect. The undeclared war eliminates the nation's painful

---

* When the Senate renounced the resolution on June 24, 1970, by a vote of 81 to 10, Senator Robert Dole, "a leading Nixon Administration strategist . . . said that the repeal would not tie the President's hands in Asia." Washington *Post,* June 25, 1970.

choice to be more safe at the risk of being less free. But a generation ago it was still the fashion to go to war by declaring it, and a generation ago (according to the Gallup Poll in 1937) 71 percent of the American people were in favor of Congressman Louis Ludlow's amendment to the Constitution of the United States providing that, "except in the event of an invasion of the United States or its territorial possessions and attack upon its citizens residing therein, the authority of Congress to declare war shall not become effective until confirmed by a majority of all votes cast therein in a nation-wide referendum." The "Ludlow Amendment," though the overwhelming majority of the American people wanted it, was kicked around in Congress until it disappeared from sight. Its opponents were not only Congressmen but all the senior officials of the executive branch of the government and most of the leading figures in the world of international affairs. Their argument was a simple one: Should there be a national emergency—even without an attack such as was to occur at Pearl Harbor in 1941—it would take too much time to inform and persuade the people to approve a declaration of war. Meanwhile the foreign enemy would have the advantage. Only Congress was expeditious enough to make the decision.

Pearl Harbor was the beginning of a war. In these latter days of the nuclear-tipped ICBM and MIRV, the "first strike" is the beginning and the end. There is no more time for Congressional deliberation and decision. Only the President is sufficiently expeditious. The undeclared war and "the blank check" have taken the place of even Congressional deliberation and decision. It is unimaginable that a Ludlow Amendment would be proposed (much less adopted) today. What is proposed (and adopted) instead, five years after the Tonkin Gulf resolution, is still another resolution that "it is the sense of the Senate that a national commitment by the United States results only from affirmative action taken by the legislative and executive branches. . . ." This toothless supplication, in no way binding upon the President, had as its "purpose" the "restoration of Constitutional balance" between the two branches. So far had an ever more republican country come from the settled conviction of its founding fathers (in The Federalist) that the "tendency of legislative authority to absorb every other . . . in governments purely republican is almost irresistible." Six years (and forty thousand dead men) after the Tonkin Gulf resolution and a year after "the restoration of Congressional balance"— Cambodia. "I knew the stakes that were involved," President Nixon told the American people after the fact. "I knew the division that would be caused in this country. I also knew the problems internationally. I knew the military risks. . . . I made this decision. I take responsibility for it. I believe it was the right decision. I believe it will work out. If it doesn't, then I'm to blame." The difference between the "King's War"—*"the King makes war, and the people die"* —is that the King used the first-person plural.

Against the Supreme Court, Congress always prevailed; against the Executive, it fell. Even after Cambodia there were measures it *could* take to recapture its authority—or to try. (Mr. Nixon's predecessor took the view that even "if the [Tonkin Gulf] resolution is repealed, I think I could still carry out our commitments.") But Tom Wicker of the New York *Times* thought that the likelihood wasn't great. "Congressional impotence," he said, "will mean that one man alone holds in the world's oldest democracy the absolute power of war and peace, life and death." *

But it would be gross oversimplification to conclude that the state power is the President's—*or* Congress'. It lies, here and there, in bits and pieces, throughout the government establishment and outside the government establishment. And the government, in the great nation-state, has become so immense that no one man can be said to govern. Not only does he have to persuade an ordinarily watchful Congress to grant him power, but within the executive agencies (whose head he is) major decisions are made, and major steps taken, without the President's knowledge. Thus President Eisenhower denied that there was a U-2 espionage flight over the Soviet Union— until the Soviets produced the flier they had shot down. President Kennedy, after the CIA had trained an army to invade Cuba and staged the invasion attempt at the Bay of Pigs, told a confidant that he wished the secret agency could be "taken to pieces and the pieces scattered to the winds"; and President Johnson likewise lamented the secret subvention of American student groups by the same agency. In his recently published book, *The Pentagon,* Pultizer Prize winner Clark Mollenhoff develops in great detail the thesis that the Depart-

---

* On March 8, 1971, Henry Steele Commager, the dean of American historians, told the Senate Foreign Relations Committee: "Five times in the past ten years Presidents have mounted major military interventions in foreign nations without prior consultation with the Congress: the Bay of Pigs, the invasion of the Dominican Republic, the attacks on North Vietnam, Cambodia, and Laos. None of these now appear to have represented a genuine emergency; none were in response to attacks upon the United States. None therefore appear to meet the requirements for the exercise of war powers by the President formulated by the makers of the Constitution. There is no ambiguity about the intent of the framers of the Constitution. They proposed to make it impossible for a 'ruler' to plunge the nation into war. They were determined that no American executive would have the power of a George III or a Frederick the Great."

ment of Defense is "now a law unto itself—beyond the control of Congress, the Supreme Court, *or the President.*" *

It is a truism that "it is of the nature of war" (as the authors of *The Federalist* wrote) "to increase the executive at the expense of the legislative authority." Congressmen who do not want to be called traitors find themselves helpless to restrain the power of the President and the powers (apparently independent of the Presidency) of the great executive departments. Senator Fulbright's lament over "the blank check" is underscored, in even more pitiful terms, by other opponents of the Vietnam war. Offering an amendment to a military appropriation bill, to forbid the continuation of the "immoral" bombing without a formal declaration of war, Senator Joseph S. Clark of Pennsylvania called the amendment (which had no chance of adoption) "a new means of Congressional protest." "I was looking," he said, "for something more we could do than write letters to the President or deliver speeches." Many a constituent who has written letters to his Congressman could sympathize with the Senator.

Every national emergency—real or pretended, fomented, imagined, or miscalculated as such—has always had a devastating effect upon individual liberty. If patriotism is the last refuge of a scoundrel, it is the first of a despot. The most spectacular such instance, in our time, is the burning of the German Reichstag a week before the election which gave Hitler absolute power. The Nazis called it the beginning of a Communist revolution, and the day after the fire Hitler obtained from President Hindenburg a decree "for the Protection of the People and the State," suspending the seven sections of the Weimar Constitution which guaranteed liberties. The terror of Bolshevism threw the German people into the arms of Hitler. Subsequent evidence has persuaded historians that the Nazis themselves planned and executed the arson.

But something like it, under similar conditions, is not unimaginable here or anywhere else. The Alien and Sedition Acts—which Supreme Court Justice William O. Douglas calls "the first reign of terror in this country"—were passed in 1798, when war with France seemed imminent, and continued in force until after Jefferson's election in

* "Meanwhile, however, the White House, according to Republican Senators, has been preventing representatives of the opposition [to the deployment of the Anti-Ballistic Missile system] from seeing President Nixon—a policy that has only contributed to the new adamant stand of the opposition." (New York *Times,* July 7, 1969.) Meanwhile, too, Pulitzer Prize winner Mollenhoff was appointed a White House assistant and was found doing his bit for Presidential control by having got access to supposedly secret income-tax returns to uncover "wrongdoing by [unnamed] Government officials or those [unnamed] persons] close to the Government."—New York *Times,* April 14, 1970.

1800. After the fall of Fort Sumter in 1860 President Lincoln suspended the right of *habeas corpus* and ordered arrest without warrant and imprisonment without trial. The Supreme Court condemned the suspension as unconstitutional, but it was helpless against the President and the military authority. Lincoln went right on exercising the power, saying that "certain proceedings are constitutional when in case of rebellion or invasion the public safety requires them, which would not be constitutional when, in the absence of rebellion or invasion, the public safety does not require them." (Long after the fact, Congress authorized the President to suspend the writ.) So, too, in the case of the Emancipation Proclamation, though it never came before the Court; widely attacked as a usurpation of power, it had (Lincoln himself said later) "no constitutional or legal justification, except as a military measure."

Hysterical peoples—like hysterical persons—may not be expected to know that they are hysterical. And when they recover, they are unenthusiastic about being told of the things they did. Thus the defeated Germans; thus the victorious Americans, and thus all peoples everywhere. (The deportation of the Nisei from the U.S. West Coast in 1942 does not play a prominent role in modern history textbooks.) In World War I, it was criminal in the United States, according to Professor Chafee in *The Blessings of Liberty,* "to advocate heavier taxation instead of bond issues, to state that conscription was unconstitutional (though the Supreme Court had not yet held it valid) . . . to urge that a referendum should have preceded our declaration of war, to say that war was contrary to the teachings of Christ. Men were punished for criticizing the Red Cross and the Y.M.C.A., while under the Minnesota Espionage Act it was held a crime to discourage women from knitting by the remark, 'No soldier ever sees these socks.' It was in no way necessary that these expressions of opinion should be addressed to soldiers or men on the point of enlisting or being drafted. Most judges held it enough if the words might conceivably reach such men." After the martial spasm, Chief Justice Charles Evans Hughes wondered, "in view of the precedents now established whether constitutional government as hitherto maintained in this Republic could survive another great war even victoriously waged."

The Supreme Court defied Lincoln in vain. It did not even defy President Wilson in World War I. Congress gave him every power he pressed for, and where there was any question raised the judiciary sustained him. Objection to conscription as repugnant to the First Amendment guarantee of religious freedom was brushed aside, in *Arver* v. *United States* (1918), with the statement that it was too

unsound to require rebuttal. And the most Olympian of all libertarians, Justice Holmes, in upholding the conviction of a citizen for
writing and circulating an anti-conscription leaflet, said (for the
unanimous Court) that "when a nation is at war many things that
might be said in time of peace are such a hindrance to its effort that
their utterance will not be endured so long as men fight. . . . No
court can regard them as protected by any constitutional right." The
other "great dissenter" of that day, Justice Louis D. Brandeis, in a
later case, said, "Only emergency can justify repression"; the omis-
sion of "only" makes the point here, without changing the meaning
of the dictum.

The circumscription of liberty in the name of national emergency
has a way of outliving the emergency. The U.S. Sedition Act of 1917
provided for the punishment of anyone who might obstruct the sale
of war bonds, incite insubordination, discourage recruiting, "wilfully
utter, print, write, or publish any disloyal, profane, scurrilous, or
abusive language about the form of government of the United States,
or the Constitution . . . or the flag . . . or the uniform of the
Army or Navy . . . or bring the form of government . . . or the
Constitution into contempt . . . or advocate any curtailment of
production in this country of anything necessary or essential to the
prosecution of the war." (The American Civil Liberties Union came
into being to fight the use of the Act as an unconstitutional violation
of the First Amendment.) The 1917 Act saw service in World War II
and was still on the books when it was amended during the Korean
war to remain in effect "until six months after the termination of the
national emergency proclaimed by President Truman December 16,
1950." That emergency has not yet been "terminated" and the Act
has never been repealed. "This is no longer a Wartime Sedition Act,"
said the ACLU long after Korea. "Although framed in those terms, it
is for all intents and purposes a permanent Sedition Act." In 1933
the Reichstag suspended the German Constitution and handed absolute power to Hitler *for a period of four years;* the power lasted
twelve, until the death of Hitler. Lenin's "war communism" was to
have lasted five years after the Bolshevik seizure of power because
"suppression is still necessary during the transition from capitalism to
Communism"; the five years have become fifty-five.

In the name of never-ending emergency, martial law on Taiwan—
"Nationalist China"—has sustained the Chiang despotism during the
entire twenty-year history of a country which held a great power's
seat on the Security Council of the United Nations. In the Republic
of South Korea, rescued from the threat of Communist tyranny by

the "UN police action" of the 1950s, the mention of the name of Pablo Picasso—or any other Communist—is illegal. Statutes dealing with national emergency are commonly drawn so loosely as to permit any state action whatever. The Greek Constitution promulgated by the Papadopoulos dictatorship provides that the press is free unless it "creates defeatism." Article 30 of the French Penal Code, giving regional prefects almost unlimited power to investigate subversion, provides for the dispersal of any gathering that *could* lead to revolution and bans organizations that advocate violence. Article 190 of the Soviet Penal Code forbids "spreading of defamatory inventions against the Soviet State and participation in group activities harmful to public order."

Although the Preamble to the Constitution of the United States does not explicate the powers of any department in the government, the Supreme Court has often cited its wording (especially the "general welfare" clause) in support of its decisions. The Preamble commits the government to—*inter alia*—"insure domestic tranquillity." Could Congress have had domestic tranquillity in view when it passed the 1950 Internal Security Act providing for detention camps—six are known to have been set up—for the internment of persons suspected of *probably* engaging in espionage or sabotage in time of war, insurrection, or "internal security emergency"? Never before had Americans been threatened with imprisonment for *probably* being criminals—except for the detention of the Nisei in 1942. But with "crime in the streets" rampant in 1969, President Nixon, after one month in office, asked Congress for authority to take action in the District of Columbia "whereby dangerous hard-core recidivists could be held in temporary pre-trial detention when they have been charged with crimes and when their continued pre-trial release presents a clear danger to the community." This was another never-before. The presumption of innocence (until proof of guilt) is an established principle of American law; but so is the authority of the government to "insure domestic tranquillity." *

True, the history of national emergency has been much less bale-

* Congress granted the President not only the power of pre-trial detention but, on the eve of the 1970 Congressional election, the "no-knock" police power to break into premises without warning or identification and the power to tap telephones in criminal cases. In addition, federal courts were empowered to sentence up to twenty-five years' imprisonment any person convicted of a felony who should be found, *in the opinion of the sentencing judge,* to be "a dangerous special offender." The vote on this last measure, in the Organized Crime Control Act of 1970, was 341 to 26 in the House of Representatives and 76 to 1 in the Senate. The President signed the act into law nineteen days before the election.—New York *Times,* October 15, 1970.

ful in traditionally free than in unfree societies. No reasonably objective historian would attempt to strike a balance between the suppression of Constitutional rights under Lincoln and the repressive horrors of the Nazis or the Bolsheviks. The grievous record of the Wilson Administration, with the mass imprisonment of Socialists and the lynching of conscientious objectors in the "virginal fervor" of America's first great foreign war, are as nothing to the massacres of Hitler and Stalin. And World War II was marked by so little repression—censorship was voluntary, and there were journals which never complied with it—that the Nisei deportation is made all the more spectacular by contrast. What is more, the free society, if it loses or surrenders much of its liberty to its own government, shows a salubrious tendency to regain a great deal, or even all, of it; e.g., the detention camp provision of the 1950 Internal Security Act was repealed by Congress in 1971 with almost the same unanimity with which it had been enacted. But that is not the point. The point is twofold. First, every society, however free, does come under the heel of the state power, however gently this or that state may tread here and now. And, second, though liberty is recovered, by the time it is recovered I may be gone and my liberty with me. The eternally vigilant citizen is no match for the eternally vigilant state.

9: Hell or High Water

T H E H O B B E S I A N doctrine of the indivisibility of sovereignty—
he used it to argue for absolute monarchy—is as good a way as any
of demonstrating that the affirmation of liberty is (just as Creon says)
"the ruin of cities." Man is to the state (or the individual to society)
as the states or provinces are to the nation. The divided sovereignty of
the Articles of Confederation brought the new United States to the
point of collapse, and the unworkability of the system was so clear
that a Constitution, reposing much greater sovereignty in the central
government, was adopted. But the right reserved to the separate states
—slavery in particular—led to the Civil War and the transfer of substantial sovereignty to Washington. What we are witnessing in our
time, in the civil-rights struggle, appears to be the slow death throes
of the states, exemplified by such headlines as "U.S. Threatens Aid
Cutoff to Alabama" and "Florida Governor Surrenders to U.S.
Marshals." *

The more homely way of stating the proposition is that somebody
in the family has to wear the pants—the truth of which homily is a
shade less elegant than the falsehood of Illinois' state motto, "State
Sovereignty—National Union," and several shades less eloquent than

* As it was the first of the American colonies to defy the Mother Country,
so Massachusetts may be the last (though it has a different Mother Country
nowadays). On April 2, 1970, Governor Francis W. Sargent signed into law
an act of the Massachusetts legislature exempting residents of that state from
foreign combat without a declaration of war. The act was seen by its sponsors
as a Supreme Court challenge to the constitutionality of the American war in
Vietnam. (The Court, divided as usual, subsequently refused to hear a case
brought under the act.)

Daniel Webster's fallacy of "liberty and union, now and forever, one and inseparable." The reason why the state would fall to pieces if it acknowledged absolute, inalienable rights to its citizens or its provinces is that the uncoerced unanimity of its citizens would be required for its operation.

The unanimity presupposed by liberty would have to be real unanimity representing the free choice of each and every individual, and not hypothetical or customary or the "dead man's obedience" of the soldier who (even though he may be a volunteer) disobeys his officer at the peril of his liberty or his life.* But true unanimity in a constituted society of many millions is inconceivable. No community, even aside from emergency, could withhold action until every member had made up his mind. A nation of two hundred million wise men would be hamstrung by the dissent, or merely by the dilly-dallying, of one fool. John Stuart Mill sought to alleviate the difficulty by allowing an increased suffrage, with a graduated number of votes, to the individual of "mental superiority"; assuming that Demos would agree and that mental superiority could be determined in matters of morals and politics, the essential difficulty inherent in what Mill called "the tyranny of the majority" would remain: Those who lost the election, be they the many with few votes or the few with many, would in essence have lost their liberty when a matter affecting their liberty was at issue.

The one nation-state in all history—as far as I have been able to discover—that actually tried to operate on the basis of unanimity (or absolute liberty) was Poland in the seventeenth and eighteenth centuries. The Polish state literally destroyed itself in the process and in doing so brought on (in considerable part) the agonies of the modern world. Poland was not, of course, a democracy but an elective monarchy in fact ruled by the *sejm* (parliament) of the *szlachta* class (military landowning gentry) which comprised perhaps 10 percent of the country's population. (The rest of the populace had neither rule nor rights.) On the assumption of the absolute political equality of every Polish gentleman, the *liberum veto* (free veto) was adopted, requiring that every measure introduced into the *sejm* must receive a unanimous vote to pass. With one member's *"Nie pozwalam,"* "I disapprove," the measure died. Subsequently the *liberum veto* was extended to dissolve or "explode" the *sejm*—some-

---

* The false unanimity displayed by a 99 percent *Ja* or *Da* in a mobocracy election has the same ultimate significance, as regards the difference between choice and consent, as the election of a President, e.g., in 1968 by 43 percent of the votes cast (and, of course, a much smaller minority of eligible votes).

thing that happened to forty-five out of the fifty-five Polish parliaments between 1652 and 1772.

The "country"—that is, the *szlachta*—was so gloriously corrupt that it was no great problem to find one member of the *sejm* to vote against any measure for a consideration, and the unabating struggle of Russia, Austria, and Prussia to devour paralyzed Poland introduced the decisive element of external corruption again and again. The struggle of patriot reformers against the *liberum veto* was futile. The monstrosity expired only with the expiration of Poland itself. After the last of its three partitions among the great powers in 1796, the Polish nation disappeared from the map of Europe for more than a century.

On two other notable occasions in history the attempt to maintain peace was similarly wrecked by the principle of divided sovereignty. The requirement of a unanimous vote by the Council of the League of Nations in all decisions of substance was the death of that organization when Germany and Japan "walked out" and Mussolini defied the League and conquered Ethiopia in the early 1930s. The similarly unhappy history of the United Nations, in which the Great Powers through the veto have all maintained their "liberty of action," is too well known to need recapitulation. On February 5, 1962, Prime Minister Harold Macmillan of Great Britain put the facts of life plainly, if painfully, to the House of Commons:

> The [UN] is not a sovereign body. It is not even an alliance.
> . . . It is an association of sovereign states whose sovereignty is especially emphasized by the Charter. . . . The whole foundation on which the UN was built has been undermined [by the Cold War]. . . . The UN can never be made to work unless political conditions can be created in the world which allow the Council to operate, not for perpetual propaganda purposes, not as a body permanently divided, but as a team. . . .

Nor is it only the veto that immobilizes the UN, but the Charter provision (like the League Covenant's) forbidding the organization's intervention in the "internal affairs" of any of its sovereign members. Sovereign Germany may massacre *its* Jews, the sovereign Soviet Union *its* kulaks, without any right whatever of the "United" Nations even to address itself to the matter—precisely as each of the antebellum Southern states enslaved *its* Negroes, with the "United" States helpless under a Constitution which reserved to the separate states their liberties *qua* states. A century after its opening guns on the battlefield the American Civil War continues; the weight of arms provided a triumph for undivided sovereignty at Appomattox, but more than a hundred years passed before the U.S. Senate outlawed the intrastate murder of civil-rights workers (over the solid vote of Southern Senators from states which refused to indict the accused murderers under their own laws).

The American struggle for civil-rights legislation was frustrated for years by Senate Rule 22—the "liberum veto" of the filibuster. Rule 22, requiring the affirmative vote of two-thirds of the present-and-voting Senators before debate can be cut off and the roll called, by preventing a vote enables a small group of determined opponents to kill an act supported by the majority. In 1968 a partisan filibuster prevented the confirmation of President Johnson's nomination of Abe Fortas as Chief Justice of the Supreme Court. (It proved to have been a disguised blessing when Justice Fortas, involved in a conflict-of-interests scandal a few months later, was forced to resign.) Twenty years before the Fortas case a principled stand by one man, Senator Robert Taft, prevented the conscription of striking railroad workers, and thirty years before that another principled filibuster by a mere half-dozen Senators kept the United States out of the League of Nations. In 1971 a variation of the senatorial filibuster interrupted the conscription of soldiers for a nation then waging war in Indochina.

Why doesn't the absolute liberty of the filibuster bring the state down? In theory, it does. In practice, it is broken (as it was in the passage of the civil-rights legislation of the 1960s) by the application of the central principle being argued here: Whenever a big enough majority wants badly enough to do anything, it does it. The pressure of the electorate, the federal executive, and the federal courts for desegregation became irresistible, and so the proponents of the majority view, when the opposition rose in the Senate to exercise liberty in the form of the "right of unlimited debate," were at last ready to talk that liberty to death.

There are three *subsocietal* institutions which in theory preserve the uncoerced rights of every member—but none of them is the "team" which Prime Minister Macmillan analogized. (Nor, indeed, is the team on the playing field.) The connotation of the team as a group (of animals or men) pulling together and remaining always united in its decisions without the sacrifice of the individual's liberties is a happy one. Men like to think of the ideal society, and even of the operating organization, in this way. But the eleven men in the football huddle are no more a team than is a Congress or a Parliament debating the national budget. At some point action has to be taken, and at that point the freedom of discussion ends. The referee, stop watch in hand, blows the whistle for play and the captain (or, likelier, the quarterback) says to his team mates, "Here's what we'll do. . . ."

Apart from the short-lived "utopias," with their overt or implied motivation of religion, there are a few (very few) small religious sects which proceed on the basis of absolute liberty and, therefore, of absolute unanimity. The best known is the Religious Society of Friends (Quakers), which, without stated dogma or ordained ministry, conducts even its business affairs in the religious spirit of pure democracy. Quakers hold that since "there is that of God in every man," no man's will may be violated by men—be they a majority, a minority, a priest, or a pope. No man may represent—and, possibly, misrepresent—any other. When the local meeting of Friends assembles, not for worship but for business, no decision may be taken if as few as one Friend is "uneasy," or undecided.

This principle, obviously impossible of application to the community, the state, or the nation, is, at bottom, also the principle of the family. In theory (and in primitive cultures) the family sovereignty is undivided, the husband ("Mister" or "Master" to his wife) exacting the fulfillment of her promise to love, honor, and *obey;* but in all societies (and much more so under modern social conditions) the wife has a "veto," however guilefully she may exercise it, and, upon close analysis, the children, too. Family decisions—including the husband's job—are taken with the "advice and *consent,*" if no more, of the wife; and as the children develop to the point of maturational competence, they play an ever increasing role in the family's governance. The small boy whose mother coerces him to brush his teeth may demur on this point—or the henpecked husband, or the rooster-pecked wife. The principle of unanimity is nevertheless operative, in modern domestic theory and to an increasing degree in modern domestic practice.

The advantage of free unanimity is obvious: The organization which acts only with the express approval of every one of its members, and only when dissent is overcome by honest convincement, is a powerhouse. The truly united family has the strength that the great society hasn't; the ambition of the free nation's President to achieve "consensus" (like the ambition of the tyrant to achieve *Einheit* or unity) looks to a degree of effectiveness which the great society cannot achieve. Thus it is that a small sect like the Quakers—with perhaps 200,000 members in the whole world—is as well known as it is throughout the world for its social-action programs. Nothing is harder to stop than a freely and fully united band of human beings.

But the family, like the Quaker Meeting, *need* not "work." First, it is rarely called upon to reach *a decision* at any given temporal point (except, in the case of the family, in the emergencies which come to every family); domestic or congregational decisions can ordinarily be debated for weeks or months, or even years. But the state must act, and act every day, on a thousand and one fronts or perish. Distant matters it may postpone for a time, but immediate matters require the innumerable immediate decisions of government at every level. And second, the family and the sect need not "work" at all: The veto, arbitrarily exercised, means divorce in the one and dissolution in the other; and the world, and its nation-states, goes on. The relationship among individuals in both cases (though its potentiality is natural to them) is an artifact in the sense that it is freely entered into and freely dissoluble, as that of man and the state is not. He who would divorce himself from the state finds it fearfully difficult to do so, if, for example, he objects to its taxes, or its wars, or its interference with his Saturday-night bath when the town is on fire. And if he succeeds in doing so, as most men cannot hope to, where will he go but to another state whose denial of his individual sovereignty is identical, in principle, with the one he left?

Let the marriage collapse or the congregation dissolve, and the previously contracting parties go their way without, necessarily, ever coming into further contact or conflict with one another. The citizen is in no such situation; he cannot walk out and never see the state again. Neither can all the citizens (or some of them, by revolution) dissolve the state without proceeding to organize another. Nor can the sovereign nation-states of the world divorce one another—that is, "break off relations"—without inducing a train of tremendous consequences including, sooner or later, war. The law and custom that hold the state (and the community of nation-states) together are human and as fragile as all human bonds, while the bonds of the family and the religious sect are those of love and of God, which are less susceptible to rupture. I once heard of a devout Christian (whose wife was a notorious trial to him) who said to a friend, "If it were not for the canons of the Church I'd have taken a meat ax to her on a hundred occasions"; the canons of the state are not so deterrent.

The third subsocietal institution in which the liberty of the individual is supreme is the closest to our concern here because, like the state, it is secular, and, indeed, an organ of the state. This is the trial jury, every one of whose twelve members must agree on a verdict. This most singular of public bodies is constituted to give the accused (in a criminal case) the benefit of the doubt, and the requirement of unanimity is intended to enhance that benefit: Better that ten guilty go free than that one innocent be convicted.

But jury membership, too, like that of the family and the sect, is free and dissoluble. A venireman may be excused—in practice, excuse himself—if he cannot on his own affirmation accept the burden of the jury, say, to inflict capital punishment (or even to send a man to prison). And the "hung jury," which cannot reach a decision, may be dismissed by the court and the case retried.

The *liberum veto* of the one "holdout" juror, exercising absolute liberty, may "hang" the jury or even, if his fellow jurors despair of bringing him over to their view, result in an actual reversal of the majority's position. What are the consequences of this untrammeled liberty which, in the conduct of the state as a whole, would be anarchy? The worst foreseeable consequence is that a guilty man will be acquitted and returned to society, perhaps to continue his depredations. In the ordinary course of society such acquittal constitutes no clear and present danger to society's survival, or to the maintenance of law and order. One more criminal is at large. Society endures the jeopardy rather than abolish the unanimity safeguard of the rights of the accused.

The trial juror is a truly phenomenal figure in that he, and he alone, as juror enjoys inalienable rights—greater, incidentally, than a Supreme Court Justice, who cannot prevent a verdict of the Court but only record his dissent and bow to majority rule. The juror—the single juror—is sovereign, and sovereignty is power. And power unchecked is dangerous. Just as one of the great powers interested in Poland's destruction had only to corrupt one sovereign member of the *sejm,* so a defendant in a jury case has to "reach" only one member of the jury to escape conviction. And however circumspectly the jurors may be isolated during their service, there are a dozen ways of getting to one of them (even before they are formally impaneled). So commonplace is jury tampering that in 1967 England replaced the unanimous verdict with the requirement of agreement by ten of the twelve jurors; it is harder to corrupt three jurors than one. (During the Parliamentary debate, an opponent of the measure, protesting that the unanimous verdict had been an English law for six hundred years, was reminded that the Scots had had the majority verdict for a thousand.)

In practice, of course, the situation of the honest juror is far from free, just as it is in the family and the congregation. The "holdout" is under the greatest pressure from his fellow jurors. Studies of the jury system all support the supposition that one or two of the twelve, standing alone, tend to yield, if not to the arguments, to the *weight* of the ten or eleven (and the plea to agree so that they can all be discharged and go home). So, too, the husband probably dominates the wife (at least on a percentage basis). And the "uneasy" Quaker may grow uneasier still under the burden of hamstringing action, especially when the strong advocates of action are "weighty Friends." So even in these three bodies, whose members are uniquely endowed with freedom of action, liberty yields to authority more often than not.

On even the happiest reading of their experience, the three truly free types of human relationship are too far from that of man with the state to suggest a resolution of the great dilemma. There is, and can be, no sovereign state which does not at some point sacrifice the individual to the real or imagined general welfare. The beating-a-dead-horse complaint remains: "What of it? Don't we rock along pretty well? Haven't the centuries, and especially the last few, shown progress in our political institutions?" The issue of progress may be debated, but not at this level. In respect of the essential relationship of man and the state, we are precisely where we were a century ago when Abraham Lincoln, in his first message to Congress, asked, "Must a government of necessity be too *strong* for the liberties of its own people, or too *weak* to maintain its own existence?" And where Lincoln was in 1860 (and Socrates twenty-two centuries earlier) mankind has always been.

Our reader may then say, "So we don't rock along pretty well, and there is no progress—still, what of it? You don't argue with necessity, with breath, or with death. You accept the insolubility of the problem and make the best of it and keep pushing for individual liberty as hard as you can." But why for liberty? Why not for authority? Why for the individual and not for the state? And here, I think, the case is clinched. Men all proclaim liberty, fight for it, and even die for it, because they believe that the state is the inherent enemy of liberty; that eternal vigilance which Jefferson termed the price of liberty was vigilance against the state. They do not believe that the state needs to be stronger, unless they are frightened of still stronger enemies from without or within. The reasoned argument for the stronger state—like that of *The Federalist*—is based squarely on the stronger state's increased capacity to preserve and advance the liberties of the citizen.

There may be those who have no qualms about the headlong increase of the state power, spurred by technology and its consequent centralization, by war and the threat of war, and by the demand for social justice through the medium of "welfare." Individuals and factions to whom these developments are immediately advantageous are not likely to be hesitant to accept them. But the power waxes, be it well or badly used. And the most thoughtful of those who concede the inevitability of that historical process are disturbed by what they take to be its inevitable concomitant—the reduction of the liberties of the individual by law and of the individual himself by custom and conformity proceeding from the same causes.

The conscious consideration of the issue raised here may, in addition, have certain specific implications for the conduct of the national life. The irreconcilable divergence in the highest decisions of their country's highest court has often been cited as an occasion of failing faith on the part of the American people in their institutions. Cynicism is certainly born of the insistence of a body like the Nuremberg Tribunal that a soldier may be hanged for obeying his officer. Disenchantment certainly follows the fact that the American and Soviet (and now Chinese) supporters of opposing sides in Indochina are equally entitled to fly the UN flag. And despair cannot but be the consequence of the successive failure of "world organizations" to fulfill their splendid promises and the callous disregard of their "peace-keeping machinery" by the unilateral action of the great powers or alliances when they do not trust the organization to act to their advantage.

We speak easily of "the free world" and "the slave world," but in the absence of any clear definition of liberty the totalitarian "people's republics" and "democratic republics" are equally entitled with the nations of "the free world" to claim, as they do, that *they* have true liberty and what *we* have is in fact the tyranny of private profit. So, too, the debate on world government and world federalism goes on from generation to generation without any resolution of the question of such a system's proper powers or the individual's relationship to them. Most Americans doubtless know that there is a World Court at The Hague; what they don't know is why it is called a court and under what conditions a nation is brought into court. Their confusion is well grounded. Nations go to The Hague voluntarily or not at all. (The "Connally reservation" denies the Court's jurisdiction over the United States without the express consent of Congress.) The Court may settle issues which two contending nations are willing to have it settle, such small issues as damages in the accidental sinking of a ship of one flag by the ship of another. But let the issue be vital to one or both of the nations involved, and the Court has no power at all to bring them in, judge them, or punish them for disturbing the peace; war may be consuming the world, and the Court still sits in The Hague adjudicating disputes over postal rates, weather signals, or fishing grounds;

it is no more a court than the United Nations Organization is an organization. (France and the Soviet Union have both refused to pay duly levied UN assessments without losing their membership.) *

The immediate issue is not whether the problem of liberty and authority is soluble. Nor is it whether we are condemned to go on crying "Liberty" without knowing what we are crying. The immediate issue is whether we have any ground for asserting its solubility (or insolubility) without consciously confronting the problem instead of manipulating it for purposes of propaganda, deceit, and self-deceit.

The individual, if he is asked which he will choose, if choose he must, tyranny or anarchy, will probably reply as Socrates did when he was asked whether he would rather injure or be injured: "Rather neither." Anarchy—the absolute liberty of the individual—is outside his experience and his comprehension. The overnight anarchy (or liberty) of a Thoreau has no more reality than the life of the hermit who accepts a letter with the state's postage stamp on it.

Let Lenin, of all people, say, "While the state exists, there is no freedom. When there is freedom, there will be no state." The fact is that anarchy, if it is not that of the freak, but the condition of a whole people, is nothing more nor less than those few days or hours of transition from one social form to another (or back to the same one). It is revolution while the old regime is falling and the new one is not yet established; and the willful breaking of a law, any law, just or unjust, is revolution in principle. Whoever chooses anarchy "philosophically," because he cannot abide the alternative of totalitarianism offered him by the dialectic, must do so temperamentally and not philosophically at all. He is simply gifted (or cursed) with the classic disposition of Mr. Jones of Johnstown, Pennsylvania, whose family, perched on the roof of the house to escape the flood, pondered his derby floating back and forth along the length of the property in front of the house—until Mrs. Jones recalled that her husband had said the night before that he was going to mow the lawn the next day come hell or high water.

* In mid-1970 the World Court, which had heard only thirty-four cases since its establishment in 1946, did not have a single case on its docket. Asked (at a conference of U.S. jurists) why the Court did not establish rules to govern its proceedings, one of its members, Judge Manfred Lacks of Poland, said, "Since we are dealing with nations, it makes us reluctant to impose limits which might infringe on their sovereignty."—New York *Times,* April 6, 1970.

III

The Theory
and Practice
of Death

Ham. What a piece of work is man! How noble in reason! how infinite in faculties! in form and moving, how express and admirable! in action how like an angel! in apprehension how like a god!
—Hamlet, *Act II, Scene 2*

Ham. (*Puts down the skull*) To what base uses we may return, Horatio! Why may not imagination trace the noble dust of Alexander, till he find it stopping a bunghole?
—Hamlet, *Act V, Scene 1*

1: They Can't Do This to Me

CONSIDER ME, *I pray you. Consider that I—I, and no other— loved Helen and Io and Hecuba and created the Brandenburg concerti and the Oresteian trilogy and the Sistine ceiling and the pyramids that never perish. Yes, and salted Carthage and buried Troy and burned Berlin and Indochina, and cut down continents and paved them, and planted my feet on the moon. And installed another man's heart into a breathing man, and found the miracle drugs and the neutron and the secret of life in DNA.*

Only consider, I pray you, and then judge between me and fleshless sneakthief Death, and tell me if I am to be done down by a shadow and become the dirt from which my marvelous carpetmakers with their deathless dyes protected my powdered and perfumed feet.

I tell you that I am Man and there is none like me.

I tell you that I will not take death lying down.

I will not—but I shall. I shall die like the first and last ant and not even know what it is to die—like Alexander, who first shook the whole world, and Galileo, who first saw it whole, and like Plato and Plato's disciple and Plato's master: "All men are mortal. Socrates is a man. Therefore Socrates is mortal."

Let me have but my lawyer, though I be a fool, and I can break the closest contract. Let me have but my accountant and I can dodge my taxes. Death, and death alone, I shall not escape—the one contract I have that is more honored in the observance than it is in the breach, the tax I shall pay when I am most embarrassed to do so.

Inexorable insult, and its whimsy adds injury to insult. It comes at its random pleasure and interrupts me in the middle of the banquet and pulls me away with it. I am here today—and gone today. I turn a carefree freeway curve (or a corner in Dallas, the best-guarded man on earth) and I am ambushed, snatched, and finished. Dishonorable, skulking shade, come out, come out, I say, and fight like a red-blooded man and I will wipe your Death's-head grin from your insolent visage.

I rage, and rage the more against the sweet deceit, "Say Yes to life," as if I might say No to death and come home with my shield instead of on it, my prize—the wages of sin and of sinlessness, of all virtue, all vice, all wisdom, all wiles—abominate Death. I put it to you: Am I, Odysseus, so sage and so splendid, to be pulled down in the end, to be one with my puling victims and they with me, and all of us together in the contemptible democracy of the dust?

(Not even the gods can help a man then, however they love him, said Athena.) (And she said it of her darling, Odysseus.)

Man—*stupor mundi:* the stunner of the earth—the conqueror of every adversary save one. How is Death to be beaten, if not by man? Is he to be beaten at all? Only the believer believes that he is to be; but not by man even then, rather by a power which is vested in one who was taunted, as he writhed and died, with being able to save others but not himself. And even to the believer, Death is "the last enemy that shall be destroyed"—and be destroyed only by the mystery of Easter. (And who among the stunners of the earth more than half-believes *that?*)

Consider, then: consider that no life would be led as it is if there were no death (or if we only foreknew its date). No other problem is so critical, none, by comparison, critical at all. No other investigation would be so eagerly attended or so universally supported, no other knowledge so highly prized. But we are precisely where we were in the Garden when the first investigator died for his presumption and man was condemned to death.

Death is the one idea that has no history. Human experience has affected every other, not just in the exact sciences or in mathematics, but in every field. Even life has something fundamental to be said about it that was not (and could not have been) said of old. Death, the ultimate whodunit, stands unmoved by man's relentless compulsion to solve or even to say; among its other offenses, death is a long litany of platitudes.

The paper-thin bibliography of the subject is eloquent testimony to the invincibility of our ignorance. We do not know what to say about death because we do not know what to think about it, and we do not know what to think about it because we do not know what it is. Of all the ideas Mark Twain says the Greeks stole from us, this is the one they stole entire. It is the only area of human wonderment in which there is intellectual despair, all the deeper in view of the stupendous advances that have been made in medicine and its related fields.

One explanation of the limited discussion of death is that it is generally viewed as the negation of an idea—the idea of life—rather than an idea in itself. And even in this respect it is singular. There are other ideas (ignorance, for instance, or evil, or disease) that as negations appear to stand to their contradictories (knowledge, good, health) as death appears to stand to life; but the appearance is deceptive. Ignorance, for example, has the character of being a remediable deprivation, evil (in Manichaeus and Freud) of having an at least arguable existence of its own, disease of being susceptible to attack. But the congenital disease of Adam—except in theology and (in a technical sense) in law and medicine—is commonly regarded as an unremediable deprivation, possessed of no sense of existence, no possibility of an antidote.

It is easier than that to explain the rarity of death *qua* death in the tradition of metaphysical, moral, and philosophical discourse. All such discourse requires a starting point which in death is missing: the report of common experience. We may acknowledge the validity of the modern physiologist's assertion that "it is impossible to define life without death"; but death is impossible to describe, much less define. The enigma of one enigmatizes the other. Here is the most decisive fact of life—death—and we cannot begin a discussion of it in the sense that discussion has knowledge as its object. And because we cannot begin a discussion of it, our discussion of life comes soon or late to a dead end.

We can ruminate and speculate and dream—and how persistently even the most prosaic man dreams of it—but we cannot *think* of death. There is no science of necrology. Death belongs to the poets.

What is death? Why, death is a "fell sergeant" and "an end of woes," a "curse" and a "cure," a "veil," a "gulf," a "valley," an "old nurse," and a "drunken sleep"; an "untimely frost" and a "dearest friend"; yes, and a "wall," and a "doorway," and a "night" and a "daybreak." What is death? Death is "cold," it is "grand," it is "abhorred," it is "soft," it is "lovely," "easeful," "delicate," "stealthy," "foul," and "fiendish." Say you Yea or say you Nay, you say it to the poets, who scrutinize it as nearly as a man can, who burn their candles and their wits to search it, smell it, taste it, embrace it, and at last say good morning to it. Dante, Shakespeare, Milton, Goethe, Hawthorne, Melville, Tolstoy, Mann—these are the great authorities on death, along with the little child with the unanswered question, "Where do we go when we die?"

Ours is the Age of Man, Man the Knower, Man the Doer, Man the Master—all the greater, then, his one frustration. There are certain limited conditions under which he can prolong life for weeks or months or even, on occasion, years; *this* is on the whole new. There are still broader conditions under which he can fend off the environmental predisposition to early death due to dietary deficiency, infection, and epidemic. There are very broad conditions under which he can reduce physical suffering. But death still comes. The confidence that stubborn cancer will yield its secret abounds, that death will do so is heard nowhere. Man is the measure of all things—but death is the measure of man.

The Age of Man has had a novel effect upon the traditional conditions of death. Longevity, secularization, and total war distinguish us from all of our forebears in their availability to the general run of men. And this availability is both cause and effect of the sudden flowering, at the end of the eighteenth century, of the Biblical plea for the dignity of the individual and the sanctity of every least human life. The privileged bones of the past rattled their protest when the authors of the American Declaration of Independence proclaimed the inalienable right of man to life. (By the end of 1971, the number of American military dead in Vietnam, almost all of them alienably conscripted, had almost reached the annual highway toll of 50,000 Americans exercising their inalienable right to ride in automobiles.)

The new status of "citizen" conspired with industrialization, urbanization, and the development of aerial bombardment to substitute block-busting—and now city-busting—for the modest mayhem of the professional soldier's suddenly primitive battlefield. Economic justice sent the general life expectancy slowly (and then rapidly) upward wherever the doctrine of human dignity was popularized. And the great revolution of the rights of man diverted men's awe from providence to progress, with freedom of contract, work laws, child-labor legislation, and workmen's-compensation and social-security programs.

But social reformation was largely nonreligious and even antireligious. Expressions like "reverence for life" found a flamboyant response. It is questionable whether men were becoming more reverential toward other men than they ever had been, but there was no doubt that in the advanced societies they were transferring their worship from the Living God, whose handiwork was Life and Death, to the Living Man, whose handiwork was A Better Life. The promise of man's sufficiency in the temporal order necessarily vitiated his sense of subsistence in the eternal. By the end of the last century the schism between intellectualism and fideism had become a dogma: The thinker was the skeptic, and the devout were the unregenerate (or stubborn) victims of ancient superstition. It wasn't Marx, but man, who identified secularism with civilization.

Politically the assertion of human dignity had at least as much to do with equality as with rights; and the democracy of one man, one vote gave rise to a new kind of mass consciousness and mass power in which the exalted value of the individual life was transmuted into the degraded value of the individual ballot. Dignified man found himself a nameless, undifferentiated means to other men's power. The industrial revolution was a concomitant paradox: It reduced the once independent contractor—even the miserable farm tenant—to the status of a disposable appendage to the machine. The "junk heap" of worn-out and cast-off and interchangeable men rose alongside the mountainous profession of respect for the status of man as man. Now, with automation, he can be "got rid of" altogether, occupationally consigned to death; and with the computer, he loses the personal recognition that even the house slave of old enjoyed, his very name; he is identified like a corpse in the morgue.

Still, this tagged and numbered man enjoyed a stupendous increase of goods, leisure, and mobility, even if these mass-produced and mass-distributed blessings contributed to the effacement of the individual personality in which dignity resides. Life was sweeter. Man's resistance to morbidity—to the expectation of a hard life and a hard death—was stiffened. And then came the cataclysmic turn. The time: 1916. The place: Verdun.

For a hundred years, beginning at Waterloo, the doctrine of the dignity of man was ascendant while the grotesque indignity of death went on claiming a man at a time (and once in a while a large or small batch). We may assume that man's impertinent claim to dignity was an affront to the ancient Enemy. But we may also assume that the Enemy was too old a hand at the game to spend a century of evenings sitting by the fire and nursing his pique. If he would bring modern man to heel, he would have to retool. At Verdun he unveiled his own assembly line for mass production.

Two million healthy young men—the apotheosis of Life—had been driven into a colosseum without spectators and handed the triumphant product of the Age of Man, the machine gun, and set at each other's throats at a distance too great for the distinction of persons or the personal bestiality of single combat in the Roman arena. One million of them dutifully killed the other million, and when the million were dead a few hundred yards of mud and blood had changed hands a half dozen times and Death was the winner again. Mass man had met his mass master and human dignity its denudation.

Nothing like Verdun had ever happened before; the most devastating of all prior calamities was the Great Plague of Europe, which killed a quarter of the people of that continent in the fourteenth century. But its twenty-year toll was "only" some 25,000,000 lives; Verdun's over twenty years would have been of the order of 220,000,000. And Verdun was man's own doing—point of which (we may be sure) Death took judicial notice for future reference.

When it "all" ended on Armistice (now Veterans') Day, and the lark, still bravely singing of life, was able again to make itself heard, there were eight and a half million bits and pieces of soldiers who could be counted (if not found); they were numbered. But so handsome was the reaper's swath in those four years that the civilians who also died are forever assessed at a variable ten to twenty millions. It was, says historian George F. Kennan, "the determining tragedy of our century."

Was Verdun man's surrender to death? Did modern man—the most modern man of all, the German, the Frenchman, the Englishman, the American—want to kill and die? Had death overtaken life?

Freud was saturnine after Verdun: "When the frenzied conflict of this war shall have been decided, every one of the victorious warriors will joyfully return to his home, his wife and his children, undelayed and undisturbed by any thought of the enemy he has slain either at close quarters or by distant weapons of destruction. It is worthy of note that such primitive races as still inhabit the earth, who are undoubtedly closer than we to primitive man, act differently in this respect, or did so act until they came under the influence of our civilization. The savage—Australian Bushman, Tierra del Fuegan—is by no means a remorseless murderer; when he returns victorious from the war-path he may not set foot in his village nor touch his wife until he has atoned for the murders committed in war by penances which are often prolonged and toilsome. . . . Behind this superstition lurks a vein of ethical sensitiveness which has been lost by us civilized men."

No; nothing like Verdun had ever happened before. But something like it, and even more congenial to death, was to happen again, and that within a generation: Auschwitz, Belsen, Treblinka. The mechanized mass extermination of the unarmed mass by men stripped of every trait but massiveness was a long, long stride from Verdun. Death had never done better. But before the stench of the secret ovens could offend the nostrils of the rest of the civilized world, the Nuclear Age began in Asia. August 6, the city of Hiroshima: 20 of its 200 doctors able to attend the dying, and 1,650 of its 1,750 nurses killed or maimed; and August 9, the city of Nagasaki: 600 of its 800 medical students killed, and 44 of its 47 hospitals destroyed.

Death no longer "struck." Man struck—one man attached to an unseen machine touched a button and hadn't even to see what he'd done. Modern death had only to program the computers, read the numbers, and affix the tags.

Alexander conquered the world and died for want of a four-day dose of drugstore antibiotics. What were the Civil War's 600,000 dead to World War I's 6,000,000, World War II's 60,000,000, or World War III's 600,000,000?

Has the Bomb changed man's attitude toward death?

Hans Morgenthau thinks that the possibility of nuclear destruction "destroys the meaning of death by depriving it of its individuality." The prospect that mankind itself can be annihilated suggests the ultimate irony of the Organization Man: Let's all go together and nobody will be out of step with anybody else. With this all-systems-go prospect, the meaning of death is indeed transformed. It loses not only its individuality but its sociality. Men think of dying for home and family, or for love of country, or for liberty or glory or morality . . . or dignity. But all of these values are outlawed by the assurance that to attempt to define them by thermonuclear means is at once to destroy them. Human dignity presupposes a human race and a human measure. A nonhuman world—a dead world—would honor equally the patriot and the traitor. It would be a world of homogeneous heroes, or, equally, of cowards and fools—a world in which death would signify nothing.*

A few years ago the *Journal of Gerontology* published a symposium of "death attitudes." The contributors agreed that there was a prevalent rejection, among modern Americans, of the thought of dying. True, more and more people die old. But true, too, more and more people die in hospitals or "rest homes" and die alone. Modern death isolated in the drugged asepsis of the hospital is one of the symbols

* "The antigrief posture is the hallmark of strategic defense in the nuclear age, on both sides of the cold war, since deterrence predicates the ability and intention to exterminate tens of millions of innocent civilians on one side moments after the same thing has happened to the other."—E. J. Lieberman, M.D., "War and the Family," in *Modern Medicine*, April 19, 1971.

of that shapeless philosophy which finds each individual alienated from all the rest.* None of existentialism's exponents has achieved a systematic statement of this "new" view of life and death. It seems to combine the more inclement aspects of Antisthenes' Cynic, Epictetus' Stoic, and Plotinus' Sage with the sorrowing sighs of Ecclesiastes: Man's struggle to escape from the meaninglessness of life ends in the absurdity of death, and estrangement from his kind is the dominant condition of both. "Man," says Sartre, "is alone, abandoned. . . ." Alone, abandoned . . . in his human dignity.

* In the August 1970 *British Medical Journal,* Prof. W. A. Cramond called for the training of doctors and nurses in "therapy for the dying" as "essential in a modern technical hospital, with its ever-present risk of impersonal efficiency." Eighty percent of the dying patients (Prof. Cramond wrote) know that they are dying and would like to talk about it, but 80 percent of the doctors believe that patients should not be told about it.—London *Times,* August 14, 1970.

2: A Dialectic of Death

IMMORTALITY is the hinge on which death turns. If man survives death, death is one thing (as, indeed, is life); if he doesn't, it's another.

Immortality does not presuppose God's existence (whether or not it implies it). It does presuppose and require a nonmaterial element of man which is traditionally called "soul" or "spirit" (or "mind," "understanding," "consciousness," or "personality")—the Latin *anima* (which also means "breath") or the Greek ψυχή, "psyche." In this naturalistic sense of the term, the soul, taken simply as the principle of animation, certainly exists—which is not to say anything about its genesis, its nature, its properties, or its destiny. It is the X which is present and operable in Jones alive and is absent (or inoperable) in Jones dead. Hebrew uses the same word for "life" and "soul."

What the soul is, precisely, where it comes from and where it goes, how it exists and subsists—these are questions so ramiform that they involve not only psychology and theology but almost every other field of intellectual investigation, metaphysics, physics, chemistry, physiology, and genetics, anthropology, sociology, law, and even geology. But death does not compel our consideration of these questions beyond the issue of immortality. There *seems* to be a nonmaterial being or power in living things, and a line (however difficult it is to situate) between life and death. One is careful to say *seems* here, for to say anything more (even to say, as we have, that a principle of animation "certainly exists") is to invite hot disagreement; the discontinuity between living and nonliving (or organic and inorganic) is widely contested, and even the absolute distinction between living and dead. (Though we don't have much of a fight on our hands when we ask our quarrelsome friend to pick up the squirming babe from its cradle and, a thousand years later, to pick up the dust that was that babe.)

Now the legendary caliph was determined to settle the issue of the soul's existence for once and all. He had a dying man encased in a hermetically sealed glass vault and set all his scientists on the death watch. If the soul was the principle of life and it could not escape the body, death would not occur. Death occurred. When the scientists were sure that the soul had not escaped the vault, they made a minuscule opening and maintained a prolonged watch at it. Nothing emerged. There was no soul. (Socrates performed the same experiment, in his own way, a thousand years earlier. If, he said, we agree that the soul rules and moves the body, and is therefore its superior, can we easily believe that it disintegrates or decomposes at the instant of death, when the body does not?)

What Socrates and the caliph *knew* about the soul, modern man knows—no more, no less. But the transcendent question of immortality cannot be approached (outside of Revelation) without a definition and description of the soul. And he who embarks upon the venture finds that he does not stir until he has answered two antecedent questions. First, is the world natural or supernatural (or both, and in what relationship)? Second, if the world is natural, is it material or spiritual (or both, and in what relationship)? If the world is partly or wholly supernatural, the answer to the second question does not affect either the soul's existence or its immortality; both may be argued even if the world is wholly material. Similarly, if the world is wholly natural, both the soul and its immortality may be argued if the naturalist, denying God, accepts both matter and spirit and the separability of the two.

But the supernaturalist materialist, when he says "the world," means the world we apprehend sensibly—that is, the physical (or "created") world. His supernaturalism is challenged by his materialism: What is the nature of the supernatural? Is God, too, material, corporeal? If not, the wholly material world is governed by (or otherwise related to) a spiritual being; if so, the nature of a material, corporeal God sets in train a whole procession of radical questions in the realm of being—that is, metaphysics—and theology. The Homeric gods were certainly corporeal, with attributes of incorporeality such as invisibility and transformation. (Their immortality and their power over the elements were not necessarily spiritual; they *could* have been a race of imperishable giants.)

Every one of these doctrinal positions has been maintained in the history of thought, and no great thinker has failed to maintain one or another of them in one permutation or another. But the extreme view that the world is wholly supernatural is as uncommon as the opposite extreme is common. (It appears in the Vedic doctrine of *Maya* and is suggested by Plato's ascription of reality to "forms," or ideas, alone.) To assert that God is everything requires a denial that there is an order of nature about which anything may be known apart from God. This doctrine, though it is more familiar to the Orient than it is to the Occident, has always had its sectarian votaries, who couple the all-embracing supernatural with the corollary that the world is wholly immaterial and that bodies are mere appearance or shadow. The doctrine of philosophical idealism, beginning with Plato, in the course of its tortuous history has often approached supernatural extremism by ascribing reality (or the highest reality) to universals, or abstract ideas or concepts, and confining the reality of sensible objects to their participation in those ideas. Berkeley denied matter's existence altogether. Marcus Aurelius and, in the Christian era, Hegel, Spinoza, and others posit a "world soul," a "universal spirit," or a "world nature" in which all things have their being.

That the world is wholly natural—apart from the issue of materialism—is as popular (and as anciently maintained) as the phrase "common sense." The Soviet astronaut who returned from outer space and announced that he had not seen God there is no better a Marxist than he is a Lucretian; the pre-Christian Roman saw human life lying "foully prostrate upon earth crushed down by the weight of religion" and raised his voice in praise of that speculative astronaut, Epicurus of Greece: "Him neither story of gods nor thunderbolts nor heaven with threatening roar could quell: they only chafed the more the eager courage of his soul, filling him with desire to burst the fast bars of nature's portals. . . . On he passed far beyond the flaming walls of the world and traversed throughout in mind and spirit the immeasurable universe; whence he returns a conqueror to tell us what can, what cannot come into being. . . . Us his victory brings level with heaven."

The all-out naturalist does not *necessarily* deny immaterialism, the existence of an incorporeal substance or power or principle of life. What he denies is the existence of an order outside of nature, a supernature. He does not necessarily insist that seeing is believing; he may, and usually does, in conscience recognize the soul; but it is a natural soul and as perishable as every other natural substance. He may be the gentle humanist, or he may be the fighting atheist who proves his case by defying God to strike him dead. (He is not struck dead, and thus "proves" equally that there is no God *and* that man proposes and God disposes.)

Between the two extremes lies the consensus of traditional thought: The world is partly supernatural and partly natural. The critical issue is the relationship of the two orders, and on that relationship the issue of freedom turns. Does God, having created the world, govern it, and in what fashion and to what degree? Does Divinity include Divine Providence? Does it watch over creation or merely watch it? Judeo-Christianity asserts God's will for men, *together* with man's freedom to obey or disobey on pain of Divine judgment, while the Greco-Roman view, though it ascribes creation to the supernatural, loosely limits intervention in the affairs of men to the sporadic whim of the gods, who are otherwise busy with their own affairs on and off Olympus.

All-out immaterialism—denying corporeal reality—is as rare as all-out supernaturalism. But all-out materialism is (and always has been) as intellectually popular as all-out naturalism; more so. The doctrine that the world is nothing but sensible bodies (though we may not yet have the instruments or techniques for sensing them) goes back at least as far as Lucretius. In his *De Rerum Natura* he distinguished soul and mind from the other parts of the body (and from each other) but only as parts of the body. The world consists of a fortuitous concourse of atomic particles in motion.

The modern materialist is more sophisticated than the Roman poet; but the lineal descent is undeniable in the contemporary assertion that mind and soul are an emanation of the nervous system, that "man is a neuro-physiological console of electric charges." Is life, then, reducible to matter? Where does life (*or* matter) come from? What is the cause of motion in Lucretius' "atoms in motion"? What is the first cause, the "uncaused cause" that alone saves philosophical speculation from the pitfall of infinite regression? Pasteur's historic proof of the impossibility of the spontaneous generation of the ultimate elements of life has yet to be overturned: Life arises only from life.

The dialectic of death turns out to be the dialectic of being: There is nothing that has a beginning and does not have an end, nothing that has an end and does not have a beginning. (On different readings of the first four verses of Genesis, theologians argue whether Chaos had no beginning and was ended by God.) If the existential chain is broken—if there is something that has neither a beginning nor an end—there is a supernatural order in which the immortality of the immaterial is acceptable.

Between the extremes of materialism and immaterialism again lies the great body of opinion, including common opinion: The world is partly material and partly immaterial, partly body and partly soul or spirit, or mind; but again, in what relationship? Historically the domination of the body by the soul, of the material by the immaterial, has been generally accepted: The spiritual principle determines the nature of the substance. Man is only described—not defined —as a featherless biped. He is defined by his rationality; a rational creature with feathers or fur and any number of legs would still be a man. It is only in the past century or so, partly as the result of what William James called the "evolutionary afflatus," partly as the result of empirical advance, and partly as the result of theoretical Marxism, that matter has been at all widely held to be the sovereign element, existing prior to spirit and shaping and determining it. This most modern of doctrines was lampooned by Socrates (who found it in Anaxagoras). In his death cell he observed that "these muscles and bones of mine would have gone off long ago to Megara or Boeotia— by the dog they would—if they had been moved only by their own idea of what was best, and if I had not chosen the better and nobler part [of remaining in Athens, to suffer death]." He knew, he said, that without bones and muscles and the other parts of the body he could not execute his purposes, "but to say that I do as I do because of them, and that this is the way in which mind acts, and not from the choice of the best, is a very careless and idle mode of speaking. . . ."

In both the materialism and the naturalism issues the decisive question regarding death is the same: Is man one or two—a simple or a composite substance? Is man Aristotle's "besouled body"—and if so, how besouled? Or is he Plato's body and a soul—and if so, how conjoined? If he is one, and that one dies and is dead, how can he survive death? If he is two, his survival of death can be argued, but the protagonist is hard put to explain human nature as regards man's consciousness of his own identity and integrity.

As death turns on immortality, so immortality turns on the separability of body and soul; and the controversy between the dualists and the monists is probably as old as controversy itself. W. E. Hocking opens his *Meaning of Immortality in Human Experience* with the statement that "the problem of the survival of death by human persons is an empirical problem for which we have no empirical evidence. It is a question of fact, and of fact in time, for which there are no antecedent probabilities one way or the other. Human survival is neither probable nor improbable, because we have to approach it through those same questions of world order which include the basis of probability."

This logic is hard to take—and at least as hard for the naturalist materialist as it is for the supernaturalist immaterialist. But it is irrefutable. The atheist who accuses the believer of wishful thinking or superstition is a victim of pot-and-kettle complaint. And the agnostic, or skeptic, has his own troubles: Apart from the worldly calluses of fence-sitting, he just *might* land in that unenviable vestibule in which Dante found the trimmers, rejected by both Heaven and Hell.

The idea of immortality, then, and therefore the idea of death, is an idea only by extension, or courtesy. In the first and controlling instance it is "only" a transcendental belief. It depends, not partly but wholly, on one's world-view or creed or "philosophy of life." If, says Hocking, men "believe that the universe has a unity and a dominating purpose, or makes on the whole some sort of sense, they are prone to conclude that the minds of men must be able somehow to carry on their adventure. If they adopt the view that human life and consciousness are episodes in a world which as a whole has no purposive structure, but is in its last analysis plain physical fact, they are bound to consider survival both meaningless and impossible." Death, and death alone, is at once a totally objective and totally subjective reality. It is the one idea belonging to the order of indisputable events about which we can know nothing of significance without knowing the individual who has the idea. *His* outlook upon this common—this unexceptionable—experience is the heart of the matter. Is it better to be alive than dead, or dead than alive? Go then, *in parvo,* to the poet, he will serve you as well as any. For as a man sees life—and what two men see it the same?—so he will see the end of it.

The belief in the supernatural (and the immaterial) probably had its origin in death. Freud, drawing heavily on Frazer's *Golden Bough* for his raw materials, concluded in *Thoughts on War and Death* that primitive man, when he saw someone who belonged to him die, "in his pain had to learn that one can indeed die oneself, an admission against which his whole being revolted; for each of these loved ones was, in very truth, a part of his own beloved ego. . . . By the body of his slain enemy, primitive man would have triumphed, without racking his brains about the enigma of life and death. . . . Of this conflict of feeling, psychology was the direct offspring. Man could no longer keep death at a distance, for he had tasted of it in his grief for the dead; but still he did not consent entirely to acknowledge it, for he could not conceive of himself as dead. So he devised a compromise; he conceded the fact of death, even his own death, but denied it the significance of annihilation. . . . The changes wrought by death [of a loved one] suggested to him the disjunction of the individuality into

a body and a soul. . . . Beside the corpse of the beloved were gen-
erated not only the idea of the soul, the belief in immortality, and a
great part of man's deep-rooted sense of guilt, but also the earliest
inkling of ethical law."

Neither archaeology nor anthropology has found an unbelieving
culture. The very universality of belief is sometimes advanced as an
argument for its validity—a suggestive argument, but unpersuasive in
both reason and history. (War, too, is as old as man, and slavery and
epidemic disease; and there is some evidence, at least as regards the
two last, of fundamental progress in their eradication.) Nevertheless,
the faith that man (and often the other forms of life) survives death
is the faith of the human race as a whole, in Freud's opinion "the
oldest, strongest, and most insistent wish of mankind."

But one massive element of that faith has already all but disappeared in the West. That is the transmigration of souls, which in the
ancient West (and in the ancient and modern East) doubtless followed, in its timeless origin, from the observation that bodies seemed
to receive life, or a soul or spirit, at conception or birth and lose it
at death; what would be more natural than to conclude that this life
or soul or spirit moved from one body to another? Like the meta-
physicians of advanced ages, primitive man probably concluded that
where there was no end there was no beginning. Unable to accept an
end of the soul or spirit, he had to reject its beginning. If it always
would be, it followed, like the eternity of the gods or of God, that it
always was. But in that case it stood to reason—or to common experience—that it had to be somewhere. Why not in a "new" body?

The "theory of reminiscence" (in Plato's *Meno*) argues that the
soul existed before its embodiment, and in the *Phaedo* the soul returns to earth in a body appropriate to its deserts. In the ancient
Hindu bible-epic, the *Bhagavad-Gita,* Krishna says, "I myself never
was not, nor thou . . . nor shall we ever cease to be . . . as the
lord of this mortal frame experienceth therein infancy, youth, and old
age, so in future incarnations will it meet the same," and in the *Upanishads* the Self or "knower," "unborn, eternal, immemorial," through
his past works in this life "shall return once more to birth, entering
whatever form his heart is set on."

Transmigration was always beset by one logical difficulty (whose
circumvention may be the origin of ghosts as "migrating" souls): If
there is not a birth at the very instant of a death, what becomes of the
decedent's soul before it is re-embodied? But the decline of transmigration in Western belief probably paralleled the rise of individualism
and the recognition of the human personality as distinct in the eyes

of God or the gods. "If the soul were imagined as common to two or more persons," said the great theology-baiter H. L. Mencken, in his *Treatise on the Gods,* "then the last judgment would present judicial difficulties beyond the ingenuity even of God." It may be significant that the doctrine of transmigration survives most hardily in those cultures which ascribe a low value to mortal individuality.

The Egyptians even combined transmigration with resurrection: During the three thousand years for which mummification and pyramid burial were designed, the soul of the Pharaoh (and later of lesser royalty and nobility) would move from animal to animal (at the instant of death in each case) and from element to element, returning at last to earth in human form. There is later Egyptian (and abundant Greek) evidence of a kind of O.E.O., an Office of Eternal Opportunity, for an ever increasing proportion of men, their salvation depending not on their rank but on their virtue. Gibbon is convinced, however, that immortality "was scarcely considered among the devout polytheists of Greece and Rome as a fundamental article of faith." It "might serve to amuse the leisure of a philosophic mind; or, in the silence of solitude, it might sometimes impart a ray of comfort to desponding virtue; but the faint impression which had been received in the schools was soon obliterated by the commerce and business of active life." And Santayana's epitome of the Greek attitude undoubtedly applies to the Roman: "Mortality belonged to man, as immortality to the gods; and the one was the complement of the other."

The doctrine of a future state nowhere appears in the Mosaic Law of the Jews and can only be inferred (and that dimly) from the later books of the Old Testament. The Mosaic Law is the law of this life, the law of impersonal justice and of righteous living and, with the emphasis of the prophets, the restoration of spirituality upon the earth in place of the pantheon of all-too-human gods who ruled after the manner of all-too-human kings in the ritualistic and cultic creed of the highly advanced civilization of Mesopotamia. The promise to Abraham and his seed was a worldly promise. It was only after Cyrus ended the exile that the Pharisees arose among the Jews and, accepting tradition along with Scripture, introduced the doctrine of immortality.

It was with Christianity—and later with Islam—that Western man as a whole was carried away in the death and resurrection of Jesus Christ. The "New Jerusalem" would see the reign of Christ and his saints, the Last Judgment, and the general resurrection of the saved on what the Negro spiritual calls "that great gettin'-up mornin'." It would be a worldly morning, and, as the ecstasy of the early Christians envisaged it, it would afford the delights of the present life without any of its sorrows and, of course, without death. Since the end of the "Gospel age" of Satan was expected soon, to be marked by the destruction of all the kingdoms of this world, conversion to the strange new faith had the added urgency of readiness.

The new faith raised questions which are not answered yet. The resurrected would, presumably, be as he had been here below, known to himself and his loved ones and neighbors—the happiest of all prospects compared with the earlier doctrines in which the soul, though it survived, might be, without corporeal integument, unrecognizable to others or even to oneself. Such discontinuity, with the elimination of memory, had always seemed a kind of sell to the cynical, who argued that under such unrewarding conditions a man might just as well be dead—or alive. Of course it has its—shall we say?—sunny side too: If I do not know that I have died and am dead, am I (the "I" that resides in consciousness and knows only life) not immortal "for all practical purposes"?

But the present-day Christian whose contact with theology is remote—if that—as like as not clings to the pre-Christian doctrine of immortality and regards it as the crux, if not actually the contributor, of his own faith. It is not improbable that most modern believers would register amazement, even rejection, of the exegesis provided in capsule form by the following editorial in the leading Protestant publication in America, the *Christian Century:*

RESURRECTION

. . . Five times the New Testament uses the word "immortality" and five times the word is applied not to man's present state but to his future being. Indeed, I Timothy categorically denies survival to anyone or anything except God "who alone has immortality." The New Testament, then, knows little about the immortality of the soul, but it is saturated with proclamations of the resurrection of the body. So on this side of his Easter no man is immortal, but through his Easter, made possible by Christ's resurrection, "this mortal must put on immortality." In the main, doctrines of immortality have little but mortal man for their justification. All intimations of pre-Easter immortality assert man's supreme worth, decry the infinite waste man's death entails, demand that a just God satisfy man's innate craving for the infinite, insist that the metamorphosis seen in nature is duplicated in nature's man. Such arguments transform the creature into a creator and use the dying to prove that man does not die. Easter is another story altogether. It is the story of him who, being dead, yet lives, and of the God who raised him from the dead. It is the story of men who are not immortal, who die, but upon whom God bestows the promise of immortality through the resurrection of Christ. . . .

Theologian Paul Tillich is even sharper in his rejection of the common concept of life after death. Calling it "pseudo-Christian" and "a popular superstition," he asserts that immortality is God's alone and that life "is strictly a gift, and not a natural or inherent part of man." Eternity is not timelessness, nor continuation, nor extinction; it is "an eternal now," and the idea of an endless heaven and hell "splits God and separates one part of reality from his spirit of love." While absolute intelligibility is not to be hoped for in such matters, it would appear that the American Tillich and the Swiss Karl Barth are on this point (if not on most others) in substantial agreement. "Resurrection," says Barth, "means not the continuation of life, but life's completion. The Christian hope is the conquest of death, not a flight into the beyond."

If, then, modern man could only accept the God of Abraham, Isaac, and Jacob, and the Christian and Islamic "fundamentalism" that goes by the Bible alone, he could reject immortality, ignore the petristic and patristic dogmas of heaven and hell, and stand on theologically invulnerable ground with reference to death. Too late, too late: Herbert Spencer is come a century since, with his assertion of the evolutionary development of the cosmos from an "incoherent, disorganized homogeneity to a well-differentiated and thoroughly coordinated heterogeneity." The literal Bible's mixed supernaturalism and naturalism has given way to a naturalistic faith in the growth, even in the origin, of the world and of men.

No aspect of the universal religious dogmas of old was more vulnerable than immortality, none less resistant to the "process" concept of the world that had its philosophical beginnings in the ancient Greece of Heraclitus, Anaxagoras, and Empedocles. The hypothesis of the mutability of species—attacking the special creation, nature, and destiny of man—can also be traced to pre-modern origins in Aristotle, Albertus Magnus, and Francis Bacon. But the past three centuries of natural science and higher mathematics have seen a world (under Galileo's telescope) and man (under Leeuwenhoek's microscope) so steadily and radically reduced to Lucretius' "atoms in motion" that the inference against the supernatural (above all, against human immortality) was ineluctable.

In the seventeenth century, says Toynbee, Western civilization "broke out of its traditional Western Christian chrysalis and abstracted from it a new secular version of itself, in which Religion was replaced by Technology as Man's paramount interest and pursuit." Sociologist C. Wright Mills says that Western man is "neither pro-religious nor antireligious; he is simply areligious. . . ." The present Archbishop of Canterbury calls upon African and Asian missionaries to come to England "to convert the post-Christian heathen. The whole world is a mission." American Unitarianism, which does not affirm an afterlife, has a current membership increase seven times as high as Protestantism's and twice as high as Catholicism's; 77 percent of its members have college degrees.

Modern times? In 1747 the French physician La Mettrie published his *L'Homme Machine,* in which he drew the profession of absolute (and, of course, atheistic) materialism from his original research: The soul is only "the thinking part" of the body, and with death *la farce est jouée,* the farce is over. And as long ago as 1890 the French historian Taine found that only a hundred thousand of Paris' two million Catholics appeared for the all-important Easter sacraments and that only two million of the thirty-two million Catholics in France went to Confession.

But urban, industrial, technological man, educated in (or at least infected by) the reality, the faith, and the imagery of science—he, too, will die. If he cannot believe in immortality or resurrection, he will die believing (without ever knowing) that he is clay—intricately constructed clay, to be sure, but clay. And this, too, is hard. But if it is truth, and hard truth, it must be borne—*if he can bear it.*

There's the rub—"if he can bear it." If he is going nowhere, why hurry? Or, why not hurry? Or, simply, why? Is the assertion that death is nothingness an unconscious assertion that life is, too? Samuel Butler said that the question "Is life worth living?" should be put to a fetus, not to a man. A man, then, must drag his meaningless way through it to its meaningless conclusion, deprived of the sustenance the "Wobblies" of the old IWW ironically offered in their "hymn": "Work and pray/Live on hay/You'll have pie in the sky/When you die." To work and pray purposelessly; to live on hay (or honey) without a "reason," without an end in view or imagined, without even a hidden star to beckon; to scurry and scrabble and scratch like the uncounted and uncounting ant—is this hard lot what being modern man adds up to? "Without the hope of an afterlife," said Bismarck, "this life is not even worth the effort of getting dressed in the morning."

Modern man's not so remote ancestor always demonstrated an ardent preoccupation with worldly survival—except for the martyrs and ecstatics—but the hoped-for salvation of his soul always took an unchallenged, if matter-of-fact, place in his matter-of-fact life. His religion held him comfortably in its matrix; it was a system, before the rise of the nation-state, larger, more meaningful, and *more* comprehensible than worldly association; indeed, all such associations had their center of gravity in his religion, and John Dewey says that "the thing new in history, the thing once unheard of, is that [the church] is a special institution within a secular community."

Can man die—and live—with this downgraded picture of himself and his situation? Or does the spread of the new "theologies," Fascism, Nazism, Communism, prove that he can't, that his hunger for meaning will not tolerate the loss of his divine status unrequited? Must he have *something* more to live and die for than the ant has? In his *Psychoanalysis and Religion,* Erich Fromm assures us that "the psychoanalytic cure of the soul aims at helping the patient to achieve an attitude which can be called religious in the humanistic though not in the authoritarian sense of the word. . . . It is [the] process of breaking through the confines of one's organized self— the ego—and of getting in touch with the excluded and disassociated part of oneself, the unconscious, which is closely related to the religious experience of breaking down individuation and feeling one with the All. . . ." But existentialism, often called "the philosophy of death," confronts the "excluded and disassociated" part of man more simply: In the works of Sartre and Camus, and in the earlier writing of Heidegger, conscious man, conscious of his being alone, must first of all achieve "freedom-toward-death" to achieve his liberation from the terror that is quite real and quite conscious at the apogee of the Age of Man. Once he accepts the proximity—and absurdity—of death he can achieve an "authentic existence." Then and only then, still alone, but unterrified, he is able, in effect, to produce himself, his essence, through his existence.

Does the "religious revival"—*or* the totalitarian innovation—simply mean that man has to go somewhere, anywhere, in his new situation and come to terms somehow, anyhow, with the lost intelligibility of death and the new persuasion of finitude? The conflicting visions of Heaven on earth and Heaven hereafter were not the exhaustive alternatives of the pre-post-Christian man. Christ assured his followers that the Kingdom of God was *within them.* And before Christ the Greeks argued, apart from immortality, that happiness was possible in this life through the harmony of the soul achieved, like the harmony of the state, through the habitual virtues of its hierarchical components. Such was the message of Plato's *Republic;* and Aristotle went further and maintained that *blessedness* (the highest form of happiness, which Christianity reserves to the next world) was achievable here and now through the gods' gift of good fortune to the man of transcendent goodness. If the prescientific possibilities of life are real, death even in the Age of Man, even as the end of the "biochemical entity," may still crown something more than a farce.

3: Where the Dead People Live

DEATH is no laughing—or even crying—matter. It is deadly serious and always has been. Its seriousness is veiled in war or in mass catastrophe, where the event that causes death is more traumatic to the survivors than death itself; Verdun's million, the half million of a Pakistan cyclone, the quarter million of Hiroshima and Nagasaki, are easier far to cope with than the spectacle of a simple funeral procession on the road. Solemnity seems to involve the contemplation not of windrows of dead men but of one: If he, then I.

We repress the attendant exultation—he, but, ah, not I. We repress it partly because we know that we ourselves are "next," but partly because this is the one occasion, of all of life's, in which it is as privately as it is publicly scandalous to indulge the cruel *Schadenfreude* that takes comfort in the misfortune of another. Whoever rejoices at another's death—let the victim be his or the public's worst enemy— debases himself. And the sense of the most awful subhumanity attaches to the desecration of a dead body. The methodical conversion of slaughtered Jews into needed soap—whatever else it is—is less horrifying to us than the jubilant mutilation of a dead Mussolini or the festive depravity of a lynch mob. We find antiquity's nadir not in the gladiatorial arena of a games-mad Rome; rather, on the primitive field of Troy, where the dead body of Hector, gratuitously stabbed by one Greek after another, is fastened head down to a chariot and dragged through the dust; and the perpetrator is glorious Achilles, beloved of the gods.

Man alone celebrates death, and celebrates it with luster; he alone is "splendid in ashes and pompous in the grave." He alone disposes of his own cadavers, and does so ritualistically. Why? The ritual of burial appears so early, so universally, and so persistently in human history (and pre-history) that its existence, says Joseph Wood Krutch in *Human Nature and the Human Condition,* "may be one of the criteria for distinguishing between men and mere half-men, and some sort of respect for his dead may have been part of the nature of man for as long as there has been man to have a nature." Custom? Whence the custom? Ego-satisfaction? Whence the ego-satisfaction? Piety, fear, guilt, grief, honor, ostentation, "wishful thinking"? Whence all of them that they should take this ubiquitous form in man alone?

Not in his physiology, for many other creatures (such as the burying beetle, *Necrophorus*) are more adept by nature at burying. Not in his imagination or his memory, for many of the other creatures are just as imaginative and most of them more retentive. Not in his respect for another's life; in his disrespect for it he outstrips the other creatures of earth, and the ancient Scythians (so Herodotus takes the trouble to inform us) strangled their dead king's concubine, his cup-bearer, his cook, his groom, his lackey, and his messenger and buried them with him, and on the first anniversary of his death strangled fifty of the best of his attendants (with fifty of their most beautiful horses) to mark the occasion. What is there, then, in man that calls for the *decent* burial of his corpses?

"It is," Patrick O'Donovan wrote in the London *Observer* on the occasion of Winston Churchill's funeral, "a gesture, made over and over again by Christians and Communists and humanists and the unconcerned. It is a proud half-conscious assertion that man is not an animal that dies alone in a hole."

Here is an oddity—if nothing more—of cosmic proportion. Supernaturalist and naturalist, materialist and immaterialist are *in practice* agreed with the "half-conscious assertion." He who denies immortality and he who affirms it might both be expected to reject utterly the importance of the dead body; but they both accept it. The immortalist, through the Church, pays ponderous and elaborate homage to the worthless clay, and the mortalist does the same. The atheist materialist ideologues of the Soviet Union restored the lost art of mummification to the inert matter that was once Nikolai Lenin and Joseph Stalin, and, to house it, reared a structure that more closely than any other modern mausoleum compares with the pyramids of Egypt. "For political purposes," you say; but in that case the politics were in head-on collision with the ideology. And when the *soul* of Stalin was disgraced, his *body* was thrust from the shrine and cast into the ground. These atheists, forbidding a hallowed burial to the *body* that once housed a villainous *soul!*

Man the burier seems to be saying, "You can't do this to *me*." Man the mourner, too. Anecdotes recur—going back to Patroclus' horse, which wept over his body—of the grief of lower animals, especially of dogs for their masters, birds for their mates, and mother monkeys, horses, and cows for their young; but its incidence usually suggests so simple an explanation as the loss of the food source or the incomprehension of the "loved one's" failure to respond or return. Though the lower animals "manifestly feel pleasure and pain, happiness and misery"—this is Darwin in *The Descent of Man*—the notion of bereavement among undomesticated animals generally yields to the account of the pair of starlings "one of which was shot in the morning; by noon a new mate was found; this was again shot, but before night the pair was complete; so that the disconsolate widow or widower was thrice consoled in the same day"; but, then, Darwin had not heard of Hollywood or Women's Lib.

Just as man's acknowledged or unacknowledged belief in immortality (or resurrection) ought to relieve him of concern for the disposal of a corpse, so ought it to relieve him of the burden of bereavement; and, conversely, bereavement ought to pervade the lives of the survivors in the lower species of animal which show no sign of such belief. "I mourn'd, and yet shall mourn with ever-returning spring," says Walt Whitman on the death of Lincoln. Why man and not the starling? If there is not immortality or resurrection—yes. But if there is—what more is there to say than "The Lord giveth, The Lord taketh away. Blessed be the name of the Lord"? "Toward the dead person we take up a special attitude," says Freud. "We suspend criticism of him, overlook his possible misdoings, issue the command: *De mortuis nil nisi bene,* and regard it as justifiable to set forth in the funeral oration and upon the tombstone only that which is most favorable to his memory. Consideration for the dead, who no longer need it, is dearer to us than the truth, and certainly, for most of us, is dearer also than consideration of the living."

Our attitude toward death, he adds, "has a powerful effect upon our lives. Life is impoverished, it loses interest, when the highest stake in the game of living, life itself, may not be risked. . . ." But "this conventional treatment of death" was being swept away by the world war (not yet known as World War I): "Death will no longer be denied; we are forced to believe in him. People really are dying, and now not one by one, but many at a time, often ten thousand in a single day. Nor is it any longer an accident. . . . Life has, in truth, become interesting again; it has regained its full significance."

These words, in *Thoughts on War and Death,* were written in 1915; just thirty years later two hundred thousand died in a Japanese city in a single day, with a single bomb. "Life has, in truth, become interesting again." Freud was a better psychologist than the visiting Englishman who asked recently, "Why are you Americans so interested in death?" It is life that is interesting to Americans, so interesting that a large proportion of their two-billion-dollar annual expenditure on funerals goes into gussying up the corpse to effect the undertaker's "living sleep." In *The Doctor and Death,* August M. Kasper says that the average American's outlook on life and death changed in the first quarter of the present century: "With great optimism we embraced science and reason. Sin went out the window, and with it, its wages— death. Sickness became preventable and curable, and its companion, death, seemed equally vulnerable to our attack, an attack which was largely an elaborate denial of death." The undertaker—now a "grief therapist"—undertook to demonstrate that what is isn't and what isn't is, and society to "hustle the dead off the scene," in the words of Margaret Mead, "without an opportunity for young and old to realize that death is as much a fact of life as is birth." The widow's weeds went before the year was out, and then the widow (and the widower); quick remarriage, unthinkable a half century ago, became the order of the day and the dead were settling down in the churchyard when the wedding procession entered the church.

For centuries the church was the living center of the living community—how incongruously it still stands at the main four corners of many towns—and the churchyard was integral to the church. Here lovers sat, friends strolled, children romped, and poets pondered. The parishioners went home by way of it after worship and shared its care with the sexton. Everyone knew who lay where—and who would lie where—and who everyone lying there was. Its stones were the community's history; children identified their greatest-grandfathers. The immortality of remembrance was assured.

Then came the great deracination, which populated the American coast and then the interior. "Everyone" was in motion and still is. (In Europe, too, now, since the world wars.) Country towns, and country churchyards, were abandoned. In the swelling cities the cemeteries were moved to, or beyond, the periphery—out of sight and out of mind. To reach them by buggy, or by trolley or interurban, was a Sunday's excursion. And when it became an hour's trip by car, there were still fewer visitors. Now there are almost none.

The church relinquished these inaccessible "churchyards" and commercial corporations took them over. Real-estate promoters who could not promote the living promoted the dead. "Chapels" were equipped with quick scene changes to accommodate denominational rigamaroles. When the undertakers had got theirs, the cemeterians moved in with Perpetual Care. (A cemetery in Topeka, Kansas, had the most sensational sales pitch ever made by man: "Perpetual Care Guaranteed.")

Now it is no longer necessary ever to *have to* go to the cemetery. "It" was taken care of. In 1967 the showman Billy Rose was interred in a mausoleum of "white Carolina mahogany granite" on a 4,000-square-foot plot, the sarcophagus "bathed by the light of three stained-glass windows." "This mausoleum," said the presiding clergyman, "will stand for ages, proof against the ravages of time and clime. . . ." The last Billy Rose spectacular cost $125,000—including Perpetual Care.

Perpetual Care—by the Corporation. I suppose that most urban American children have never been in a cemetery. "What's a cemetery?" my four-year-old asked. "It's where the dead people live," said his eight-year-old brother. Everybody *lives* somewhere.

So amiable old Death, making his door-to-door rounds with the fidelity of the Fuller Brush Man, finds his wares unpeddlable: "Nobody here but us live ones." What is this bent on the assuagement of grief and the belief that it can be assuaged by rouging the earthly remains of its object? "Never a bone the less dry for all the tears." Sympathy, yes; but *therapy?* Only a fool quarrels with necessity, and death is the one necessity; the only thing we can say for sure of the newborn babe is: "He will die."

Whoever purports to peddle assuagement in the marketplace would seem to do so with intent to defraud; he cannot deliver the goods to sober men and women. But it is done and, it would seem, quite profitably. Marshall McLuhan, in *The Mechanical Bride,* has preserved an advertisement of a manufacturer of metal grave vaults "scientifically designed to use the pressure of air in the dome to keep seeping water from the rains and melting snows from reaching the casket." At the window of her home stands a gorgeous young widow with plunging neckline in her black dress. With the countenance of a debutante wondering what to wear, she is looking up into a storming sky: "There's deep consolation . . . serene through shower or heavy rain . . . for those who know the casket of a dear one is protected against *water* in the ground by a Clark *Metal* Grave Vault." Mr. McLuhan suggests alternative copy: "I cried until they told me it was watertight."

The scandal of American (and Canadian) funerary practices erupted with the sensational publication of Jessica Mitford's *The American Way of Death* in 1963, but the small "protest" segment of society had been fighting them for several years with funeral societies offering burial as low as $150 (compared with the private undertaker's average of close to $1,500) and cremation as low as $35.* The undertakers' lobbies are the deadly enemies of the practice, and effectively so; through restrictive legislation in many states they have pushed its price up to the burial range. Church uneasiness about cremation may be theologically dubious,† but that of the undertakers in the *National Funeral Service Journal* is economically intelligible: "A funeral is not an occasion for a display of cheapness. It is, in fact, an opportunity for the display of a status symbol which, by bolstering family pride, does much to assuage grief." (John F. Kennedy was buried in a wooden coffin, and when the matter was last heard of, two or three years later, the U.S. government was still contesting the undertaker's bill for a "status symbol" casket.)

The sumptuous funeral was opposed ineffectually by Solon in Greece and by Constantine in Rome; but only the general acceptance of monotheism overcame it to any significant and durable extent. Among the Jews the simplest burial was the rule—it still is in modern Israel—and was handled by the synagogue. Christians, of course, rejected the show and splendor of this life in their disposal of the dust of their dead. In early America—as in Europe—burial was wholly a family matter. Lavish ritual is still a rarity in Europe (where the American "open casket" is very rare) except for funerals of state, in which the ceremony is profoundly political, demonstrating the majesty and continuity of royalty or rule.

The ancients associated funeral rites with propitiation of the gods— a likely heritage of the primitive feat of spectral vengeance—and in modern burial the scarcely separable roles of debt and guilt undoubtedly play a part in the disposition of the survivors to have their dead live it up. Gratitude, never fully expressed or expressible, takes the common form of gifts, and, in unprogressive societies without arma-

* Between 1960 and 1970 American cremations rose by 44 percent—still involving only 4.5 percent of the total number of deaths. In the tight little island of England, where "the dead were pushing the living off the earth," half of all those who died in 1970 were cremated.—New York *Times*, December 6, 1970.

† In 1963 the Roman Catholic Church abandoned its prohibition and now tolerates cremation. The Churches' view that the practice was a specific rejection of resurrection was undermined—according to Miss Mitford—when an English clergyman "made the acute observation that if burning prevents resurrection, what about our blessed martyrs who were burned at the stake?"

ment races or drag races, children still bury their parents (rather than parents their children) and piety tends to persuade the distraught to empty effort. Guilt, too; we all mistreat one another, by neglect if in no ruder way, and we seize a "last" (which we know is an after-last) occasion to relieve ourselves and, if we have given him nothing else, give the unrousable a rousing send-off.

There is no real mystery about the American funeral and much democracy of a kind. We are still, even now, more restrained than the Scythian kings with their strangled concubines and cup-bearers and cooks in their tombs, but in the society which considers every man a king, and in which the generality of men have a princely income, it is not unnatural that the fashion of the blooded mighty should become the fashion of the bankrolled many, and both gratitude and guilt encumber the dead with baubles and baggage. The sociological motivation is more readily acceptable than the religious; what, in a nominally Christian country, has a procession of Cadillacs or an "impermeable casket" got to do with the Gospel of Christ crucified *and risen?*

Denominational dogma segregates the suicide and the unrepentant from sacred ground, and the bodies of these sinners (unless their survivors have money) share the shame of the unforgivable paupers in potter's field. Beyond that one dogma, the Church as a whole says nothing in the matter—and it is the Church whose hope is the soonest possible permeability of *every* casket come the Last Day. The Eternal Flame must be extinguished *before* the promise of Eternity is realized, and Perpetual Care is impossible until the last caretaker is gone. But men will have Parian marble to commemorate the spirit, though the marble begins its perishing as soon as the flesh it anchors, and the imperishable spirit (if not its commemorators' cash) has eluded the grasp of the speediest undertaker.

4: The Undiscover'd Country

MEN want to live on, in their children, in their friends, in the memory of men. And they will sacrifice everything to do it, their lives included. Take immortality away from them, and they will die for the closest thing to it they can get. Leave them their belief in the genuine article and they will still die for its substitute. The gods told Achilles before Troy that "if I stay here and fight, I shall not return alive but my name will live forever." But in Hades he changed his mind: "I prized that wretched chimera, glory, higher than life. I had not yet experienced how affairs stand here. . . . We are all immersed in the same darkness, without the least preference or distinction." (An old High Church joke has the churchman saying: "The Methodists preach universal salvation, but we Anglicans look forward to a happier prospect.")

But we are speaking here as mortals, unlike Achilles, and fame is our immortality. How much fame is worth one's life? A few hundred million have heard of Homer's Achilles, but billions in the past three thousand years have not. But, says Bacon, to achieve the immortality to which man's nature most aspires you want to be not a warrior but a writer like Homer, whose verses "have continued without the loss of a syllable or letter." Ah, but as many as have never heard of Achilles have never heard of Homer. How much shall I give—my life, or how much less?—to be famous in Greece but not in Rome, in Rome but not in Europe, in Europe but not in Asia or Africa or America? Or in a crossroads village, where ten will speak of me a thousand years from now, when only nine in all the world remember the name of the man whom millions remembered the day after he died?

The duration is as much the essence of my mortal immortality as its spread. How long do I want my fame to last? Why, forever, of course. But this is the chanciest of all worldly enterprises, requiring me to invest everything I have with no certainty whatever of a dividend or (should there be one) of its size or continuity. Worse yet, I shall have no enjoyment of it. A man once called upon fame to comfort him "by a solemn assurance, that when the little parlour in which I sit at this instant shall be reduced to a worse furnished box, I shall be read with honour by those who never knew nor saw me," and that man, Henry Fielding, enjoyed a very small fame, and then his *Tom Jones* was made into a movie, and I doubt not that more people read his words (or at least heard them spoken) in two nights than in two centuries.

The immortalists cite the chase of undying fame as a suggestive, if shadowed, evidence of the existence of the real thing, but this just-as-good substitute is terrible trouble to pursue and most unsurely got. It sometimes seems that its best guarantee is notoriety won by an unrelieved life of consummate wickedness. Mark Twain—that unlicensed poet—serves up the verity in a yarn of old New Orleans about a bloody pirate who reformed and was at last elected alderman of the city; "but today the loyal and generous remember only what he was, and charitably forget what he became."

History does even better by the point than the humorist. Consult your encyclopedia and your history book—but consult them in vain—for the name of the man whose life was the most eminent as well for the greatness of his virtue as his power, who saw his country victorious under his command and whose honors and triumphs brought him to the happiest possible end of a life which (so far as human life may be) had been full of all that is good and honorable; a man whose riches were nobly acquired and nobly dispersed to the needy, a man juster than Solon himself, a man profoundly beloved and even more profoundly mourned by the greatest city in all history. Atrocious Nero lives on everywhere, but who outside of Italy (and perhaps in it) remembers that Poplicola whose praises I have sung on no less authority, and in no other's very words, then Plutarch's? There is more immortality in burning Rome than in saving it.

An end to all of them—Achilles with Homer, Poplicola with Nero, the poet with the peasant. But is there no hint at all of their survival, then, outside of divine revelation? There is a hint, and more than one—a hint within nature and experience, and a peculiarly hard one to document. There is a persistent hint of actual communication from and with the dead.

There is no end of instances of biological "revival," more every day,* but no report from the revived to confirm even Hamlet's fear that the dead might dream. Cryobiology, the science of life at low temperatures, is developed to the point where human tissue and whole organs and even whole animals have been frozen and revived. Robert A. Ettinger, in his *Prospect of Immortality,* argues that freezing will preserve human life in suspension indefinitely. Quick-freezing immediately after death (assuming revivability after longer periods than has yet been demonstrated in man) offers the distant prospect of the cure of the mortal affliction by future undiscovered medical procedures.† A firm in Phoenix, Arizona, is now in the business of deep-freezing the dead, and at least three Californians are known to have put themselves on ice (at fantastic expense).

Mr. Ettinger's proposal has encountered the intensely self-conscious jocularity (such as "God's frozen people") that always greets frauds, incompetents, and wise men alike in respect to "cheating death" or communicating with the dead. So the claims of psychic research, or parapsychology, are generally hooted at by professors of the established sciences. Though most "occultists" are naturalists, they are regarded as supernaturalists by naturalists in other fields, and most psychologists ‡ spurn psychic research as neuroticism—or charlatanry —in spite of the assertive warning of their great colleague, C. G. Jung, that "anyone who has the least knowledge of the parapsychological material which already exists and has been thoroughly verified will know that so-called telepathic phenomena are undeniable facts. . . . The ideas and doubts of theoretical physicists in our own day should prompt a cautious mood in psychologists, too. . . ."

Nor is Jung alone among the intellectual giants in insisting that the

* On July 13, 1964, Dr. Charles Drew of Westminster Hospital in London performed a nine-hour heart operation on Robert Macklin, aged forty-one. For two hours and twenty-two minutes, with the patient's body temperature reduced from 98.6° to about 50°, there was no pulse, no breathing, and no blood flow. "In every accepted sense of the word," Dr. Drew is quoted as saying, "Macklin was physically dead. . . . There was no life whatsoever." The operation was successful.—*National Enquirer,* November 22, 1964.

† While transplantation of organs immediately after death is now a commonplace, Dr. Richard Lillehei of the University of Minnesota has taken kidneys from human corpses, preserved them for up to eleven hours after the patient's death at temperatures just above freezing, and then transplanted them into patients facing death from kidney ailments. According to the Associated Press, he predicts that eventually victims of organic ailments may be frozen in suspended animation and returned to life when replacement organs are available.

‡ "Some people go to a psychologist. Others come to see me," says Madame Frederika, one of the fifty thousand practicing clairvoyants in France. There is reported—in the New York *Times*—to be one practitioner of "occultism" to every 120 Parisians, compared to one physician for every 514 and one priest for every 5,000. A French statute of 1895, still on the books, illegalizes interpretation of dreams or forecast of the future.

door be left open to the procedures whose validity, if it is ever demonstrated, will affect the life of man more profoundly than all the breakthroughs of science together. William James was one of the founders of the American Society for Psychical Research and was fully convinced of the reality of psychic phenomena (though he admitted that his years of study of them had left him "baffled"). Reports of psychic experimentations were "simply howled down" in James's day, and it is still almost impossible to make a career of parapsychology. But we are hard put to ascribe victimization or fraud to such moderns as Sir William Crookes, inventor of the X-ray tube (and president of the Royal Academy of Science), astronomer Camille Flammarion of the French Academy of Science, physicist Sir Oliver Lodge, and the inventor of the incandescent lamp, Thomas Edison, all of whom, along with Sir Arthur Conan Doyle, were satisfied as to the genuineness of spirit communication. According to the *Encyclopædia Britannica,* it *appears* that there *may be* "a strong *prima facie* case for some communication from human spirits that have survived death"; and Alexis Carrel, "quite unconvinced" by spiritualist claims, nevertheless concluded that "it is far from being unreasonable that some part of human personality may escape death."

Every now and again the "strong *prima facie* case" receives support in the form of a sensational testimony which passes instantly from the front page to that special oblivion reserved for things we simply can't believe. In 1967 the press reported that Bishop James A. Pike of the Episcopal Church believed that he had been in communication with his dead son. In a televised seance in Toronto he received "some general ideas and a loving affirmation" directly from his son, he said, and, through the medium of the Reverend Arthur Ford, a Disciples of Christ minister who participated in the program, messages that "had the ring of truth" from the late Right Reverend Karl Block, Mr. Pike's predecessor as Bishop of California. Mr. Ford's powers as a medium, the New York *Times* said, "have been pronounced authentic by several American psychiatrists." (Mr. Pike subsequently resigned his bishopric, and then left the church to pursue his psychic research and Biblical studies. In 1969 he died in a touring accident in the Holy Land.)

Asserting that he had been in communication with his son on "at least half a dozen occasions" after the latter's death, Bishop Pike said he would have leaned over backward to explain these conversations had he himself not read and written about psychic phenomena. "But," he went on, "in the context of what we know about man's psyche transcending the space-time continuum, about mystical experience and the accumulating evidence of extrasensory perception, plus all the data about apparent communication with the deceased—not excluding the Resurrection—one can say that it is the most plausible explanation to accept it as true. . . . It is too much to ask for proof of life after death. But the evidence is strong enough to warrant a modest leap of faith—as in science—and to make a faith affirmation." But "on the surface," said the past president of the American Society of Magicians, an organization active in the exposure of fraudulent mediums, "it almost looks like a conspiracy by someone trying to play on the feelings he had after his son's death, possibly to draw him into spiritualism."

The possibility that there are sense perceptions stimulated "interiorly," by the brain or the nervous system and not by the known stimulators of sense, can be discountenanced by easy scoffers but not by those who know that we know little of the human subconscious. What we call sensory hallucination may be real in an order of reality we cannot yet reach. According to F. S. Edsall in *The World of Psychic Phenomena,* "Parapsychologists are convinced that ghosts and apparitions are psychic creations, not spirits wilfully wandering in the world of the living, or somehow separated from a living body and straying about erratically in some other place."

Mankind as a whole (taken over the whole of its history) disagrees on the last point: Ghosts are; and they are spirits of the dead. They seem to be of seven distinct kinds: (1) wrongdoers, especially murderers, who cannot rest away from the scene of their crime; (2) their victims, haunting the wrongdoers; (3) the spirits of carnal creatures, so enamored of the bodily appetites that they cannot survive death without carrying about some semblance of their bodies; (4) the spirits who, troubled over the unfinished worldly business they left behind them, come back to take care of it; (5) the spirits of those who foresee trouble for their loved ones and wish to warn them; (6) the unburied; and (7) the maladjusted spirits clinging to the places of their worldly habitation.

Of course *you* and *I* do not believe in ghosts; only primitive peoples believe in ghosts, such as the inhabitants of present-day England (whose Church of England has established a Fellowship for Psychical Studies, with fourteen Anglican bishops as members). "Few Britons think ghosts are purely imaginary," the New York *Times* reported in the fourteenth year of the second half of the twentieth century. "One fifth of the [British ghosts], according to a recent survey, appear in daylight. More than half are middle-aged. Five percent are children. And, as would be expected of a nation so universally fond of man's best friend, two percent of ghosts are believed to be dogs." The best antidote is, of course, exorcism, their damnation by "bell, Book and candle," occasionally conducted by church officials.

To the extent that the Church recognizes a ghost when it sees one, it justifies its reputation for tolerance; the supernaturalists (including theologians and churchmen generally) deny the existence of ghosts on the ground that only God can raise spirits. The materialist likewise rejects them because he does not accept the existence of incorporeality. The naturalist will have none of them, because natural processes afford no ground for their possibility. And the immaterialist, of course, cannot abide the matter (however wispy) that they trail. So all of us hard-boiled modern realists—Englishmen excepted—disbelieve in spooks and take a picnic to the nearby haunted house—preferably, to be sure, a noonday picnic with a coterie of noisy friends.

5: The Uses of Death

IF THERE is a deadlier enemy than death, it is dying. But dying is something that man thinks he knows a little something about. He has seen and studied the performance under a variety of conditions, and often under the optimum conditions of a hospital and an operating room. We don't know how many men die with their boots on, but Sir William Osler, the great clinician, says that of those who die with them off, as most of us do, "a few, very few, suffer severely in the body and still fewer in the mind." Dying is "always easy at the last . . . almost always preceded by a perfect willingness to die. . . . All competent observers agree that except in imagination there is no such thing as death agony. . . . The patient may hear"—watch that "may"—"the ringing of nonexistent bells or see the flashing of non-existent lights. He may feel a slight restlessness. Gradually he drifts into darkness, without pain, without sensation. . . ." *

We lay this body down every evening, and what is more, we can come pretty close to knowing the last wakeful instant (though not the first or any other instant of sleep). We are stretched out prone and prostrate a third of our lives—"dead to the world"—in something like rehearsal for the long run. We actually court sleep, and at some point in the day we prefer its emptiness to the fullness of being awake;

* O. A. Battista, "What Happens When You Die," *Science Digest*, May 1964. Within a few minutes of circulatory stoppage, the oxygen starvation of the human brain at ordinary temperature is (as far as we now know) functionally irreparable; this, determinable by electroencephalogram, is death, and not (as Harvey discovered three hundred years ago) the cessation of the "heartbeat," which may be restored by artificial respiration, heart massage, massive blood transfusion, or drugs. Soviet scientists are reported to have used refrigeration successfully to extend the survival of brain function to as much as an hour after anoxia (the deprivation of oxygen).—San Francisco *Chronicle*, June 24, 1964, report of American Medical Association convention; "The Reversal of Death," *Saturday Review*, August 4, 1962.

but, lest we let the analogy carry us away, be it said that we "know" that we shall awaken and that the worst bad dream will end. We have always slept . . . and always awakened. Montaigne wonders if this is a foretaste. (But he does not ask whether we shall hate to get up on the Last Day, and do it as bad-naturedly as on every other.)

We are well practiced in sleep, says Montaigne, but "in dying, which is the greatest work we have to do, practice can give us no assistance at all. A man may by custom fortify himself against pain, shame, necessity, and such like accidents, but, as to death, we can experience it but once, and are all apprentices when we come to it." It has been thus up to now. Will it always be? There are two kinds of mysteries, says Carrel: those we can conquer and those that are forever beyond our reach, the Unknown and the Unknowable. "There is a frontier between these two worlds, a wall that we will never climb. On which side of this wall is death located? We do not know. To find an answer to this question will be a long and difficult task. However, in the course of a few hundred years, science may be capable of ascertaining whether death is to remain forever a mystery."

There are dunderheads who maintain that it is better to be alive than dead (and, equally, dunderheads who maintain that it is better to be dead than alive)—an opinion which, on its very face, is nothing but local pride (or wanderlust). For he who knows only his own side of the case knows little of that, and in the case at bar the witnesses for the Adversary have not yet taken the stand. Strictly speaking, we cannot have an opinion that we are going to be dead. Opinion demands consciousness first of all. We know that it is impossible to be at once conscious and not conscious of the future; but it is this impossible situation which presumably obtains at the last conscious moment that precedes death. We may be of the opinion that we are going to die— but the opinion that we are going to be dead is mere presumption.

There are one or two things of secondary consequence which we are pretty sure we know about being dead. It is a state involving no pain of a sensible nature. (And no pleasure.) If there is spiritual torment or ecstasy, it is a kind that the spirit does not know on earth, for the spiritual torments and ecstasies which we indulge here are all dependent upon corporeality, from which the responses of the five external senses and the two internal senses of memory and imagination are inseparable. Thus death, barring bodily resurrection, would seem to be eternal rest, as advertised—at least from worldly attractions and distractions. The man being tortured to death, or the man on the scaffold, or the man in terminal illness with great pain, likelier than not prefers death by, so to say, dis-preferring life. Not release, but only release from present horrors; not liberation, but only liberation from the present conditions. "Whatever it is, it can't be worse than this"; the sooner 'tis over (as the Bard puts it) the sooner to sleep. Whoever is beset—and who isn't?—by the incessance of hubbub and the inescapable entertainment of every public and private place (even unto the musical treacle in the office-building elevator) and yearns for a little peace and quiet may (or may not) be consoled by the near certainty of someday having as much as man could want of one or the other (or both).

But there are men who know to a certainty when the thief cometh, men condemned by man's law to die at a given hour of a given day; as a newspaperman, I have known a few such men, and I think of none who wished they were dead that day rather than the next. They, like the rest of us—perhaps the dying, too, to the last split second of consciousness—think that a reprieve is not impossible. How long a reprieve? An hour's, a day's, or a year's or a hundred, but a reprieve. Abdul was sentenced to death, and on his last day he sent a message to the Caliph: If the Caliph would grant him a thirty-day reprieve, he would teach him to fly. "You must be mad," said Abdul's friend, "to make such an offer." "Look," said Abdul, "in thirty days the Caliph might die, or I might die, or (who knows?) I might teach him to fly."

Is death ever itself a desideratum, or does it only seem so under apparently hopeless conditions? Is it wished for more commonly in "backward" societies, where labor is unrelieved and suffering irremediable, or in "advanced" societies which, by reducing labor and suffering, perhaps weaken men's will to endure it? Is the poor man's desire for death a case of sour grapes (as the Stoic says) and only the rich man's genuine? The Green Pastures may or may not be green; we paint them here and their verdure depends upon the brownness of those we are grazing.

Modern man is made acutely anticipative, perhaps the first in all history really to accept the ancient dictum that "this, too, shall pass away." Motion has hold of him, including the motion of the neon sign on the fence of a California cemetery that flashes the words "Rest in Peace," "Rest in Peace," "Rest in Peace," on and off. He thinks that there will be a big change any day now—and there usually is. But the great change in his life, and the end of all change, is unchanged: death.

In his habituation to change, and his anticipation of it, he comes to love change and pursue it. The great change (if it is change he wants) is still death. Now a man who is worth very much as a man has always been relatively indifferent to his life—the frontiersman of science and discovery and money and fame and revolution and religion and love. But the persistent fascination of Homer's Odysseus is his daredeviltry for daredeviltry's sake, his aimless adventure, his taking a gander at the Cyclops for kicks. A man who risks his life should risk it with an intelligence that comprehends both the value of the end and the choice of the means. But we seem to see something more often now—or is it only that we who see it are getting old?—than we ever did before: a whole breed of Odysseuses, playing "chicken" on the highways and racing cars on the ice.

Wealth and leisure provide the possibility of enlarged experience of life and a shot at the bizarre for ever more men in the advanced societies. The thrills that were once vicarious—in the Circus or the Colosseum of ancient Rome—are now available to most of those who were then mere spectators. But that is not necessarily to say that we find life worthier; the "punishment-provoking behaviour" of children (and of elderly teenagers, on and off the campus) is at least as pervasive among the rich as it is among the poor. Neither is there a necessary contradiction between the frantic pursuit of life's multifarious manifestations and its *ultimate* manifestation in the exercise of its power to kill oneself or others. (It wasn't Adolf Hitler who said, "Perform those deeds of blood, of valor, which above everything else bring national renown. . . . By war alone can we acquire those virile qualities necessary to win in the stern strife of actual life." It was Theodore Roosevelt.)

There is some suggestion of a mark-down on human life in the conduct of modern war. "Total war" was a commonplace among the ancients, without restriction, restraint, or discrimination between combatants and noncombatants. But the concept of "civilized warfare" appeared as early as the late Middle Ages and flowered after Napoleon. Its conduct was fairly rigidly codified more than a century ago, and, until recently, it showed steady progress in the international agreements to which all the advanced nations adhered.

Wars were fought on battlefields; the succor of the wounded was sacrosanct; and the treatment of prisoners was regulated in terms of rights. Civilian life and liberty were exempt in principle, civilian property likewise, though both suffered if they happened to be in the way of contending armies. In World War I the perfection of long-range artillery and the rapid advance of the German armies through Belgium and northern France wrought immense destruction of civilian life and property. But this destruction was viewed—on both sides—as unavoidable and unfortunate. The first purposive attack on a noncombatant population was the British blockade of Germany for almost a year after the surrender; at least a million Germans died of starvation.

The record since then is one of precipitate decline and is too well known to require elucidation; the massacre of My Lai was one that "leaked." The total war of the ancient barbarians has become the practice of civilized nations generally. The whole world—cities and towns, hospitals, orphanages, schools, and churches—is now the battlefield. The short-lived myth of "pinpoint bombing" has long since given way to the generally accepted reality of "saturation bombing." It is all still deplored as unavoidable and unfortunate—unfortunate that more civilians than soldiers were killed and wounded in South Vietnam *without* enemy bombing of population centers. But it has come to be accepted with a shoulder shrug as "the nature of war."

If we are setting a lower value on life than those before us—or those around us whose lives are poorer than ours—we are making the most radical of all changes. This is not to say that it may not be the right change; those before and around us may have overvalued life and therefore tended it more carefully (within their much more limited abilities) than it deserves. Modern man's valuation not of death but of life is not necessarily wrong, and the spread of secularism may be a blessing in its liberation of him to look at life (which he knows) entirely apart from death (which he doesn't). Life as seen may be La Mettrie's farce, after all, and well shut of.

Passing strange, if life should be losing esteem among the very people who have access to its blessings in measure undreamed of— unless, of course, what we take to be blessings are not blessings at all.* But the fact is that the devaluation of life—if we may judge by their indulgence in murder, manslaughter, war, alcoholism, suicide, and "the pace that kills" at work or play—is the world's highest in those societies that enjoy the widest spread of comfort, leisure, diversion, and a splendid living standard. The speculation on the paradox is abundant enough, ranging in form from man's inability to survive without the perpetual challenge of hardship to his inability to maintain the *persona,* the sense of individual identity, against the depersonalization of the machine and its products.

Man does not *really* accept the old and honorable bromide about the individual's dying and the race's living on. The "race" theme has always had political currency, either to spur a people on to hardy adventure (and investment) or to console them for the loss of their loved ones in war. But it has never known philosophical or psycho-

---

* "The flush toilet has been stirring increasing concern because of the damage it has done and is continuing to do to the environment. 'There are two crimes against humanity which at their inception seemed like real boons,' Dr. Donaldson Koons, chairman of Maine's Environmental Improvement Commission, said in an interview. 'They are the internal combustion engine and the flush toilet.' "—New York *Times,* July 27, 1971.

logical respectability. It is not a philosopher but a homespun littera-
teur of philosophy, Will Durant, who says, "We are temporary organs
of the race, cells in the body of life; we die and drop away that life
may remain young and strong. . . . Death, like style, is the removal
of rubbish, and excision of the superfluous. . . . Life itself is deathless while we die. . . ."

The individual, in consciousness no less than in conscience, rejects
the "race" mythos, and rightly, both as a man and as a citizen. No
"cell in the body of life," he. He senses his entity, his identity, his independence—the Crusoe, if not the God, within him. He knows what
it is to live alone with *his* consciousness, always isolated unbridgeably
from his neighbor's or his countrymen's; to be glad or guilty or fearful or troubled or satisfied when no one else is, not even the companion of his bosom. He has his own sore throat, his own grudge, his own
pleasure of a sunset or a book, and the rest of the world has only
his report of them.

But the race mythos is not all hogwash. The community *is* a continuum and our lives are in considerable measure devoted to its continuity, most obviously in the provision we make, or would like to
make, for our descendants born and unborn. An aged man plants an
oak whose shade he will never know. We do not envision a cut-off
point, though there is one somewhere. In twenty, thirty, forty years
this generation will be gone—all of it. In a hundred, forgotten—ancestors whose very photographs have crumbled. We date our letters
1/14/72; no need for 1/14/1972.

We who make the world go 'round—when we are not here to make
it go, it must surely stop. These children, these babes, *they* can't run
the country, or the bank, or the store. But they will, and we testify to
our admission with our testaments and our ninety-nine-year leases
(and our twenty-year mortgages) and our "long-term" constructions
and welfare and military and population projections. "By the year
2000 we . . . " No; not we. The transition goes on, and on, and on,
and the W. E. Jones Company, after being W. E. Jones and Sons, will
be W. E. Jones' Sons and, after that, very possibly the W. E. Jones
Company again. Whoever lives or dies, tomorrow's paper will be
published, tomorrow's race will be run, tomorrow's January white
sale will open at Macy's. (And where is Macy?)

Those who went before and those who come after us have a shadow
or dream existence of a kind categorically different from our own.
Augustus could never have heard of Charlemagne, or Alexander of
Napoleon; Gandhi, Einstein, Churchill could have heard of me, as I
heard of them. Gandhi, Einstein, Churchill, you, and I. In a hundred

years we are lumped with Augustus and Charlemagne as "history," except that you and I uncelebrated are lumped with the leaves of the trees—not in history, in homogeneous oblivion. *Spurlos versunken*— gone without a trace the living generations that must have been. "These pegs, now, they must have used them for nails." *They?*

6: The Love of Life

THESE MEDITATIONS (or vaporings) compel us to the trickiest question that man confronting death has any competence to try to answer: Is one uncelebrated life cheaper or dearer now than it was "then"? The answer, on its face, would seem to be: dearer. Certainly so, if we are becoming more secular. The immortalist does not need Euclid *or* Dante to tell him that seventy years are nothing compared with eternity; but the mortalist may be expected to hold those seventy years dearly as being all that he has or ever will have. And these seventy are thirty more than they were "then"; thirty more, indeed, "here" than "there" even now.

On this showing, the answer to the tricky question is monstrous easy. But it fails to satisfy—in part, perhaps, because of some contrary signs, in greater part because it fails to inspect the question closely. What is the currency we are to use to measure cheapness and dearness? What makes life meaningful (and meaningless) to us? What do we want "out of" it that we can or can't get? Wealth? Health? Fame? Power? Private influence? Popularity? Friends? Love? Variety? Excitement? Steadiness? Quietude? Intelligence? Beauty? Virtue? Or some or all of them (or still others, such as suffering, sorrow, sacrifice) and in what combination? "Happiness" tells us nothing until we have said what will make us happy (or what we think will); no more does "the full life," for life may be full of any or all of these things (and of years besides) and utterly empty of others we value higher (or come, at a date too late, to value higher); or it may be short and sweet.

Take personal identity as a desideratum—individuality. Its ingredients are many, and some of them are subtle. To be one's own boss; to be known by one's first (not to say last) name; to have one's own home and one's own possessions; to be recognized by elevation to special trust or responsibility among one's neighbors or associates or in the larger local community; even, perhaps, to dress or walk or talk (or think) "differently"; even, perhaps, to have a distinctive automobile license or telephone number.

Anything (or almost anything) rather than be a leaf of the tree— of a tree that cannot be seen for the forest. Is *my* life to be oozed not of *its* meaning but of *mine?* Am I to know the man next door only by the color of his door and be known by mine? Am I to be tagged with a number, and then another number, and then another number, as a dog is tagged or a tin can? Are all those around me to undergo the same homogenization? At some point I am one with my wall-to-wall carpet and my automatic transmission and my Disposal (which has already eliminated my garbage man). My life has become so comfortable, so nameless, so interchangeable with every other as to be imperceptible to me. In terms of individuality, life in an advanced urban-suburban society is emptier far than Crusoe's. I am bored—to *death*—and death's shares rise ineluctably as life's sink. They are the only two issues offered, and I buy into the one as surely as I sell off the other.

How cheap or dear do we hold another's life as against our own? We all kill men, directly or indirectly, advertently or inadvertently. As sovereign members of an organized society we execute criminals, and if, in war, we do none of the bombing, we are all accessories in providing the bombers and the bombardiers. Some of our neighbors are in want. A little farther away some of our fellow citizens starve; still farther away, hunger's toll takes some ten thousand human beings every twenty-four hours. And our philanthropy, domestic and foreign, does not affect our living standard; we are not so concerned as to bereave ourselves of capital when surplus eases us of our concern.

Of course, those with whom we are at war we at once reduce to the status of submen who "don't understand anything but force." Wild beasts, by nature or corruption the enemies of humanity. First we demote them from manhood in sufficient degree to justify our killing them in conscience.* Few men otherwise ever kill a man or condone his killing.

The immortalist should, in reason, value his own life lower than

* Q. (Asked on television of a South African mercenary in the Congo): "Wally, how do you feel when you're out there fighting? How do you feel about killing anyone?" A.: "The first time I felt a bit squeamish, but after that it was like, well, I'd done a lot of cattle farming, you know, and killing a lot of beasts, it's just like, you know, cattle farming, and just seeing dead beasts all over the place. It didn't worry me at all."
"A psychiatric report . . . described [Lieutenant William Calley's] state of mind [at My Lai]: 'He did not feel as if he were killing humans, but rather that they were animals. . . .' "—*Time,* April 12, 1971.

the mortalist his (but the other's no higher); but the case is infrequently encountered historically, except among the relatively few religious martyrs. Like the Hindu *suttee,* in which the widow places herself on her husband's funeral pyre, the self-immolation of Buddhist monks in Vietnam or students in Prague astounds us roundly: How can life be so worthless that a healthy man would throw it away? But so the behavior of the early Christians astounded the Romans, though the modern jargon may relieve us of a little of our astonishment by substituting "martyr complex" for "martyr."

Killer of self or another, man is a killer. (Freud thought that the lust to kill is older than love.) He kills all his life and lives by killing. He kills purposively, he kills accidentally (and "accidentally"), and he kills just to kill. He kills—or drools in front of his TV screen—to prove that he is alive with the power of life and death in his fist or at his fingertip. Why, then, shouldn't man the killer be killed—the hunter hunted down, the trapper trapped, the catcher caught, the fly-swatter swatted? Why shouldn't the eater be eaten, to cure him of his illusion that the power to kill is the power to create (rather than merely expedite) death? He is the great killer, always more adept at killing other kinds and his own. The German, if he was once distressed to hear of his country's gas ovens for Jews, does not seem to mind killing his countrymen on the highways (four times as many, proportionately, as the American); and the American learns with apparent equanimity from his Secretary of Defense—Defense, mind you—that a Soviet nuclear attack would kill 140,000,000 of the 200,000,000 Americans.

The great killer kills dutifully and professionally, in peace no less than in war, and not, like the brutes, just for food or a mate. The public executioner may send a real or affected shudder through us, but his post is never vacant for want of applicants. In seventeenth-century England more than 200 crimes were capital—including the stealing of a handkerchief by a "malicious" seven-year-old. But for all the rigor of the penalty, crime did not decline (nor has it yet). The abandonment of the death penalty by the Netherlands a hundred years ago has been followed by most of Europe and by most American states. The causes of the trend against capital punishment (apart from the demonstrability of the failure of deterrence) are not clear. What is perhaps clearer is man's rejection of his own image as a killer except in war and in play (including prize-fighting, against which legislation is urged with growing ardor).* Either he does not like to kill, or he

* The "bare-knuckle" bout, which originated in England and has long since been forbidden there, was always a bit strong for the American stomach, though it was not outlawed in the United States until a century ago.

is ashamed of liking to (or of being seen liking to); or, with the growth of understanding of the unconscious, he is afraid to stimulate his own blood lust by doing so. Public execution was always an occasion of general degradation.

But if (as Arthur Koestler says in his *Reflections on Hanging*) there is "a spoonful of sadism at the bottom of every human heart," a "little Stone Age man inside us," we may still want men killed and even to be in on the killing. Newspapermen know to what lengths some men (and women) go to find a way to be admitted to an execution.* The mob that waits outside a prison when a notorious execution occurs—and that cheers when the hearse comes out the prison gates, as it did in the Lindbergh-Hauptmann case in 1935—undoubtedly contains a fair number of persons who would like to be in immediate, and even participatory, attendance. And if we do not want to see others killed, or kill them, it may still be possible that we want them dead (though we may repress the wish or sublimate it by deciding that they would be "better off").

Still, the closed execution and the use of humane instruments to perform it seem to testify to man's progressive effort to control his blood lust, as do the conventions (however widely breached) for the treatment of prisoners of war. Even stronger testimony is the modern reprobation of torture. Torture to bring about death with maximum pain was the common practice of our savage ancestors. Those savages had a wisdom we civilized have lost: Like us, they wanted to inflict the worst possible punishment on their enemies. But whether death— above all, a quick death—was in fact punishment, they knew no more than we do. What they did know was that pain was punishment, and for centuries the art of torture, like all human arts, was steadily refined by man's admirable ingenuity.

Torture, not as punishment but as a device to obtain criminal or military information, is still practiced everywhere, though it is forbidden by the law of civilized societies. But there is not much evidence, outside of the statutes, that civilized societies as a whole are disturbed by the quiet employment of "a little arm- [or neck-] twisting" in criminal cases or war,† and almost no evidence that modern man has any

* Assigned—the night my first child was born—to cover the country's first triple electrocution, at the Illinois State Penitentiary, I stuck it out for the first two "burnings" and then went for an unsteady walk in the prison yard, wincing as the searchlights suddenly went dim and on again. I suppose that half the "witnesses" in the commodious auditorium were pretty thoroughly drunk, and most of the rest partially oiled. I can't say, in the event, that I blamed them, except for their being there. The character of the crowd was clear: I recognized a dozen minor politicos from Chicago, who were making a party of it with a few similarly choice and, of course, fortunate friends.

† Although the actual conduct of the Vietnam war was largely inaccessible to the press, accounts of excruciating torture of Vietnamese by Vietnamese

compunction against the "blind" or "saturation" bombing of civilian populations. Even the Nazi practice of genocide, in the wartime slaughter of six million Jews, cannot be shown actually to have outraged an "outraged" world (or the mass of the German people, themselves wartime sufferers). But the world sentiment toward *mercy* killing is different.

The practice of euthanasia on mental and physical defectives, either at birth or afterward, is traceable, like all killing, to man's recorded beginnings; and its advocacy, especially for the dying (with their own permission or, *in extremis,* without it), but also in cases of hopeless monstrosity at birth, is considerable among modern secular humanitarians. But the churches in the Western world are adamant against it, either on the miraculous power of the Lord to produce recovery or on the related dogma that He alone has the right to take life—though just how they square this pious sentiment with their acceptance of capital punishment (not to say war) is one of those nice points on which apostasy battens.

The argument for euthanasia is, of course, mercy; and the works of mercy are sternly required by Scripture. So the believer is torn; and many an individual cleric is a euthanasiast. The argument turns on the question of suffering in what medicine calls the "terminal" situation. Its measurement is impossible, and those who ordinarily measure it tend to be hopelessly subjective. *They* may be suffering more than the dying, especially in an era of sedatives freely and effectively used. And the suffering of "mind" may be far more intense than that of the body. The man who is told that he has three months or six to live may at that point be feeling fine physiologically and, in those three or six months, suffer the most acute agonies of spirit. Should he be "put out of his misery" and when? And at whose decision? Shall we let even *him* decide, in his tormented condition? *

(both North and South) were photographically confirmed. In addition, charges appeared down the years—especially by French and Scandinavian journalists—that the United States not only condoned their ally's practices but took part in them. On August 11, 1969, the charges "surfaced" when the commandant of the U.S. Special Forces ("Green Berets") and two of his officers were arrested in connection with the alleged murder of a Vietnamese member of their unit who was said to have been accused by the Americans of being a double spy. In a dispatch from Washington the Times-Post Service reported "possible torture" of the supposed victim and added, "While no one talks about it in public, torture and murder are part of the clandestine activities of the Special Forces established as an elite group by the United States Government. . . . The public reaction to disclosure about some Green Berets' activities is likely to be one of shock. . . ." The case never came to trial.

* "To the people who are active in this country's two major euthanasia groups (the Euthanasia Educational Fund and the Euthanasia Society of America), euthanasia generally means one thing: the right to die with dignity.

The introduction of euthanasia—literally, "good death"—as a social program was attempted (along with sterilization) by no less than the Nazi dictator at the beginning of World War II. Its first victims—or beneficiaries—were mental defectives. Popular opinion resisted it—which meant only that it proceeded as decorously as possible. But church opposition was vehement and implacable, even among churchmen who "swam along" with the regime, and the euthanasia program was abandoned in August of 1941. There is little doubt that there were powerful proponents, within the Nazi leadership, of its extension to the dying and ultimately to the unemployable aged.

The *prima facie* argument against euthanasia is easy enough: We cannot know that the "dying," even in the last extremities, will in fact die. Nor can we know that either mental or physical defectiveness is, or will be, incurable. But the religious position more accurately reflects the general unease. The Commandment reads, "Thou shalt not kill." (There is exegesis to substitute "murder" for "kill.") But John Locke's contention that men, as God's handiwork, "are His property . . . made to last during His, not one another's pleasure," as it challenges capital punishment, war, and suicide, challenges euthanasia, too. If Locke is right, man, including the exegesist, is, and always has been, wrong—dead wrong.

If the love of life tells us something not about death but about our view of it, it is in order to ask how cheap (or dear) life was held in the past compared with the present. The historical inference would seem to be irresistible: In the ages of primitive or nonexistent medicine, sanitation, drainage, and disinfection, of murderous conditions of labor (slave or "free"), and of implacable and recurrent plague, epidemic, famine, flood, and fire, men could not have valued life anything as highly as we do. But wait. Why isn't the opposite as likely to be true? Why wouldn't the very hazards and hardships of life make it that much more precious? If a man anticipates no more than thirty years on earth—the life expectancy of ancient Rome— why wouldn't he hold each of those thirty, and each day and hour of them, dearer than we do with an expectancy of almost seventy?

But we may turn the argument on itself yet again. Up to (and into) the present century, 20 to 40 percent of all infants born alive died

---

Indignity, to them, means deterioration, dependence, and hopeless pain. . . . Almost 20,000 persons have requested the 'living wills' in the 18 months that they have been available. . . .' The 'living will,' which is not legally binding, provides that the testator, if he becomes ill and there is no reasonable expectation of recovery, be allowed to die and not be kept alive by 'artificial means' or 'heroic measures.' "—New York *Times,* February 28, 1971.

during their first year, and three out of four of all deaths were those of children under twelve. Only two of Jefferson's six children survived infancy; Edward Gibbon was the only one of seven siblings to do so; more than half of Judge Samuel Sewall's fifteen children in the Massachusetts Bay Colony were lost. And this was the fact of death among the favored few. In the Dublin Foundling Asylum, forty-five babies survived of 10,272 admitted between 1775 and 1796—a mortality rate of 99.6 percent. Small wonder that even the relatively prosperous New England colonial, not to say the suffering masses of most of the rest of the world, rejoiced mightily in death's approach and yielded himself "with unaffected cheerfulness." *

Perhaps the incidence of suicide is an index to the value a people put upon life. But only perhaps. Its inducements may be the consequence not of life's depreciation but, in an environment of tension, its unendurability. At least this is a possible explanation of the phenomenally high—and rising—suicide rate in such advanced societies as America's and Sweden's. We are pretty sure that suicide in the past was much rarer than it is now, in spite of the physical hardness of life, and in spite, too, of the fact that earlier religions did not undertake so sternly as ours to dishearten its indulgence.

But we can't really *think* about suicide, any more than we can *think* about death. Is it brave or cowardly? Shameful or honorable? Defiant or escapist? A "bang" or a whimper? The ancients disagreed among themselves, as do we. Oriental religions did not forbid it, and Shintoism enjoined the excruciating act of hara-kiri—"honorable departure"—upon a gentleman who had disgraced himself. (The observance is still known in Japan.) And, while Athens denied funeral rites to suicides, Plato justified self-destruction in cases of intolerable distress or public shame. Aristotle condemned it as cowardly and treasonable; and Roman law forbade it as an escape from criminal punishment or military duty. But the Epicureans and the Stoics approved of it as the act of a truly free man. "No one," said Seneca, "need be wretched by choice. Do you like it not? It is in your power to return from whence you came." Pliny held that the choice of death was the greatest gift of God. The Stoic writings doubtless accounted, at least in part, for the spread of suicide in the last age of the Roman Empire.

But the rise of Christianity reversed the trend. While the six occasions of suicide in the Old Testament are recited without condemnation, the single suicide in the New Testament put the seal of horror on

* Alice M. Earle, *Customs and Fashions in Old New England*, New York, Charles Scribner's Sons, 1894, p. 386.

the act as the abomination of despair: The religion of Christ could not condone the behavior of his betrayer, and St. Thomas Aquinas in his *Summa Theologica* characterizes the taking of one's own life as "the most fatal of sins, because it cannot be repented of." Nor did Protestantism take a more temperate position. In Europe—even in the United States—it was common in the not remote past to bury the suicide in an unmarked grave at a crossroads between communities, and even to "punish" him by driving a stake through his heart. (Plato, in his *Laws,* specified that suicides, except for those whose act was prompted by intolerable stress or public shame, should be "buried ignominiously in waste and nameless spots on the boundaries between the twelve districts and the tomb to be marked by neither headstone nor name.")

We know that among primitive peoples of our own era suicide is almost unknown and that its incidence among the traditionally oppressed, such as the American Negro, is only a fraction of that of their "happier" countrymen. In San Francisco, which leads the United States in suicide and which enjoys the reputation of being one of the world's most delightful cities, a compilation made in the mid-1960s revealed that the suicide rate of whites was almost thirty-five times as high as that of Negroes. But a year later the Negro magazine *Ebony* reported that, while the white suicide rate the country over was almost three times that of the Negro, the Negro rate had almost doubled since the end of World War II: "It is even more significant that of the thousand Negro suicides each year, almost two-thirds take place in the financially secure, even wealthy, group. For as the Negro wins his way into the material plenty of American middle- and upper-class life, he inherits economic, social, and psychological tensions possessed by his white counterparts. . . . Suicide in this country is a kind of luxury."

We do know something about past man's evaluation of *another's* life than his own. It was lower far than ours. In and out of the dangerous trades—the workers called them deadly, not dangerous—wage-labor was a mercilessly used commodity like any other. And from the beginning of time the conqueror had been deemed to have the right to the life of the conquered. At his discretion he might spare his enemy's life (which, however, remained forfeit) and enslave him. Whole populations went into slavery (unless they were put to the sword), and their care was strictly a matter of their animal worth to their masters. On these counts, at least, modern man respects human life in a way that his early forebears did not. But "respect" may not be the right word. The man who says—or thinks—"Fry 'em" or

"Too bad they didn't break his neck," or "They should have shot more of them," is, ordinarily, restrained by the mores from fulfilling (or from having others fulfill) his wish. How much more or less serious than his ancestor's is his wish? To what extent does his restraint reflect respect? And whence the tenderer mores of modern man?

The highest reward of the competitive life is the domination of others; at the top of the ladder is the job of *boss*. But the absolute domination of another is the power of life and death and, ultimately, the exercise of that power. When I stand over my dead competitor, dead by my hand, I have bested him for keeps. If I cannot take his life, his liberty will do as the token of my competitive success. Civilized men stop—or are estopped—short of enslavement and murder, but their implication is within us, somewhere beneath the veneer. If we do not dream of committing them, when our competitors or foremen appear in our dreams, it may be a sign that they are buried deep, or it may be a sign that we are afraid that we might be the loser instead of the winner.

How far beneath the veneer of civilization is killing buried? The apparent reversion in our time to the ancient—and pre-ancient—indifference to other men's lives in war is painfully suggestive. Mass slaughter by remote control came in with artillery and the aerial bomb and chemical and biological warfare; we do not need to go to the trouble of lopping off a hundred thousand heads one at a time. And, far from there being a general revulsion of mankind, the acceptance of streamlined massacre seems to be suddenly universal. It would be a reckless philosopher of history who would say today that the rising esteem for another's life that preceded our own time was secure. The earnest observer sees all about him the triumphant recognition of mortal worth, above all in the acknowledged right to medical care (which as recently as a century ago was reserved to the rich); and he sees all about him the acknowledgment (even the embrace) of total war, the rapidly rising tide of crime ("in"—and out of—"the streets"), and the addiction to the play of violence in the press, the cinema, and on television. (*Mother: "Johnny, your grandpa is dead." Johnny: "Who shot him?"*)

The last of the tricky questions involving the value of life is no easier than the others: How cheap or dear do we hold an old man's life, a young one's, an infant's? I was once (when I was very young) engaged in a discussion of the fate of Socrates, at the point of his refusal to escape from the death cell. I argued that he had made a simple calculation to achieve immortality at the expense of a few more years of life. After all, he was an old man; why should he mind dying?

"Young man," said an old man in the group, "you have never been an old man." I am old now, and I think I know what the old man meant.

Bright, bedazzled youth. Try to tell the young (as Hegel does) that "the nature of finite things as such is to have the seed of their passing away as their essential being; the hour of their birth is the hour of their death." Only try to tell them that "the first minute after noon is night." Only try to tell them what they are in in the midst of life. Death is impossible to the young. Their lives are charmed and so we call their deaths. Movie star James Dean—even the brothers Kennedy—"had it made." Impossible and, more important, unimaginable. For how far away is youth from the years of childhood in which you are dead, bang, bang, every day in cops-and-robbers, cowboy-and-Indian? What has death to do with the world of cheerleaders, hot-rods, plunging halfbacks, and all-night sessions with the books or the band? Ask rather what it has *not* to do with the middle-aged twisters and drinkers, fighting the wearisome fight, and the losing fight, to recapture the dead-and-gone reality of youth.

The young understand death well enough; what they don't understand is the necessity to look both ways before crossing the street. They understand death well enough, but not the necessity to brush their teeth or lay off drugs (or hot dogs or cigarettes). They understand death well enough, but not the necessity to apportion their time and treasure their days, their hours, their minutes. Why shouldn't they be prodigal of them? They have "all of life" left. Death is too far in the distance to be seen on the clearest day. On the clearest day—and all days are clear—they see the day. The past was childhood and done with; the future is age and afar. The present, the now, is bubbling, effervescent. What the old barber said in *Zuleika Dobson* is all that there is or ever will be to be said: "Youth! Youth!"

Youth is rising to command, to take over. The future belongs to it—not it to the future. It is climbing the hill of life with such strides as middle age takes on the other side and hobbled senility remembers as a dream. The summit, the peak of man's power, is above the clouds, invisible, but it is there, and youth will be there with it and fasten its standard to it. And there it is, sure enough. He gets out of the play pen; life is beginning. He goes to school, to college; life is beginning. He gets his first job; life is beginning (unless the job is at Vimy Ridge, Bataan, or Dak To, where death is a dirty trick and if you could only escape it you'd live forever). He has his first love affair, and then marriage and the hand-to-mouth glory of the kitchenette; life is just beginning. In a few years we see him at the peak of his power. Lusty lord of the universe, he flails about him for another fast few years, say, from twenty-five to thirty-five or forty. And then, one day or, likelier, one night, a disconsoling vision . . .

Maybe it is only a crick in his back or a stitch in his side that doesn't disappear, and he has to lie abed a few days and still it doesn't disappear; or it disappears and reappears. Maybe a classmate, a friend his own age, is suddenly dead: "Joe? Why, I saw Joe last Thursday, and he was as healthy as I am." *And so he was.* Somewhere between thirty-five and forty (or, if he is a little less introspective, before forty-five) he realizes that he will die. It doesn't dawn on him—it comes much less perceptibly than the dawn. But it comes. Its mark is a settled, solitary wistfulness; he is over, just over, but over, the unmarked watershed. Death is born.

The wistfulness will sharpen, little by little, until it stabs him again and again, more and more frequently. He no longer means to do this, that, and the other thing, but to do them "while he can"; and then, to do them "before he dies." The "time of diminishment." The children are gone. The house is too large. A smaller house, then, and then a smaller, until, one day, he asks himself, "Will this be the last one?" And then, one day, his wife sees a new overcoat she thinks he'd like to have, and for the first time in his life it occurs to him that the coat he has will . . . will last. Maybe more than last. Another beachhead or two established. He who had known so many illnesses and accidents as incidents, events, misfortunes one *recovers* from, is told by the doctor, "You'll be all right if you take it a little easier. . . ." And now, when his friends ask him how he is, he says, with careful affability, "Hanging on, hanging on." And to himself: "Why, I've got thirty . . . twenty . . . ten good years in me yet."

He was always doomed. Now he knows it. Life is fading slow away.

Our ancestors expected to die when their "time" was come, and their time was come at whatever age above thirty-five or forty they were stricken by illness or, as was so often the case, malnutrition. At forty, said Montaigne in the sixteenth century, and what he said was as true in the first half of the nineteenth, "we are pretty well advanced; and since we have exceeded the ordinary bounds, which is the just measure of life, we ought not to expect to go much further. . . . We should acknowledge that so extraordinary a fortune . . . is not likely to continue long." It is not that we do not expect nowadays to die at forty, or at fifty, or at sixty, but rather that we do not expect to die.

We could not live if we did, living as most of us do in an ever accumulating tumble of large and small matters. We plan to go on living as if we knew so much of the future as the next five minutes. We plant a garden in the spring and mulch it in the fall. This morning we made an appointment—a doctor's appointment?—for tomorrow and this afternoon we sent away for a book or a subscription. And this evening we missed a plane—and took the next one or, perhaps, a ride home from the station with a friend whose brakes were worn and who had an appointment to have them relined tomorrow.

But there is no other way to live. Only the monk is ready to die; his affairs alone are in order, ours in cataract. And how hopeless an undertaking it is for our survivors to straighten them out. We all carry our files under our hats, unassorted. Now they will never be sorted. The paper we were going to sign (or not sign) . . . the charity we were going to support . . . the letter half written . . . the sonnet wanting a fourteenth line . . . All, all into the fire, all the things we were going to take care of in the next week or so (or any time now). No time now. No time for a long talk with an old friend; or a reconciliation over an old misunderstanding or a trifle; or a confession to a wife or a husband or a father or a son . . . postponed just a little too long. I think of no one I should treat as I do now if, instead of knowing I am going to die, I expected to.

Medicine, in the past one hundred years—above all, in the past twenty-five—has done one wonder after another. The "killer" diseases of the old have been beaten further and further back. The great killers nowadays—heart disease, cancer, and stroke—are not in the first instance the diseases of age at all but of middle life. These three afflictions account for 71 percent of all American deaths, and we read headlines daily like "Surgeon General Forecasts Era of Hope in Ending Disease," statements like former President Johnson's that "we can look to science for the health programs which will eventually conquer disease and disability"; and we accept the hyperbole because we have seen the validity of so many previous hyperboles in medicine. What, then, if we must die of *some* thing *some* time, shall we die of? Old age?

But we no longer know where to put the finger on old age, not in the era of Senior Citizenry. There are too many active, even strapping, men in their eighties to be seen in every community. Nor do they die of *old age*. Our forefathers would have been incredulous, as we are not, to hear from President E. L. Bortz of the American Geriatrics Society that "there is no known case of death from old age. No pathologist has ever established at the autopsy table that a person dying of natural causes had body tissues correct and adequate in every way except that they had worn out in the process of aging."

The process of aging, if it is ever understood, may be blocked—or so we hear nowadays in ordinarily cautious scientific circles. In a symposium at the New York Academy of Sciences, Dr. Bernard L. Strehler of the National Institutes of Health asserted that the determination of the biological causes of aging "could be achieved within this decade"; Dr. William J. Kolff of the Cleveland Clinic predicted that "an irreparably sick human heart will be replaced in the near future by a mechanical pump"; and Dr. Joel D. Nobel of the Pennsylvania Hospital in Philadelphia urged the establishment of a national commission for aging research whose object "would be to achieve an understanding of the mechanisms of aging and, if possible, of ways by which the mechanisms may be deliberately manipulated." The sober-sided participants all agreed that they saw no insuperable obstacle—assuming the provision of research facilities—to what they called (in the symposium's title) "The New Medical and Scientific Attack against Aging and Death." The decade ended—the symposium was held in 1966—without the attack's having been launched and without a breakthrough in the determination of the causes of aging, but with the transplantation of the human heart an increasingly common, if still uncertain, procedure in major surgery (and the year-and-a-half survival of a recipient after the operation by a team of South African doctors).

The fact is that man's life span, in contrast with his life expectancy, has lengthened very little. What has happened, with the past half century's spectacular reduction of infant mortality and communicable disease, is that more people in the advanced countries are living out the life span of the Biblical threescore and ten. (The average length of life in the United States is 70.5 years—67 for men, 74.2 for women.) Once a man reaches fifty or so now, his expectancy is almost exactly what it was one hundred and fifty years ago—about twenty-five years. As far back as the human record goes, some few men have always lived to be 100 or even 120; more and more are now. In well-fed societies the percentage of the population over sixty-five will continue to grow, and their life expectancy, once they have reached that age, rises steadily; where only one-fourth of the American people reached seventy-five at the turn of the century, one-half do now. The population is exploding at both ends. ("It's getting so," said a friend of mine, "that you've got to shoot a couple of centenarians to start a cemetery.")

We do not know the limit of human life or whether there is one, though there is no scientific evidence whatever to support the persistent predictions that "research" will any day (or any century) now extend life expectancy much beyond the Scriptural limit. We know that aging is an accumulation of bodily changes that increase one's chances of dying *of disease,* but we do not understand the nature of the changes themselves: why, for instance, a canary, which is about the same size as a mouse and has a much higher metabolic rate—i.e., lives "faster"—should live six to seven times longer.

But age we do, canary, mouse, and man, and for a man to grow old—above all, in an age of youth and mobility and tempo—is to take on an abiding melancholia. I am "on the shelf," and the shelf itself grows bare. I am less and less urgently necessary, less and less often sought. I am not wanted *badly* by anyone except my true love (while she or he lasts). I may not be a nuisance to others, but I may be a bit of a bother. Or I may be a nuisance and know that they would be better off with me out of the way. I, too, would be better off without me—sinking more and more of what I have and am into staying alive. I have surrendered myself to the high priesthood of the doctors, who hold the keys of life and death. And between the doctor and the undertaker, the confrontation of either's bills is enough to discourage the confrontation of the other's.

And so my substance—and my grandchildren's—is surrendered for another week or two of a life that no one values much. I am not wanted badly, except to baby-sit; and then, by and by, not to baby-sit. "She can't hear them cry." "He dozes off all the time." Another five years and I am not wanted at all; and in those five years I have changed from a bit of a bother to a bit of a nuisance; I overhear them refer to me, inevitably, as *querulous.* And in another five—or two or one—I'll be more than a bit of a nuisance to those who have no more need of the very old than they have, in the affluent society, of their teenagers.

It used to be different. It still is, in the "backward" societies, where families do not move from place to place and confront the wretched problem of carrying their old and useless with them. It is different even in the remoter areas of the advanced societies. Grandparents—even great-grandparents—are needed to help peel the potatoes, chop the stove kindling, and, with near-sightless eyes, darn the socks and mend the clothes. Where life has not changed much between generations, the ancient wisdom is something more than ancient crotchet. Grandfather—even great-grandfather—is the ceremonial head of the family. More than ceremonial: Until he dies the property is his, and he knows *its* crotchets and its needs, and the community's. The family does not meet without him to consider its affairs, and now he has the time the community can call on for its counsels. He needs care. But he gives care appropriate to his condition.

It is categorically different in the rapidly changed and changing culture. Now the old are seen first of all—if not exclusively at first— as having to be taken care of. They are superfluous, devalued; they are burdensome. Gunmen have their way of "taking care of" the unwanted. We have devised our own: the Convalescent Home, whose inmates (called guests) are left to convalesce from life. This is not the Old People's Home of times past, where those who had survived their young (or who had none) went. The Convalescent Home is where the old go now because the young cannot survive with them in the house. It is a very expensive indulgence but, apparently, worth it. They are "taken care of," and we visit them for a half hour once a week—"or so."

This is modern life—and death. The end may be wonderfully drugged, but the last years en route are bitter. The realization that one has been read out of the circle of the living—that no one has time to listen—may lead to impotent regrets at first: I might have lived more honorably, or more honestly, or more generously, or less quarrelsomely. But the impotence of regret is angering. My life is getting even with me. I writhe under its torment. Very well: I shall do what I can to get even with it. The contest grows steadily more unequal against me, and I seize whatever weapon comes to hand.

Money. My savings. They all want my money, and all they want is my money. George Eliot's *Middlemarch,* in which the miser on his deathbed actually tries to "take it with him," is only one of a hundred such classics. My money is all I have now, and I'll never have more. How do I know how much I'll need? *They* can earn. Let *them* do it, with their lives ahead of them. In my bitterness I reduce or eliminate my philanthropies. Estate lawyers know well the story of the will redrawn from year to year—or month to month—with progressively meaner provisions. "Then," says Goneril to her sister in *Lear,* "must we look from his age to receive not alone the imperfections of longingrafted condition, but therewithal the unruly waywardness that infirm and choleric years bring with them."

It doesn't always happen, but often enough. And why shouldn't it, until the time arrives, like as not from one day to the next, to know at last that you are beaten? Nobody cares any more what you do or don't do. Neither do you now. Once more—as in childhood and infancy—the long future recedes and with it the immediate past. Only the present remains, with the long past and the immediate future that belongs properly to the present. The web of relationships, broken a thread at a time, is gone now. Friends, enemies, praise, dispraise;

snubs, jilts, compliments, hand-pats; allotments, assignments, letters, calls, numbers, forms, bills, credits, taxes, cars, houses; war, peace— all gone now. The newspaper lies on the table unopened.

When society was relatively stable and knowledge relatively unchanging, the wisdom of the aged was profoundly prized, and when West finally met East, it turned out that age in the Orient was not only respected for its wisdom but revered as a bridge to holy ancestry. But the tempo of technological change in the past two hundred years or so has accelerated to the point where Elder Statesman Herbert Hoover, an engineer by trade, had to say of satellite television, "I belong to a generation that just doesn't understand all that." It is no longer an open question whether the old are old fogies. It is a fact. And it will be from now on, as electronic man, walking the moon, reaches out for the planets: Each generation of us in our dotage will belong to a generation that just does not understand "all that."

7: The Love of Death

THAT LIVING should grow no more perfect with our practice of it—and, unlike all of our other undertakings, be most difficult when we have had the most practice of it—is enough to touch every satisfaction with conscious or unconscious dejection, every joy with evanescence. The agreement of the thoughtful men of all times is general, if not universal: Life is hard, *la vie est dure, ernst ist das Leben.*

Oh, there are passages of exquisite pleasure, and others of contentment, and others of rest; occasions (and not a few, to give it its due) when the gods and the muses bestow nepenthe and even nirvana, for a day or a night, or a week or a month or two; but they are occasions, and they pass and leave us with envy and pride tormented, ambition dismayed, humiliation sustained and recalled, betrayal suspected, loss and the fear of loss suffered; withal a perpetual irritation that boards the boat with us in the frenzied seizure of a holiday from it. The monotony alone persuaded Francis Bacon that "a man would die, though he were neither valiant nor miserable, only upon a weariness to do the same thing so oft over and over"; and a great university president of our own time to answer a young man's question as to the aim of life by saying, "The aim of life is to get through it."

Or let the gods smile more incessantly than their wont, and let the middle years be a continuum of delights; what do they bring, every day closer, than the time of incapacity of those delights, of subsidence of every appetite and the perpetual petulance of their recollection? Recall in misery ecstasy; Francesca and Paolo were condemned in Dante's Hell to suffer nothing worse than this. The slow but ever accelerating increment of limitations, to be capstoned and concluded by the absolute limitation that alone liberates us from the process. The physical torments may be ameliorable, but not the "mental"; for them no sedative is surcease.

It is likely, these days, that I shall know for some months or years that I am a "terminal case." The term approaches. I have nothing to do but wait, and the days that rushed me on implacably, each shorter than the last, are long now, as they were in early June in my childhood when I *couldn't wait* for school to be out. Wait—and stare reprehensively at the things that I know will outwait me. This ten-cent bowl of clay, this pot, this pan, this shoelace; and this bulb will bloom; and this grass will grow, this tree, this puppy, and yes, on the last day, this day will break. . . . The whole world—only not I—will get up, brush its teeth, eat its breakfast, and set off for work or school. The weather will be forecast, the bread baked, the cows milked. Streets and shops will be crowded, traffic lights will change from green to red to green. . . . I shall not be here. (Or anywhere?) *Le moulin n'y est plus, mais le vent y est encore.*

Only see how the thorn outlasts the rose.

If I could live my life over again. Yes? And what, pray tell, would you do that you didn't do this time around, and what wouldn't you do that you did? ("If I had to live my life over again," said a Frenchman who had lived his life, "I would shoot myself.") What you mean, my friend, is "If I could live that part of my life over again when I was having the time of my life," or, perhaps more accurately, "when I was having the time of my life as I now remember it." What you want is to put between you and death the years that you would gain by living them over, not then, but right now.

Do you envy the young? I do. I envy them their powers, and their failure to use them profitably horrifies me (as mine horrified my elders). The books I might have mastered (and the girls?). The arts I might have learned (and the tricks?). Envy them, unlined, unwrinkled, unsagged, undieted, unoperated. Why? For those few years? It will be their turn to be lined and wrinkled and confront what you confront: the coming of death. Socrates slyly asked his friends if they believed that he would live forever if only he got away from his jailers this time.

You are greedy. (I, too.) You have had enough, like the child at the cookie jar. You are already surfeited, even queasy. And you want more. Very well, then: Retire to the vomitorium and come back for more. But the process, as the Romans discovered, and as the monkey, alternatively itching and scratching, discovered before them, is a wasting pleasure; and in any case there is no spewing your sorrows like your cookies.

Ah, but you would not make all the mistakes of excess and deficiency you made this time around; you know better now. Do you, indeed? I submit that your assurance rests on sand. It involves the implicit assumption that there is such a thing as an increase in the knowledge of living—an assumption which implies (a) that there is such a thing as the knowledge of living and (b) that it binds us to obey its law like the multiplication table—i.e., that a "reasonable man" does what he knows. On these dubious assumptions rests the grand assumption that living teaches us how to live. If it did, the old would be wise, and the world which they rule would be a wise old world. No; the hypothesis, indemonstrable in fact, is undemonstrated in analogy. You might live better the next time, or the same, or much worse. And fate, or chance, or accident, will determine it in all events, just as it did this time.

Great Goethe at seventy-five assayed the course of his existence as "nothing but pain and a burden . . . the perpetual rolling of a rock that must be raised up again forever"; he had not, he insisted, had as much as four weeks of genuine well-being. And who was greater or more successful than he, unless it was Martin Luther, who, when the Electress Dowager said to him, "Doctor, I wish you may live forty years more," replied, "Madame, rather than live forty years more, I would give up my chance of Paradise." Schopenhauer likened life to a pendulum swinging between pain and boredom and thought that to desire immortality "is to desire the eternal perpetuation of a great mistake"; and Mark Twain topped *him* to say that "whoever has lived long enough to find out what life is, knows how deep a debt of gratitude we owe to Adam, the first great benefactor of our race. He brought death into the world."

You quote me Plato and Cicero—and, of course, Abou Ben Adhem —and a hundred or a thousand other old men in praise of old age. I say more power to them (and wonder if they were praising or defending). You have heard of the masterpieces Michelangelo and Verdi and Goethe and Tennyson produced in their eighties—and Titian and Holmes in their nineties. I say more power to them (and wonder if you could name another half dozen). You have known men who died serenely. I say more power (and wonder how well you knew them, and recall how well I finally got to know old Harry Herndon, full of years and directorates, who, at the last, sat there and mumbled and remumbled the tale of his fraternity brothers' scheme to have him deflowered sixty-five years before, and how he turned and ran, and how they taunted him).

How many of these serene old men could say, "It is finished," meaning (as Christ seems to have meant) that all they needed to do here was done? The shorter the time, the greater the hurry; but the time is shortest when the ability to hurry is lowest. Heine called, "Paper! Pencil!" and died. Which of us lesser men is satisfied to leave lesser works unfinished, to know no more of the future, how a war or an election or a world's series will end, or how our children or grandchildren will fare, or whether our survivors will be financially secure? Who does not "have" to do some small or great thing yet, or see another spring or a friend again or hear a sonata or drain a glass or write a letter or repair the roof?

So we hang on, *for dear life*. At any and every cost, we hang on. We lower our sights, cut the cloth to fit the condition, and hang by an ever slenderer thread. With Faust we plead, "Stay—thou art so fair." What, then, of life's reprobation by the Goethes and the Luthers? Can they be right? It would seem not, for even in modern America, with its high suicide rate, only one person in ten thousand takes the advice of the Roman Stoics and unencumbers himself of life; and of these few some several do so in derangement or panic and not in settled determination. Proof enough of the life instinct, if the bargain is a bad one *and still we cling to it*. Did not Satan say of Job, "All a man hath he will give for his life," and the Lord reply, "Save his life"?

We cannot say, because all men have died, that all men will. A nice point—as the lawyers say—but a point. Who of us of *a certain age* has not wondered off the battlefield, like the soldier on it, if he might not be spared, or his whole generation? Dying of cancer, or dreading it, we or our loved ones wonder if a cure will not be found in time, in the last week, or the last day. But Shakespeare died, and Shelley at twenty-six, and many a mute, inglorious Shelley at six, or at six months. Why they and not you and I? There is little enough justice here below as it is; shall I be left in profligate possession of my life and my worthy grandfather deprived of his?

The obstacles to eternal life on earth are not theological (as witness the doctrine of resurrection). Augustinian theology (among others) suggests that man in the Garden was corporeally immortal and lost his immortality, in which case death may be said to be older than life. But natural man, born of woman, is no longer innocent; he is only ignorant, knowing only enough to know that he is not innocent. He is not, however, content to be ignorant, and his presumption (that got him into trouble in the first place) knows no end. He has no hesitation to take hold of the tree of life and convert it into knowledge, pulp, or plastics. The Man in Black may be willing to wait for the return of the Second Adam to be born again; not the Man in White.

Death is the failure of a system or, more precisely, a system of systems. Every part depends upon every other, and accident or disease (if it is serious enough) cannot be localized. The special difficulty—and this is the central distinction between the living organism and the inorganic system—is that the parts are in constant motion. We don't know if at some point nature, the master mechanic, finds it just too expensive to keep the old bus going. We have supposed so.

So strong has the supposition always been that irreversible chemical changes are assumed to be responsible for man's embryonic development, his growth, his decline, and his death. These changes—which we don't understand—are supposed to constitute a kind of mechanism. As man turns his intellectual engines on death and looks for its causes, he bethinks him of every possible kind of "antibody." Is there, for example, a "death hormone," produced (like other hormones) by the organism, that kills us either by its own action or by activating what we now take to be the causes of death? (In reporting this hypothesis in the *Saturday Review,* one writer made the understatement of the ages when he said that a drug designed to counteract that hypothetical hormone "would be of considerable interest.")

Fifty years ago Freud was "astonished to find how little agreement exists among biologists on the question of natural death," and it is a pretty fair guess that he would be at least as astonished today. As we learn more about the causes of the "causes" of death, and attack those causes, with faltering success, we wonder more and more often whether man without whiskey, whipped cream, war, and a few other ancient and modern conveniences would have to die. This is not to suggest that Rousseau's noble savage lived forever, for the wild animals do not; he would have to be able to protect himself against accident, infection, and (hardest of all) against other men, in addition to his being protected against his own tastes and passions. But take a man's whiskey, whipped cream, and war away from him—Winston Churchill went to a resplendent ninety on some such diet—and it is not certain that he would not be interested in living very long, or at all. (When Philip Blaiberg died in August 1969, as the longest-lived survivor of a heart-transplant operation performed in January 1968, his doctors said he never recovered from a relapse which they blamed on his "living it up too much" after the original operation.)

There are thousands of kinds of living creatures that die "as sure as you're born" and thousands that don't die and live on, as far as we know, forever. The living immortals are the untold number of almost all the classes and orders of Protozoa, and unicellular (or, to be zoologically more particular, noncellular) animalcules almost all of which reproduce by fission, or a splitting or division of the "mother" into two or more "daughters." Given access to temperate water and not too much salt—and, of course, food, but they are not at all choosy—they are immortal in the sense that they go on living and never die. (Of course, they lose their personality when they divide, but they don't seem to have had much to begin with.)

Assume the hypothesis that human life as we now know it might be extended indefinitely. The world would be untenantable in no time; with no infant mortality, every generation would double the number of the living, unless birth control were universal and absolute; with the present accelerating increase of 2 percent a year, more than double. The consumer burden of the very first generation of the nonproductive aged would starve out the race, unless, in that very first generation, the hard-pressed young reverted to primitivism and killed off their parents.* But these cataclysms might well be reckoned the least of the scheme's disadvantages.

It is the prospect of death that gives life its form and its meaning, that gives love its poignancy, that occasions concern and kindness and consolation. And time; as Heidegger points out, we really know time because we know we are going to die. Without this passionate realization of our mortality, time would simply be a meaningless circle of the clock. For man is not in time, but time in man. It is not time that marches on, but we.

Love, and kindness, and time; and biography, the shape of life. Without death we should never have the measure of a man. We should not know what a good or a bad, successful or unsuccessful, happy or unhappy human life was, or what we might do (or try to do) to achieve the one and avoid the other. We should have no models of childhood, youth, maturity, old age, or the whole of life seen as a whole, because there would be no whole. We are witnessing, these days, an increasing, and an increasingly unsatisfying, wholelessness in our lives, with the dislocations of protracted adolescence and suppressed senility, with childish thirty-year-olds at one end and childish sixty-year-olds at the other; with television advertisements for soap-

---

* Nobel Prize-winning geneticist Herman J. Muller, asked about the "prospect of immortality" through freezing, thought that it should be more readily possible in the future "to use both genetics and methods of treatment of the developing individual as well as improved educational methods to produce better people than to reform revived individuals whose past was in an earlier age. . . . It seems to me that we would be extremely selfish in a misguided way to want to intrude upon these later generations. Moreover, I think they would quietly wipe us away, and we, of course, would never know the difference. I would not blame them a bit for this."

suds in which the mother's hands cannot be told from the daughter's. The generations blend and merge on the surface, parents affecting chumminess with their children (a chumminess which the younger party rejects with, quite literally, a vengeance). The rambunctiousness of the too-long young is the corollary of the rambunctiousness of the not-soon-enough old.

Love, kindness, time, biography—and progress. The *mortmain* of the living dead: Without death there would be a geriocracy—the tyranny of the old bores whose grip on power and prestige could not be shaken and whose wealth could not be subjected to distribution. They would, even as we, mere octogenarians and nonagenarians, "belong to a generation that just doesn't understand all that"; and what they did not understand they would not encourage. And they would be hated for their domineering uncomprehension. An end, to be sure, to recklessness and to ruinous abandon; but an end, too, to discovery and exploration and experimentation and invention and daring.

An end to love, kindness, time, biography, progress; and to deadline and decision, choice and consequences, fulfillment and failure, sorrow and the memory of a spray of mignonette. An end to the momentousness of the moment, "this-is-it," to what the German calls *Einmaligkeit,* once-onliness.

Don't we live long enough, on the whole? What would most of us do with more time? When men lived to be thirty or so, men did great things at thirty or so—Jesus, Alexander, Mozart, Napoleon—and when they live to be seventy or so, they do not do many more great things than these. What do we do with the time that Jesus, Alexander, Napoleon, and Mozart did not have? Why, we kill time. But only in our spare time, we say. But if we have time to spare, what do we want more time for? To spare? What we would do with more time is probably what we have done all along. So we lose the great efforts of a Dr. Tom Dooley at thirty-five or of a T. S. Eliot at seventy-five; but we lose the mischievous efforts of others who, like them, might live on—and the empty efforts of most. Would we *dare* to have time without end?

The record thus far is one of animadversions. Goethe, Luther, and a train of great and small men before and since have so persuasively advanced the disconsolate view that the only dry eye in the house is Death's; the rest of us are reduced to the swan song of the dying swan, echoing Swinburne's *Garden of Proserpine:*

> From too much love of living,
> From hope and fear set free,

> We thank with brief thanksgiving
>> Whatever gods may be
> That no life lives forever;
> That dead men rise up never;
> That even the weariest river
> Winds somewhere safe to sea.

But what is this about "too much love of living"? We lift our eyes from the stanzas of dilapidation and look about us and see the lusty bustle of men—and women and children—at work and play. We see the everyday contentment on the faces of most of those we meet; their lives are satisfying enough. They have their bad moments and their bad spells and their bad luck, but the bad passes, too, and retrospect soon softens it. Of course there are difficulties and handicaps and disappointments. But see how little they come to: See the paralyzed and the paraplegic enjoying the kaleidoscopic spectacle of nature and art; see the blind invigorated by music; see the old catching up on their reading and their conversation, as vividly engaged by their checkers or their shuffleboard or their crocheting as you by your first day in kindergarten or your last day in college or your appointment as executive vice-president.

Life is good!

Old Faust in his closet says, "I long for death, existence I detest," but Mephisto the Traveling Man replies from the eternal experience which polls the opinion of the race: "And yet Death never is a wholly welcome guest." And I, too, though I have been told that there have been men who wanted to die, and have heard some say so themselves, have never known one, not one, of whom I was sure that he would not want to live tomorrow, or ten minutes from now, unless he was dying just then and in excruciation. "I could have died laughing"; could he have?

We conscious *mortals* have everything to lose by dying and nothing to gain. We conscious mortals . . . But what of us *unconscious* mortals, every one of us, whose unconsciousness is of the proportions of the iceberg beneath the surface? What of the cliff-hanger, clinging by his fingertips—is he working as hard to hang on as he is to repress the wish to let go and lie down to rest? "I am dying," said St. Theresa, "of not being able to die."

Many a pre-Freudian recognized the Freudian death instinct, among them Montaigne in the sixteenth century. Montaigne's Mother Nature is speaking to man: "If you had not death, you would eternally curse me for having deprived you of it; I have mixed a little bitterness with it, to the end that, seeing of what convenience it is, you might not too greedily and indiscreetly seek and embrace it. . . ." But Freud gave the instinct its name and traced its genesis in *Beyond the Pleasure Principle:* "At one time or another, by some operation of force which still completely baffles conjecture, the properties of life were awakened in lifeless matter. . . . The tension then aroused in the previously inanimate matter strove to attain an equilibrium; the first instinct was present, that to return to lifelessness. The living substance at that time had death within easy reach. . . . So through a long period of time the living substance may have been constantly created anew, and easily extinguished, until decisive external influences altered in such a way as to compel the still surviving substance to ever greater deviations from the original path of life, and to ever more complicated and circuitous routes to the attainment of the goal of death."

Thus, "the goal of all life is death," and the phenomena we know as life are nothing but these circuitous ways to the goal. What happens, then, to the famous first law of nature? "The postulate of the self-preservative instincts we ascribe to every living being stands in remarkable contrast to the supposition that the whole life of instinct serves the one end of bringing about death. The theoretic significance of the instincts of self-preservation, power, and self-assertion, shrinks to nothing, seen in this light. . . . The organism is resolved to die only in its own way. . . . Hence, the paradox comes about that the living organism resists with all its energy influences (dangers) which could help it to reach its life-goal by a short way (a short circuit, so to speak); but this is just the behaviour that characterizes a pure instinct as contrasted with an intelligent striving."

In his *New Introductory Lectures,* Freud denies that death is the only aim of life: "We do not overlook the presence of life by the side of death. We recognize two fundamental instincts, and ascribe to each of them its own aim." But the life instincts, the erotic or sexual, are the younger and, in the end, the weaker of the two. They "are always trying to collect living substance together into ever larger unities, [while] the death instincts, which act against that tendency, try to bring living matter back into an inorganic condition. The co-operation and opposition of these two forces produce the phenomena of life to which death puts an end." The winner: Death.

The analyst's "self-destructive tendency" is not the *wish* to die but the *need* or *necessity.* We know what it is to wish consciously to die and the ambivalence that attends it. Death's praise, too, and life's dispraise are not manifestations of the death instinct at all; they are

Freud's "intelligent striving." The matter turns on the unconscious. Here is *ennui*—the noun for which English has no precise equivalent —that a man feels consciously. He is simply tired, tired of "it all," and he knows it. Here is the adjective *blasé*—again with no English equivalent—which the man feels, and knows he feels, who is not merely tired of it all but thinks that he has seen and known it all and has, in the American vulgate, "had it." But even to act out this sentiment in the form of suicide is not the death instinct.

Indeed, suicide, under extreme provocation of one kind or another of suffering, may be the recourse of the "part-instincts" of self-preservation against what is felt to be destroying the self. But purposive suicide, "getting it over with," probably represents the smallest proportion of all self-destructive patterns of behavior. The forces of adventuresomeness may be destructive or constructive, and they may inspire the daredeviltry (or self-sacrifice) that is sure or almost sure to be fatal, death being the one adventure the daredevil hasn't had. We approach the death instinct a little closer in the "accident-prone" person or the man who is drinking himself to death.

The Freudian hypothesis is, in effect, that every human being is a suicide. Without knowing it, we are trying harder to die than to live. Death is the only cure for what ails us all. We don't want to go back to the living womb, to a sheltered life; what we want to go back to is the Biblical dust. It is all right for a sentimentalist like Tennyson to say that "no life that breathes with human breath/Has ever truly longed for death," but a hard-boiled old hand like Satan ought to know better than to say that "all that a man hath will he give for his life." On the contrary, say the Freudians; you are taking man's *word* for it; he will, in fact, give all that he has to die.

Look at it this way: My whole life long I invite the Devil to try to destroy my soul. (Not that he wouldn't try uninvited.) It is a game we play, he and I, he with his fatal temptations and I with my surrender to them right up to the point where they might be fatal; and then, ah-ha, foxed him again. The Devil, with his works and pomps, interests us. We can admit it privately, can we not? Why, then, shouldn't death, which my whole life long is trying to destroy my body, be an interesting part of life? Why shouldn't I flirt with it, as I do with the Devil, and, as the bullfighter does, with the crowd spellbound? Is the Spaniard less civilized than the Swiss or the Swede, or is he not, rather, more interested in living (and in death as a seamless part of life), a *livelier* man than his neighbors to the frostbitten north?

Many, perhaps most, of Freud's eminent successors came to downgrade the master's death-instinct theory, arguing (as does Bruno

Bettelheim) that "it is not the battle between the sex and death instincts that govern man's life, but a struggle of the life drives against
fear of death." In short, there is a fear of, not a drive toward, extinction. But the orthodox Freudians may have many common folk with
them these recent days. Thirty years after the beginning of World
War II (which began twenty-five years after World War I) we
see that the unabating preparation for the war that will end the
world is the leading activity of every great government, and we
know that every previous such armaments race has ended in war.
While each "side" blamed the other for the failure of disarmament
discussions and each side challenged the other with new "ultimate"
weapons, the President of the United States solemnly announced that
the United States could "deliver" three times as many missiles as
the Soviet Union—and just as solemnly added that the population
centers of both nations would be destroyed. But man, and man everywhere, sits in the midst of this gathering gloom and says, "What can a
man do? Nothing."

Reporting "a long conversation with a leading university consultant
to the State Department and a major bureau chief of one of the big
news magazines," John McDermott wrote in the *New York Review:*
"Both agreed that the war [in Vietnam] would either go on indefinitely
or lead to war with China. Both agreed nothing could be done.
Through his magazine the bureau chief had good intelligence on the
more political segments of the business community. . . . What about
them? What are they doing about it? 'Nothing,' he replied, 'there is
nothing that can be done.' " The bureau chief was wrong about the
immobility of the business community. In August of 1969—man had
just walked the moon—the Bekins Company announced its Survival
West project, to preserve and process the records of two thousand
major American business firms in a self-sustaining underground city
near the small town of Coalinga, California. Construction (including
a computer center) would be completed in 1971, and the corporate
tenants (represented by a thousand "lucky" programmers and their
families) would be able to conduct their operations for thirty days
after a "catastrophe" destroyed their surface operations. Distinguishing Survival West from the civil-defense bomb-shelter fiasco of the
1950s, the Bekins spokesman said, "Our purpose is to serve business,
not people. . . . There is nothing in government planning to preserve
business and industry. National defense policies are aimed at preserving the ability to attack."

Those who say "Nothing can be done" may be right or wrong; they
are probably right. But that is not the point. The point is that man,

not as an individual but as a species, has got to this point—to the point of what Herbert Marcuse calls "the exalted acceptance of death." Is may saying, "Better dead than Red [or white, or blue]," or is he saying, without knowing it, simply, "Better dead"?

From time to time an animal psychologist reports the extraordinary behavior of a mouse cornered by a cat. The game, as the cat sees it (and—who knows?—perhaps the mouse, too), has gone on until the cat is bored with it. The mouse seems to sense that his time has come. The cat sits back on his haunches and stares at his victim. And the mouse proceeds to preen himself sedately, like a fop before the mirror. He smoothes his coat and his whiskers with his forepaws—and takes his exquisite time about it. The cat seems to appreciate the gesture and never moves a muscle. At last the mouse's preparation is finished, and he faces the cat.

8: Who's Afraid?

THE REAL pre-Freudian was Sir Thomas Browne, the seventeenth-century physician and putter-of-things-in-their-place. "The long habit of living," he wrote, in his *Vanity of Earthly Monuments,* "indisposeth us for dying." Life *is* a habit, and every habit binds us the tighter the longer we practice it. Twentieth-century man should, on this count, be more indisposed for dying than his ancestors, for he has more of the habit of living by some thirty years per man. And the habit of gung-ho, or living it up, which was confined to the seventeenth-century few, is nowadays extended to the many.

But there is little doubting that, as machinery has replaced bodily exertion, man's life has been becoming progressively less physical and crude and progressively more mental and aesthetic. Those who deplore the whoop-and-holler of modern culture tend to ignore the much more stupendous spread of education and the arts. The Old Adam is still there, beating the drums; but the Egghead is cooking on a scale beyond the wildest hopes of those who first thought that man was more than an incorrigible brute.

Modern, mental man probably pays more attention to death than the physical man of yore. That is, he probably thinks about it more, though the physical man of yore (and of now) was (and is) probably more fearful of the sure deprivation of the more obvious long habit of corporeal activity. Modern, mental man has found a thousand ways to conceal the indelicacies of life. But dying is nearly always indelicate and undignified. Its ugliness mocks every beauty, real and cosmeticked. Every disguise and pretense falls in inexorable ruin as he proceeds, little by little, to the indistinguishable condition of the cave man and the composer of the "Ode on a Grecian Urn." In the process he must be "attended to," the continent man incontinent, the temperate man intemperate, the aesthetic man unaesthetic; the operator operated, the manipulator manipulated, and proud man prone and lowered.

And he does not bear pain as well as he thought he might—or, in any case, he is afraid that he won't. He may comport himself like a child, utterly incapable of the advice he admired when Marcus Aurelius pointed out that the complaints of the body are *its* complaints, not his. Man is not nearly as stolid as the lower animals which suffer pain unmurmuring or with only a whimper; so, it would seem, the further his civilized life is from theirs, the less stolid. Besides, the ubiquitous and effective pain-killers of our time relieve him of the habit; only a "masochist" would have a tooth out (not to say a leg off) without an analgesic.

But by the same token the physical pain of dying is minimized. The painless extraction of teeth has been extended to the painless extraction of people. These days we may die happily forever after, under constant, increasing sedation. We have not yet had a treatise entitled "Dying Can Be Fun"; but we know that it need not be agony. Then, too, life seems to prepare itself, perhaps for death, but in any case for dying: It releases us, little by little, from the needs that, little by little, become incapable of fulfillment. We have been letting our old friends go, our old interests unclutch as we develop what Lewis Mumford calls an "inner deafness and blindness" to the coming and going of captains and kings and the crises of personal, social, and political life. Life consists of falling further and further behind, in any case. Why not drop out, like the student with a hopeless record of Incompletes in his courses? The fatigue of age brings its own relief. Time loses its urgency, and the hand that can still turn the calendar leaves it unturned. This is the "providential amnesia" of common medical observation, the gradual withdrawal to the point where (as Hazlitt says) death consigns only the last fragment of what we were to the grave.

And still we are afraid to die. The timeless Chinese custom on celebrative occasions—to wish the celebrant a happy death—would ruin the party anywhere in the Western world. A happy death; what would a happy death be? A quick one? Give me my choice, to die tonight in an airplane crash or ten years from now in long lonely pain, and I will try my cunning and say, "Make it fifteen . . . make it twenty. . . ." We live always with both death and dying, and modern medicine gives us increasingly longer notice of the appointment; types of cancer and cardiovascular diseases that only a generation ago carried a man off on the instant or in three months have so far yielded to research that their progress may be restrained for ten years or twenty and, in the direst of them, for many months. Death sits longer at our bedside than it did before, and makes itself at home; it can wait.

And we with it. There are two worlds—the world of the living and the world of the dying. And "they," the living, and "we," the dying, both know it. They visit us ever less frequently, and speak with us ever more perfunctorily. What have they to say to us, or we to them? In the Rest-in-Peace Home or Convalescent Hospital we are abandoned; but it is life that has abandoned us, and the living can no more help themselves than us. They smile "cheerfully" and ask us if we "want anything." No; we smile wanly and shake our heads. Do we want anything? Only to be alive—or maybe dead. We are waiting. They are waiting. Death is waiting. Life alone has moved on.

Men, says Epictetus, are disturbed not by the things which happen but by the opinions about the things. "Death," he adds airily, "is nothing so terrible . . . the opinion about death, that it is terrible, is the terrible thing." But Santayana, in our own time, insists upon looking at the matter in a different way entirely from Epictetus *and* from Freud. In his essay on Lucretius, he says that "nothing could be more futile than to marshal arguments against that fear of death which is merely another name for the energy of life. . . . [If] the love of life were extinguished, the fear of death, like smoke rising from that fire, would have vanished also." Precisely the opposite, says Plutarch (b. A.D. 46), taking issue with Santayana (b. A.D. 1863): "It is fear of death, not craving for life," says our ancient Greek in his *Contentment,* "that makes a fool hang on to his body and wind himself about it. . . ."

Plutarch and Santayana cannot agree. Can you and I? Hardly. But we can agree on some subsidiary issues involving the nature of the fear of death. We can agree that we see death—as mortalists, now —as an everlasting kind of night. Night and the unknown . . . the *dead of night* . . . Hamlet's "witching time of night, when churchyards yawn, and hell itself breathes out contagion to this world." Night and the unknown . . . the two things we fear with good reason . . . The time of helplessness, when our blinded senses deceive and disarm us against the enemy . . . the time of the stealthy attack . . . the time when we are defenseless against disaster striking at us while we sleep, against crime in a hidden doorway or around a corner. This dread of the dark—so readily seen in childhood, so hollowly defied later on—is intensified by darkness; silence. The racket of the day reassures us; now the world is spectral-still. The time of all despair, "the prisoner's hour," the time when we are prey

to that awful affliction, middle-of-the-nightis, that raises up every real
or imaginary evil. The dead of night.

But perhaps the greater terror arises in our impotence to imagine
incorporeality, the nonpossession of the body with its senses. Non-
sensitivity is inconceivable; conception begins in the senses. We cannot imagine not being hurt or hurtable. The worms, the sharks, the
buzzards torment us while we live, as they will not when we are dead
and they have their way; * and thus the hospital eye-banks (and now
kidney-banks) beg the sensitive living for their sense-less organs and
the medical schools beg for cadavers, and there are not enough; we
are afraid of being hurt when we know that we won't be.† We cannot
believe that "it" won't hurt, and this in spite of our universal experience with anesthesia.

Under local anesthetic we have seen ourselves cut and sutured and
we know that anesthesia intercepts pain, but neither seeing nor knowing is believing: In order to prepare my mother's grave, the diggers
had to move my father's headstone; they lifted the stone, and underneath it was a maggot, white and fat, curling itself against the daylight, and I shuddered. As, on another occasion, an intelligent woman
of my acquaintance shuddered when the discussion, after a friend's
funeral, turned on cremation: "Fire," she said, "seems to me such a
horrible way to die."

The terror of the endless dark and the terror of being chewed or
nibbled or torn to pieces are terror enough; but they are not the
ultimate terror. The ultimate terror is not to be *dead and gone;* the
ultimate terror is to be *gone*. Death means that I shall be no more—
not you, or he, or they, but *I*. Your death, his, and theirs I can bear,

---

* Inquiry up and down the block indicates that small boys no longer sing
the words to the classic dirge which I sang, with uncertain and therefore
exaggerated gaiety in my small boyhood. (But maybe I canvassed the wrong
block.) I don't remember all of them, or any of them exactly: *Did you ever
think/when the hearse rolls by/that the next time/it may be/you or I? The
worms crawl in/the worms crawl out/they crawl/all over your/face and
snout/Your teeth fall out/and your eyes fall in/They crawl/all over your/
mouth and chin. . . .*

† Writing on "Our Shameful Waste of Human Tissues" in *The Religious
Situation 1969,* Massachusetts theologian Joseph Fletcher quotes Dr. Abraham
Kantrowitz of Brooklyn's Maimonides Hospital: "It is not right to bury seventeen good organs when a man dies." Apart from the prospective donor's
queasiness, the Reverend Mr. Fletcher blames what he calls the "bier barons"
—"When there is no body, there is no funeral"—and their embalmers, "who
find it easier to inject their fluid into a single and undivided system." Typical
organ shortage for transplantation: "In New York City fifty to a hundred
victims of kidney disease each day and only 700 renal transfers each year; four
thousand livers needed a year and almost none donated. U.S. medical schools
need 7,400 cadavers a year; they get 2,000 unclaimed from the morgues and
six hundred bequeathed."

however hardly; my wife's, my husband's, however desperately—but mine I cannot. This *I* is really all there is; the whole world otherwise is a procession that passes, and I alone fixed, like the dignitary in the reviewing stand. Is not mankind divided into "I" and "thou," and is not all the rest of mankind "thou"?

Of course I love others, and my good will toward the rest is enormous. But I *can* live without them all—only not without myself. *My* annihilation is out of the question. I won't hear of it. I am only a small man, but I am *some*body, am I not? And only think of the great man, the indispensable great man, wielding great power and surrounded by thousands or millions to do his bidding. In his biography of William Randolph Hearst, W. A. Swanberg tells us that the Newspaper King would not allow death to be mentioned in his presence.

Just see what it is that death asks of me. It asks not all that I have, but the very I that have it. Who knows what it is to be I? None. None can. I alone, always alone, with my inalienable identity, my consciousness my only infallible and immutable informant that I am Jones, not Smith. And death will murder it.

That I should *not be.* No. Ask everything else of me, my husband's life or my wife's, my mother's, my father's, my child's. When they die, I am bereft. *I,* not they; and this, in honesty, is the meaning of their deaths as my perception and embrace of them is the meaning of their lives. You have crushed a finger, stubbed a toe? I sympathize. But *I* have crushed a finger, stubbed a toe. I *suffer.* Every man is an island. All life is private life. What is closest-related to me *is,* in proportion to its closeness; what isn't related to me *isn't,* be it fire or flood or battle or the rustling of a tree in the forest.

This *I,* this essence, this ego is more than what I love best; it is, when the chips are down, what I love alone; in it, and in it alone, resides all the rest of my love. And the modern psychological and philosophical arts—if existentialism may be said to be a philosophical art—pay it all their compliments. They call for its recognition of its alienness and its solitariness. They urge its liberation from myth and superstition and dependence, its development, its realization, its fulfillment—even though its fulfillment may prove to deny my social responsibility and the preciousness of others.

The existentialist commitment to "being yourself"—or its hippie counterpart, to "be what you are"—squares ill with the existentialist thesis that life is meaningless. You say that I am an aggregate of mucus, calcium salts, and corpuscles, in the process of becoming a handful of dust. I say that if this is what I am, to be what I am is unacceptable to me. No; rather cast my lot with the self-consciousness

of the romantics or the subjective transcendentalism of the phenome-
nologists and proclaim that egocentricity is the only reality. The night
is nothing; the worms are nothing; the loss of *I myself* is unbearable.

"In the final reduction I go a long way with the man to whom I had
once to say that his wife was dead. He gave me a puzzled look. 'Dead,
eh?' he said, and then with a wistful glance into the middle distance,
he said, 'Dead, eh? Blimey, it's a funny old life.' " * This is what is
known as "taking it philosophically"—by which expression we mean
not philosophically but stolidly. Your philosopher, like your scientist,
has got to be stolid in order to do his work; but his work is reasoning,
not blimeying, and with respect to life and death it is philosophical
reasoning that pursues "the final reduction." But in vain. For your
philosopher has got to reason about death, because his proper work
is the meaning of life, and life without death would mean something
very different from anything it might mean now. So philosophy ends
in the mystery and is forever circumscribed by the human condition.
There may be a philosophy of history, but (except chronologically)
there is no history of philosophy; knowing no more of death than
Adam, we know no more of life.

"Teach us to number the days of our years" is the Psalmist's
prayer. No man knows when (as we say these days) his number is
up. (And what if the airline pilot's number comes up while we are
aboard?) Is it not philosophically plain, then—to us as it was to
Marcus Aurelius—that we must live this day as if it would be our
last? Plain as a pikestaff; but we do not do it; and neither did Marcus;
still less the Psalmist. We do not do it, nor did they, because the soul
is the prisoner of the body, its servant instead of its master. What we
must do, then, says the philosopher, is spend our lives loosening the
body's fetters and liberating the soul. We must learn to live without
that vermiform appendix, the body. We must spend our lives learning
—imperfectly, to be sure, for it is always with us—to resist its petulant
yammer and say No to its petulant claims. We must learn to live
without it, giving no thought to what *it* shall eat or *it* shall wear or *it*
shall cry out for or against. Only thus can a man approach the realm
of being instead of flailing fruitlessly about in the world of becoming.
The instant he says, "I am ready to die," he is free; and the sooner he
says it, the longer his freedom. *His resignation is on the table.* Now he
can turn to the things that are proper to a man: the pure things un-
mixed with clay, accessible only to the instrument which itself is un-

* John Lydgate, M.D., "Where Is Thy Sting?" London *Spectator,* 1961, No.
206.

mixed with clay—the soul. Philosophy, which seeks the disembodied good, seeks it best of all when the philosopher is undisturbed by the wants and grievances of the body. The philosopher—and so he comes down to us from the greatest of them—is "a lover of death."

So living, or striving to live, we may hope, with Socrates, to outgrow life and be dead to the world before we are dying. The modern scientific analyst finds empirically that there are two psychological aspects of dying that seem to be of special significance. One is that "the dying patient, even in the face of death, remains more or less true to his basic personality (the term 'basic personality' is used here to describe an individual's total responsive attitude to his environment and his habitual behavior patterns regarding his physical and mental activities irrespective of the picture he presents to the outside world); the other is the tragic realization of how many people enter their terminal disease with a sense of defeat, failure, and unfulfillment." * The Socratic recipe is the recipe for satisfying the first aspect of dying and avoiding the second.

The modern philosopher does not disagree at bottom with the ancient. But he puts an ever so slight turn upon the perennial doctrine. In general he accepts the condition of resignation on realistic grounds, only arguing that it is resignation to the end of many good things. He substitutes *carpe diem* for the injunction to live every day as if it were the last. And yet there is no irreconcilable quarrel here, for both the ancient and the modern enjoin us to seize the day; the question is only what to do with it.

We suppose we like day-to-day life better nowadays than the ancients did. There are things to savor that our ancestors never had, and devices for escaping their crude inconvenience (if not their refined sorrows). Your old Marcus Aurelius tells me that I shall lie in my tomb tomorrow? Very well—tomorrow, then. The ancient's craven courtship of death, in any conscious degree, is gone. We accept death, yes, but as a proud people accept an enemy occupation. We fraternize with it for the purpose of frustrating it and—who knows?—by some miracle driving it away.

Renunciation survives; a Gandhi says that "man lives freely only by his readiness to die." Words, these, that might have been, and often have been, spoken in ancient days, and they are spoken just as commonly today. But the modern turn upon them is momentous. The modern turn is directed away from outgrowing life and toward the assimilation of death into it. The really modern philosopher enjoins

* Dr. Arnold A. Hutschnecker, "Personality Factors in Dying Patients," in *The Meaning of Death, op. cit.,* p. 237.

us to "embrace death within life." * *Avanti! Sempre avanti!* Death belongs to me, not I to death. Heidegger himself—the existentialist forebear of Sartre and Camus—has described his *Being and Time* as an interpretation of the poet Rilke's Elegies, which close with these lines:

> But if the countless dead were to waken a symbol for us,
> See, they might point to the drooping catkin
> Hanging from the bare hazel; or they might show us
> Rain, as it falls on the dark soil in the spring
> And we, who think of *rising* joy
> Would feel the same emotion
> That almost overcomes us
> When a joyful thing falls.†

Have we not come full circle, then? We are told to compass our falling into our rising. We are told that the whole work of man is to *exist,* and to *exist* he "must direct his life to no other goal but death." ‡ Is not our last philosopher, then, like our first, a lover of death?

---

* Frans Rosenzweig, quoted in *The Shadowed Valley,* by H. J. Schachtel. New York, Alfred A. Knopf, 1962, pp. 180–81.
† N. Wydenbruk. *Rilke—Man and Poet,* New York, Appleton-Century-Crofts, Inc., 1950, pp. 326–30.
‡ Rosenzweig, *op. cit.,* p. 180.

9: The Carrot
and the Stick

DYING may take some doing. Why shouldn't we try to figure out how best to do it? It would seem that the Boy Scout has the heavier assignment; he is expected to be prepared for every contingency. We have only to prepare ourselves for a certainty.

The easiest way, beyond a doubt, is to believe that it isn't going to happen; the next easiest, to be steeled; easiest of all, to be assured that we'll be all right when it's over with. A painful operation, but a minor one. So we are back, at the end, where we started: Dying, like death, turns on the survival of death. What is a little fear, a little pain, a little loss, or even a great deal of all of them, when we know that we shall soon be home in glory?

But the rub is that the immortalist, like the mortalist, must die a *mortal* death, and mortal man is weak. The historical literature of death is, however, persuasive (as is reason) on the point that the believer is at least a little likelier to die easy than the nonbeliever. But the record is replete with the instances of nonbelievers who carried the thing off with as much aplomb as the devout. There is a case to be made that the mundane virtues that carry us well through life carry us well through the mundane exertion of dying.

The moral virtues enable man to resist the pleasures of this life and bear its pains (not the least of which is the pain of resisting pleasure). The agnostic and atheist view of dying puts great store by these virtues, and with considerable weight. For we know that virtues are habits (as are vices) and that virtues (and vices) are formed by repetition of the acts of which they are the habit; the more often we do a thing, the easier it is to do it (and the harder it is not to). He who has the habits of fortitude, temperance, justice, and wisdom is not likely to lose them of a sudden; they have become his settled disposition, James's "second nature." Thus he should be equable in his contemplation of the loss of the pleasures of life and of the pain of its leaving. Let him be virtuous and a philosopher; enough. He requires no crutch and no goad; no hope of heaven, no fear of hell. He has been able to live, and live exemplarily, without religion. Why should he not be able to die without it?

The immortalist is generally pessimistic about man, the mortalist optimistic. The immortalist usually accepts the hope of divine bliss and the fear of divine retribution as the necessary tension to which original sin reduced us all. The mortalist, on the other hand, cannot believe that a grown man must become as a little child in the sense that his righteousness must be induced by bubble gum and bumps; what more, under such conditions, is righteousness than calculation? Israel Zangwill makes the point in his story of the wise man who, upon being informed by the Lord that he would not go to heaven, said, "At last I can do good without fear of reward."

After the eager and ecstatic death of the primitive Christians who believed themselves saved, the history of the Church showed a precipitate decline in the hope of heaven and a precipitate rise in the fear of hell. Piety among nonecstatics seems to be more effectively enjoined by the promise of punishment than it is by the promise of reward. The stick is mightier than the carrot. For a great many centuries Protestants no less than Catholics painted the horrors of damnation in vivider colors than the joys of salvation. The result was a dread of death so strong that many writers (some of them on some sort of sampling basis *) have maintained that it is deeper among believers than nonbelievers—a paradox, but far from an impossibility.

The modern Church tends to re-examine some of its dogmas, and its consideration of eternal damnation may in part reflect its long concern with the apostasy of men and women who simply cannot stomach the traditional outlook. Among the eminent believers who have taken a hard look at the matter is none other than Teilhard de Chardin, the Roman Catholic theologian (and paleontologist) whose *Phenomenon of Man* and *Divine Milieu* have made so great a world impact in the past few years. In the latter work he writes: "Of all the mysteries which we have to believe, O Lord, there is none, without a doubt, that so affronts our human views as that of damna-

* See *The Meaning of Death,* H. Feifel, ed., New York, McGraw-Hill, 1959, pp. 120–22.

tion. . . . We could perhaps understand falling back into nonexistence . . . but what are we to make of eternal uselessness and eternal
suffering? . . . You have told me, O God, to believe in hell. But
You have forbidden me to hold with absolute certainty that a single
man has been damned." Here is a new look, indeed, one which in
many theologies of recent ages goes so far as to ask whether Hell is
anything more than eternal death and the deprivation of the beatific
vision of God.

"The whole creation groaneth in travail until now," said Paul in
the Apostolic age, and in an age that has left the apostles behind,
Karl Barth says that "we live in a sick old world which cries from its
soul, Heal me! . . . In all men, whoever and wherever and whatever
and however they may be, there is a longing for exactly that which is
here within the Bible." Is religious faith only (as Freud has it) "fulfillment of the oldest, strongest, and most insistent wishes of mankind"? Is it an intoxicant to deaden neurosis, an intoxicant without
which "man will have to confess his *utter helplessness* [italics mine]
and his insignificant part in the working of the universe"? "Man," he
goes on, "cannot remain a child forever; he must venture at last into
a hostile world. . . . It is at least something to know that one is
thrown on one's own resources. . . ." And just what resources (the
believer asks) will this *utterly helpless* man have; with what weapons
will he, in Freud's *utter helplessness,* meet Freud's hostile world?

Santayana says that some of man's ills are essentially incurable,
requiring not imaginary cures by secular devices but only help to be
borne. Is Barth's "longing for exactly that which is here within the
Bible" only a defense mechanism against death? To the religious man
this life is nothing but a preparation for the painful birth of death.
Religion is death-centered; the one decoration in the monk's cell is
the skull on his table: *Memento mori.* Macabre, you say, and the
skull replies: "Remember that thou shalt die." Are the modern—and
ancient—"pagans" any less macabre in their nonreligious insistence
that "the goal of life is death"? The religious man thinks that the goal
of death is life. So insisting, he can say that where there's death there's
hope. So insisting, he can answer the mortalist's "live and learn" with
his own "die and learn." To his confessor on the Nazi scaffold, the
Jesuit Father Delp said, "In a moment, Father, I shall know more
than you"; in the midst of death he was in life.

But the fact that immortality may both please us and plead with us
for its acceptance makes it neither more nor less likely; it merely pin-
points the realization (as Niebuhr puts it in his *Beyond Tragedy*) of
"the total human situation which the modern mind has not fathomed.

. . . Man cannot exist without having his eyes upon the future." Consider, on the one hand, the worth we ascribe to the human person and, on the other, the ease with which that person's life is destroyed. "What," says Jacques Maritain, "is the meaning of this paradox? It is perfectly clear. We have a sign here that man knows very well that death is not an end, but a beginning." But we know by faith and by faith alone.

Agreed that the mortalist is in danger of the deadliest sin in both the supernatural and the natural lexicons: despair, despair of others, of trust and friendship and help and finally of life itself. Suicide is left, as the Stoics never wearied of reminding us. But canon law forbids us to take the life that does not belong to us, and not, apparently, canon law alone: A Cuban Communist, dismissed as Labor Minister, killed himself, and this interesting communiqué was issued by the Castro government: "We believe Comrade Augusto Martinez Sanchez could not have consciously committed this act, since every revolutionary knows that he does not have the right to deprive his cause of a life that does not belong to him. . . ." *

Agreed, if you will. Let a Camus say that "life will be lived all the better if it has no meaning" † and an Einstein counter with "The man who regards his own life and that of his fellow-creatures as meaningless is not merely unhappy, but hardly fit for life." ‡ Who would side with the former's sentiment against the latter's? Agreed, then; but the agreement does not make Einstein right and Camus wrong. We may need meaning and want it—and want immortality as the condition of it; but none of that is to say that the meaning or the immortality exists.

We may even agree with the believer's best "argument" of all and still have proved nothing: that without immortality there would be no moral order in the universe. We see—as did Job and all men before and since—how often the wicked prosper and the good suffer in this life. And, seeing it, we say with Socrates that "if death were the end of all, the wicked would have a good bargain in dying, for they would be happily quit not only of their body, but of their own evil together with their souls." Where, then, would there be any justice, truth, or honor? Where, indeed, would such universal concepts ever have originated? What motivation would men have for decency except for the dolt's recognition of his own inability to get away with indecency? Thus Kant's rational requirement of immortality as the practical ne-

---

* New York *Times*, December 9, 1964.
† Albert Camus, *The Myth of Sisyphus*, New York, Knopf, 1961, p. 53.
‡ New York *Times Magazine*, April 24, 1955.

cessity for man's progress toward "the perfect accordance of the will with the moral law . . . a perfection of which no rational being of the sensible world is capable at any moment of his existence."

Agreed, if you will. Agreed, upon hard analysis, that Dostoevsky is right when he says, "If God is dead, everything is allowed," and that the modern mortalist is on shaky or, at least, slippery ground when he replies, "If man is alive he knows what is allowed; and to be alive means to be productive, to use one's powers not for any purpose transcending man, but for oneself, to make sense of one's existence, to be human." * All agreed, if you will; we do not *know,* we have not been *shown,* that God exists and that man survives death, and the probability of both is not advanced, though comfort may be, by the greater problems posed by the contrary propositions.

"Very well, then," says the believer, "how about betting on it?" We are wary at once—wary, and even contemptuous. Is this what your holy faith comes to—a sporting guess as to probability? Do you hold it so uncertainly that the best you can do for it is subject it to the procedure whose very essence is uncertainty? Perhaps the believer blushes a bit—or ought to—as he replies that it is *you,* not *he,* who needs to bet. And some of the most famous of hard-rock thinkers, beginning with Socrates and the Stoics, have not scrupled to advance what is known in the great tradition as "the wager."

Pascal asks us to "weigh the gain and the loss in wagering that God is. Let us estimate these two chances. If you gain, you gain all; if you lose, you lose nothing. Wager, then, without hesitation that He is." If the believer wins the wager, what a triumph for him! And what a defeat for his opponent! But if he loses, and God does not exist, and death is the end, he gets off scot free, for he is not there, or anywhere, when the time comes to settle the account; and his opponent, the dis-believer, is cheated of the fruits of *his* victory by the same token. A horse racer's trick this wager, which might as easily be used to advance the argument (prior to the space age) that the moon is made of green cheese. We have a repugnance, if not in reason, then in proper pride, to this aw-come-on,-what-have-you-got-to-lose formula, to this dangled prospect of a perpetual gala in preference to an occasional ball. Rather with Job proclaim, "Though he slay me, yet will I believe on Him."

Immortality does not follow from God's existence, in any case; im-materiality, yes, but not immortality, and still less the personal im-mortality that seems to be peculiarly rooted in Western individualism.

---

* Erich Fromm, *Man for Himself,* New York, Rinehart, 1947, pp. 248–49.

Herbert Muller, in his *The Uses of the Past,* argues that the modern Westerner rejects the anonymous immortality of the World Soul offered by Hinduism and Platonism because "John Smith not only wants to live forever—he wants to be forever John Smith, hanging on to everything except his warts; and in a heaven swarming with Smiths he still wants to be set apart, or even catch the eye of the Super-Smith." Tillich (among others) points out in *The Eternal Now* that the Bible does not speak of the "hereafter" or of the "life after death." What it does speak of, and with repeated precision, is what follows least of all from God's existence—namely, the resurrection of the body.

"Far be it from us," says Augustine, "to fear that the omnipotence of the Creator cannot, for the resuscitation and reanimation of our bodies, recall all the portions which have been consumed by beasts or fire, or have been dissolved into dust or ashes, or have decomposed into water, or evaporated into the air." True, resurrection of the body is much further from man's comprehension than immortality of the disembodied soul, for the main and simple reason (as Penrod would say) that the perishing of the body is abundantly familiar to us. But the doctrine of corporeal resurrection *of the dead* is bounteously grounded in the New Testament wonder of the Second Coming, the Last Judgment, and the Second Death of the unredeemed, as the immortality of man's soul is not.*

The Creeds recited in nearly all the Western churches sustain the resurrection and fortify the faithful in the harder of the two doctrines. But the harder is at the same time the easier, for it pictures man as he knows himself, and at least appears to circumvent the metaphysical difficulties of separability of soul and body and the independent existence of the soul. A New Jerusalem of *people*—however crowded by space-occupying bodies—makes less of a demand upon our imagination-circumscribed piety than a gathering of even the blithest spirits.

The assemblage of my dust is no mean miracle and is second in splendor only to the Creation itself. Here I am—or was—in the course of a long and peripatetic life having left a fingertip here, an earlobe there, and teeth and hair everywhere, and, in the end having had the disconcerting experience of falling among cannibals, who, having

---

* If the Old Testament is ambiguous on immortality, it is less ambiguous on resurrection. Amid its many stern proclamations of the body's last end in the grave, there are, I think, only two contrary suggestions, if we take Ezekiel's experience in the Valley of the Dry Bones as symbolic: Isaiah 26:19 ("Thy dead men shall live, together with my dead body shall they arise. Awake and sing, ye that dwell in the dust: for thy dew is as the dew of herbs, and the earth shall cast out the dead") and Daniel 12:2 ("And many of them that sleep in the dust of the earth shall awake, some in everlasting life, and some to shame and everlasting contempt").

severally consumed *and assimilated* morsels of me, fell out among themselves and were variously consumed and assimilated. The credulity of the credulous seems to be sore taxed by the doctrine of hale-and-hearty resurrection, as witness the prevalent religious opposition to cremation.

Why is cremation, the proper burial of ancient Greeks (and of ancient and modern Hindus), frowned upon? If, to be sure, the bones and dry dust of my decomposed body are snugly ensconced in one place, I suppose that they are easier reassembled *if it is men who are doing the reassembling.* But it is God, to Whom all such things are equally effortless. Why, then, undertake to keep me from the quick, clean fire? Because—I am told—the disposition of my dead body is no more the proper business of men than the disposition of my live one by suicide. But see how the faithful, with the sanction and co-operation of the Church, embalm me and perfume me and preserve me, even with stout caskets and still stouter caskets around the caskets; is not this a disposition of the body, with as much attempted interference in God's work as cremation itself, and much more lost trouble and lost money besides?

Nature shows us its winnowing ways on every hand, as it did in the Scripture on the seed's need to fall to the ground and die in order to be reborn or to fructify the life-bearing earth. We are not seeds (or leaves or trees). But we are bodies, and the more we get to know about bodies, including falling bodies, the more difficult it is to cling to the belief in their arising. With the increase of scientific knowledge, modern man (including the modern man of faith) grows increasingly ambivalent toward the tradition of death which he inherited.

Nowhere is the ambivalence plainer than in the India of Gandhi and the India of Nehru. In his *All Men Are Brothers,* the Mahatma said that the living faith in God "sustains us in life, is our one solace in death. . . . You may pluck out my eyes, but that cannot kill me. But blast my belief in God, and I am dead." It went without saying that Gandhi's ashes would be ritualistically consigned to the sacred Ganges. But his successor and disciple, dying fifteen years later as the Prime Minister of India, declared that he did not want any religious ceremonies performed for him after his death: "I do not believe in any such ceremonies, and to submit to them, even as a matter of form, would be hypocrisy. . . ." *But* he asked that his ashes (should he die abroad) be sent back to Allahabad and "a small portion of them thrown into the Ganges." This desire, he added, had "no religious significance. . . . I have no religious sentiment in that matter. I have been attached to the Ganges . . . ever since my childhood

and, as I have grown older, this attachment has also grown. . . ."
And so the unbelieving Pandit joined the believing Mahatma in the
flow of the sacred (or, as you will, sentimental) river.

We believe in immortality, said James, because we believe that we
are *fit* for it, that, apart from reward and retribution, we believe that
our life somehow deserves it.* "Can things whose end is always dust
and disappointment be the real goods which our souls require?" Let
man have faith and hope and "his days pass by with zest; they stir
with prospects, they thrill with remoter values. Place round them on
the contrary the curdling cold and gloom and absence of all permanent
meaning which for pure naturalism and the popular science evolu-
tionism of our time are all that is visible ultimately, and the thrill stops
short, or turns rather to an anxious trembling. . . ." †

There is an anxious trembling in the world today. Whatever may
have been man's psychic estate when his atmosphere was faith and
hope, the deliquescence of that faith and hope does not by itself, or
even with the increase of knowledge, appear to have met his most dire
needs—at least not yet. And Jung says, "As a physician I am convinced that it is hygienic—if I may use the word—to discover in death
a goal towards which one can strive; and that shrinking away from it
is something unhealthy and abnormal which robs the second half of
life of its purpose. I therefore consider the religious teaching of a life
hereafter consonant with the standpoint of psychic hygiene. When I
live in a house which I know will fall about my head within the next
two weeks, all my vital functions will be impaired by this thought.
. . . Among all my patients in the second half of life—that is to say,
over thirty-five—there has not been one whose problem in the last
resort was not that of finding a religious outlook on life. It is safe to
say that every one of them fell ill because he had lost that which the
living religions of every age have given to their followers, and none of
them has been really healed who did not regain his religious outlook"
(*Modern Man in Search of a Soul*).

* *Cf.* the hoary thesis that there is no universal wish of man—for food,
shelter, mate, sociality, community—which nature does not gratify, and immortality is such a wish. (The modern critics call this the delusion of the
self-fulfilling wish.)

† *The Varieties of Religious Experience*, New York, Modern Library, 1929,
pp. 136–39.

10: The Art of Dying

IN THE FOXHOLE where we all die, today's nonbeliever may be tomorrow's believer—maybe not. In either event each of us will, some time soon now, join the great majority, and it is not unbecoming (for the flesh is weak) to wonder whether some of the sting can be taken out of the procedure. If Death cannot be cheated, maybe he can be talked into taking it a little easy—and, again, maybe not. It wouldn't seem so, for the art of dying graciously is nowhere advertised, in spite of the fact that its market potential is greater than gracious living's.

The art of dying is a self-evident misnomer. An art has artists, and dying (though we are all its practitioners) has none that we know of. Like death, it is wholly outside our communicable experience; by definition, none who lives (including him who has lain at death's door) can know anything about dying. By definition, then, dying is the one do-it-yourself kit for which the manual of instruction is a preachment and nothing but a preachment—regrettably but unavoidably.

Those who "know"—that is, by analogy and extrapolation—are almost all agreed that the best way to die is not to shuffle and lag but to be hurrying to do something useful (or something *else* useful), or at least something urgent that preoccupies the victim. This is, of course, a happy concatenation that is hard to arrange—but ever easier, it appears, in the more civilized industrial societies. Sudden death by violence is standard front-page fare these days. It frightens us, as the long list of death notices among the want ads do not; but the fear is probably the product of the spectacularity.

I asked a friend of mine, whose hobby is flying, how he would like to die. "By crashing my plane," he said. "Intentionally?" "Why not?" *Getting it over with* is said to be one of the—usually unconscious—inducements to wartime soldiering, as it is the conscious inducement to suicide. Accident, if it would only occur (as it never does) at the right time and with instantaneous effect, is the supreme boon; alas, it is outside our power, though suicide disguised as accident is not uncommon, nearly always with a view to cheating the insurance companies which pay double indemnity for accidental death and none at all for its self-infliction. The suicide wave which followed the 1929 stock-market crash—many the "ruined" wretch who assumed (still more wretchedly if he was right) that his wife and children preferred his money to his life—resulted in a tightening of insurance-policy restrictions to discourage the practice.

Sudden death has the redeeming feature of being unanticipated, and anticipation is almost certainly the hardest part of dying. But we encounter an occasional dissent on the point. The famous last words of the dying may not have been their last words nor their last thoughts. But an occasional doomed man, usually a writer, undertakes to make a written record. To be sure, the record, whenever it ends, ends a moment too soon to be satisfactory, but it does tell us something—all the more if the writer is dying, as most of us do (even nowadays), of natural causes. One of the most recent, novelist Thomas Bell, a professing atheist, in his account of his last months registered an eloquent exception to the prevailing view: "Those who drop dead in their tracks . . . have missed dying altogether. And dying—not death . . . but dying—must surely be placed high among the two or three supreme human experiences. It's one I would willingly forgo for another twenty years. Since I can't, I may as well make the best of it by regarding it as an opportunity, an uncommon one, but by no means unique. . . ." * We may quarrel gently with Bell and ask what the third of "the two or three supreme human experiences" might be if one is dying and the other is, presumably, being born. Love? And why would anyone willingly forgo any supreme human experience for another twenty years? But we can at least grope for the understanding of the opportunity—hard as it is to arrange to come by—of dying rather than dropping dead.

We are told (by the Greek tragedians) that man learns through suffering (and by the idiomatic Christian that you can't get to heaven on roller skates). True, what we are not told is what stead the suffering of death will stand us in. But it may be that a man can learn a little something useful by suffering the sense of dying, and even that the longer he attends its school the more he will learn both about the conduct of this life and the demeanor of its close. What is indicated,

* Thomas Bell, *In the Midst of Life,* New York, Atheneum, 1961, p. 123.

on this hypothesis, is a lifelong expectation, and a conscious expectation, of death.

Whatever else may be said for war—and I am sure that there are a great many things to be said for it—it habituates the fighting man to the steady prospect of death. Like the momentary relief of the incurably ill, his two weeks' home leave is as busy with his death as the battlefront—perhaps busier. But the battlefront is immediate. The fighting man is afraid; but fear is not the same as funk. He is ready, or, if not ready, readier than the upholstered civilian; he has the habit. But if he survives the war, he loses the habit. The vividness of day-to-day life in the peacetime world—more so in the wartime world for most civilians—is consuming. Life does all that it can to bury death.

But physiologically we are all practicing dying all the time. It is the habit of the end that is hard. Well, then, practice is indicated. *But that is impossible?* Is it? Directly—yes. But indirectly—perhaps. But very hard. It takes concentration, in the midst of life, to be *willing* to remember that thou shalt die. And it takes unaccustomed practice (itself painful) to bring the reminder to consciousness and keep it under conscious contemplation. The contemplation must be steady and in both senses of the word: It must be continuous, and it must be composed. Now the involuntary or nonvoluntary contemplation of death is a nocturnal commonplace. We may ascribe its incidence to something we ate instead of to the struggle of the repressed unconscious to get a hearing. Do we begrudge it its irruption? But it is at least as much an active part of life as love and labor and sleep itself. Does it trouble our sleep? Why shouldn't it? Do we really expect a living man to sleep like a log?

Your only chance of sleeping like a log—and it is still a chance which Hamlet wouldn't take—is to be dead. Say that it is certain, that "there is no consciousness, but a sleep like the sleep of him who is undisturbed even by dreams." Then—it is Socrates again, under sentence of death—"death will be an unspeakable gain. For if a person were to select the night in which his sleep was undisturbed even by dreams, and were to compare with this the other days and nights of his life, and then were to tell us how many days and nights he had passed in the course of his life better and more pleasantly than this one, I think that any man, I will not say a private man, but even the great king will not find many such days or nights, when compared with the others. Now if death be of such a nature, I say that to die is a gain; for eternity is then only a single night."

Hamlet is still restrained from suicide by the "perchance to dream." Is it immortality—for to dream is to live—that we dread? Is it the dream, unconscious by night, subconscious by day, that terrifies us?

But the assault of the day-dream or night-dream is very far from being the same thing as steady contemplation. Steady contemplation is purposive, intentional, effortful. Otherwise I am everlastingly taken by surprise and distressed by my dreams and just the opposite of composed. I am agitated, and to be agitated is profitable preparation for panic, not for steady contemplation.

Dying will come of itself in the night to perturb us when our defenses are down. If we need the steady contemplation of it, we need it in the daytime, in the course of the diversions and distractions that bind us to life. "Why not forget about it? You'll just worry yourself sick." Just try not to worry and see if you don't get sick. Besides, we are talking not about worry but about contemplation. We *worry* about things we can or might do something about; death is not one of them. "Forget about it"? As easily the blind man forget that he is blind or the black man that he's black. "Forget about it"? It will not forget about you, and it will force its reminders on you in the tossing of night, the twinges of the day. You don't mean *forget*—you mean *repress*. We suppose that we cannot live with death, knowing the consuming and immobilizing effect of any uncertainty—of an illness, a lawsuit, a courtship, an application. And death, certain as it is, is a lifelong uncertainty as to its time and place, its undergoing, and its character. To do our daily work and live our daily lives, we suppose that we have got not to think about death at all or think about nothing else.

But the price of repression is demonstrably high in other areas of our activity; why not in this one? Won't it "out," as it does in other things, and distemper and discolor our lives from start to finish? Would it not be more salubrious to *choose* to live with what lives with us anyway, like an uncongenial couple forbidden divorce? We know how much better off the hungry man is who is hardened to hunger than he who is not. Why wouldn't we be better off to harden ourselves to death by facing it as we do the other inconveniences of daily life?

Why shouldn't a man forget about death "once in a while" and have a little fun? Why not, indeed? Escapism is a fine thing, provided that the escapee escapes. There is nothing wrong with hedonism if you get any pleasure out of it. The only trouble with fun and its pursuit is that you get out of condition—not for living but for dying. It keeps your eye on the main chance instead of on the main certainty, and the law of antithesis would seem to suggest that the better we live the worse we die. Remember that thou shalt die, and when thou enjoyest the amenities of the Roaring River Inn,* tote them up and ask thyself how many of them thou canst take with thee.

We don't want to let dying spoil our lives. Very well; then we must live with it, as we do with any other disability. To reject death is to reject life for delusion. What goes up must come down; you, too. So, precisely when you are at the peak of a good day's fishing or work, or a perfectly lovely party, or a delightful evening of meat and drink and companionship or love, precisely then, gung-ho and à-go-go, remember that thou shalt surely come all the way down from the peak. Take a look at your watch, if you have forgotten to bring the skull from your table. You are exactly an hour closer to the grave than you were an hour ago.

Then enjoy yourself, disillusioned but without delusion. You are thirty-five years old; you are half dead. Those telltale aches, those telltale wrinkles, that telltale weariness that wants external titillation to see it through—the tale they tell is told to practice and prepare you. Will you listen? Will you act your age? Or will you cling to the shortening shadows of the *dolce vita* which in fact ended with your birth? Ever since then you have had troubles. Some of them have given way to more exasperating and expensive troubles, and some of them have remained from that day to this. And will remain. Forward is death; yes, but backward is the greed for a combination of the irretrievably gone and the never possessed.

Would you be practiced to go? Then be packed and, remembering that thou shalt die, remember that he travels best who travels lightest. Every attachment will be broken, and they will be broken easiest if they are loose. The dear attachments, too; and even the dearest of all, that was made until death do you part. It will part you. Will you cling to it hopelessly to the end and intensify your agony? But this is the hardest practice of all, the most nearly impossible; for when the struggles of wedlock are past (if they pass) and life is tired and friends are few, there is the one bond that takes the place of every other; and it, too, must at the last be broken. Very well, then; disengage yourself at least from the others, children, employers, employees, associates, whose domination, of them by you or of you by them, was only an effort to stave off death.

---

* "All Hotel Services, Superb Food, Cocktail Lounge, 24-hour Coffee Shop, Black Panther Room, Entertainment Nightly, Oversized Beds, Direct Dial Telephone, Day-and-Night Valet, Free TV, Free Radio, Free Ice Cubes, Heated Swimming Pool, Steam Bath, Swedish Massage, Shuffle Board, Tennis, Riding, Golf (Two Courses), Putting Green, Free Parking, Children's Play Area, Private Dining Rooms, Banquet & Convention Facilities, Beauty and Barber Shops, Gift Shops, Rent-A-Car Service, Elevator to Second Floor."

He travels best who travels lightest. We mock the man who makes a fetish of his car or his golf clubs or his fishing tackle or his books or his clothes, but we respect the man who loves his home. Must we be packed to leave it, disengaged from it as we were the day before we saw it first? He travels best who travels lightest. Are we laden with self-importance, our standing in the community, our indispensability to enterprises? We shall be dispensed with. If we were indispensable, we would not die; if we think we are important, we will die that much harder and be that much worse practiced for it.

He travels best who travels lightest. Has your self-importance been swollen by adulation? Have you been told—by people who didn't know you—that you are courageous? When it comes time to die, your basic personality will assert itself, and dying may be harder if you try to bend it to the image. Valor, even reckless valor, on the battlefield does not ensure your heroic dying at home; indeed, of all occupations, the military probably does the least to prepare a man to die alone. Casper Milquetoast, having retreated his whole life long, may turn in a better performance at the last retreat than the hero of Sebastopol or Bataan. Not how many you killed but how you died will measure you. Be not puffed up—not yet.

Why shouldn't the tried and true recipe for old age be tried for dying? Why not avoid going glumly and idly into the one as into the other? The fewer hours you have left, the fewer you have to be idle. Now you may know the measured urgency whose knowledge is denied to youth. On his ninetieth birthday Justice Holmes said that "to live is to function. That is all there is in living. . . . 'Death plucks at my ears and says, Live—I am coming.' " You will not finish your work; no man has. Your stamp collection, your reading, your music, your chess game will not be complete; no man's has been. But you will have made Death hustle for you. You will have been moving; he will have to catch you on the fly. And, like Lady Mary Wortley Montague, the eighteenth-century English wit, you will be able to die saying, or at least knowing, "It has all been very interesting"—with the accent on the *all*.

Dying, then, is an argument for living well—intellectually and artistically and not just morally. Whatever inner resources you have cultivated may come in handy at the end, if not one, then another. This function may fail you, and you may still have that one. You can no longer read or speak articulately; you can, perhaps, listen articulately. You can no longer follow prose; perhaps you can follow poetry, or music. Or your own richly and rigorously developed imagination. Have you pondered the wonder of a flower or a fern in your out-of-door days? There is one at your bedside. The difficulty is not only to remember that thou shalt die, but to remember that thou hast lived: *memento vixisse*. The difficulty is to find *all* of life interesting, and if you have been ardently interested in all of it up to the end, your interest may sustain you then.

Remember that thou shalt die. Why not "practice" it in the death of others? A somber business, sitting with the dying; more somber still, sitting with the dead. Our earliest (and even some of our recent) ancestors did it; "simple people," we say as we hurry by. I know a brilliant married woman of forty-odd, with a substantial family "on both sides," who has never seen a corpse and has, she says, no present intention of ever seeing one.

But to be simple is not the same as to be stupid, and being somber is not the same as being morbid. We learn by seeing and feeling and pondering what we see and feel and not just by doing. See others die and feel it, then. See and feel, not in reluctant duty or in righteous care, but in open curiosity. There, with the grace of God, go you. Life has given the old an assist: They have been "through it" many times, and it has not been entirely vicarious. The experience of another, when the same experience awaits you, is something much more than vicarious. Most of them have tended to the dying, or have helped. It is not so strange to them as a consequence; and it is the strangeness that makes it hard, if not for the dying, for the living.

See and feel yourself really dying, once in a while, of a bump or a lump, during those hours, or days, or weeks before the doctor comes out of the laboratory and says, "I've got good news for you." Whoever has had *this* experience has practiced dying as has no one else but the man who has been told, "I've got bad news for you." Stiff-upper-lip time. But see to it that the lip trembles on appropriate occasion, lest you have deceived yourself and only mastered the art of repression.

Best of all, but as difficult to manage as sudden death, is the chronic illness of half a lifetime or a whole. You have known, as the sound man hasn't, what it is to be prone and alone, to have given over the perpetual motion of the body and the mind. You are in practice for the long stretch of being prone and alone. Or practice it, sound as you are, ten minutes, a half hour a day, without books and papers. Doing nothing, emptied, as far as possible, of concerns, regrets, rejoicing, hopes, and plans. The seventeenth-century Quakers, who found it facilitated by the practice of silent worship in community, called it "setting loose."

It wants patience. You and I—I address this entire preachment to myself—want patience. The frenzy of the lives we lead wears away the native patience we had as children. It is we, not they, who can no longer sit still, set loose. Here is your opportunity, in the dentist's, or the bureaucrat's or the boss's or the garage mechanic's anteroom, to recover some of the patience that dying may require of you. Why do you leaf through that magazine while you wait? And then, when you're called, lay it down and forget it? In those ten minutes, in that half hour, you could have practiced being still. The Oriental knows what it is to do it, and he is said to die easier than the Westerner; but it is not an Oriental scripture that reads, "Be still, and know that I am God."

"He who should teach men to die would at the same time teach them to live." But dying is self-taught, and he who, having learned it, should teach it is unavailable. We are told that the thing for a man to do, when he finds himself with a lemon, is to make lemonade out of it. We do *not* know that there are *no* worse things than dying. We do know that it would be nice to be rid of the blemishes of this life, and we know (unless we are fools clear out to the rind) that we shall not be in this happy case while we live. The Great Frederick of Prussia thought that German was a language fit for servants and horses, so he found a French name for his palace, Sans Souci; and there, care-ridden, he died. What life couldn't do for him, death did—or so we suppose.

I V

The Young: Their Cause and Cure

. . . grow old with me—
The best of life is yet to be.
                    —Hunt, *Abou Ben Adhem*

To be young was very heaven.
—Wordsworth, *On the French Revolution*

1: Why We Hate Them

H O W T H E generation gap (which goes back to the Beginning) so suddenly became a chasm takes a little accounting for, but not very much. We have, I think, only to remind ourselves that these whelps of ours are the first who ever were who cannot remember a continuum in a changing world.

They are the first who cannot remember no television (and no radio), no airplane (and no aerospace), no superpower (and no superbomb), no balance of terror, no hot-and-cold running war with no light at the end of the tunnel (and no end of the tunnel); no Secretary of *Defense* (and no tutor to teach him to say *protective reaction strike*), no CIA, no FBI, no bugs, no taps, no finger prints, no anti-Communist jihad, no loyalty oath, no un-American Activity, no uppity niggers, no dope endemic, no 'round-the-clock crime in and out of the streets and above and below and between them;

—the first who cannot remember no divorce without scandal, no j.p. wedding (if any), no cremation (and no napalm), no throwaway bottles, no his-and-her lung cancer, no comic books, no freeways, no psychiatrists off the freeways, no psychiatrists, no supermarkets, no sleeping pills in the supermarkets, no sleeping-around pills over the counter;

—the first who cannot remember no picture magazines with ten-second captions (and no *Reader's Digest* with ten-minute happiness), no Muzak, no Kleenex, no detergents (and no allergy to detergents) (and no pollution by detergents) (and no plankton deficiency to explain the pollution), no polls (and no computers or microfilm or data processing or area or zip codes or social-security numbers), no social security (and no rest homes), no forty-hour week (and no any-hour week), no washers, dryers, laundromats, freezers (and no refrigerators), no college turned high school (and called university), no two-car garage runneth over, no two-day weekend runneth over;

—the first who cannot remember no instant coffee, no instant deodorant, no instant blond, no instant relief, no neon at all, no—oh, no, not that—cellophane. (What's celluloid, Pop?)

They are the first who ever were who cannot remember, and we who are over thirty, sixty, ninety are the last who ever will be who cannot forget.

We are the revolutionizees, and the revolutionizees are always, above everything else, indignant. Had up before the *Directoire,* hauled off in the tumbrils, thrown down on the block, the revolutionizees proceed in classic crescendo from astonishment to outrage to inconsolable indignation. They had agreed, to be sure, that revolution was inevitable—and (with Thomas Jefferson) a good thing, on the whole, and the very essence of our heritage; but that it should take place just now, when they were willing to meet the rebels halfway (certainly a third of the way), and that it should take the ridiculous form it is taking, and that they should be its victims—their case is painful.

Their case is painful because age is wasted on the old. They should have known, in their dotage, that the belly-ache bespeaks an abscessed tooth whose only cure is removal of the slipped disk (itself the consequence of a fluid imbalance in the inner ear). The trouble wasn't where they thought it was, and no sooner is it diagnosed and its treatment submitted to when it proves to be something else somewhere else and there is no catching up with it. What is the matter with them? Had they never read "The Katzenjammer Kids" in the Sunday funnies of their youth?

What is the matter with them is that age is wasted on the old. Is, and must be: Their acuity has failed as fast as their experience has accumulated. On the Great Chinese Wall of the medical school of the Sorbonne in the Bloody May of 1968 was the whitewash legend *Vous êtes ancien, Professeur.*

Having succeeded in forgetting that their parents did not know what to do about them, the old are then pleasantly positioned to deny the first fact of progenitive life. What the wisdom of the second half of the twentieth century amounts to is that man, unlike the guppy, does not know what to do with his young. He never did, but he used to know that he didn't. The Greeks knew it and said so, in the *Meno,* and four hundred years before the Greeks the Lord God Jehovah knew it (and said so to Isaiah): "I have nourished and brought up children, and they have rebelled against me . . . lying children, children that will not hear the law of the Lord. They have chosen their own ways, and their soul delighteth in their transgression." Stendhal's young hero ran away from home in order to escape the sorrows that were poisoning his life, especially on Sundays.

Nothing to do with them, and at last we know what the Greeks and the Lord and Stendhal knew. And, ah, Shakespeare of the serpent's tooth: "You have taught me language, and my profit on't is I know how to curse."

The parson's son turned out to be a reprobate—or a parson like his pa. The English have the world's highest level of civilized behavior and the highest proportion (71 percent) of people who left school at fifteen or before. *And* the greatest tolerance of the young—and the lowest disapproval of corporal punishment of children (21 percent, compared with 88 percent in Italy).* But the English are the most law-abiding of people and the Italians the least. The Italians don't love their children; they love their *bambini* and turn them loose as soon as they can forage. The French love to keep the business in the family, and the Germans love to break somebody's spirit.

You have but to turn to the right page in the right edition of Dr. Benjamin Spock's baby bible to discover that Dr. Benjamin Spock, a man and a hero, did not know how one makes a man of a child or a hero of a pediatrician: "A great change in attitude has occurred," said Dr. Spock on the right page of the 1957 edition, "and nowadays there seems to be more chance of a conscientious parent getting into trouble with permissiveness than with strictness, so I have tried to give a more balanced view. By keeping children on the right track, firmness keeps them lovable."

Too late. Too late to be firm. Too late to keep them lovable. To late to unspoil the child by unsparing the rod. Too late to do anything but discover, on the right page of the 1957 edition, that Dr. Spock had discovered that if you couldn't do anything with the carrot you might, for all he knew, do something with the stick, or, for all he knew, vice versa. And if he, then you, then I, then all of us. End of

---

* "Mr. Percy Wood, aged 63, whose pupils accused him of excessive punishment and humiliation . . . told the Cheshire Education Committee that he had not kept a cane since 1960 'because I was tempted to use it too often.' He did not regret inflicting punishment. It was in his pupils' best interest. . . . The only regulation governing corporal punishment in primary schools is that all beatings must be recorded in a punishment book. There are no rules laying down what instruments can be used or what parts of the body may be beaten."
—London *Times*, August 15, 1970.

the science of bringing up children—except in the schools of Child Psychology. (Ph.D. in Child Psychology, dissertation on "Dr. Spock from Year to Year.") The wisdom of the end of the twentieth century—still to be recovered from the Greeks and the Lord and Stendhal and, ah, Shakespeare of the serpent's tooth.

New York *Times* scientific survey: Children of happy homes "have as many problems" as children of unhappy homes. (Might as well relax and have an unhappy home.) New York *Times* scientific survey: Children of nonconformist (or conformist) homes "have as many problems" as children of conformist (or nonconformist) homes. New York *Times* survey: Conformism at the end of the twentieth century means abandonment of religion (not of church) and of traditional values of hard work, thrift, simplicity, sobriety, familiality, and geographic, occupational, and economic stability; and nonconformism at the end of the twentieth century means abandonment of religion (and of church) and of traditional values of hard work, thrift, simplicity, sobriety, familiality, and geographic, occupational, and economic stability. Take the desponding case of Jones, the noble old liberal crusader who fathered identical twins, one of whom is presently in the bank (School of Business Administration), the other (College of Soft Knocks) in the East Village when last (and Jones hopes it's the last) heard of (not from). Jones was the best of his generation and was therefore, in his season, rebellious against reactionary Smith. An exemplary father, he signaled his rebellion to his identical twins, and they were the best of *their* generation. And they responded with rebellion against Jones *and* Smith.

Whoever in the American (or any other) middle (or any other) class dreamed of living on in his (or her) children has, as my Aunt Jennie used to say, another think coming. Nothing for it now but to shudder. The young lady's eyes were well glazed as she awaited her turn at the long-distance phone at Woodstock. The man asked her whom she was calling, and she said, "My mother." "What are you calling her for?" "To tell her I'm fine." "Are you?" "*Fine,* man? I'm, like, y'know, *beautiful.*" "Does she understand you?" "Who?" "Your mother." "My *mother?* She thinks I'm, like, y'know, going to hell. Like she doesn't understand, y'know, like there's no such thing for me." Hell is where the old folks go when they live. Hell is guilt: *We didn't read the 1957 edition.* Hell is shame: *My son the pusheh.* Hell is falsehood: *He's taking the year off for travel . . . experimental farm . . . independent study . . . enroll at Berkeley . . . film work . . . new college in Mexico.* Hell is failure: *All the advantages, and she just . . .* Hell is disgrace: *No, we haven't heard from her recently*. Hell is a wall that rises faster than you can climb it.

Why do we hate them? Why shouldn't we, when they despise us and disgrace us and lie and lie and lie and love and love and love? They are spitting images of—and at—us. We loaded them up with all the junk we live by. Such as the 340-h.p. two-seater, the pornucopia of the magazines and the ads, the sacrament of Holy Matrimony (with every second marriage in California ending in divorce). Such as the preprandial souse and the postprandial embrace by the idiot box, the blank stare at table, and then the measured alternation of the bottle and the bromide, the psychiatrist and the bridge. Such as the you-can't-af*ford*-not-to-trade-it-in, and We-Fly-You-To-Vegas-Free, and the $64,000 Question, and the $64,000,000,000 Answer in Vietnam, and the J. Edgar Hoovers to hot up the hippodrome. That's *our* bag—and the cat's out of it: A bigger buck for a bang. While Dr. Spock was compiling the 1957 edition, somebody was singing, "Stop the World—I Want to Get Off," and it was listed under "Songs."

"They hate hippies," said the hippie triumphant. It was hate them or hate ourselves, and they wanted so much more to be hated than we did. What is so bad about having it out in the open, after all the centuries of our being *proud* to *see them go* into *the service of their country* for which they *gave* their lives and, if they didn't want to give their lives (with a gun at the back of their heads), disowned, cast off, cast out by the mother they'd deprived of her Gold Star and the father deprived of *giving* his boy. How is that for hating under the craggy old Cross-and-Skull of the homemade Calvary lovingly mown by Dad and watered by Mom against the day when Johnny (or a piece or two of Johnny) comes marching home full of holes or hashish? What Johnny, Most Likely to Succeed, succeeded in doing was our thing, all those years, all those decades, all those man-eating millennia.*

How really nice of Johnny now to let us hate him alive instead of love him dead. "They hate hippies"; that's why Johnny went hippie. It was a gas, it put him in the aisles when W. C. Fields said, "A man who hates children and loves whiskey can't be all bad," and he stayed for the second time around just to hear it again. Beautiful little baby burdens, germinated in dutiful coitus, carried in long loveless gesta-

---

* As of September 30, 1970, Prof. E. James Lieberman of the Harvard University School of Medicine calculated on the basis of life tables used by public health statisticians that there were 80,000 mothers and fathers, 60,000 grandparents, and 30,000 widows and orphans surviving the American dead in Vietnam—and another 750,000 immediate family members of the seriously wounded. "About 2.5 million families (5% of the total) have sent a member to Vietnam."—"War and the Family," *Modern Medicine*, April 19, 1971.

tion, expelled at agonized expense, carried home muling and puking in pink and blue, and from then on carried, carried, carried until the great day of the Greetings from Our President, Johnny on the mailing list, Johnny off our backs and where they'll let him have if it he tries any more of his tricks. Gold Star Johnny, germinated, gestated, expelled, scrubbed, laundered, foddered, carried (*"carry* me"), paid for and paid for and paid for; and asserting more of his contrariness all the time, setting himself up against his betters first by howling No, then by saying No, and by the time he had holes in the knees of his pants, by doing No. Before he was two my cousin Harry had learned to turn himself blue by holding his breath; * he "had problems."

In the world of equality, dedicated to the equal treatment of unequals, the doctrine spilled over into the playpen. The blooded nobility, if they had less difficulty with their young, may (I say may) have had the less difficulty because they believed in the unequal treatment of unequals. A blooded nobleman, in his way, was my friend Sampson Lightning of About-a-Mile-and-a-Half-from-Here in Dallas County, Alabama. He was setting in front of his nigger-shack when I met him—not whittling, just setting. I showed him a bird I had shot and said, without knowing then that his name was Sampson Lightning, "Uncle"—all niggers in that Pleistocene day being darkies and old darkies uncle—"what kind of bird is this, some kind of snipe?" He said, "Naw, suh, boss, that ain' no snipe, tha's a kildee, tha's what that is." "They any good to eat?" "Naw, *suh.* Ah feeds 'em to mah chillun." Thus the blooded nobility, whose truly beautiful babies were drapped in the cotton patch. Thus the unequal treatment of unequals in Dallas County, not five miles from Selma, Alabama, in that day of darkies and uncles. Thus the unnecessity to hate the young.

Rejecting them, instead of letting them drop and letting them go, shipping them bound and gagged off to the Parent-Teacher Association, to college to prepare them to be my son the dokteh, and to find

---

* ". . . The toddler who develops breath-holding attacks is always bright and strong willed. . . . The attack is brought on by anything which annoys him. . . . Like any actor these children must have an audience for their performance so that they do not have attacks when on their own. In fact, they seldom have an attack unless mother or father is present. . . . Parents of such children find themselves in a cleft stick resulting from their fear of doing anything which may precipitate their child's temper and subsequent very alarming breath-holding attacks. However, they and the child soon become aware of the consequences of this policy so that the child becomes increasingly unmanageable. . . . Most parents will find that slapping the child to make him breathe or throwing cold water at him makes little difference. . . . It is some relief to parents faced with these alarming attacks to know that the child will always come round. He will also always lose the habit as he grows older, although his strong determination is likely to continue to show itself in other ways. . . ."—"Our Paediatrician," London *Times*, August 29, 1970.

a Nice Girl ("She's a Falter from Detroit"), to the Front to Serve Their Country by killing their opposite numbers on what, there being no war any more, is called the Other Side, or, between no wars any more, to pushing a quill or a hand truck ("He's with General Motors now")—rejecting them for their insolence in being equals, in being at all, we are all at once indignant that they have rejected us. They don't dig us, and they say so. They don't love us, they don't honor us, they don't obey us. And they say so in their four four-letter words and their two six-letter words dedicated to Mother.

To father . . . There wasn't room in the road, like, y'know, for both Laius and Oedipus, nor was there room in the parking lot for both the young man in his Porsche and the old man in his Cadillac. While the old man was maneuvering into the only parking space left the young man zipped in around him and took it, jumped out of his car, and said to the old man, "You have to be young and fast to do that," and the old man thereupon smashed into the Porsche a half dozen times and wrecked it and said to the young man, "You have to be old and rich to do that." They reciprocated, and we reciprocated, and they reciprocated, a blind eye for a sharp one, a snaggle tooth for a baby tooth.

And they were all we had, all we had to *live for:* They left us for dead.

The day we brought them home, all pink, all blue, they slept and slept. They were beautiful. This wino on the curb, this bruiser with his beer can, this crabbed cadaver taking his effluviant time to die, this gung-ho go-getter, this paunched and flatulent pater of a disorganized familia, tail of the TV dog, this Nixon, this Sinatra, this Manson, this Mayer—this was the beautiful baby that somebody brought home from the hospital, skin so soft, eyes unbagged and unbloodied, gossamer hair, *who didn't stay that way* (who broke his proud parents' hearts by not staying that way). Proudly given to his country, Our Oldest, Our Youngest, Our Baby. To Our Baby we clung. Our Baby we stunted, Our Baby we carried and would not put him down. "He's breaking my back." ("He's breaking my heart.") Our dreadful, disgraceful Baby. He had to jump from our arms, the little tyke of eighteen, seventeen, fifteen, twenty-five, hardly hatched from the egg; and mopheaded she, our little girl, somebody's chick now, everybody's chick now, into the hay and the Village and the dirt and the dope and the mentionable diseases, and hardly time for the mumps and the measles. "You should have seen her when she was a Baby." You shouldn't have seen her when she wasn't.

Do you suppose our old folks didn't hate us? Did we or didn't we put a 100 percent mark-down on them to make room in the declining market and box them and ship them to St. Petersburg and Long Beach to sit on the green benches and dry in the sun, and when they fell off the green benches did we or didn't we put them into the Rest-in-Peace home where they'd be *taken care of*—and by somebody else? And whatever it cost, it was worth it to get them out of the house and off our backs (now that we couldn't ride theirs any more) with their Ancient Wisdom and their Ancient Complaints.

Did we or didn't we want our parents to die—and somewhere else, and had they or hadn't they brought us home once, all pink and blue and gossamer? Why wouldn't our young want us to die, too, a little earlier on since we were more than a little more dispensable to them than our old folks were to us?

More than a little more dispensable to them, since they would go somewhere else to live if we wouldn't go somewhere else to die:

Dear Mother,
I meant to write you before this and I hope you haven't been worried. I am in [San Francisco, Los Angeles, New York, Arizona, a Hopi Indian Reservation!!!! New York, Ajijic, San Miguel de Allende, Mazatlán, Mexico!!!!] and it is really beautiful here. It is a beautiful scene. We've been here a week. I won't bore you with the whole thing, how it happened, but I really tried, because I knew you wanted me to, but it just didn't work out with [school, college, my job, me and Danny] and so I have come here and it [sic] a really beautiful scene. I don't want you to worry about me. I have met some BEAUTIFUL PEOPLE and . . .*

* Tom Wolfe, *The Electric Kool-Aid Acid Test*, New York, Bantam, 1969, p. 121.

2: Descendant Worship

WE OF THE world wars produced more history than we could consume. Spengler's ship of Western civilization wasn't slowly settling now; it was plunging. We locked ourselves in our first-class cabins and watched the Big Picture. What else was there to do? Go overboard? Our little ones went overboard.

Consider us as they considered us. We weren't quaint and skinflint and fideistic as our waltzing fathers (and grandfathers) (and great-grandfathers) were. We were mortally dangerous, mortally faithless, and mortally liquored on buying and selling. Fifty years after Adolf Hitler said that the ancients would be remembered for their philosophy, the Middle Age for its cathedrals, and modern man for his department stores and his banks,* the incendiaries in Berlin were crying, "The *Warenhaus,* the *Warenhaus,*" and in Santa Barbara, "The bank, the bank." Hitler had been wrong (as always); modern man would be remembered for the *burning* of his characteristic institutions.

We were the first generation as a whole people, in America (which became the world), to have leisure and to suppose that leisure must mean pleasure instead of respite. We were so rich we didn't need

* It didn't occur to him to include the Grand Hotels; like the railroad stations they were *too* awesome to be attacked by the old Schicklgrubers. But not by the new Schicklgrubers: "One of Paris' luxury hotels, the Plaza Athénée, was spattered with red paint today by a group of demonstrators wearing red scarves over their faces. They broke eight large windows, threw a smoke bomb into the lobby, and left behind boards protesting against the 'France of Money' and 'Rich Men's Holidays.'"—London *Times,* August 15, 1970. (The French student slogan, *"Rabol,"* is derived from the slang phrase, *"ras le bol,"* meaning "fed up to the back teeth.")

Grandma—*or* ourselves—around the house or anywhere else. "Primitive" men neither work nor play until they drop; they just go on, each day, each night, each life, until it is time to slow down and then to stop. We were the first whole people to think of living it up and on up in a world of open-ended possibilities. What had always been (or seemed) open to the few was now (or now seemed to be) open to the many. With techniques on our hands and inventive time, we could at last get even with our tiger cubs for not being the originally sinless butterballs we brought home from the hospital. We could be pink and blue ourselves and spoil their cruel fun by hanging on to what they were taking away from us, instead of letting them take it. We'll see— the wars went on killing them—who buries who.* We could defeat them by staying young if (as it did) it killed us.

Nary a silver thread among the gold, nary a telltale wrinkle. Mother and daughter—which hands are whose? Jack's widow in her miniskirt weeds, and ageless Dickie with an ageless touch of honest Republican gray at the temples. We—not our young—invented the jive and the twist and the frug and the Madison. "Them too I hate," says Euripides, "who desire to lengthen out the span of life, seeking to turn the tide of death aside by philters, drugs, and magic spells." The philters, drugs, and magic spells kept us from looking our age for a year, or two, or five, and then the fact of life fading fast away, forcing itself through the masquerade—fingernails creasing, liver spots on the dishwater-free hands. . . . And then the desperation. What good was it anyway? We would always be young and fair—well, middling—to each other. But we knew; we knew each other. And *they* knew; *they* knew us at home with our hair down, they knew which hands were whose and never took the wrong hand in theirs.

Boy Scouts ought to give their seats to old ladies in the streetcar because the old ladies are old and tired and need them and the Boy Scout will be an old lady himself some day. The young respect the old because the old are old. If the old are young, they are not respected

---

* "When a 'savage' feels that he is a burden to his tribe; when every morning his share of food is taken from the mouths of children—and the little ones are not so stoical as their fathers: they cry when they are hungry; when every day he has to be carried across the stony beach, or the virgin forests, on the shoulders of younger people—in savage lands there are no invalid carriages, nor destitutes to wheel them—he begins to repeat what the old Russian peasants still say: 'Tchujoi vek zayedayu, pora na pokoi" ('I live others' life, it is time to retire'). And he retires. . . . He himself asks to die; he himself insists upon this last duty towards the community, and obtains the consent of the tribe; he digs out his grave; he invites his kinfolk to the last parting meal. His father has done so; it is now his turn. . . . West European men of science, when coming across these facts, are absolutely unable to understand them. . . ."—Kropotkin, *Mutual Aid,* London, 1914, Chapter III.

by the young (who have no need to respect one another). And if the old pretend to be young, they are pretending not to be respectable and don't want to be respected. They will have their wish, and they have it. *Mocked*—who needs hatred?—by Our Babies with their necks unlined, uncrow's-footed their eyes, ungnarled their dishwater-unfree hands, unknobbled their knees, and, oh, bitter, bitter, untired their joints and unhardened their arteries. Now we would hate them with a hate impossible to Grandma and Grandpa and Laius.

But the worst was to come (as it always is). If we wanted to hang on to our youth so badly, why, youth (though the young hadn't noticed it themselves) must be beautiful, or at least so much less miserable than age that it was worth an old man's while (and still more an old woman's) to make a fool of himself for. Beautiful. Beautiful to see them trying to relate, trying to identify, trying to be unidentified, nobody here but us kids, jiving, jumping, rocking, rolling. Mom's a teenybopper. Bridge that gap. Whoops—didn't make it, Mom's down. Bingo, Pop swung too hard at the tetherball. Pop's down. Take it easy, folks, you're old. Act your age.

Now you're really old, as those alone are really old who are old all at once.

The oldest man I've seen in my life was a young middle-aged honky running a worthy project in the black ghetto of Watts. He came to a rip-roaring campus outside Los Angeles to persuade the collegians to join him in his crusade. He had studied up assiduously on their patter, but he had done his studying too soon; "groovy" had been dead for two or three years ("groove" as an intransitive verb was still permitted) and he told them how groovy it was. They jeered him, they hooted him, they cursed him, and they drove him from the platform at San Fernando Valley State College a broken old man. He'd had a go at relating, identifying; no go. One way to grow very old very fast is to do it gracelessly.

Unrespectable old fools, who wouldn't let their babies be children or their children grow up, who wouldn't age and die and had to die without aging. The serpent's tooth, and the society built on descendant worship blown up in our faces when we tried to be the descendants and transfer the worship to ourselves. We couldn't lick 'em another way, so we tried to do it by joining 'em. Blackballed. Was it the baby-sitter or the schools or the Communists that spoiled them? Or that wrinkled us? The gap is no gap, the chasm no chasm; it is straight extrapolation of our own misled lives and the missiled world we made. The millionaire's son who hid in San Francisco's old Hashbury under a false name, with a deliveryman's job, no beard, no sandals, no grass, no acid, explained his being there by saying mildly that he simply couldn't bear the way his parents lived. Oh, serpent's tooth. Oh, sharper still in the society that betook itself to feast forever off its young, to give them more love than Sampson Lightning knew that there was in a parent to give, to repress more hate than the rich old man in the Cadillac knew he could repress when the fast young man took his parking place.

Permissiveness was not conjured up by subversive psychologists. The doctrine, like all doctrines, was *post hoc propter hoc*. Having abjured respectability by our children, we had no ground for withholding permission to them. Pot isn't "the car key Dad wouldn't give him"; pot must be something else, because Dad *did* give him the car key to keep him from hating him. (But irreparable disaffection followed irreparable disrespect.) Why not give him the car key anyway (or the keys to one of the cars)? No reason not to. No telling him— never any telling anybody—that he ought to stay home and do his homework or help his mother or read a book. We lived for our jollies, why shouldn't he for his? No telling him we needed him to mind the store or hoe the corn; we didn't. We were rich (unlike the blooded nobility who *need* their children to carry on the tradition). Permissiveness, which would not have been the inexorable consequence of our being rich, was the inexorable consequence of our being rich and unrespectable in combination.

Permissiveness doesn't have to be parental. Our generation achieved it on its own, having granted ourselves the great permission to kill as many people as we could of every age and condition. After the saturation bombing of open Dresden—to notify the Russians that *that's* how far east we could do it—why not Hiroshima? After Hiroshima, why not My Lai? After My Lai, why not? Having steeped ourselves in the irresponsibility of total war under total government taking adult choice off our shoulders, we were set for the blast-off. What we permitted ourselves we thought sensible to permit our little ones. Let them grow—we had had to transplant ourselves—like a flower (and be a Flower Child?). If the little one should be allowed to grow, as we hadn't been, he would surely be an Integrated Personality. His father would be his pal instead of his Oedipal, and Mother Jocasta party with him. His schooling would be interest-centered, and its maxim, "Learning is fun." ("Learning," said Aristotle, "is accompanied by pain.")

The seed was the War to End War, the sprout its Jazz Age aftermath. It ripened until, when the War *after* the War to End War was over, it produced its first fruit in the adolescent apathy of the Fifties.

Apathetic adolescence? It wasn't the adolescents who set the somnambulant pace of the Eisenhower Years, and neither they nor their parents were apathetic about absolutely everything. Like their parents, they were crowding into the Great Big Peacetime PX. The new ten-billion-dollar-a-year teenage market with its teenage charge accounts required no adult signature. And below that market was another market for those who had to pay cash. The *juvenile delinquent* was discovered, drinking (ah, happy days) beer and playing "chicken" on the highways—first to turn aside coming head-on was it.

The charge-account set and the cash-on-the barrel-head set had something in common. The car was the message, and you couldn't steal them like you used to when there was no driver's license. Every one of a gang of seventeen young burglars run to earth in New Jersey—this was 1956—came from economically more-than-adequate homes. They got their getaway wheels from good old apathetic Dad. The high-school parking lot was as big as the high school—just as the factory parking lot was as big as the factory. Everything and everybody was rolling. The Hell's Angels ride what *they* call their "bikes."

What the gung-ho society produced was the World's Oldest Child. The protraction of adolescence was already a sociological theme song of the luxus Twenties. The question that should have been before the house was, Could you love them when you needed them to need you and they didn't? Could you love them when they were twenty and twenty-five—and you were still wheeling them? I was a product of the Late Jazz Age, complete with collapsible Ford (and raccoon coat), and I wrote a song for the college show that ended, "I'll stay here in college forever/ If you'll stay in college too." Who wouldn't stay here in college forever rather than get hit by a pitched ball in the Great Game of Life? Who—though we called ourselves *men,* not *kids*—wanted to hurry it up so that he could be like the old folks? (We knew, vaguely or sharply, that in time we would be; no species mutation for us.) But twenty-one was the statutory limit, twenty-three for the bar, twenty-four for a Ph.D.,* twenty-six for a sawbones. "The typical Ph.D.," said the Carnegie Commission on Higher Education in 1970, "is won at 32 years of age, 14 years after the student enters college"—and six years after the twenty-sixth birthday on which his

---

* As the "third degree" sank steadily to the level of the old high-school certificate, the genuine diploma mills found themselves pushed to the wall by the actual institutions of higher learning, one of which, in 1969, offered to convert earned Bachelor of Law degrees of past graduates into Doctorates of Jurisprudence on the strength of a mail application—and the payment of a fee. The institution: Harvard University.—New York *Times,* December 14, 1969.

eligibility to be shipped out to Perforation Paddy expires.

A generation after we would stay here in college—on dear old Dad's back—forever, our tiny tots did. *Kids,* with health and pep and time on their hands. No hurry. Life need never begin. Graffito: *Don't worry. You've got plenty of time. At thirty-five Gauguin was a waiter.* And underneath, in another hand: *At thirty-five Mozart was dead.* And Seurat and Shelley at thirty-one. And Billy Budd (and Billy the Kid) at twenty-one. If they dropped out of school and became remittance children, and you had to keep them in doughnuts and dope, at least they were doing their nothing somewhere else and you were ahead by most of the $2,000, $3,000, $4,000 per annum it cost you to keep them in any kind of college at all.

Kids, little kids who *have* to go to school and stay there because Mom and Dad make them go to school and because they can't get that drag of a clean-collar job if they leave the ivy-clad hiring hall and because their King and Country need them in Vietnam. Rest homes for rich adolescents. Jumping shut-ins. President Brewster of. Yale University came to the disconsolate conclusion that "the involuntary campus" was a major factor in student disorders of the late 1960s and quoted an SDS member at Berkeley: "Like don't give me that stuff about how I'm here to learn. I'm here because I have to be." * The chicks had always been there because they had to be; the premature Women's Lib girl was the one who dropped out of Texas A&M in her first year because, as she said, "I come to be went with and I ain't."

Because I say so—Mom and Dad and the Placement Office and the Presidential Greetings and You've Got to Get a Man. *Because I say so.* Who taught them to call themselves kids when they were twenty going on ten? Who went on and on loving them and showed it by going on and on telling them that they had to wash their ears *and their feet* and brush their baby teeth and hurry to school and stay there until school was out and they could go out and play? "I haven't got anything to do, I don't know what to do."

Stay the same as you are—or I'll kill you in Perforation Paddy. But they wouldn't—and couldn't, if they would—stay the same as they were. The kids grew until they were elderly kids and saw Ma and Pa and the Placement Office and the Presidential Greetings through a glass brightly. Purposeless kids, but impossible now to put to the old folks' purposes. Irresponsible kids, as what kid isn't, but impossible now to saddle with the old folks' responsibility to wash their ears and

* New York *Times,* December 14, 1969.

hurry to school and not play hooky. It wasn't hooky after you were sixteen or fifteen or, if there were enough of you, fourteen.

The first thing a *little* kid learns in this vale of tears is what John F. Kennedy knew when he delivered a three-word speech (which he wrote himself) before an audience of one rejected applicant for political preferment. The rejected applicant said it wasn't fair, and John F. Kennedy, about to be assassinated, made his speech, which I quote here in full: "Life isn't fair."

Life isn't fair. Your beautiful son wants to know why you won't let his good friend Sammy—his *good* friend Sammy; they didn't know each other Tuesday, and this is Thursday—borrow your car or your books (or your house), and you're in for it. You are going to say, "Because I don't know him," and your son is going to say, "You mean you don't trust him," and you, in for it, are going to say, "Actually, I don't," and he is going to say, "Why don't you? Why don't you *trust* people? Why are you *afraid* of people?" No way out of it now, even when you say the only thing that there is to say—that life is unfair. Your beautiful students want to know why you insist on grading them if you don't want to play God, and you are in for it when you say, "You don't want to be judged, eh?" And when they shout "Right" (or with black fists, "Right on"), and you say, "But *you* judge the grading system," and they say that you know as well as they do that the system is bad, and you acknowledge that it is bad, and even execrable, and they say, "Well, then," there is no way out of it even if you say the only thing that there is to say—that life is unfair.

Life isn't fair. "Jimmy got a bike for Christmas and he doesn't even have to help his mother on Saturday." "Joey's got a cold too and *his* mother lets him out." "Jerry did it too and nothing happened to him because he didn't get caught." Is—as Milt Gross's Mowriss said—diss a system? The little kid (the really little really kid) is an enemy of the system years before he gets to be a big enough kid to be an enemy of his elders and then a superannuated kid who says so. Life isn't fair; but the proposition is not susceptible to normative conversion because there is no getting even with it.

But you can try by rejecting the system on the sly. The system is hypocritical, and the thing about it that rowels the young is its hypocrisy. *Do it in the road,* let them see you doing it, make them see you doing it. In the road, and not on the sneak—unless the system absolutely makes you. But the system absolutely makes you. Before the Flower Children wilted, a non-*garde* group called the Living Theatre (so long ago that they still wore G-strings on stage) sang a song the burden of which was that the system tried to persuade you hypocritically that you can't live without money. (The title of the song: "You Can't Live Without Money.") If you can't, the system's got you. But you can. You can live without Bread by begging bread, or, in a pinch, by ripping it off the counter and tucking it under your Karma Yogin robe.

One system says, "Work, for the night is coming," but when you've got things to do nights you have to sleep days. Another system says, "From each according to his ability, to each according to his need," but if you don't need much and you're unable to be able, you have to get what you need however you can get it. Both systems say, "He who will not work, neither shall he eat," but the rich have found a way to eat without working and only the deserving poor don't eat, so there must be a way for the undeserving poor to eat without working. So the Lilies of the Sidewalk, "shamelessly" panhandling the old straights, and not doing too badly until the old straights, who hated them as they had never hated before, had had it up to here and decided to try starving them into the system (or at least off the sidewalks and into the alleys with the winos). But the Flower Child wasn't fuddled; he was a fuddler. Life isn't fair, and it won't be until the system is destroyed. And until then . . .

Beautiful, Beautiful People pushing bad dope to the teenyboppers—"He told me he'd had it before and I believed him"—and sharing good dope with their truly beautiful friends. Beautiful, Beautiful People (including one of my close acquaintance) stealing Thanksgiving turkeys from a turkey farmer (also of my acquaintance) who is having a terrible hard time making it. Beautiful People forging foodstamp applications, getting a Beautiful-People-Sympathizer to hire and fire them so that they can live on California unemployment insurance. Beautiful People faking freakout (or homosexuality) (or starving down weight) (or smoking up emphysema) at the Induction Center. ("Nobody here," said a denizen of one of the big noburbs, "has been inducted in the two years I've been here.") Beautiful People using long-distance charge numbers and moving on fast. Beautiful People borrowing youth-fare cards and wrapping a hand in a bandage so as to be unable to duplicate the signature at the airport. Oh, Beautiful People filing for bankruptcy—"You can do it every seven years and they can't touch you"—just like the Penn Central Railroad and leaving the railroad's doctor, the railroad's dentist, and the railroad's starving grocer on the corner to survive as they can.

Beautiful, but *People?* All the lying, all the stealing, all the dodges, all the capers—all the hypocrisy that the system absolutely demands and *gets from them*—from them and from their hypocritical elders, except that their elders were not hypocritical *about* their hypocrisy. Life is unfair, and it always has been, and it always will be. You play the game "their" way or "they" run you down. Life is unfair: a while back, when I was avuncularly involved with a Youth Commune, one of the Communitarians raised himself up on an elbow and rapped at (not with) me and said, "I'm as good a man as you are. I feel and think the same things you do, and I believe in equality and democracy. But look at me and look at you—and the only difference between us is that you've got money." I told him I had to go to work now, if he'd excuse me.

But this frankness, this brutality, is *closing* the classic gap between generations, not opening it at all, and when did *this* ever happen before: a merger of infantile grownups and broken-down kids, neither of them Beautiful? If I could get away with it—if Ike could have got away with the U-2 flights . . . But I could and did get away with it when I was what in my day was called a kid, because I was what in my day was called a kid. Puppies aren't immoral; puppies are naughty. But an old dog has to be careful, play the game carefully, lest he be caught. Kids get caught and get cuffed, but grownups get caught and get handcuffed.

Graffito: "I want to be what I was when I wanted to be what I am now." Be what you were, with temple bells, headbands, goldilocks, bare feet. *You wash your feet when you come in from playing; they're filthy.* I was a pink-and-blue and filthy-footed attention-getting device myself once, but I do not recall that I got the attention after I cut my second teeth. When I was *high* Pa told me to get out and come back when I could behave myself, and when I was *down* he told me to get out and come back when I could be more sociable. Ma dropped me in the suds every night and got my farina down me; Pa threatened to hone his razor strap on me pretty regularly; but they had their own little lives to lead, Pa on the streetcar with his paper-box samples and Ma over the washtubs in the basement. Pretty soon I'd grow up—or I wouldn't—and be off their backs and they could settle down to a little serious cribbage. *Nobody's paying attention to me.*

A ball while it lasted. A costume ball, but whoever wore a costume except to be seen in it? You preen in your pad and head for the ball, and so does the duchess. So even before the ball is over—and why does it ever have to be over?—it operates on mummery, psychedelic or just plain carnival. *How do I look? said the duchess to the duke. Fuss and feathers,* said the duke. Fuss and feathers. And like all mummery it depends for its effect on antithesis. No washerwoman, no duchess; no straight, no groovy. We live off each other, we sorrowful old clowns wearing our paint, *Look at that Caddy,* the sorrowful young clowns, wearing theirs, *Look at those shark's-teeth.*

Sorrowful. Nobody pays any attention to the new car *or* the new god's-eye, everybody's got one now, just as everybody's got a pecker or a vagina (and sometimes both). Nobody pays any attention to morals, everybody's lost 'em now. What's left is manners, the last refuge of an attention-loser. At the White House garden party it was into the pool in evening dress—why not no dress at all? We chanted our heads off when I was what in my day was called a kid, any old chant, One Two Three Four Who Are We For, or when the girls were around, I See England I see France, I See Susie's Underpants. *Ho! Ho! Ho Chi Minh!* When I was what in my day was called a very little kid and I couldn't get any attention chanting, I turned to dirty words until nobody paid any attention to them. I remember screaming "Nekkid! Nekkid!" (*Six*-letter word.) And when I was what in my day was called an extremely little kid and didn't do well syntactically, I couldn't begin a sentence without saying, "Like, y'know."

I couldn't get any attention after a while, no matter (like the junkie) how much harder and harder I hit it. Fortunately for all hands my own attention span was short, and the system had a thousand ways of diverting me from what, at six and at six weeks, were my non-negotiable demands. Its diversionary strategy was bottomed squarely (oh, squarely) on my being, at six and at six weeks, a member of the Now Generation. What I wanted I wanted *now,* and what I had to have I had to have *now* and here. A chocolate ice-cream cone in front of Joseph's Ice Cream Parlor—"Let's stop at Joseph's" on the corner of 55th and Prairie in Chicago—and Ma, who didn't have the money for the chocky then and there, picked me up and licked me then and there and took me home and gave me a piece of sponge cake on the supposition that I'd then and there forget all about the chocky and the licking. I forgot the singular incident but not the generic. It wasn't fair, life wasn't, but when I grew up I'd see to it that it was (at least to me)—a doctrine to which Pa solemnly subscribed when he said, "If you don't like the world the way it is, boy, all you have to do is wait until you grow up and change it."

But the Now Generation couldn't wait when I was six, and didn't. And the world changed, sure enough; and I never learned to accept being judged lest I judge; but I was judged and I judged, and I still was and still did when the Now Generation became the Was Generation.

Dirty feet, stealing pennies, playing hooky, laying down on the job

Saturday morning, playing dress-up Saturday afternoon in the old folks' old clothes, cowboy and Indian, somebody's ragged old evening gown and floppy hat, howling *"Chocky! Chocky!* in front of Let's-Stop-at-Joseph's and *Nekkid! Nekkid!* in back of Susie—why, I'd know myself anywhere. Or any time. Fifteen years after I joined the Now Generation at six, we went in a select body from the fraternity house to see *Beau Geste,* with Clark Gable as Douglas Fairbanks, and came back to the house and drank too little gin to get too much drunk and have drunkenness as an excuse for chasing each other around the roof with swords. Any time, Ma: "What's this Sammy's last name?" "Huh?" *"What's this Sammy's last name?"* "Sammy's?" "Yes, *Sammy's."* "I dunno, gosh, Ma, he's Sammy." Fifty years later my son introduces me to his Sammy (and Sammy is twenty years older than he was when I knew my Sammy). "Sammy—Milton." "Hi." "Hi." "You know Sammy's father—teaches at Wisconsin." "Oh." Maybe Sammy's father's name is Sammy, too, and maybe I'd know that I knew him if I knew what his name was. Or: I walk into the living room of my house. A dozen Sammys occupy the chairs and the floor drinking (out of bowls) Zen-Zen tea. None of them gets up. None of them says hello. No conversation going on and no meditation. Just sitting there. I stand for a minute or two and go out. Or: I'm trying to do my desperate lengths in the local pool, along with the other old desperate length-doers, and the Young Adult members cut across us and capsize us and hit us head on and come up from under us and dive in on top of us. Playing tag. I used to play tag in the pool myself and, while nobody called me a Young Adult, by the time I was twelve the ancient mariner I landed on top of told me to act my age or get out of the pool.

I had no manners, either, but the ancient mariner wasn't afraid to tell me so; he wasn't afraid I wouldn't love him if he did, or much interested if I didn't.

3: Cold Comfort

THERE IS one place where the Now Generation has always been the Right Now Generation, and that is the United States of America. As an accident of both history and geography, American society was the sole occupant (except for a few savages without gunpowder) not of an immeasurably rich land but of an immeasurably rich continent at the time of the birth of technology. Rich and (with the genocide of the savages) uncontestable except by Americans. Rich and unreachable except by Americans. Rich and moated and its moats impassable by (among others) the British Navy. It could not be invaded or its own invasion of its hemisphere impeded. It could not be colonized except by Americans or kept from colonizing within its own immeasurable boundaries. It could not be settled by anybody else, only by Americans.

It was the only inherently revolutionary society in history, and the only thing it ever did that was not revolutionary was fight the Revolutionary War. Its revolution was (to put Trotsky's expression where it belongs) permanent revolution. The uninstructed American whom Tocqueville encountered a century and a half ago swept the New York skyline with his hand and said, "All this will be changed in twenty years." He was right. And he would have been right had he said it every twenty years before or thereafter.

Conservatism was unthinkable in America; its tories were upstart, its robber barons radical. Law and order were unthinkable as soon as the Appalachians were crossed. The state motto of Illinois, "Here I Rest," is a libel on America, and the state motto of California, "I Have Found It," should have been "Kilroy Was Here—and Kept Going." On and on into the sun and the next day's dawn somewhere else. "Do It!" wasn't invented by the Yippies; it's more American than apple pie *or* violence. Every kind of utopia—"Do It!"—came and went and came again, leaving its detritus uncollected and uncovered behind it. New. Now.

Open, openhearted, open spaces. Quick hospitality. Quick friendship, "my good friend Sammy." Quick generosity. Quick adventure. Quick recklessness. Quick frenzy as the summit of the next range was achieved, and quick fury as the Wild West spread to the East and the melting pot seethed with new feuds on old. As American as "Do It!," apple pie, and violence is: volatility. The unthinkable of unthinkables was stability. The Admirable Crichton—the servant's son a *servant?*— was the first Un-American. "By God"—or "By damn"—"my son is going to have the advantages that I didn't have." I hear you, oh, how I hear you now. Take advantage of those advantages, son. I'll take advantage, Dad. Beautiful instability. Everything—everybody?—up for grabs. Every dream the next generation's reality, and we'll beat 'em this time around, too, and beat 'em for keeps; we are not, as President Nixon said, going to suffer the first humiliation in America's proud history. Cataclysm, maybe—humiliation, never.

Open, openhearted, open spaces. Turkey and buffalo and timber and tobacco and cotton and wheat and oil and gold and golden spike and the gold-plated Cadillac. Not only in America, but never any place else. *Do It!* Strive and succeed, nothing succeeds like success, there is no substitute for victory. Don't tread on me (I'll tread on you). Poland to polo in three generations, free land, free men, free women. Every man a king. Too much? *Too* much. Pa never made more than forty dollars a week in his life, Pa wasn't very far off the bottom, and he pushed back his chair after supper every night and said, "I et like a fool." The stewardship of half the world's wealth was too much for a twentieth of its people. No time to ponder it—*Do It!* No time to contemplate the past. No past. No time to contemplate the future, only to keep up with it. The Romans had it easy; the Americans would have to be their own barbarians.

I am told that Cassandra was an unattractive girl. She may have been unattractive, but she was right. There are unattractive Cassandras who are saying that the Born Sick Society has entered the terminal stage, that the big boys are rolling the barrel over the falls with the Silent Majority inside the barrel. May be. But may be that the heavens—or the hells—are not going to fall in on America (and if America, everywhere). May be that the Youth Revolution is no more a revolution than the Revolutionary War was and is only, like the country itself, an excruciating case of growing pains. May be that it is only the Old Adam (or the Old Nick) in Living Color. And it may be that it isn't a revolution of youth, but only a rumble perpetrated by that minority of troublemakers—President Nixon's "bums," Vice President Agnew's "rotten apples"—to whom the flat-earthers always ascribe the troubles that they themselves don't make. As the 1960s went into high gear the minority of troublemakers was invariably computed at 10 percent. But the computation involved the Romanoff Error, as it always does. It is not the troublemakers who need to be computed, but those who, in addition to the makers of it, are perfectly willing, for reasons of their own, or for no reason at all, to see the trouble made.

The Romanoff Error is never made by the J. Edgar Hoovers, who bother to familiarize themselves, within limits, with the fate of the Romanoffs. Like the Bolsheviks of October, the combined forces of the disorganized SDS, the never organized Yippies, the Socialist Workers Party (not to be confused, but no matter, with the Socialist Labor Party, least of all with the Socialist Party), and the adherents of Chairman Mao, together with (but together with only for purposes of computation) the Communist Party of the U.S.A.—all together they did not comprise 10 percent (or 1 percent) of the American populace. The critical datum is the number, always, of fellow travelers. When Sergeant John Harrington, national president of the Fraternal Order of Police, labels pop-music festivals "a communistic plot to destroy our youth," * he is standing on firm computational ground; it takes no more than two to make, and even execute, a plot. He is standing on equally firm ground when he goes on to say, "Khrushchev said that he could not destroy us from without so he would decay our youth so he could destroy us from within. I think Khrushchev"—when Khrushchev had no job at all—"is doing a good job." † It takes no more than one to do a good job (as witness the Creation). But to tote up the placard-carrying members of the SDS and the other visibly decayed youth, and multiply by 1,000 or 1,000,000 for good measure, is punk computation, as the Romanoffs learned at Ekaterinenburg.‡

Public-opinion polls fail to exclude the Romanoff Error. In roaring, riotous 1970 the Gallup Poll found the greatest approval for President Nixon's performance in Americans under thirty and that that

---

* New York *Times*, August 5, 1970.
† *Ibid.*
‡ Russians and Americans have no monopoly on the Romanoff Error: "As the [French] Minister of Education, M. Olivier Guichard, said last month, [the *lycées* rocked by pupil demonstrations] number hardly more than thirty of the 2,258 establishments of secondary education in France, and, if all of their pupils were involved, which is far from being the case, there would still be only a tiny minority of the 647,000 *lycéens* and *lycéenes* in the country."—Manchester *Guardian Weekly*, April 24, 1971.

same category was the most hawkish of all age groups and the
harshest advocates of stiff penalties for draft evaders.* But by June
of 1970 Khrushchev had decayed the young hawks in windrows
and left their cadavers to the bare-breasted buzzards: "Without any
public announcement, President Nixon dispatched eight young members of his White House staff to sound out students on more than a
score of college campuses after the U.S. incursion into Cambodia and
the killings at Kent State University. The findings were not encourag-
ing: 'Total hostility to the Administration among young people—just
as strong among those who supported him during his campaign as
those who opposed him,' according to one member of the White House
staff." † Even academic surveys may be academic. In the fall of 1969
the American Council on Education questioned 169,000 college freshmen and found that fewer than one in ten expected to engage in any
kind of protest while in college. Three out of five thought that colleges had been "too lax" with student protesters, and fewer than one
in five placed much importance on influencing the country's political
structure.‡ But in the spring of 1970, when some 450 American colleges and universities—including most of the biggest—were demoral-
ized by student strikes, I summoned the members of my freshmen
class to a command performance to find out how the American Council on Education was doing. Of my twenty-two freshmen, twelve appeared, one with books and eleven without. The eleven said they were
on strike, and the one was not (or not yet) engaging in any kind of
protest while in college. When I asked the eleven what they were *doing*
while they were striking, three said they were picketing, organizing, or
"attending workshops," and eight said, in the words of one of them,
"Not going to classes." I never did catch up with the ten no-shows
at the command performance.

There is no computing the incomputable; there is only the utiliza-
tion of the sixth sense that was missing among the Romanoffs and is
never missing among the J. Edgar Hoovers and the Sergeant Har-
ringtons. The beatniks, in their day, were minuscule in number. The
Free Speech Movement on the Berkeley campus—was it no longer
ago than 1964?—numbered between twenty and fifty participants, as
computations went (including my own). What was significant in all
these Californian (always Californian) *vanguardista* of the Youth
Revolution was that they were not repudiated by their coevals. They
weren't taunted. They weren't ostracized. They weren't attacked. The

* New York *Times*, July 15, 1970.
† *Newsweek*, June 8, 1970.
‡ International *Herald Tribune, loc. cit.*

90 percent (or 95 percent or 99 percent, or more) of their coevals who were still square, in terms of appearance and action, from the first appearance of the phenomenon stood still for it, stood still and watched the 10 percent (or 1 percent or 1/10 of 1 percent, or less) do their deviationist thing. In its summation that what most of the entering freshmen of 1969 valued most was developing a philosophy of life, raising a family, helping people who were in trouble, and acquiring friends who were unlike themselves, the Council on Education, having already fallen victim to the Romanoff Error, fell further victim to the Hit-and-Run Fallacy; it should have asked the freshmen of 1969, "Tell us more about that 'acquiring friends who are unlike yourselves.' "

So it was, when the student strike struck the next spring, that management was unprepared to manage. The freaks had been few, and the barn burners fewer, but millions of upstanding (or, rather, downstanding) young squares were even then all unwitting in the process of being decayed by Khrushchev to the point where they would one day gather up their noisome flesh and march to the anti-success anti-music of the few and the fewer. If the millions themselves were all unwitting, why not the Gallup Poll and the Council on Education? The University of California is the best-computerized university in the world—as the biggest it had better be—but its president was able to astonish the Commonwealth Club of San Francisco on May 29, 1970, midway between the Gallup Poll and the findings of eight young White House staff members, when, having taken a reading from his cuff, he told them what every college boy knew, that protest on the nine university campuses of the Golden State now involved a majority of the students. "A broad cross-section of the campus population has been galvanized," he said; apparently Khrushchev was now using electrodes. Activist ranks had now attracted "engineers as well as humanities students, athletes as well as student government officers, sorority and fraternity members." *

The cold comfort of the 10 percent computation was gone. The decayed had infected the sugar-coated supercleans and become epidemic. The 1968 Democratic convention in Chicago might be seen

---

* Washington *Post,* May 30, 1970. The cuff-reading may have been conservative. A scholarly survey made at the same time of 1,542 graduating seniors, "predominantly white, middle-class young men and women with above-average academic records attending campuses in the West, Midwest, and East with varied characteristics," found that 80 percent of them "believe confrontation tactics—ranging from nonviolent mass demonstrations to physical violence —are necessary to bring social change."—New York *Times,* September 20, 1970.

some time again, but never the 1964 Republican convention in San Francisco with its buttoned-up collegians proclaiming their readiness to follow Goldwater and What's-his-name to save the country for what Huey Long said fascism would be called if it ever came to America: Americanism. Six hairy years after the 90 percent (or 99 percent) watched the freaks freaking out in Berkeley, their number went down to no more than 49.99 percent (according to the University of California president's reading of his cuff). There was no likelihood any more that the Young Americans for Freedom would take their intrepid place at the police strong points or just behind them; the thin anti-Red line collapsed on the college green. The fat cats trotting out their Old Timey darlings, Bob Hope, Kate Smith, Jack Benny, would be able to rustle up hundreds of thousands of Americanists at the Washington Monument for, of course, the Fourth of July, and the age level of the entertainees was as high as the entertainers'. The hep cats had only to war-whoop to rustle up twice as many hundreds of thousands of Unamericanists anywhere any time. The body count was warmer comfort abroad than at home.

Cold comfort, too, that the freaks were abominated by their noncollegiate contemporaries in the land where everybody who was going to stay out of Viet was in college. The shipouts shipped out in wrath at the dodgers—but in greater wrath at their elders who shipped them out; and they shipped back in, if at all, in still greater wrath at their elders. Epidemia became endemia; whoever wants to knock it over, for whatever reason, has more in common with whoever else wants to knock it over, be the reasons however incompatible, than either of them has with whoever wants to keep it propped up. What began with the elite spread fast to the canaille. Whoever is outlawed is a fellow outlaw of whoever is outlawed. The dreadful hippies brought the drug culture to the dreaded Hell's Angels, and the Hell's Angels brought the motor-bike culture to the hippies. On the campuses, nonviolent activists amiably argued strategy, not principle, with their terrorist classmates (or former classmates) determined to "bring the war home."

On the perimeter of the army camps the freaks opened coffeehouses (with names like The Pentagon) and the conscript skinheads, instead of kicking them to pieces, came crowding in; the kicking to pieces had to be done by the Chamber of Commerce via the sheriff. In Vietnam U.S. courts-martial were running overtime, and, by the end of 1971, universal urinalysis, to try to cope with drug use by what has variously been estimated at 30 percent (the Pentagon figure) to 80 percent of the American soldiers. Desperate measures were taken "stateside" to try to check army desertions and AWOL's (250,000 in 1969, the last year a figure was announced) attributed in considerable degree to the student-sponsored Movement for a Democratic Military ("a serious threat to the defense of this country," according to the Department of Defense). The visible evidence of contamination began to sprout, shyly at first and then aggressively, from the pates and the chins and the chaps of bus drivers, ticket-takers, office workers, technicians, chiropodists' assistants, even young mailmen and clerks and manual laborers and firemen, even an occasional young policeman—none of them (except possibly the last) motivated like the teachers and preachers trying to "identify" (or, rather, conceal their identity) by shaggy means.*

Way-out dress began to be the fashion, the world dividing between, on the one hand, whoever was young or wanted not to be old and, on the other, whoever was old or wanted not to be young. Middle-aged matrons and patrons stalked the boutiques. Fashionable stores psychedelicized their doornail-dead Teen-Age and Youth Salons and hustled to rename them the With-It Shop. It was no longer possible to separate the shearing sheep from the slinkies by looking at them, and the car dealer might regret having given the brushoff to a tatterdemalion who sidled across the street and paid cash for a Porsche. And vice versa. The two Beautiful People who hitched a ride on the Big Sur and killed their benefactor and ate his heart may have been born killers—but they *may* have been post-graduate anthropologists topping off their research in Inca civilization. Charlie Manson's background was socially deplorable, but his "family" back at the abandoned movie ranch included the daughters of a scientist, a property developer, a psychiatrist, an auctioneer, and, naturally, a clergyman. Oh-oh-it-went-off bombs, together with murder, suicide, overdrug, and the other hazards of being With It, left lacunae in the social register, the relief rolls, and the police records.

Wherever the dropouts dropped out, they all dropped in together and found the togetherness that the straights had been advertising ever since the modern desolation began. The Youth Anti-Culture had ready-made the cheapest come-on yet, its raw materials nothing but the totems and taboos of primitive American society. Against the Age Anti-Culture it had only to uncork and do what comes naturally on a twenty-four-hour show-and-tell basis, and it had its endemia

* "The number of barbers in Chicago has been trimmed by the long-hair fad, so their union is urging them to cut their patronage of the shaggy-maned. . . . 'We're telling our barbers not to patronize long-hairs,' the union's president said. 'They don't give us any business. Why should we give them any?'" —New York *Times,* September 20, 1970.

going. All America "over thirty" turned out to be Middle America, egg-heads and no-heads and two-heads wringing their heads over the hopheads they'd brought home twenty, eighteen, sixteen, fourteen years ago all pink and blue. Another togetherness, as rich and poor crossed and recrossed the wrong side of the tracks to police stations, clinics, communes, and festivals; the déclassé kids were welding their elders into the classless society.

In America, and if in America, then around the world, the old were still able numerically, and with their monopoly of paramilitary power, to hold back the flood tide at the turn of the decade, but the increasing use of the power produced decreasingly salubrious consequences, as it always does, and, as it always does, stiffened the resistance of those who know that they have time on their side. In spite of the advance of geriatrics, the 1970s would tell the story unless "they grew up." (There was always less evidence that they would and more that they wouldn't.) Concessions were fuel to the fire, and eighteen-year-olds were no more to be bought off with the right to vote for Nixon or Humphrey than they were with a plastic flag on the moon, no more to be crushed with truncheons than they were to be washed away in Governor Reagan's bloodbath. Implacable and irresponsible—while the responsible citizens who spawned them, and whose responsibility consisted of Waiting with Baited Breath and of buying bumper stickers reading Support Our President, Our Local Police, and Our Boys in Vietnam, went on hoping against hope, and praying against the gathering gloom, that their brats would come back and settle down on the burning fuse under the wall-to-wall carpet. They wouldn't. They had enrolled, for a season, or for all seasons, in Bad Apple Training School to study their own (and one another's) navels. When the navel shriveled for want of sustenance, they came home more imprecative than ever to sojourn for a season on the bent back of Dear Old Dad and revive Mother's enfeebled illusion that it had only been a *phase*. In the decade after it all began I never met an ex-freak, only some who had landed to refuel or restyle and lift off again to come down, if not on the barricades, in burgeoning rabbit hutches as far away from it all as possible.

Cold and ever colder comfort to assemble Sunday mornings in the Middle American Church and sing the old hymns and drop a Pittsburgh streetcar token into the collection plate—and then have to assemble Wednesday evening to dismiss the pastor for leading the Vietnam demonstration or for getting married (or for not getting married) or for getting a divorce from the organist twice his age to marry a choir girl half his age; or to accept his resignation because he was moving to a Black Pulpit or a Ghetto Pulpit or the Office of Economic Opportunity or the Council on Human Relations. Cold and ever colder comfort to welcome the flag-wavers to the White House and see one's own banal Middle American patriotism, the patriotism of God Save America, give way to the malevolent idioticization of Love It or Leave It. Colder and colder comfort to see the tribe increase whether you gave them all a passing grade, or went down to the Monument before breakfast to talk it all over with them, or clubbed, or gassed, or shot them, or unleashed the yahoos whose disposition to get it over with would, if you left them unleashed, join the issue with the lintheads at some point in the imminent future and between them, under the contending banners of some Man on Horseback and some Kid on Horseback, crush the Middle out of America, out of France, out of Germany, England, Italy, Japan.

Ever colder comfort to hear of the Acid Graduation—into Transcendental Meditation or the Psychedelic Mass, and to hear *Timothy Leary* say, "The real trip is the God trip." "Jesus said, 'I am the truth,' and that's where it's at, man, that's where it's at." The Swinging Church was their church, not yours; if you wanted to *do it,* you did it their way. Ever colder comfort in the "Jesus freaks" hopefully heralded by *Time* (in four colors) and Leonard Bernstein (in forty-four colors at the four-hundred-forty-four-million-dollar Kennedy Center) and, yes, Billy Graham. The new Pentecostalism—"Maybe they're on their way back, Mother, what's Pentecostalism?"—which bypassed the Church Eternal for Jesus *Now*—"What's *captism,* Mother?"—in the Holy Spirit that drives out the demons. ("I had a vision of them flying out the window like a cloud. It sure cleared the air, man. I'd gone the political route and the drug route and the Hare Krishna route. They're counterfeits for what you feel when there's an angel in the room.") Another island of the blessed young; another door locked as tight against the sociologized soft-shell Sherry-Hour red-noses of the Friendly Come-as-You-Are Church as it was against the cold-water blue-noses of the Come-As-You-Would-Be Old-Time Religion. Frigid comfort.

Bone-chilling comfort that the Movement was hopelessly divided between the hideaway communards and the do-it-now Robespierres, with the latter selling off as the Vietnam War was "wound down." Either way they would go would spell disaster for the Then Generation. Whether they were cultivating organic turnips or breaking bricks into handy halves, they were through throwing roses. What divided them was the methodology of saying No; they were one in their nay-saying. So, too, coldest comfort of all, the division between the Movement (white) and the Movement (black). It ought to have been good news to the totterers that the young honkies, for all their eagerness to be accepted, for all the all-out Robespierreianism of the Robespierre branch, were rejected by the young Afros. It ought to have been good news that all the Woodstocks were 100 percent white (except for entertainers). It ought to have been good news that Our Little Ones, whatever else they were and did, were uninfected (though not for want of their trying) by the sleepless maniacs of the Black Ghetto, pouring out of their hutches at midnight to burn, baby, burn, and shoot back at policemen and guardsmen and smash the shop windows and latch on to the dream of the Madison Avenue mass-market slob—a color TV set. It ought to have been good news—but it wasn't. It was only a difference—however enormous—in the methodology of saying No.

The young honkies leaped off the ladder of Madison Avenue's soap-scrubbed slobs while the blacks, young and old, were on their way up it. (Every Negro seventh-grader in San Francisco's Roosevelt Junior High School, in an essay, "My Thoughts on Hippies," said, "They're dirty.") After three hundred years in line at the bottom of the ladder, the blacks were still at the end of the line. The young honkies wanted to move them up—without, of course surrendering the rungs that Mom and Dad were holding for them while they were tripping. Enthusiasm unlimited for black jobs—for blacks, for black studies—for blacks, for black dormitories—for blacks. The classic white liberal patter updated, and the conscientious white liberal, young and old, marched behind Martin Luther King in the splendid short-lived days of civil rights prayerfully pursued against the gunmen of the white bourgeoisie both petite and grande. An end to Martin Luther King and overcoming *someday* and all that jazz. An end to concern and to dedication and to sacrifice and all that jazz. At the beginning of the 1960s a young man of my acquaintance (lovely family) began his career by going to jail for thirty days for a civil-rights sit-in in San Francisco and reported, on his emergence, that the honest black criminals he met persuaded him that *civil* disobedience wouldn't help the blacks (still Negroes, that prehistoric decade ago); he dropped out of graduate school and into the honky Hashbury he dropped to stay. At the end of the decade I had daily contact with a commune in New England, and I never heard race mentioned, not so much as once, by any of the members of its continually changing (but always white) population. Chairman Mao, neither white nor black, graced the walls of the Maoists, who were neither black nor yellow.

The black campus killings of black collegians produced no massive protest on the country's desegregated—i.e., white—campuses; it took the white campus killings of white collegians to do that. At least our pink-and-blue toddlers would not make common cause with the brown niggers (who wouldn't make common cause with them). Fast-frozen comfort again, as the Caucasian babies began burning the banks and the ROTC buildings and smashing the shopwindows (*and* the color-TV sets). Better prayerful desegregation—oh, for Martin Luther King now—than segregated militancy. Now our toddlers were infected, after all, but by whom and by what? Hadn't all their happenings been secure against the unbeautiful spades who told each other that black (which is no more beautiful than blue) was beautiful? Comfort frozen stiff; similar subjectivities produced similar attitudes and similar behavior without reference to color, creed, or condition of previous, present, or future servitude. Whether it was Vietnam, and "Hell, no, we won't go," or the ghetto, and "Hell, no, we won't stay," common cause wrote the unlove letter to an America that was promises made with its fingers crossed. *Our* little pink-and-blue babies and *their* little brown ones, in their separate modes, but ever more similarly, were saying No.

4: The Sellout

THE customary view of life is that you're turned on when you're born and you're turned off when you die. If you have to be turned on again when you're twenty (as you do when you're nearly dead at forty) you must have died somewhere along the line. Somebody—or something—killed the young.

If you want to try to figure out what it was, you can do worse than take America and the year 1968, when the assassinations of the last of the faith-healers, black and white, were followed by riots (including the police riot at the Democratic convention in Chicago) and the first of the mass demonstrations that ended not with the V-sign but with the clenched fist. The days all hell broke loose, the birthdays of the Age of Confrontation. It was the second decade of the lives of the young. They were born *circa* 1948. If you want to try to figure out what it was that turned them off when they were twenty, you have got to look at them not as they were in 1968 but as they were twenty years before, all pink and blue and destined to the human lot of turning brown.

1948. The war—*the* war—was on. The barbarous Russians had rejected Mr. Bernard Baruch's perfectly reasonable proposal to stop the armaments race right where it was, with the Americans with the Bomb and the Russians without it. But the war was incidental. The primary differences between 1948 and, say, 1928, or 1908 were these: (1) peacetime conscription; (2) the postwar baby boom; (3) automation; (4) television; and (5) the possibility and (with the possibility) the prospect of the end of the world. There were, in addition, two other facts of life not then pressingly present at the cradles of 1948 but hovering above them. One was the self-enslavement of the higher learning to the truth that makes men dead, the colleges having been bountifully underwritten to convert themselves into firing ranges, the universities even more bountifully underwritten to produce the two-billion-dollar incineration of Hiroshima. The other was the unaccountable restlessness of the newly liberated natives of Indochina —it wasn't just the babies who didn't know where *that* was—from the frightful Japs now that they were restored to the bounteous bosom of France.

In contrast to these seven wonders of the America of 1948, I give you the America of 1908 and of 1928, the years in which I was, respectively, born and turned twenty without having been turned off. The America of my childhood was, of course, an unjust America. The rich were richer than they would be again and the poor poorer. Blacks were Negroes, Negroes were niggers, and niggers were ineducable and would, therefore, always be menial. Jews knew their place and did not take forcible possession of the university president's office or the country club that refused to practice participatory democracy. And if there was anything lower than a Jew, or Yid, it was a Jap or a Chink and nobody could tell the difference. An unjust and an uncouth America, and, for a white man with money or even the prospect of money, a grossly insensitive America—a drugged culture.

"Better than Europe, anyway"; worse than Europe, because it professed to be so much better. Exactly what kind of America it was I have known in my own person and my own history. I have lived in one Jim Crow locality or another all my life, in what I was brought up to recognize as a Nice Neighborhood. In all the years I have lived in the Nice Neighborhood nobody did or said anything about the contradiction between the national practice and the national pretension to civil rights. The churches, the schools, the office holders, the office seekers, the businessmen, the unions, the service clubs, the social clubs, and, of course, the hotels and the restaurants and the shops all did nothing and all said nothing; and the realtors lived in terror of so much as a suntan. The townspeople were as quiet as clams, and the press did nothing to disquiet them. In the Nice Neighborhood Nice Boys and Girls were not told—and did not ask—about conditions at the county hospital or the county jail or among the sharecroppers or the migrant workers or the sweatshops. The unattended agitation of Outside Agitators demonstrated that America was the Land of the Free. Once every twenty or thirty years a guilty spasm—a New Freedom, a New Deal, a New Frontier—ended with a Rally 'Round the Flag. When the Rally ended and the Flag was lowered, a third of a nation was back where it started and the repression of Outside Agitators began. And this was the richest society that ever was; what was it like to be really poor, in Asia, Africa, Latin America, eastern and southern Europe? Nobody asked, and nobody answered except Export and Import and Balance of Payments—and *their* answer was to wait until the famous evening of August 15, 1971, when the American President would announce devaluation, and there would be headlines in Europe reading: THE DOLLAR IS DEAD!

An insensitive and shortsighted America—but still a generous and visionary one where I was born in 1908. Its golden door was open and the lamp of opportunity (even, in some rare but beguiling respects, of equal opportunity) was bright beside it. Its very existence was a terror to tyranny everywhere, lest its spirit be infectious—as indeed it was. (In Indochina a rebellious student who later called himself Ho Chi Minh was secretly plastering the village walls with the preamble of the American Declaration of Independence.) It was an America which, in its sumptuous isolation, was able to cultivate and perfect the techniques, if not the arts, of perpetual peace; in the first eight years of my life in the city of Chicago, I never once saw a soldier. America was still, as it was intended to be, a refuge from chauvinist horrors. If someone had told my Chicago-born father that he had to take a loyalty oath, he would have said, "What do you think this is—Russia?"

There, all there, in 1908. There, all there, if perceptibly fading, in 1928. Gone, all gone, in 1948, never there to be seen again or even (twenty years after 1968?) remembered. Gone, and in its place, in 1948, the superpower whose lesson to all the world, including its black and white babies, was superpower. Superpower and the responsibilities of superpower (but the superpower first and *then* the responsibilities); the new bought-and-sold imperialism whose colonials were paraded as sovereigns, committed to preserve the *status quo ante* all over the world; the great engine of destruction, all its moving parts geared for war, the *garrison state* the world had shuddered at when it arose in Germany.

Peacetime conscription, said Woodrow Wilson at Versailles, was "the root evil of Prussianism." In 1948, after Prussianism had been destroyed not once but twice, the American people fastened its root evil on their newborn babes; and its opponents were ridiculed when they predicted that it would change the very character of American society and would never come unfastened. Peacetime conscription was not just one more mincing little step down the primrose path to perdition. It was the end of the New World. And it provided the upcoming American young with the first impulse the American young had ever had to drop out of American society. It had done just that in continental Europe for a century, populating the United States with enterprising lads who split the scene on which Napoleon (the actual inventor of the root evil of Prussianism) said that he could now afford to spend a hundred thousand men a year.

1948. In 1968 conscription would (as it always has everywhere) exempt the elite in college. Now add the two other factors projected in 1948: the postwar baby boom (and the dispensability of teenagers as the consequence of Cold War prosperity) plus a labor market radically reduced by automation. Result: The American college elite in 1968 would be more than half of the country's age group. In 1948 the country's educational facilities needed to be expanded as fast and as far as possible to accommodate the college population in 1968. Nothing was done.

By 1968, then, the lower learning already wrecked, the higher would be so jampacked with (you should forgive the term) students, and so frantic to expand its physical plant, and so wretchedly staffed with uneducated and uneducating instructors, that what it would be operating would be an assembly line. Whatever could be done to computerize ebullient young human beings would be done; the four-foot hair, the four-letter word, the fist, and the fire bomb were the way, and the only way, that a spirited young human being could impede the processing process and say, "I am." (Graffito: *I Am a Human Being. Do Not Fold, Staple, or Mutilate.*) The debasement of the higher learning would be capped by the cynicism of its male *enragés* who, to hang on to their military deferment (i.e., exemption), would elevate to an art the traditional goof-off's unrelenting search for a foolproof curriculum—the pipe courses of my day—and further debase an educational system in which the customer was always right. The state universities and colleges, dependent on legislative support, transformed themselves unashamedly into service institutions: You want it?—We got it.

The service institution was the ultimate debasement of the higher learning. Education is not vocational training, because training is not education. Animals and slaves are trained. Men are educated. The purpose of education is not a job—that's the purpose of apprenticeship—or the housing of its students or the entertainment of its alumni or the national defense or the advancement of industry. The purpose of education is human freedom in so far as human freedom may be achievable through the cultivation of the intellect directed to the intelligent judgment of public and private affairs. The problem is not to get ROTC or Dow Chemical off the campus. The problem is to keep everything off the campus that has nothing to do with education for human freedom. That takes care of ROTC and war research and industrial and commercial and labor research. It takes care of the placement office (and of Dow Chemical) and home economics and physical education and business administration and three miles of beach and four years of fraternities and all the other goodies with which a holy profession perverted by public pressure has tricked out the higher learning in the hope that the young could be kept quiet.

In the universities, which set the pace for the colleges, the big spender, the red-white-and-blue right customer, was in Washington. He liked what he had got for his two-billion-dollar purchase of the bomb-in-a-poke in 1945. Now that he had it (invention being the mother of necessity) he had to have more. The sellout of the contemptible eggheads was foregone. Chemists, biochemists, geologists, and textbook writers had had it going for fifty years.* (In my nonage I knew a scandalously incompetent educationalist who produced a cheesy textbook a year and admitted to a $20,000 income on a $2,500 salary, the lowest faculty wage in the institution whose great name adorned the colophon of his books.) Before the New Deal, professors of psychology, economics, and business administration had got to the trough. With the New Deal subsidy (sometimes sacrificially modest) of social scientists, government for the first time undertook to buy brains over the counter. With the onset of the War Effort after Pearl Harbor—does anyone know how wars got to be called War Efforts?—the physicists wrote their own tickets and government reached out for every hand and heart in biological and sociological sight. By the time the babes of 1948 were twenty, the universities were all of them unabashed war plants; three-fourths of all their research (and *all* of their candidates for doctorates of science) were being supported by federal agencies. The Massachusetts Institute of Technology had a $218,000,000 budget, $170,000,000 of which was supplied by the government for something other than the Elizabethan Sonnet, the Pre-Socratics, or Advanced Ethics.

The babes of 1948 who would constitute the student body of 1968 would not, in 1968, be supposed to be any more interested in what the university was studying than they would be in what it was teach-

---

* There will always be an England—fifty years late: "[Prime Minister] Wilson said that a particularly important development in higher education was the growing awareness in the universities of the vital role they can play directly in Britain's economic and social life through closer links with industry and commerce. 'There has been growing interest in collaborating directly with industry. Many university staff act as consultants for industry. . . .' "—London *Times,* June 4, 1968.

ing. They were supposed to be interested in football, goldfish-swallow-
ing, panty raids, and in staying in college forever if you'll stay in
college too and Charlie stays in Viet. They were not supposed to be
interested in knowledge; they were not supposed to be interested in
the enrichment of human life; they were not supposed to be interested
in the motto of my Alma Mater, "Let Knowledge Grow from More to
More, That Human Life May Be Enriched." (As a service institution,
given over, like its German counterparts, to the service of its country,
my Alma Mater in 1942 achieved the first self-sustaining nuclear
chain reaction, whose enrichment of human life in Hiroshima three
years later memorialized the end of the medieval dream of *universus*.)

The professor had once been—whatever else he was—a disinterested codger without enough take-home pay to keep body and body
together—a put-upon man as much to be pitied as scorned (unless
his research produced a sure cure at home or a sure kill abroad).
He had a collar-turning slattern of a wife who despised his unworldly
pretensions, a litter of Raggedy-Anns with prematurely weak eyes,
and a thin red line of debit at the shoe store and the grog shop. The
reason he wore shaggy tweeds with elbow patches and sucked on a
pipe was that tweeds were durable, his elbows were out, and Granger
Rough Cut was a nickel a shtickle; and it was cheaper to suck the
pipe than to light it.

No more. He was a marketable go-getter now with chicken every
Sunday. The Nobel physicist who said of Hiroshima, "If anyone
should feel guilty, it is God, who put the facts there," with that
pleasantry made a bigger bomb than he made for Hiroshima. What
was good for the teacher was good for the pupil; they could cop out
together, and if anyone should feel guilty, it is God, who put the
cop-out there (and the self-indulgence there, and the rebellion there,
and the rocks and the fire there, and, of course, the pot and the hash
there, and, before that, the juniper berry). The students were not
supposed to be interested in God *or* the antics in the laboratories, or
in goodness, or in beauty, or in truth for sale, and most of them
weren't and aren't. But some of them began to writhe to see their
own cynicism compounded by the institutions in which they had hid
themselves from Vietnam.*

---

* "Higher education is in deep trouble today, not only because of activist
students or disenchanted alumni, but in large measure because of the shift in
the nature of higher education brought about by the activities of the Federal
Government. Before the Government entered the research field in force,
research grants were usually given to individuals. The Government continued
this concept in theory, but in practice grants have since been administered by
institutions. . . . The universities have been allowed to charge administrative

In 1968 the sellout of the medieval *universus* came home to roost. Young Whitey—Young Blackie had other things on his mind—made for the "defense" research projects on the campus and hammered them. A year later the director of the Stanford Research Institute, which took the first hammering, informed the eight hundred industrial and engineering executives attending the Seventeenth Annual Western Electronics Show and Convention that researchers bullyragged by campus militants were leaving university laboratories to work in industry or private research institutions, and, since research projects usually go where the researchers are, this could mean more federal funds available to electronics firms. *But*—"When federal research funds come into your plants, you might be well advised to see if there are militants close behind. . . . They have new ideas about incentives for working, about rewards, about the social responsibilities of the business world. . . . They were active in efforts to achieve control of Stanford Research Institute's research programs so as to concentrate them on areas that they felt would be morally acceptable." *

If anyone should feel guilty, it is God, who put the "new" ideas into the heads of the babes in the federal research-funds toyland of 1968. The babes in the toyland of the federal research funds were not supposed to have had ideas, new or old, about incentives for working or rewards or the social responsibilities of the business world or moral acceptability. The professors' ideas about such things were received doctrine which had not been seriously challenged since Christ challenged them, and Christ (as the Scottish judge said to the radical who said he was trying to follow his Lord) was hangéd for it.

---

costs, which in recent years have amounted to as much as fifty per cent of the grant. . . . Individuals were recruited for faculties because they had access to Government grants or knew how to get them, not because they met any student demand; an increasing number of them never even offered courses. . . . Stanford has 375 full-time faculty members in its medical school and 357 medical students."—Vern L. Bullough, "Financial Crisis on the Campus," *Progressive*, October 1971.

* San Francisco *Chronicle*, August 20, 1969.

5: To Know and
to Do

THE received doctrine of 1948 was the doctrine of the adequacy
of knowledge to the pursuit of the proper purposes of human life:
To do the right thing, it was enough to know the right thing. And if
it wasn't, if knowledge was an inadequate compulsion to action, that
was not the concern of the schools, whose concern was knowledge.
It had not been ever thus.

In 1908, when I was born, higher education had not yet broken
the bonds of its denominational beginnings. The proper object of
education (as distinguished from literacy) was still the good man (or,
occasionally, woman). There were learned rogues, as there always had
been, but the schools that had harbored them turned their pictures to
the wall and even declined their bequests. In 1928, when I was
twenty, the good man was still a vestigial concern of the schools, but
still a concern; colleges still had chaplains and student chapel was
still compulsory in the private institutions and something furtively
like it in the public. (When I was a freshman we had a chaplain with
a lisp who said, "Stay in the woad and stay out of the wut.") Moral
relativism was already a philosophical cult, but the dean of students
had not yet heard of it and the burgeoning rogue who felt his wrath
did not advance it as a defense; but by 1948 it was universal. The
fogey who maintained that good and evil were absolute, the same for
the Trobrian Islander and the American, was the scorn of his colleagues and, what is more to the point, of his students. He may have
enjoyed a season of renewed grace when King and Country called
him to mortal combat against the *absolute evil* of Hitlerism, but only

a season. By 1948 the Now Philosophy was the Philosophy of Science. Science had made the Now World and won the Now War; the men of science were the Now Gods and the Now Dogma the dogma of unbelief.

It's a long story and a very old one, a story that does not begin with Bacon's dictum that knowledge is power, with Descartes's *Cogito,* with Locke's *homo rationalis,* with Rousseau's faculty of self-improvement, or with Hegel's perfectibility. It is only its modern identification of knowledge with empirical science that dates from the Renaissance. At one end of the era stands Laplace: "If we were able to make an exact catalogue of all particles and forces in a speck of dust, the laws of the universe would hold no more mysteries for us"; at the other, two centuries later, Justice Holmes, who saw "no reason for attributing to man a significance different in kind from that which belongs to a baboon or a grain of sand"; and in between them Kant's "sovereignty in which reason alone shall have sway." This was twentieth-century man's twentieth-century credo. Its beginnings went back many more than twenty centuries to the Greek hypothesis that virtue is nothing but knowledge and to the explanation (by Lucretius) of the world as atoms in motion.

Knowledge is power—no doubt about that. But what are you going to do with the power? This is the question that science doesn't answer, the question of human action. Science is amoral. It makes— or at least can make—no pretense of instructing action except as to means. It can tell us how to build or blow up a bridge, how to kill a man or cure him—but not whether to. It can tell us what is and how to do what ought to be done, but it cannot tell us what ought (or ought not) to be done. At its best, it is a neutral implement; at its undirected or misdirected worst, a diabolical. When Thomas Arnold introduced mathematics, history, and modern languages at Rugby in 1828—and in doing so changed the whole course of classical education—he excluded science on the ground that it ought not to be studied "parenthetically"; it had either to dominate the curriculum or be omitted altogether. "Rather than have physical science the principal thing in my son's mind," he said, "I would gladly have him think that the sun went round the earth, and that the stars were so many spangles set in the bright blue firmament." Sacrilege!

The votaries of science, if they are morally sensitive men, do not get their morality from their science. If they are morally insensitive, they are no less scientific and no less scientists. One of the geniuses of the Nazi V-2 rocket surrendered to the Americans in 1945 and was soon a genius of the American missile program; a fellow genius of the V-2 surrendered to the Russians and was soon a genius of the Russian missile program. But it is not the scientist alone who may equally be a decent or indecent human being. The separability of knowledge from action is obvious in every discipline, in the shyster lawyer, the bigoted logician, the faithless philosopher, the gluttonous physician, the physicist who rounds a sharp curve at 80 m.p.h.—and the tax-dodging political *scientist* (and the domestic *scientist* who steals from the larder). If there were any causal, or even correlative, connection between knowledge and action, a weighted analysis should show (at least tendentially) that college graduates are better behaved in later life than noncollege graduates and the top of the class better behaved than the bottom. But there is no evidence that this is the case. Avid readers of John Marquand are aware that disgraceful young men may leave the academic grove (and return for the Alumni Reunion) no less disgraceful than they entered it. The academy *qua* academy, if the communication of knowledge is its objective, is guilty of moral nonfeasance—nothing more, but nothing less.

By 1948 all this went without saying; whatever education did for the young, if it did anything, it did not make silk purses or sow's ears out of them. Neither the arts nor the sciences of which the graduate was a bachelor, a master, or a doctor had anything demonstrable to do with morality public or private. Governor Wallace of Alabama was a graduate of its university and its law school and might be assumed to have a passing acquaintance with ethnology. The restrictive real-estate covenant in the North was not a product of the unschooled, nor the "restricted" country club their special province. The late Rabbi Emil G. Hirsch was once asked—in the dining room of an exclusive organization whose members were all university men—the meaning of the Hebrew with which one of the ornamental wall plaques was inscribed. "It says," he replied, " 'We Don't Take Jews.' " "We supposed," said G. A. Borgese, the author of *Goliath: The March of Fascism*, "that the universities would be the last to surrender in Italy. They were the first."

The lifelong crisis of man is moral—i.e., the choice of opposite or contrary acts of the will by men who are so far free to make them that they are conscious of at least having to ponder them when they make them. If, then, what the young need most is what they will need when they are older—for they will be older much longer than they are young—it would seem that education should, if possible, in some way be trained upon morality. We should not make any such requirement of bingo, or tap dancing, or swinging on the old front gate. We might make it of education because education is, apart from war, the great public enterprise, and the learned lout is more dangerous than the unlearned.

The schoolhouse is the national ground cover and schooling the national habit. Jefferson was as fearful as Adams—their correspondence is conclusive—of the democratic form of government. In his fearfulness he talked up education (and Madison with him) beyond either its known efficacy or his own proposal of three years of basic skills for every child. The American devotion to the schoolhouse was the result and a model to the world: the consuming faith that the more schools there were and the longer they confined their charges (even unto the "lifelong education" of the book sets), the better off we should be.

We pedagogues were willing to exploit the national habit in so far as we could cozen the moneyed—and the taxpayer's name leads all the rest—out of their money. We did not ask them to examine the national habit's premise, or even to ask themselves (or us) what it meant to be *better off;* nor did we examine it ourselves after the disappearance of the denominational vestige. Our trade secret consisted of our being supposed to have a secret when we hadn't one. What we had, and kept, was a skeleton in the multipurpose closet. We did not want to argue with the taxpayer, and the taxpayer's pressure filled the schools, and the colleges, and the universities, with junk.

Even before the federal cornucopia was tilted our way, the public pressure was irresistible because we had nothing to resist it with. In the mounting moral crisis of the society we were unable to argue that we were doing something useful. Why shouldn't driver training be compulsory in the curriculum? Driving is a moral problem, without intellectual content beyond the grasp of a high-grade moron; the public wanted the moral problem solved and believed, in its childlike faith in the schoolhouse, that the moral problem could be solved by something's being taught; and we pedagogues were unable to plead that we were preoccupied with much more pressing moral problems than driving and unwilling to confess that this one could not be solved pedagogically (as it couldn't be and hasn't been).

The new humanist, too, denominationally unfettered, made no pretense of teaching (or trying to teach) morality; but his subject matter was such that he could not help teaching *about* it. He, too, like the scientist, might be an uneducated specialist, teaching Shakespearean form to students who needed (and, before they took his course, wanted) to study its content. If, however, he was himself liberally educated and, on top of that, a morally sensitive man, he might cherish the secret hope that a little of the content that went into the student's head might, by means of some sort of nasal drainage, seep down into the student's heart. A few institutions like the University of Chicago fought to preserve the teaching of the content of the humanities. It was an uphill fight in the secular age of Value-Free Science. (The "soft" social sciences, bucking for the respectability enjoyed by the "hard" natural sciences, were, of course, in the Value-Free camp.) But Value-Free Science was losing caste as the world slowly awakened from the binge of the Bomb and wondered not what science would do *for* it but what it would do *to* it.

Ten years after the bomb a Nobel physicist, I. I. Rabi, observed with humane satisfaction that "nowadays everyone connected with education, whether in the public schools or the colleges, is pressing for greater emphasis on the humanities." Then came Sputnik, and everyone connected with education, whether in the public schools or the colleges, pressed for greater emphasis on science. On December 27, 1957, the Kiplinger *Washington Newsletter* predicted that "education will swing heavily to science from this time out," and three days later President Eisenhower submitted to an enthusiastic Congress a plan for "expanding scientific education at a federal-state cost of about $1,800,000,000 over the next four years."

Out went the humanities (or the superficial survey courses that passed for humanities), in went science (or the superficial surveys of science), and up went the professional training of technicians and mechanics. Why not? Had the educational plant been doing anything so important—besides maintaining custody of the young dispossessed by their elders—that the curriculum should not be transformed the instant the Russians presented a moral problem that the American people wanted solved? There was no question that the *evil* of Communist success was a moral problem, no question that it had to be solved, and no question that the schools needed money. Mortarboards in hand, the schools stood ready to leap into the breach, requiring only the replacement of library by laboratory and of one mode of investigation by another.

The "emphasis on science from this time out"—the babes of 1948 were ten years old—was a pitfall prepared by the sequence of gratifying suppositions that science was knowledge, knowledge power, and power progress. True, man armed with scientific knowledge was, and is, as a god. Freed from demonology and dogma, he poured forth, in ever-increasing tempo, a cascade of marvels and transformed "the world" of the medieval (and Mesopotamian) oxcart. But his sorrows abode and his terrors multiplied. The rarest of all birds was the commencement orator of the mid-twentieth century who did not wag his head over the discrepancy between scientific and moral progress.* The implication was that morality, like science, was progressive, that the difficulty was morality's pace rather than its nature; the inference was irresistible that there was an integral connection between morality and science that needed tightening up a little.† But when President Kennedy said that "science has no conscience of its own," he was doing more than quoting Arnold (and Jeremiah and Goethe); he was saying something revolutionary about the schoolhouse. He was calling upon it to de-emphasize science and emphasize something else.

The modern idolization of scientific method was the idolization of a procedure that in its application placed sophisticated tools in the hands of unsophisticated men. How they used the tools was a consideration wholly alien to the very nature of the procedure that in its application produced the tools. Scientific investigation is experimental. Humanistic investigation is not. The Nazi physicians who tried to investigate human materials scientifically were as reprehensible as the dream book that tries to investigate scientific materials humanistically is ridiculous. Empirical research on man as man is inaccessible to science because the conditions under which we study man are not controlled conditions. We may shoot a cabbage full of enzymes and see what happens, but not a man. Human life is not an experiment—at least not an experiment of ours.

What the modern pedagogues were doing, and what government bought them up to do more of and to do it faster, was abjure the human crisis for the tool crisis and the moral predicament for the military. Education—including college education—had long since degenerated into real or pretended preparation for making money. That the young might be more interested in other things than making money was inconceivable to the up-to-date school. That the time might come when the young would be in open rebellion against making money was, of course, unimaginable. What was education for? What was everything for? Hiroshima set the seal upon the abdication of what the Schoolmen of the thirteenth century called the last end toward which all human action was directed. Sputnik set the seal

* "How can the scientific mind produce such precision, and the political mind produce such confusion—both centered on this same great city [of Washington]?"—James Reston in the New York *Times,* February 8, 1971.

† "The trouble is that man, by a series of enormous technological advances made in recent times, has acquired almost unlimited power at a time when his social progress gives no guarantee that this power will be wisely used. The nub of our problem is fantastically rapid technological advance coupled with relatively slow social progress."—Lord Todd, in the Presidential Address to the British Association for the Advancement of Science, September 2, 1970.

upon the tergiversations that engrossed Jeremiah, Goethe, and the commencement orators (including President Kennedy).

What was missing from American education in 1958, when the babes of 1948 were ten years old, was an understood purpose, aggressively advanced against all comers—a purpose that would justify either their going on doing what they were doing or their doing something else. Beyond the unappetizing objective of a job in the bowels of industry, in the bladder of commerce, or in the vermiform appendix of school teaching, what did the schools think they were schooling people for? Could they prove it, or even argue it? In the order of human action the end is the first principle. What was missing was that battered old shuttlecock, a philosophy of education.

Ours is the first secular age in history and the first since that of Greece and Rome in which schooling is ostentatiously secular; and America's the only public schooling now or ever that is unexceptionably secular. (Westerners are invariably astonished to learn that religious instruction is still given by clerics in the schools of the *atheist* Communist countries.) The Americans are, in a word, the only people on earth who *believe* so ardently in the power of reason that they take learning to be the sole objective of the institution in whose hands they place their young (whether what is learned is mathematics, restaurant management, or the manual of arms). In the Christian theocracies, as in the Jewish before them and the Islamic after, the asserted objective of education was morality as a means to salvation. It was supposed, right or wrong, that works followed faith and that faith was supported (but only supported) by knowledge. When, therefore, knowledge appeared to challenge faith, there was trouble with the Holy Office. "It is your business," Cardinal Barberini is said to have told Galileo, "to teach men how the heavens go, ours to teach them how to go to heaven."

The settled conviction that men might be *taught* how to go to heaven was maintained—if never demonstrated—long after the age of the Iron Maiden. It was a settled conviction as late as the middle of the nineteenth century. Newman and Mill, the two giants of educational thought in England, were agreed, and vigorously agreed, that the intellect was the proper province of the school. But they were each of them careful to cover their bet on it. It was to be understood that the philosophical cardinal would hold that the Church founds a university "not for talent, genius, or knowledge for their own sake, but for the sake of her children, with a view to their spiritual welfare and their religious influence and usefulness." But the secular philosopher was just as pointed as the philosophical cardinal. In his inaugural at St. Andrew's, Mill asserted that the ultimate end of study is to make men "more effective combatants in the great fight which never ceases to rage between Good and Evil." He did not, however, any more than Newman, attempt to show just how the objective was to be effected by the instrument at hand.

Still, Mill, no less than Newman, meant what he said. A man simply cannot proclaim the primacy of morality (as did Mill) and *omit* it from his consideration of education, least of all the chancellor of a university in economical Scotland. For mankind will not support a public institution, including war, that does not have a moral purpose or the color of one. There are no apostles of wickedness. Capone, protesting that "Insull's doing it, everybody's doing it," is appealing his behavior to the accepted moral standard; and worse men have appealed theirs to a still higher one.

Nor is goodness, praised by hypocrites, praised hypocritically. Men want to be good and to live (if in no more elevated an interest than that of security) among good men; and if they have not found it feasible to be good themselves, they want their children to be good. Ask a man—ask a bad man—at the cradle of his son whether he would rather be the father of a clever scoundrel or a decent boor.

The instinct is just as sound publicly as privately. We know that it is good men who are wanted in the community—and only then good doctors and good hod carriers and good philologists and good votegetters. We know that what was said of old is true, that the state is not made of oak or rock, but of men; and as the men are, so will the state be. We know that goodness—and not law at all—is the bond of men in community and that even a band of thieves is held together by goodness and by goodness alone. Good men (as Penn said) will make good laws, and if they make bad laws they will correct them; but bad men will subvert good laws and good societies. We have seen, and see, it happening.

The settled conviction that men might be taught how to go to heaven was just as long and ardently maintained in America as in Europe. In 1701, Yale University undertook to transmit not only *Veritas* but *Lux;* a century later Oberlin College in Ohio was consecrated by its charter to "the total abolition of all forms of sin"; and only yesterday the Haverford College catalogue asserted that more important than the skills of learning "is the desire and moral capacity to use these skills for worthwhile ends." The prospective Haverfordian was left to understand that a church-related college would not leave the desire and moral capacity unattended to.

If a private institution like Yale, Oberlin, or Haverford thought that it could attend to such matters, there was no legal impediment to its trying; it was over the Wall of Separation upon which the safety and security of the secular state rest like Humpty Dumpty. But public education is forbidden by the First Amendment to the Constitution of the United States to abolish all forms of sin, to tamper with desire and moral capacity, and to ask which ends are worthwhile and which are not. What ever made us think that it could if it tried? What evidence has there ever been, what evidence could Newman himself adduce, that even under the most sacred auspices education could make men good *or* bad? Logomachos wants to know if God is corporeal or spiritual when we encounter Him in the Eucharist. "How should I know?" says Dondinac. "What! You don't know what a spirit is?" "Not in the least: Of what use would it be to me? Should I be more just? Should I be a better husband, a better father, a better master, a better citizen?"

The centuries of sacerdotal schooling may have produced especially good churchmen. Had the churchmen been especially good men, the first two parts of the Divine Comedy would have had a small cast of characters and Luther would have had to do without all ninety-five of his Ninety-five Theses. The parochial schools were not peripherally religious like Yale or Oberlin or Haverford. They were blatantly so, and their objective was, accordingly, the improvement of the pupil as an immortal soul which will be known by its fruits. They meant to make men good. But where was the evidence that they did? The alumni of Notre Dame were all fine fellows, but no finer than the alumni of Yale—or of City College. And they should have been, if goodness could be taught.

If the parochial objective were achievable, it should have been achieved by Father Adam. He was, in his day, the most knowledgeable of men, and he held his knowledge much more certainly than any man since. He knew all about incentives for working, about rewards (which he was already enjoying without working), about the social responsibilities of businessmen, and about moral acceptability (and he and Mrs. A. must have done what they could to transmit to their little pink-and-blue Cain as many of their virtues as were still within their power). The things Father Adam knew he knew without benefit of four years of football, fraternities, and fun. These things he knew without any of the arts and any of the sciences, and he knew them better than those of us who have all of them. And still he fell. He fell in knowledge. Indeed, we are told that there is no other way to fall; and the salvation of Abraham testifies that ignorance of the Law *is* an excuse.

6: Moping Mum

THE BABES who were twenty in 1968 were, like Father Adam, unlettered and, like Father Abraham, ignorant of the Law. What they had learned in school in the Age of Science was not humane (though it is still undemonstrated that the knowledge of what is humane would have been of much use to them in the unrelenting moral crisis of human life). What they had learned in school was a dab of value-free humanities, a dab of value-free social science, a dab of value-free natural science, and, if they were bent on making it, more than a dab of value-free technique in industry, commerce, or some other servile art. If they were not acutely conscious of financial need or greed they did not learn about the incentives for working or its rewards or the social responsibilities of businessmen or moral acceptability; these were not value-free matters and were therefore not scientific and were therefore irrelevant to an education which had been liberated from values known now to be nothing but local superstitions. As value-free as the scientific method could make them with its dabs of this and that and the other thing, and an elective system which inspired them to row their boats gently down the stream, the babes who were twenty in 1968 were brands for the burning. Or for burning.

When they were born, there was nothing on earth that science couldn't do—not after Hiroshima. When they were ten, there was nothing off the earth that science couldn't do—not after Sputnik. When they were twenty the moon was within reach of value-free science serving the competing interests of power; the Bomb's two billion was the moon's twenty-four. The incentive for working was power. The reward was power. The social responsibility was power. The moral acceptability was power. On the earth most men were hungry not for power but for bread; in the sky a few men luxuriated, the finest flower of science since Hiroshima. The old sat marveling in front of the Big Picture—itself the poor man's crumb from the feast of science. The young were not marveling; they had been looking at the Big Picture, and at nothing else, all their lives. They were bored stiff by the time they were ten; by the time they were twenty they were bored with being bored and were flexing their muscles instead of feeling John Wayne's.

If the Westerns left their elders helplessly nostalgic for a time that antedated Hiroshima and the moon, a time they could understand, as they could not understand the Age of Science, the rising generation was moved by the nostalgia without the helplessness. In the Westerns there were good men, always simple, always compassionate, always forthright, always fearless, always untutored, and in the last reel triumphant; and bad men whose badness was armored with cunning which in the last reel undid them. The old were bewildered by the modern cunning of science in the hands of the desperadoes in Washington, Moscow, and points East and West. They saw themselves chained to it and hoped against hope. The young, always unenthusiastic about chains, were turning against the marvelous monster. Unlike the old, they had been born to all of its bounties and dismayed by all its curses and promises of greater curse. Like the old, they were afraid of it; unlike them they were not afraid to say No to it.

The few fogies who observed the rising revulsion (superficially against technology) and pointed it out were themselves set down as anti-scientific. Hadn't science produced all our wonders, along with a few regrettable side effects which, however, and don't forget it, saved the lives of hundreds of thousands of Our Boys who would have been Lost but for Hiroshima? The young had no stake in those hundreds of thousands of Our Boys of a generation ago. Hadn't science created the modern world which we enjoyed? The young were not enjoying it. By the time they were twenty and throwing stones at the Massachusetts Institute of Technology, and the schools awakened to their contempt of the computer, it was too late, too late. Whatever else their rap sessions, their workshops, their communes, and their "free universities" were, they were now, as the president of Columbia University told the President's Commission on Campus Unrest, "an alienated culture, hostile to science and technology." (Like the president of California, he estimated them, two years after 1968, at as many as half of all the country's college students and "growing at a rapid pace.") * During the three days the world waited with (what

* *Time* Magazine, August 17, 1970.

else?) baited breath on the struggle to bring Apollo XIII back to earth, I encountered not so many as one student on a California campus who cared whether the moonship ever got down (or had ever gone up); they were Un-American.

Un-American, ignorant, and young—conditions which, in combination, could not help but explode them. Their ignorance alone was enough to explode them. They could not read beyond the level of the comic books they appropriated from the lip readers. They could not write at all. They could not even speak without saying "like, y'know," and not much else beyond their four four-letter words which had always indicated an impoverished vocabulary. (At ten their powers of description were limited to two adjectives, "neat" and "keen"; at twenty they were down to one, "beautiful.") They could not respond articulately but, after twenty years of the Big Picture, only stare wall-eyed when they were spoken to and, when they weren't, stare just as wall-eyed at the kaleidoscopic psychedelia of inarticulate infancy. Immobilized awake, they jerked in their spasmodic sleep to their electric tom-toms that polluted the air with a pandemonium that gorged their being and shut them away from all the world's terrors and all its turtledoves. Lovers living for love, they danced alone, each by himself; the world which separated their elders one from another and each from all separated the young from one another, too—not a generation gap, but a people gap. They could not communicate with one another except at the barnyard level of copulation, which, at its very best, is an enervating delight; and I have heard that it is better to have loved and lost, better both never to have loved *and* to have lost, than to love night and day. An enterprising New York *Times* reporter spent a day in a queue with them, waiting for one of their favorite movies to open, and found that the dominant topic of their desultory conversation was the movies they had seen. After *relating* to a class of college freshmen for a whole semester I got them sufficiently loosened up to tell me that, without exception, they had no communication with their peers, no confidants, no friends.

Miserably lonely like their elders—worse off, perhaps, than their elders, who could at least indulge themselves in the sedentary *pnyak-nyak* of real estate, cars, clothes, Communism, moon landings, weight-losing, and the dreadful behavior of the young. Incurably lonely, nothing to say and no way to say it, nothing to do and nowhere to do it, nothing to want and no spur to wanting it. No pleasure without pain, and life was too painful to be confronted for the sake of the countervailing pleasure. The dreadful truism drove their elders to drink; rejecting patriarchal vice, which would have meant patriarchal acceptance, they latched on to dope. Incapable of enjoying themselves stone sober, they tried it, like their elders, stoned and (like all Saturday-nighters) when they had had too much had had just enough to have a wonderful time and (like all Saturday-nighters) *relate* * (just as they'd been when I was young, after a much less addictive and much more sporadic half-pint of gin). But when they sobered up, their devils were waiting for them. And so on to the next trip to nirvana by way of nepenthe. And the intervals between trips—and the height and length of the trip as the pain abates the pleasure— grow shorter in the drug culture as they do in the booze culture. To live on jolts is to live on capital.

Unhappy hedonists, paralyzed by their incapacity to do with it or without it, paralyzed by their incapacity to move except reflexively against authority undistinguished from authoritarianism. The buoyancy gone out of their hippieesque salad days when, as I used to go panting past them on my way to get an extension on the mortgage or a prescription filled for my (or their) cough, I would catch snatches of their gently buoyant patter: "Pure molecular energy . . . beyond Maya . . . selective expansion . . . inner participation . . . self-realized reality . . . opens you to God. . . . That's *it,* man." A few years later, as I would go panting still faster past to get still another extension or still stronger prescription filled, the character of their *rapping* had changed; they walked or sat or lay with long non-meditative stretches of silence broken by monotone monologues devoid even of the idiot animation of the college bull session of my youth. Moping mum the merrymen: It takes more than saying *wow beautiful man* to feel *wow beautiful man.* At a cheap restaurant at breakfast time I had the privilege of sharing my table with one of them. Another joined us and, like the first, said nothing to me. He

---

* " 'Drugs help me feel close to people.' People who use drugs in groups do frequently feel a sense of community, but so do people intimately engaged in any other group activity. *Feeling* close, moreover, is not the same as *being* close. Many drug users realize after some time that their sense of being close to other people is baseless. Non-partaking observers of group drug parties have observed that many people are actually 'doing their own thing' quite independently of those around them, even though the drug users themselves report intense feelings of closeness. Intimacy is important to everyone; it's what makes us human. Whether or not today's youth have actually been more deprived of intimacy than other generations is less important than the fact that they *feel* more deprived, which is why they look for a place to belong in the 'youth culture' or 'drug culture.' Indeed, many youngsters may be aware that, without drugs, the closeness they feel even for their contemporaries is something less than genuine. It is a reality they don't want to face, so they turn on to foster the illusion of closeness. For them, while under the influence of the drug, the illusion may well be real. . . ."—Charles C. Dahlberg, M.D., of the William Alanson White Institute of Psychiatry, in *Medical Economics,* July 1970.

said to the first: "High?" "Uh-huh." "Banana peel?" "Uh-huh."
"Well, so long." "So long." (Whatever became of the banana-peel
jag?)

If there is one thing worse than growing old—or growing at all—
it is not to know how to have a Real Good Time without having to
depend on an electric guitar or an electric shock to produce it. For a
few months (as long as it lasted) I *related* to a commune sponsored
(i.e., financed) by a tax-exempt religious organization. In its concern
for its religiosity (perhaps even for its tax exemption) the organization put one condition on its loving guests: no drugs on the property.
One evening a loving visitor arrived and lovingly distributed little pink
pills to the communitarians. In the ensuing scandal (consequent upon
the ensuing freakout), hearts and hands of the uncles, aunts, nephews,
and nieces were joined in a mighty rap session. The session ended
with the weightiest of the communitarians answering the great question thus: "The real reason we use drugs is that there's no reason
not to."

No reason not to—no reason to live, no reason to die, no reason not
to. Youth in its springtime, the time to be bursting, dragging itself
through the world to its distant grave—a more solemn sight, perhaps,
than the hecatombs of the battlefield covered with the young with
reason to live, some of them even with reason to die. A solemn
generation incapable of kidding around or being kidded, burdened by
the unbearable burden of having no reason *to* or *not to*. Gone the
"old" Hashbury—the scene itself split—when to be a hippie was
Wordsworth's very heaven. Gone the gentle candor of the busted defendant who, when the judge told him to "take those stupid beads
off," said brightly, "I'll do it, Your Honor, if you'll take that stupid
necktie off." Gone the two-bit buttons that enriched American Button Consolidated—even the legends on them came out of the gag
factories before they were finished. It was hippieism that produced
them: "Jesus Saves Green Stamps," "Support Mental Health or I'll
Kill You," "Wear Pink Underwear and Avoid the Draft," "Smoking
Is Safer than Breathing," "God Is a Teeny Bopper," "Kill a Commie
for Christ," "Draft Beer—Not Students," "Help Stamp Out Thinking"
—social commentary as saturnine as Swift's and a lot more cryptic.
Gone the languid smile, come the curse and the cobblestone; gone
the thrown flower, come the thrown fist and the thrown fire. Gone the
light heart, come the heavy—and in their springtime. *Bad scene*. One
of them, a doe, sat next to me on a plane as the killings spread east-
ward from Berkeley. She couldn't get her small suitcase under the
seat, and she turned to me and said, "What will they do?" "Call out

the National Guard." "That's not funny." The new Puritan, without so much as the Puritan's reason to die.

You couldn't help loving them in their need. You couldn't help worrying about them in their need. And you couldn't help—say it not in Gath—being bored stiff by them.

7: Revolution Is
a Happening

OUR CHILDREN are so unhappy that they are unhappier than we are. And not nearly so smart, in so far as a man is smart by virtue of being better educated. Yes, yes, oh yes, we cannot understand them because we cannot understand what it is to have lived in the world they have lived in.* But they cannot understand us. They cannot understand us because they are ignorant. They were not born ignorant. They had ignorance thrust upon them by an educational system which achieved ignorance by enslaving itself to presentism—i.e., to supposed relevance. We are smarter than our children because we know more about the things that matter to them than they do—not because they know only a little something about being young while we know a little something about being old *and* young, but because as students we had had the vestigial dab of those studies that say something about incentives for working, about rewards, about the social responsibility of businessmen, about moral acceptability. They didn't; by the time they came along Hiroshima and Sputnik had exorcised the vestige from the curriculum.

That the fallen generation should be smarter than the risen is a novelty without precedent in American history; here is a gap as is a gap. It has always been the other way around. When I was a boy not

---

* "Today, nowhere in the world are there elders who know what their children know. . . . It is not only that parents are no longer guides, but that there are no guides. . . . There are no elders who know what those who have been reared within the last twenty years know about the world into which they were born."—Margaret Mead, *Culture and Commitment—A Study of the Generation Gap*, New York, 1970.

one of the one hundred Catholic bishops in the United States had a
father who had been graduated from high school; nor had I. Of all
the advantages fathers prated of, the greatest in a culture whose
national religion was schooling was more schooling. By the time I
was sixteen I had left my parents behind with their little stock of
elementary learning; by the time I was twelve and was getting the
better of the argument, my father was reduced to telling me that I
was so smart I could hear the grass grow. My father was wise. But I
was smart.

My children—let's say yours—are neither wise nor smart. They
are not wise because, while the old may not be wise, the young cannot
be. They are not smart because they have no acquaintance with the
wisdom of the race. Like the scientific director of the Stanford Research Institute, who says that their ideas are new, they have no way
of knowing that their ideas are not new. They have no way of knowing
that the world did not begin with them or that the second week of the
Creation did not begin with the production of the Model T. They do
not know that the world has been both well and badly lost for love and
that even Paolo and Francesca found the ultimate going hard. They
do not know that the anarchy of doing one's thing (or rugged individualism) no better squares with the communal ideal today than it
did when Ananias and Sapphira tried doing theirs in the commune of
the Apostles; or that identity (which they adore) is sometimes at odds
with togetherness (which they also adore). They do not know that
Thoreau was a manufacturer—not a whittler—of pencils. They do
not know that before Manson there was Raskolnikov. They do not
know what came of the nonnegotiable demands (even when they were
granted) of the Babylonians, the Persians, the Greeks, the Romans,
the Bolsheviks, and the Nazis, or why what came of them came of
them. They do not know that nihilism, monasticism, communism,
millenarianism, apocalypticism, and transcendentalism in all its forms
have been given a whirl here, there, and everywhere, rarely altering
the nature of the whirlers and never altering the nature of the world.
"I have never known a patient," says an eminent practitioner in the
field, "who had a drug-inspired transcendental experience that
changed his life." * They do not know (does the eminent practitioner?) that neither has anyone else.

They are the children of the century which did away with the Book
and then with the books, of the Free World in which, if nobody
wanted to read them, there was no need to burn them. The children,
too, of that happy land which had no politics, but only politicians.

* Dahlberg, op. cit.

Their elders had had a mild flurry of political theory when a man named Harry Hopkins—none of my students recognizes the name— decided that he was going to "make America over." But the New Deal was gone and forgotten (forgotten even by those who loved it or hated it) and unheard of by their children; a majority of my freshmen do not recognize the expression, and fewer than a fourth of them can describe it in even the roundest terms. All the New Deals. An eighteen-year-old (an honor student) stared at the plastic figure of a skinny old man seated cross-legged and wearing nothing but a loincloth and iron specs and, in answer to my question, said she had never heard the name Gandhi; and on further questioning she said she had never heard the name Mussolini. Hitler? "Oh, sure, he's in a lot of the late movies." Marx? "He started Communism." In 1968—the year the U.S.S.R. invaded Czechoslovakia—the wild and woolly days of the ever-splintering Trotskyites and Stalinists were lost in the past. (With the student riots in Paris the Fourth International bravely announced to no audience that "1968 is a turning point in the world situation.") China was as far away as possible and nobody (prior to 1971) could get there to find out what was happening; up Maoism, up, at least, the fist and the blouse. The New Left splintered before the glue was dry. The ideologues and anti-ideologues of the SDS rode off in all directions and none. Ideology? In *America?*

I know a little about all of these things because I had my nose rubbed lightly into the history of ideas and discovered that all "my" ideas had a history. As an Old Plan Boy, I had to learn enough about man to know that as long as there are men they will bear some inescapable resemblance to man. Knowing that man takes man to the moon with him, I know that there is sorrow and suffering and sleeplessness on the moon, and hate and envy and greed and terror of death there along with joy and love, and sleep and good and bad dreams. Unless man has undergone a species mutation between my youth and the young's, and something called Now Man has taken his place, the young and I each know something the other doesn't; and even there I have the advantage of them, for while they know a world that I don't, I know a little something about all worlds, including theirs.

I don't say that the little I know about all worlds improves my behavior, only that it makes it a little less bewildering to me and relieves me of having to start life from scratch every morning. But it makes me arrogant, too, and in my arrogance I am always tempted to say more about all worlds than I know. But why wouldn't I be more arrogant still if I knew nothing about any world but my own and, indeed, insisted that there was none? Is the young man who says "If it didn't happen now, it didn't happen" any better off than the old man who says "If it didn't happen in Emporia, it didn't happen"? I can win the argument with the young because I am smarter than they are, but I can't get them to argue with me, me with my "straight-line reasoning," because theirs is the only world there is. Since theirs is the only world there is, who but they has the competence to decide what they should learn and what they should know and what they should do and what books (if any) and what teachers (if any) and what courses (if any) they should submit themselves to? On their assessment, their nonnegotiable demands are proper; on mine, ridiculous. On their assessment, relevant; on mine, evanescent. Cut off from history, the man who says, "This is *it,* man," has no way of knowing that it isn't —and that nothing is.

The galloping Galahads of the campus crying out for relevant education rarely say what they want their education to be relevant to. When they are pressed they say that they want it to be relevant to them. Good enough. But pressed to say what is relevant to them, they speak of life style (though the generation that gave the language "high rise" has a dubious case against "life style"). Still further pressed, they speak of the persons and things that threaten or inspirit their way of—whoops—their life style: "Spiro Agnew," or Vietnam, or war research, or ROTC, or the ghetto, or the Black Panthers, or the Chicago Seven, or the police, or the National Guard, or Kent State College in Ohio (but not, unless they are black, of Jackson State College in Mississippi). What can their instructors do for them? Their instructors cannot figure out how to save themselves from "Spiro Agnew"; how then can they save others from him? The way to be relevant to Vietnam is to enlist—in the Green Berets if you're for it, in the Army of the Lord if you're against it. The man who will not enlist but lets himself be conscripted either for or against Vietnam is irrelevant, and nobody can make him relevant (least of all an irrelevant instructor who lets himself be conscripted by the patrons of Moloch). And the same thing goes for war research and the ROTC; whoever wants to enlist for or against enlists, and whoever doesn't enlist is conscripted (or, in the Now Argot, co-opted). The way to be relevant to the ghetto or the Black Panthers is to be black. The way to be relevant to the Chicago Seven is, like them, to have attempted to attend the 1968 Democratic National Convention.

The difficulty with all these burning issues—and they are burning issues—is that they are not educational issues. Like life style they are, at bottom, moral issues. They involve the cardinal moral virtues of courage, temperance, justice, and prudence. Socrates did not know how to teach these virtues, and neither do the heirs of Socrates. There is, to be sure, always Erasmus and his advocacy of example as the only school that men will attend. If the teacher is courageous, temperate, just, and prudent, some of his students may absorb some of his courage, temperance, justice, and prudence by staring at him; or, since he is only one of the objects at which they stare, and an ever less impressive object lesson to them, they may not.

What seems to be relevant to the Youth Revolution seems to be revolution. But revolution cannot be taught, least of all to prodigal adolescents in a prodigal society; the American young, says Chicago Sevenman Tom Hayden, are "living in the most comfortable oppression the world has ever known." * Revolution can be taught *about,* but that means the reading of books, some of them very old books, as old as revolution itself. And books, except for two or three—Hesse this season, Tolkien last season, Kierkegaard next season—are dead, man, we live where we are. The revolutionaries are not (or wouldn't be, if they knew) appreciative of the impudent observation of Logan Pearsall Smith: "Some people say life is the thing, but I prefer books." *That's not funny.* The revolution, like the three books, has its season in the sun and another revolution takes hold of the revolutionaries. The Panthers reject them. The Chicago Seven (or the Catonsville Nine, or the Pocatello Eight) want *money* for their *appeal* to the Establishment's Supreme Court. Up the Revolution. The Parisian communard asked a passer-by, "Which way did the mob go? I am their leader." Which way is the revolution going? Legalized abortion. Amnesty for political prisoners. Homosexual joy unconfined. End to war research and search warrants and dormitory rules and final examinations and dope laws and parade permits and police oppression. The revolution is like a sealed balloon; squeeze it here, and it bulges there. The only thing it never does do is deflate.†

Of a sudden the bulge is ecology. The United States—the whole industrialized world—is strangling and the ecologists have been trying to tell us so for almost a century. Since 1899 it has been illegal to use the navigable rivers of the United States for disposal. Who cared? Who cared when Rachel Carson wrote *Silent Spring?* The red-eyed reformers cared, the conservationist crazies, and the dwindling ranks of resistance to the science sellout. Now, all of a sudden, the *kids*

---

* Tom Hayden, *Trial,* London, Cape, 1971.

† "All the excitement last spring about mounting a massive campaign by students to help elect peace candidates has dwindled to a whisper."—James Reston in the New York *Times,* September 18, 1970. Observing the phenomenon, that old phenomenologist, Aristotle, said, "The passions of the young are quickly aroused, and they are just as quick to flag."

cared, not enough, to be sure, to wash their feet or tidy their rooms or do the dishes or rake the lawn, only enough to make a revolution of it. Ecology was the Now thing. Hand in hand with Burn It Down and Knock It Over went Clean It Up. *Sempre avanti* the galloping Galahads, Clean It All Up, the country, the city, the sky, and the seabed. A new automobile is buried on a campus (on an *American* campus, of course; where else in the world?). Over hill and down dale the cool crusaders ride their motor bikes and their minibuses, the air fetid with the fumes of their leaded gasoline. (Public magnificence and private squalor had given way to private pollution and public environmentalism).

A dreadful old square suggests that instead of burning their draft cards they burn their driver's licenses—a *put-down*. Another dreadful old square wonders why they don't begin by putting out their cigarette butts in the ashtray instead of on the floor or the grass or the tabletop —*put-down*. Still another dreadful old square points out that their university has long since given up trying to get them to turn off the lights—and has raised its dormitory rates accordingly—and that the electric power industry is one of the country's prime polluters—*put-down*. And yet another old square tells them that it is people, not places, that are polluted and that ecology is first and last a moral issue and that men will not live considerately until they want to, and until then they will only exploit one another's jags—*put-down*.

Put-down of put-downs when the oil companies leap into the ecological fray with their proverbial love of country and contempt of countryside, and the President of the United States, his first and last thought ever for posterity, assumes the intrepid leadership of the revolution with his "quality of life" pitch designed (so yet another old square suggests) to gather the wilted flower children in his green-and-yellow basket—a riot of roses rioting for something nice and wholesome instead of polluting the landscape by lobbing boulders at the police. It is an article of the young ecologists' faith that the big-time polluters are the people who put some of their money into electing the President (any President) because they knew they could count on him to see to it that they kept the rest. What next? Will Dow Chemical offer to subsidize the Ecology Revolution until it blows over? What next?

Ecology has its season; the new season's loss leader is Women's Liberation. Up the Revolution for Women's Liberation. Or down? Women's Liberation wants the revolutionary chick to throw her brassiere to the winds, but she hasn't got one. And while it wants to liberate her from her brassiere—this is a little confusing—it wants to liberate her from her subjection to the musky lusts of the revolutionary cat. But the revolutionary cat isn't sure about that, and what the cat isn't sure of the chick isn't; for the revolution, if it is not notably masculine, is notably male. The female of the species is its *old lady* (that is, its young lady)—that, and only that. Her appearance may not be quintessentially ladylike—she could do with a little dusting—and her vocabulary still less so in the presence of the enemy. She may be adept at passing the ammunition, even a pretty fair shot with a slate shingle. But to her torpid cowboy she is beautiful, man (like everything else, animate or inanimate, that doesn't threaten him). Whoever has had more than a grunting acquaintance with the nesting habits of the revolution knows that the *old lady* swallows her pills and gets the groceries and whither he lopest she lopest. She may be allowed to carry his guitar (but not play it) for her cowboy. At the rap sessions around the psychedelic fire she is the Silent Minority, her aggressiveness confined to the proper advances of the immemorial sex object. Her cowboy isn't at all sure about her being liberated from his lusts; what (as his grandfather asked the suffragettes) do they think a lady's for?

Her liberation from his lusts is supposed to symbolize her equality. The equality itself is supposed to consist of equal job opportunities and equal pay for equal work. Her cowboy doesn't like job opportunities and he doesn't want to think about work, equal or unequal (much less carry the picket sign for it). And what's pay for? To buy His-and-Hers junk? He prefers He-and-She, and in that order. When She does as she's told—or does it without being told—and rebels against the authority of the straights he's with her to the bitter end (or until they trade off, whichever comes first). But when she betrays the Youth Culture and carries the revolution to *him* and his already battered masculinity, he's affronted. Happily, Women's Liberation doesn't attract her much; she's as liberated as she wants to be, and she has no great compulsion to desert her pinchable post and join the Liberettes whose hard core consists of viragos singing their anti-siren to the Working Girls who regard them as the enemy—them, and not the male chauvinists in whose ranks the Working Girls hope to find a Masterful Boy.

8: What Maisie Didn't Know

LIFE HAS marvelously little to do with Vietnam, the ghetto, and war research—unless you are in them and trying to get out—and still more marvelously little to do with Women's Liberation, ecology, and dormitory hours. All these enthusiasms or distresses pass, or they don't, and life has to be got through. What is relevant to life, which has to be got through, is not to change the world but to keep the world from changing you—or, more accurately, to retard the inexorable onslaught of ineluctable corruption. Life consists of (1) falling further and further behind, not in the rat race but in the discharge of one's commonplace responsibilities, and (2) the making of choices, a dozen or so a day, which have nothing whatever to do with Vietnam, the ghetto, and war research—choices among alternatives no one of which is very good but only more or less unpalatable than another. Life may not be real, but it is appallingly earnest—a serious, and often fatal, condition. Life is, in one word, hard—not unbearable, but hard—and a man has a hard time getting through it. And public life, apart from getting dressed up to go out, is private. Life is hard, and private, and what is relevant to it is disenchantment, disappointment, bills, bronchitis, taxes, and death (and more taxes). In its course a man trims his sails and his soul, and, as his delights pass from him, with increasing intermittance, he finds himself increasingly preoccupied, not with maximizing pleasure but with minimizing pain. What is relevant to life—and is not beyond a man's reach, and is not over there somewhere, and is not confronted by crowds or committees—is a kick in the pants. (I speak as a man reputed, and, I think, justly so, much more fortunate than most.)

The young have no way of knowing this when, like me in my baby carriage in front of Let's-Stop-at-Joseph's Ice-Cream Parlor, they make their nonnegotiable demands. They have no way of knowing this because they are young, anywhere, any time. And the young who were clenching their chubby little fists in front of Let's-Stop-at-Joseph's in 1948 do not even know that their youth is the reason they don't know it; they have had no report of it in the course of their schooling. They have not heard about life any more than they have heard about man. And the schools, in their increasingly frenzied effort to meet the demand of relevance, have instructed them in the trivia that are transitory, or the marvels beyond their reach, instead of trying to acquaint them with the report of life by men who have reported it classically; and, beyond that, if possible, fortify them with the only weapons that are ever relevant: an awareness of the human condition and an irrepressible and durable curiosity about it.

In 1968 the chubby-fist-clenchers of 1948 were so preternaturally young and so badly educated that they had no way of knowing that unaccountability is of the nature of childhood, anywhere, any time, and, in an adult, the mark of childishness. They had been beaten into shapelessness by an educational drag that did not inspire their love of learning, elevate their humane sentiments, or capture their attention and distract them from childlike (and ultimately childish) horse-play—a drag that damped down curiosity, developed immediacy, disclaimed responsibility, and forced its terrible textbooks on them. They hit the deck in 1968 peculiarly crippled. They were inexperienced at second hand and, in a culture devoted to the perpetuation of infancy, inexperienced at first. Incapable of recognizing an undistributed middle when they encountered it, they could not help but arrive at two unsound conclusions from two sound premises: (1) Their elders hadn't learned from experience; therefore experience must be incapable of being learned from, (2) Their elders were fools; therefore they themselves must be wise.

Armed with these two unsound conclusions from two sound premises, they proposed to seize power from the experienced fools. There was—when wasn't there ever, with such elders and such youngsters? —no telling them that the seizure of power is not the same as its conquest. There was no telling them that men do not conquer power, but power men. When they were told, by some experienced fool, that power corrupts and that any power at all corrupts absolutely, there might be one or two of them to accuse their lecturer, falsely, of quoting Acton. When they were told that the way to get power is never to be honorable but always to seem to be, there might be one, rarely two, of them to accuse their lecturer, truly, of quoting Machiavelli. When they were told that whoever wants power wants trouble, more than one or two of them would say that the only way they could get their rights was through power; and when they were pressed as to what their rights were all of them would say that their first right was their right to power, *participatory democracy*.

They don't even want the power; their demand for it is part of their mummery. They don't want it because they know that power, whatever else it is or does, is unremitting exertion—the exertion that men assume compulsively in order to get and keep power and dress it up by calling it responsibility. Except for the Maoists, etc. (and they are only the nonlunatic fringe of the Movement), the last thing the young are looking for is unremitting exertion. But we are terrified of them, terrified and (as we should be) guilt-ridden, and in our guilty terror abase ourselves and yield them the power they want to take but don't want. At one college of my close acquaintance they demanded membership in the faculty senate, and got it, and a year later the secretary of the senate in his annual report observed that none of the student members (if, indeed, they had ever been chosen) had appeared at any of the senate meetings. Lenin found the power lying in the streets, picked it up, and found himself incapable of transferring it to anybody but Stalin.

If their war cry were "All Power to the Soviets" and they established their soviets, something half serious might be made of it. But what can be made of that beat-up banality "All Power to the People"? What do they mean, long of nothing at all? The people under thirty (and over what?)? The white people under thirty? The males under thirty? The white males under thirty? The white male collegians? The dropouts, the pushed-outs, the flunk-outs, the fallouts, the goof-offs? The ascetics, the acid-heads, the deadheads, the God-is-dead-heads, the Buddhists? The meditationists, the rappists? The macrobioticians, the doughnuticians? The solitaries, the communitarians, the fists, the pacifists, the resisters, the deserters, the dodgers? The drones, the soldiers, the queens, the stallions, the ecstatics, the social workers, the anti-social nonworkers? Are some of the People—such as the hard-hats and skinheads and rednecks—to have some of the power? (They are people, too, aren't they?) The police, or pigs? (Or aren't they people?) And how are the People, when they have the power, to exercise it differently from the way it is exercised in the nonparticipatory democracy of the present arrangement? *Straight-line reasoning*—out with it, and up the mummery.

If the war cry meant anything, it would mean, as perhaps it does, civil war, and civil war in which the revolution, on the present deployment, would be badly bloodied. For the Movement is not a Movement but a surge so motley in its composition that nothing (including the things that are said here) can be said of *it* except that it represents every kind of dissatisfaction from pimples to the Pentagon; and in so many degrees, at so many levels, that, as the 1970s got under way, what was still a bare majority of collegians at California and Columbia (if the cuff-reading of the heads of those institutions was correct) was also a bare majority at a half dozen or a dozen other universities and a modest minority of the country's collegians as a whole; and *they* were only half the age group involved. Generously add half the upper-division students of the high schools, to be sure that we have encompassed all the would-be dropouts, and the People—if the People means the people—were not the people that the warriors had in mind with their war cry. What "All Power to the People" comes to is that some of the people, presently without power, would like to take all of the power from some of the people who have some of it, and to keep others from getting any of it; and the claimants have no serious interest in exercising it. What they really want is No Power to Any People. That would be the revolution of revolutions. It has long been anticipated by the anticipators of the Second Coming.

Dealing, then, with something approaching an infinite variety of minorities within a minority, reconcilable only by the rambunctiousness common to the young anywhere any time, we are hard put to make a projection twenty years, or twenty minutes, ahead. The fact that their tribe increases irresistibly doesn't mean that it will, or that it will be the same tribe, or the same kind of tribe, in 1988 that it was in 1968. Where it will end is no more predictable than when or if. Some of its adherents will have dropped into the bag if, through the rockets' red glare, Our Bag is still there. Some of them will have died of exposure, enervation, or inanition. (A few will die of overdose, a great many of driving wild, a few in the fringe wars around the American world; a few will be shot dead on the domestic barricades.) But the big bag is time. Doing it deadbeat is trickier at forty than it is at twenty. No more money from home; no more home. And even between the bomb to kill them after they're born and the pill to kill them before, they will still nilly, if not willy, propagate. If their parents could not reproduce their kind, what makes the young think (or would, if they thought about it) that they can reproduce theirs? In 1988—itself a reckless extrapolation, four years beyond 1984—

the Now Generation will be Was, and the then Now Generation may well be in revolution against the revolution. Will the then Now Generation, like the now Now Generation, have had its teeth straightened at the insistence of the Now chicks who will be the then (and surely no less so than the now) dotty doters? The orthodontist's bill alone will catapult the revolution into the bag.

No looking forward with any assurance. Looking backward alone provides any prospect of profitable inquiry as to a—let us say—twenty-minute projection. The babes who were twenty in 1968 were not supposed to have come to the conclusion, latent as it was and already reached by a few discountenanced fogies, that the American (and, if the American, the world's) educational system was a bummer and American (and, if American, then the world's) society a sellout. They were supposed to roll off the assembly line, all of them stamped "Bachelor," and into interchangeable jobs for interchangeable young gentlemen (and young ladies). Nineteen forty-eight again: Henry Wallace had failed, the Berlin air lift succeeded, and Harry Truman had told a reporter, "I wouldn't want my daughter to marry a man who was not her own color"; the social order was secure, and the Keynesian management of the market would (once it was fully computerized) secure the economic until the end of the big bag time. Detroit's assembly line had already eliminated every incentive for working except money, every reward except money, every responsibility of the business world except to make money, and every moral acceptability except the acceptability of money. But by 1948 Detroit was already primitive. Machines worked better and cheaper than men, and the parents of the pink-and-blue babes of 1948 had discovered that work *qua* work was a lousy, lusterless way of spending time to do anything except get money, increasingly indefensible as the welfare-and-warfare state devalued thrift, and altogether indefensible if there was any other way of getting money than actually working for it. What kept the old folks at it, in 1948 (as in 1968, spavined and sagging now), was not the *Protestant ethic,* any more than Protestantism, but the congenital idiocy that everybody had always worked and what would you do if you didn't? The terrors of the five-day week were already upon them, the terrors of the four- or three-day week on the drawing board. Drink beer, look at television, go somewhere, spend some money, drink some more, go home—a working society that, having never known leisure or a leisure class, equated leisure with going crazy doing nothing.

The babes in their buggies in front of Let's-Stop-at-Joseph's were on a no-day week in 1948, a little young yet, but only a little, to come to the revolutionary conclusion that the lousy, lusterless work was not just altogether indefensible but, *if you didn't want money,* gloriously indefensible. If the lousy, lusterless work didn't turn you on—look at the Old Man—you had to depend on your leisure to do it, and you had only to look at the Old Man to see that the approved uses of leisure didn't do it. The only way out would be—the babes were a little young yet, in 1948, but they had not yet discarded the straight-line logic that led to the conclusion—the discovery of unapproved uses of leisure to make the no-day work week bearable week in and week out.

Under the iron law of omnigeniture their use of their leisure—and of their lives—was, of course, predetermined. Of all the generations that ever were in America, theirs was the surest to proceed in the (you should forgive the term) groove. What their parents foresaw (and supposed they had foreordained) would require only college and the job to deliver the *coup de grâce;* television would have rendered them comatose before they had got to high school. Commercial television would be what commercial radio has been; in twenty years, 1948–68, it would not provide its audience with a single three-hour stretch for the performance of a play by William Shakespeare (he of the serpent's tooth). But it would be much more effective—and that much more pernicious—than radio because it would be a much more effective medium as such. (As McLuhan and Aquinas [1225–1274] would be saying in 1968, the delights of the eye are categorically more seductive than the delights of the ear, and the telly would carry to the zenith power the combination of the two inaugurated by the talkies of a generation earlier.) But the combination would have a very special effect on a very special group of the babes of 1948. We shall call that group Group X, and identify it as the residuum when we have disposed of Group A, the Good Boys; Group B, the Bad Boys; and Group C, the Wide Boys.

Group A, now, numbering 95 percent of the babes of '48, would go inert into the grinder and come out round and firm and fully packed in a Levittown–Germantown–Georgetown of the prefabricated dead. While the vinegar of adolescence still stirred in them, their floating detestation of their lot would produce a perpetual hi-jinks slowdown of the collegiate assembly line. Moonflower-children, they would open by night and close by day. Nothing to worry about; weren't we young ourselves once? If only they would say something, do something—*anything.* It was the dead calm, the cease-fire, the stand-down, the stand-still. Between them and their teachers, between them and their elders, the understanding (tacit, like everything else) was total;

nobody would try to do anything, least of all rock the ship (just in case it was sinking). 1958. They were ten years old. "Where are you going?" "Out." "What are you going to do?" "Nothing."

Vast psychiatric services were installed (long since in the colleges, now in the high schools) to stir the young stumps. See your Adviser —*do* see your Adviser to be Advised to do something, *anything.* Were they in need, unresponsive? (What was there to respond to?) *Mad* comics: *What—Me Worry?* What would become of them? Nothing? Nothing. Ah, well, Levittown would take care of them. Group A would grind down nicely—if only . . . If only what? If only—they were ten years old—they would say something, do something, *anything.* (1968—say something, do something, *anything*— was still ten years away.)

Group B was something else again, something lamentably familiar, but comfortably familiar as long as we had jails and jailers. It comprised 3 percent of the collegians, 10 percent of the white noncollegians, 15 to 20 percent of the pickaninnies (who, of course, were noncollegians). They would be the incorrigibles, who were always with us, and if they were on the increase, why, so was everything else—slowly, surely. Levittown would not subdue them or even reach them; but it never had. What was wanted was more jailers, better equipped and readier to use their equipment on (this was new; the studiers were all studying it) juvenile delinquents. They would surf, dry or wet, all summer and surface in the fall to go on the prowl or the h'ist. There would be more and more of them as things got bluer and bluer. They would not stay turned off except by the Army— which got them, but only for twenty-four months. They would not stay turned off for clubs or tear gas or buckshot or for anything less than cyanide or tanks. They were the *anti-social element,* in the Soviet Union the hooligans. Group B.

Group C was one-tenth of 1 percent of the white collegians, and its number was an inconsequential constant. It consisted of the hairs, long or short, who tried to organize the campuses and succeeded in organizing ten-man splinter movements off the wormy old blocs. It was they who kept the J. Edgar Hoovers looking for them in the land where nobody over or under thirty had anything to complain of. They were the Dread Leftists, with a premature hot line to Moscow. *"But I'm not a Communist, Officer—I'm an anti-Communist." "I don't care* what *kind of a Communist you are. Come along."* They would know who Proudhon and Trotsky were. But Georgetown and Germantown (not Levittown) would take care of them, too. They would go on organizing—conglomerates and weekends and PTAs and

ACLUs and Americans for Democratic Action in behalf of Stevenson, Kennedy, Johnson, Humphrey, and Congresses for Constructive Criticism. They would become the liberal intellectuals who *used to be a Socialist myself*—or *a pacifist myself* or *a civil-rights worker myself*. Things would get bluer and bluer, and the pinkos would peter away.

That would be Group C.

(Between Group C and Group X would be the young radicals who would stick it out and never *used to be;* and lumped in with them, the few creatives in the arts in an anti-artistic culture. These would be the rugged individuals—the only rugged individuals left anywhere. Neither organizers nor organizees. Their mark would be refusal of military service and the takeover of the villages in the big cities. Their number had always been so small, and always would be, as to constitute a predictable trace in 1968. Nothing could be, or needed to be, done about them. They might even, after their teeth, or they themselves, were gone, be hoisted to their countrymen's shoulders to prove that ours was the Free World. They would scandalize the Art Establishment and raise the Constitutional Issues and command the services of the Constitutional lawyers, proving, in the Free-and-Easy World, that we were Different from the Russians. A trace.)

Group X would—among the babes of '48—be another trace. Or, since there would be nothing for them to be a trace *of,* a psycho-biological sport. Like a two-headed baby, only unbottlable. Tourists would come by Gray Line Tours to look at them. They would be hatched not in sweaty, savage New York but in elegant smelligant San Francisco, the national capital of Happy Land, with its elegant scenery, its elegant climate, its elegant flowers and fruits (fresh, dried, candied, and transvestite), its elegant restaurants with their elegant menus, its elegant women with their elegant clothes, and its elegant alcholism, suicide, and divorce rates. There in the Pleasure Dome, there and nowhere else, they would be hatched, where every pink-and-blue-blooded American boob wanted to go when he died, at the very latest. The only thing for sure would be that they would be everything (or appear to be everything) that San Francisco was not (or appeared to be not). Like, maybe, trading studied elegance for studied drab and principal (and interest) for insecurity and disinter-est. Or boycotting booze and blood and Brooks Brothers and tinted plumbing and vitamins. Or picking other people's—or the People's—peonies and giving them away. Or sleeping together out loud. Or finding some one vice—could there be one, in San Francisco?—with which their elders were not besotted.

What they would *look* like, when they dropped out of Levittown, Germantown, Georgetown and hit San Francisco, somebody bright should have foreseen in 1948. Somebody bright should have foreseen that you can get out of Levittown but not out of your skin—and television would have wrapped its skin around them and made them its own. Whatever Group X would be or do (if it came into existence), it would wear the accouterments of the Big Picture, combining Rousseau's noble savage with Cecil B. De Mille's footsore, scruffy, scrofulous saint emerging from the desert to stagger Babylon-by-the-Bay. There would be holy men, cowhands (and Annie Oakleys) and Indians (and squaws, or *old ladies*), sodbusters, prospectors, mountainmen (and mountain girls), sheriffs in holsters and kerchiefs and gamblers in the best boots that other men's money could buy, Pioneer Women in floppy hats and long cotton dresses with high waists (and no corsets); and sandaled Christs sure as shootin' to be crucified by piggish centurions on the orders of the high priests of Things as They Are.* Whatever they would be or do, they would look as if they had sidled out of the Big Picture.

What appearances are not is deceiving. The identification of decency with looking decent is the timeless obsession with the outside of the cup which within is full of uncleanness. To rebel against this identification means first of all to be dirty, or at least to look dirty, and the easiest way to look dirty is to be dirty. The dirt is the message. It is not the consequence of soaplessness. It is purposive. Christ's feet were his badge. They had to be dirty, and dirtied, so that he would be known for what he was and those who knew him could signify their recognition by kneeling to wash them. The day that he comes back in glory—and the whole world kneels—will be the day his feet are shining and the high and the mighty will grovel in the dirt. Whoever will take up arms against the Pharisees must shake them up by their perfumed feet, for Phariseeism is nothing but the scrubbed façade.

But it takes more than dirt to make a man holy. It takes renunciation of all the hypocrisies grand and small. To affect dirtiness is only to say, "I want to be holy," or, more precisely, "I want you to know that you are unholy." Dirtiness is one way of saying No. But war to the very knife against an unholy world (whose unholiness is merely symbolized by its obsession with cleanliness) calls for saying No

---

* "When Charles Manson was arraigned in Court, he 'assumed a crucifixion pose with his arms extended and his head bowed'; and one of his 'family,' pleading against the sentence imposed upon him for torturing and killing a young musician, declared, 'I've got a nail in my right hand and a nail in my left hand and I'm only waiting for the crown of thorns on my head.'"—London Sunday *Times,* September 6, 1970.

across the board. As a protest against hypocrisy, and not as an indifference to the symbolic obsession, dirtiness calls for indifferent tatters. Dirty feet encased in seventy-five-dollar boots for hitting the city's sidewalks *blow* the message; and the young man of my acquaintance who spends as much time preening for the street as his mother does, and empties the household of its hot water to wash his dirty hair every night, is having a very hard time telling the old folks that he has broken out of their bag. Like them—he doesn't believe it of them because he has never been old—he would like to be holy. Like them, he finds it a little harder to be holy than to say that somebody else isn't.

9: The Naughty Children's Crusade

I T I S sometimes easier to draw the cork than it is to replace it, but the cork of confrontation was three years in the drawing. On April 7, 1965, President Lyndon B. Johnson, already identified as the squarest corkscrew of them all, addressed His People from what he called John Hopkins University and informed them that they—i.e., he—would put a billion dollars into the development of the Mekong Delta—and before the ink was dried on the TelePrompter the translators had translated it accurately: He would do more than put a billion into the Delta's development; he would put twenty-five billion a year into razing it for development. Twenty-five billion a year—and the lives and deaths of ten, twenty, thirty, forty, fifty thousand young Americans, plus another hundred thousand of them maimed, plus another million of them turned into random butcherers of their kind.

Turned off at birth, tuned into Wagon Train, dropped out by conscription, and turned on by the noise and the grass and the acid so that they couldn't see, hear, taste, touch, or smell what had come out of Texas—nut country, as John F. Kennedy called it the night before he went on to Dallas. That's what would happen in 1968, when the whole country, and not just Texas, would be nut country, everybody in it betting that it would end before they did and eating and drinking accordingly. And having a manful try at being merry, for yesterday they died chasing the bluebird down the freeway with six lights in back and six lights in front and into the pushbutton garage and the fingertip house with the restrictive covenant and the electronic alarm in case somebody did not obey the covenant and the rumpus room in case of a rumpus. Nothing could touch such a man, and what nothing can touch is nothing.

Group A—Levittown–Germantown–Georgetown—was the first to begin moving into Group X; such nice people, too, such a lovely home, such a good upbringing. Group B—the incorrigibles—would find in Group X the only haven they would ever find anywhere and no questions asked when everybody was doing it. Group C, the organizers, would organize the New Left and be swept away with it half organized into Group X. The radical individualist trace between Group C and Group X would go on doing its irrelevant individualistic thing, but in sympathy with Group X. Group X would grow and grow and grow, always amorphously, always faster, and it would no longer be necessary to go to San Francisco and take the Gray Line Tour to look at them in their lair. Their lair, overnight, was everywhere. Lolling along, half prostrate, half educated, half starved, half dressed, and half baked, they were inheriting the earth that everybody fought for and nobody wanted, least of all they themselves.

In ten years—in three—the trace that had been Group X had become a torrent. Our pink-and-blue babies—*how fast they've grown* (and how many)—knew us for what we were and what we meant them to be whether, when they got loose, they bought the bag or they didn't. They knew us for pleasure-leisure-loving locksteppers, faultless cogs in the money-making-war-making machine, dreamers of meaning well but meaning nothing, uneasily acquiescent nudes in our imperial new clothes. You can fool anybody but children (said Freud, and he guessed he ought to know). Ours in their baby buggies had known us in 1948, but hadn't yet mastered the expletives. By 1968 they knew how to say what they'd known—and what we'd known without knowing how to say it in mixed company.

"Accumulated stress" is the post-mortem report of the structural engineers. *Too* much. Too much fat and too much fighting. Too big and too heavy to waddle around any more on spaghetti legs; too po' to tote it, as Sampson Lightning says in Dallas County, Alabama. Historically predictable. Historically repetitive. Historically monotonous and historically sure. Whether you got to the cataclysm by jet or by jenny, by bongo drum or hair-of-the-dog or Hearst, you got there. You'd been there before with the Greeks and the Persians and the Syrians and the Romans and the Spanish and the Dutch and the British and the French and the Germans and the Swedes and the Portogeezers. Next man up: Man, the Cosmopolitan Boy, homogenized out of his separate hole and his national costume by the Mix-It-All Mixer.

The American cataclysm was a uniquely short time cooking. It was, of course, irretrievable, as everything is, and its tempo, like everything's, always greater, but within the memory of men still alive it had not begun. Where and when its beginning? San Juan Hill? Manila? Vera Cruz? San Quentin, France? San Quentin, California? Wisconsin's substitution of Joe McCarthy for Robert M. LaFollette, Jr., in the United States Senate? The New York *Daily News* photograph of Ruth Hall in the electric chair? *Hold it, gentlemen: Shutter open:* Teddy Roosevelt, Edison, Firestone, and Ford. *Hold it, gentlemen:* the two-car garage. *Hold it if you can:* the three-skeleton closet.

Skeleton One: Chauvinism, the first refuge of a meatball. Love these sticks and stones (or I'll kill you), and hate those sticks and stones (or I'll kill you). Kill the bastards (or I'll kill you), and especially their sisters and their cousins and their aunts. Free-fire-zone patriotism and a decal flag for a buck (what's a buck any more, it's the least you can do) (and the most) to prove it.

Skeleton Two: Prodigality, 6 percent of the world's people consuming 40 percent of the world's means of subsistence. We fought and killed you to get it, now we'll fight and kill you to keep it and blow it. (Sixteen-Ounce Extra Cut with six ounces for the garbage can.) (Every man, woman, and child in the world has to spend forty dollars a year for war—in peacetime—and every third one of them has exactly that much annual income.) (*There's a nice little place on East Fiftieth where you can get the drinks, steak, wine, the works for twenty-five bucks for two.*)

Skeleton Three: Gnosticism—i.e., not gnosticism but intellectualism—i.e., not intellectualism but science—i.e., not science but mechanics. Knowledge is power, and all you have to do now is apply the power to your purposes, and if knowledge doesn't give you your purposes, what does—superstition?

This was the bag, and nothing else in it any more: chauvinism blind and deaf, the sixteen-ounce steak, and machinery to be machined by. You either bought the bag or you didn't. Ma and Pa bought the bag, with, perhaps, carefully reserved mental reservations about chauvinism. (*Go ahead and take the oath; it doesn't mean anything.*)

"There must not be another war," said President Harry Truman on August 6, 1945. But on June 20, 1950, he found he had time for just one more—a quick one for the road. The Korean fiasco—all defeats are fiascos—was a Bad Thing for the Country, and a few patriotic old meatballs protested it. In vain, of course. Besides being bad, it was hopeless. Its hit-and-run wilderness defused the City-

Buster Bomb and set the stage for the hard-way extinction of the world's non-Caucasians, guerrillas all, in everlasting war. Korea bolted peacetime conscription—and "peacetime"—in place for all wartime. It put the economy on a shoot-the-works binge from here on in and the polity on an irrepealable broomstick binge called Mc-Carthyism. It completed the conversion of bayonet/belly society openly engaged abroad, and sooner or later at home, in racist slaughter.

This was the society that still had time, running while it read, to see the signal hoisted in the person of the *beats,* who thought they knew when they were beaten but didn't. The beatniks were the assault wave against the wall-to-wall world. More. They were the first young Americans to face the sophisticated fact that they were turned off, the first full-time conscientious apathetes. They were the first young Americans who were not going to go through the unavailing agonies of their parents to turn on. They had no issues, no protest, and no put-on. They were the dropouts unalloyed, no turn-on, no tune-in. Their slogan was "Stay Out of the Market." If you weren't going to buy the bag, San Francisco (where else?) was your supermarket, where cleanliness was next to godlessness.

The beats were not trying to tell us something; they were telling us without trying. They were telling us that work meant clubbing yourself to death while you clubbed your fellow man from the ladder. They had all been born halfway up themselves, white, whitewashed, and ticketed for the Commuter Special with a bar car at both ends. Why kill yourself working for an elegant San Francisco woman, or for a rung on the ladder from which you fell with a coronary, or for a rosette to wear in the lapel of the suit you'd be buried in? Why—as the first Quakers asked—the lapel anyway?

Why kill yourself?

The question was the forerunner of the hippies' Why kill anybody?

The beats were the first Un-Americans since the Navajos.

They excavated the un-American guitar. They wore un-American Levis because Levis were un-American cheap (and they didn't cut fringes in the cuffs). They sat (an un-American Activity) in their un-American coffeehouses. They talked un-American talk about books and wrote a few. They played the most un-American of Games People Don't Play: chess. They lay low, in their coffeehouses, on a cup of coffee (which they didn't finish) instead of getting high on the American sauce. They didn't go near the Big American PX; they were the enemies of the American President, who said (he actually said it), "Buy—buy *anything.*" They didn't sell their labor to the highest bidder; they were the enemies of the American Adam Smith. They didn't sell their labor; they were the enemies of the American Karl Marx. They didn't live off their American folks; they were the enemies of the Remittance Children who would one day draw their allowance at the American *poste restante* on the condition that they stay away. They were what Alexander II called the French: the enemies of mankind. They did what the American sociologists are required by Canon Law to call opt out.

Nobody in America paid any attention to them, and nobody outside North Beach in San Francisco ever saw them.

Between Korea and Vietnam came the civil-rights kick—last call to American reformism. Mistaking it for another Un-American Activity, the beats began to be seduced by it, and that was their finish. Instead of sitting in their own coffeehouses, they took to sitting-in in their elders' in San Francisco—the Palace Hotel, the Cadillac showroom—and being dragged out and to jail and sat there. But while they were sitting there, all un-American, civil rights became the All-American In thing, germinated by the terror that surfaced when three young Negroes—they weren't blacks yet—sat at the counter of a white lunchroom in Greensboro, North Carolina, and sang a slave song about not being moved and another slave song about overcoming. Three white civil-rights workers—vestigial representatives of the radical trace that lay between the Group C liberals and the Group X sports—murdered by the sheriffs in Mississippi. *Lyndon Johnson was a civil rightist.* (Remember Franklin Roosevelt's asking Secretary of the Navy Knox, on Walter White's instigation, why the Navy could not use a few Negro bandsmen since Negroes were musical and Mr. White thought they shouldn't all be messboys?) *Pearl Mesta had a Nigra home to dinner.* The bag again.

The beats drifted out of the civil-rights movement and off into the sunset. They had served their turn. Too tardily to recover their stance, they saw themselves co-opted—the word had not been minted yet—by the consuming compulsion of everybody on the sinking ship to keep the ship on an even keel; if you wanted to keep first class from capsizing, you had to keep steerage from capsizing. Let it sink. The beats departed the scene belatedly *hep* and leaving behind them a hurricane heritage: The hippies were on their way to being born.

Vietnam, of course, tore it, unfurling the *white* man's slogan: "Burn, baby, burn." To a few more patriotic old meatballs Vietnam was a Very Bad Thing for the Country. Loving their country—patriots that they were—they protested it in their patriotic conformist-reformist way, and a few more Senators than had cried "No more

Koreas" while they voted the appropriations cried "No more Viet-nams" while they voted the appropriations (and a few more than had cried "No more Vietnams" would cry "No more Cambodias" while they voted the appropriations). All in vain, of course; or was it, this time? Vietnam was the end of meatballism, the bottom of the bag.

The beats hadn't seen all the way to the bottom; they had thought to do their nothing in a world that went on and on around them, to survive soundlessly in the cracks of its sidewalks. In their no-handed way they were the last chance to revivify the True Belief That Made America Great. They were willing—if no more than that—to let the Golden Gate stay hinged. They smelled the flowers and strolled the pavements and threw neither. They listened to music and played a little of it and composed no cacophony. They also served who only sat and waited. *Requiescant in Bello*. Korea spawned them—but Korea was a never-again. Vietnam, ever-again, spawned the hippies full-blown from the unwrinkled brow of Pandora.

The beatniks were walkaways; the hippies were runaways. They spurned the whole big bursting bag from bottom to top—the con-formist bag, the reformist bag, the liblab bag, the radical bag, the Students for Any Kind of Society and the Americans for Any Kind of Action. They weren't anarchists or nihilists or Socialists or Com-munists—except in J. Edgar Hoover's Desperado Book. They weren't dissenting or protesting or demonstrating. *Cool it* ultimately expanded to *Cool it, man*. Unanimated unagitators, leaning against the walls of the Hashbury and slowly slumping to the sidewalk and staying there where the inaction was. *We live where we are*—with no visible sign of life or invisible means of support, while Khrushchev decayed them (à la Sergeant Harrington) with dental decay, hoof-and-mouth dis-ease, the running sores of antiquity, and the new In contactual afflic-tions of mononucleosis (for a season) or hepatitic jaundice (for all seasons)—going softly, softly, softly to seed, and dig those decibels, man.

The teenies came tumbling into the Hashbury to go on a diet of dalliance. The San Francisco Tours were loaded with Peorians look-ing at (and sometimes for) them and life was an all-day every-day parade up and down the street. The hippies loved being looked at, didn't they? Or could it just be that they were screaming unbloody unmurder for a chocky in front of Let's-Stop-at-Joseph's and were going, if ever the chrysalis cracked, to compel Peoria to do something more than just look at them?

What did we do, what did we do, to gather such thorns from such pink roses, such thistles from such blue figs? By the time they were ten they had sunk their second teeth into us. Instead of beating them lightly and sending them to the salt mines to earn their own dime for the movie, we had bought their sulks and their pets, celebrated their birthdays instead of the saints' and the martyrs', and took them on bum trips of our own so that they could be acclimated to the diamond-is-forever degradation of the Consumer. Hippieism was their temper tantrum when they were too old to cry and too prematurely tired to laugh. Its motivation was to do unto us what we had done unto them and drive us, like them, wild. Hear ye—too late now to hear ye and heed—Mr. John J. Thompson, the twenty-two-year-old teenager credited with the original Dirty Word outbreak in Berkeley: "I was trying to arouse adults to the fact that a four-letter word like 'kill' is respectable and mine isn't."

When you asked them what they wanted, or what they wanted to do, they answered and answered serenely (as they did everything). (The glass-eyed stare of insolent incomprehension wasn't seen outside the black ghetto until 1968.) They said they wanted to *find themselves,* and you recalled that when you were a teenager (at sixteen, not twenty-twoteen) you too were red hot to find yourself, and you never did. Grandma and Grandpa said that what you were doing was looking for trouble. They'd found it, and you'd find it, too. The hippies wanted to find themselves, but they didn't go to Mississippi, or Harlem, or Watts to do it, or to Head Start or Hind Most or the Peace Corps. They didn't, in their stillborn vernacular, *go to the opera.* They went to the wall, leaned against it, and slid down on to the sidewalk and sat.

They didn't care. Oh, but they did. They cared for Careless Love. But what they appeared to love was themselves alone and their pleasuring, so that it was hard to tell their love from an alley cat's. They were hung up on the theological error of angelism: They could not face the hard-rock reality of conflict, in others or in themselves. But it was there—they wouldn't have become hippies if they weren't mad at somebody—and their passive hostility came smiling through. It proceeded by provocation, by bugging. They turned up their Hare Krishna until it brought the cops. They went gliding down to the Embarcadero, where their regalia got them beaten up by sailors; one way or another they found a way to get themselves stoned. Their consciousness that they were able to bug the straights swelled their paranoia: They were *hated*—they who *loved.*

But love is said to find itself by not seeking its own, and love is said to be the fruit of suffering, never ripened, never ready—not merely wanting, but willing, the good of the other. Up and down the

Hashbury the listless lovers went, their ankle bells tinkling to notify some shepherd somewhere that he had a ready-made flock. They held their kittens to them; happiness was a warm kitten, a cuddle a commune. A commune not of lovers but of fun-lovers, like Palm Beach, the Tuileries, and the Winter Palace. Outside the commune were the ashes of their fathers and the temples of their gods. Outside were Harlem and Watts and Vietnam. Outside was man killing and being killed and killing himself; death was the straights' bag, life and love had been abandoned to the Hashbury. Their jewelry included all kinds of icon, but never, ever, a representation of that put-down, the Passion.

But Christianity without the Cross was not the invention of the hippies. It was the invention of the Church Triumphant, perverting grace to gratification and reason to the reasonable. The hippies, too, turned upon grace and reason, taking the perversion for the pure and, all unknowing, buying the bag of the Church Triumphant. What hippieism didn't know (and so its subsidence and substitution were inevitable) is that escape from escapism is a viscous, as well as a vicious, circle.

Buddhist *nonattachment*—without, of course, the self-denial—was *It,* man. They carried those old Buddhists, Tolkien, Hesse, and Kierkegaard, around with them and read the *Zap* comic books, which were shorter and sweeter; unlike the Buddha, and like their own parents turning the dial from station to station, they had no attention span sober. So they smoked their wild oats, sowed their sperm and their sores, spun their bright cobwebs, and grunted their primordial idiom. A *religious* movement—a kind of Immobilized for Christ. Uninvolvement—can't you see Christ uninvolved, man? Until you found yourself you could not be involved. Involvement conceals existence. Becoming stunts being, and what the straights take for being is nothing but becoming. *Be* by letting your consciousness expand and letting go of your hangups. Leave the sordid static of tribulation and despair behind you. Find yourself.

The straights wagged their hard heads: Life finds you and nails you to it. Harlem and Watts and Vietnam find you. The landlord finds you. The electric-light company finds you. The garageman finds you. The insurance company's due date finds you. The publican finds you on April 15. The rheumatiz finds you, and all its relatives find you. The doctor finds you and finds you and finds you. The Grin Reaper finds you, grinning. Monday morning finds you. There was no Monday morning in the Hashbury. Monday morning was the Lost Weekday. (*La vida es sueño.*)

I knew some of these pre-revolutionary transfiguration pushers fairly intimately, and I still do. They were going to be changed or filled full of fulfillment. After two or three years of acid rock, or two or three years of graduation from it, they were just about what they were two or three years, or six, or ten or fifteen, before that. A little less bounce. A little less lovely for the premature wear and tear. A little less hopeful of making it that way—and two or three, or six, or ten or fifteen years less hopeful of making it any other. A little—older. The quick-change artist—look, Mom, no crucible—had yet to produce the quick change for the better or for the worse. The psyche-delic lighting had yet to produce the blinding flash of the road to Damascus.

Those slow-change-for-the worse artists, the old folks, kept telling themselves that it wouldn't last—and they were right, and still are, about that. It wouldn't last, not as it was, because there is no such thing as quick change or free love or happiness on the cheap, no going up high without coming down low, no getting more out of life (or less out of death) than there's in it, no chemical compound to retard human spoilage, and not even an unsure cure for the mortal affliction of Adam. The right answer is still Yes to the question "Is this all there is to it?"

The hippies weren't doing anybody any good, including them-selves—which, however, was more than you could say for their elders. But they weren't doing anybody any harm except themselves. All they had to do to do good was do what that good old togetherness chump, old Dad, wouldn't do. All they had not to do to do harm was what Dad was doing. What Dad was doing did more harm than good, and what he wouldn't do would do more good than harm. *Quod erat.* Hippieism wouldn't endure. It wouldn't endure because of its inner contradictions—between detachment and dope, for instance. It wouldn't endure because of its fluid fallout of summertime soldiers. It wouldn't endure because of its careless corelessness. But many—if far from all—of its votaries were the most sensitive and flexible and talented members of their generation. If the mode of the Hashbury wouldn't spread indefinitely, what it represented would. The sensi-bility, the flexibility, and the talents were there—there, if anywhere, and nowhere else. In some new, perhaps even less presentable, mani-festation, what it represented would not go away, not as long as what evoked it was still there, still evoking it.

In three years the Hashbury was deserted.

At last it's over.

Alas it was beginning.

It hadn't disappeared, only dispersed its armies to establish its colonies. It hadn't burned itself out, but metastasized. The whole country, and so the whole world, was the Hashbury now, in its variorum visitations adapted to local conditions (including even the young Czechs' singular support of the short-lived Dubček Establishment in Prague in early 1968).

Metastasized—and metamorphosized. Hippieism, too, had served its turn, like the beatniks. Its essentials—the hair, the feet, the rock, the dope, and the rags—would survive as the incidentals of Whatever-Would-Happen-Next: its uniform, its flag, and its password. But the serenity was done with. The infantilism of dropping dynamite would succeed the childishness of dropping acid. In the counter-revolutionary country—the capital of the counter-revolutionary world—revolution. Not yet, and not yet that spectacular. Pre-revolution. Deployment and maneuver. Harder words and harder hardware. "Incidents." Control slipping away, and contact breaking. "Polarization." Lenin's ho-hum objective conditions and Marx's equally ho-hum inevitability: It isn't necessary to want to make a revolution in order to make one.

Nineteen sixty-eight begins. It begins in Paris. It begins in Prague, Tokyo, Berlin, Rome. It begins in the black ghettos of America, where "there's going to be trouble this summer." Nineteen hundred sixty-eight begins, and the CBS panjandrum concludes his Big Report on the hippies with "Granted the shortcomings of our society. Nevertheless . . . " Oh, grant the shortcomings of our society quick, and get on to the nevertheless. Tell us about the horrors of idleness and bathlessness and truancy and sex and the serpent's tooth. Tell us about the horrors of LSD; we already know more than we want to know about the horrors of ABM and LBJ and RMN. Tell us about the Panthers and the crime in the streets, and sing us no song of Songmy. No credit to the hippies, then, or to the beatniks before them. All credit to us: Mom and Dad. We are the measure of all their things, the White Men who taught the Indians to scalp. We are the tear gas, the clubs, the buckshot, and the grave they rejected us for. We are the Careless Lovelessness that took the Rubberneck Tour to look at the prettiless practitioners of Careless Love.

My baby, my baby, what did we do, what did we do? Where were we going? Out. What were we doing? Nothing. We were the labor saved by the labor-saving device, with nothing to do but go out and do it. We were the generation that fertilized the eggs of the cockatrice in elegant San Francisco. We were the hellers who begot the children of hell.

"While we sleep," said Pope Innocent II of the Children's Crusade, "they go forth to conquer the Holy Land." Not yet; it was not yet the summer of 1968, and while we screamed *My baby!* in our pink-and-blue nightmare turned daymare the Flower Pot Children dreamed of never having left the Holy Land and never having to reconquer it. They took to the streets—"the paving-stones," said Lenin, "are the artillery of the revolution"—and lay down in them. They took their dime, which they got from the profligate society to stay away or go away, and put it in the parking meter and went to sleep in one piece of street they rented from one city for one hour, and curled up in the beautiful, man, dream of being among the few lucky Americans who were lucky enough never to have been born. Harmlessly spreading their venery among themselves,* they were the end of the harmless line. But it was our line they were the end of.

In the summer of 1968 they would suddenly be lions in the street, and the Rubberneck Tours and Tourists would be barricaded back in the barn. In the summer of 1968 you wouldn't know them.

But they would know you, in the summer of 1968, and their slow bacchanalia of a few years, a few months, before would have been an insouciant interlude. Group X would inherit the tortured earth and bring the war home to the warriors.

* "The free clinic in San Francisco's Haight-Ashbury district had just under ten thousand visits June 9–September 5, 1967. Its unpaid doctors were amazed, not at the incidence of gonorrhea (up fourfold in five years) but at the prevalence of caries and malnutrition and the universal susceptibility to upper respiratory infections."—*The Progressive, loc. cit.,* October 1967.

10: "What Do They *Want?*"

THE DIFFERENCE between my children—it is yours I'm talking about, of course, not mine—and me is that I accepted the precepts of my parents (and they were the same precepts my parents had accepted from theirs) while mine reject them. I violated the precepts, of course. But I accepted them. I was wrong and my children were right. The precepts were good precepts, but still my children were right and I was wrong. They were right and I was wrong because preceptorial is as preceptorial does. I was (and, of course, am) a pious fraud. My children are impious Abelards, though they have not read any books and do not know who Abelard was.

Their rejection of the precepts is the great discontinuity in an age whose hallmark is discontinuity in practice and continuity in pretense. The Wild Flower Children are on a berserk search for the orthodoxy pulled out from under them with the substitution of reason for faith and rationalization for reason; never in all the world, and not in the Crusades, have so many men had such good reasons *and* such good rationalization for doing such bad things as now. Humanity followed orthodoxy into the discard, not in one generation but in no more than two or three; for men who embrace the illusion that they are cunning enough to govern themselves soon embrace the delusion that they are cunning enough to govern others, and then they are devils.

The devil is a wretched devil, for he was once an angel in enjoyment of the beatific vision and his racial memory torments him; the torment makes him worse than he would be if his memory had failed him. A poor devil, the devil, condemned to the company of his kind in the society of hell, and since his companions are all of his kind each of them takes the foremost if he can; and so each of them is always alone.

With the fires of hell burning all about us, we ought to know by now where, if not what, we are. But that would be too much to bear, and we must live by self-deceit or choose suicide and *its* risks. The self-deceit is the keystone of the arch of this world. It is our law and order. Without it, we are lost. But with it, too, for see where we are and, in our nightmare turned daymare, who.

Man is a social devil who has sacrificed his sociality to the lostness of fuck-you-Jack-*I'm*-all-right. A personal devil who has sacrificed his personality in the pressure cooker of conformity. And an individual devil who has sacrificed his individuality to a system that prates individuality and cannibalizes it. He is alone, alone and lonely, without even himself for company but only the identical maskharah that is the only mask worn in hell.

His secrecy is the sanctimonium of his private hell: how much he makes, how much he has, how much he gives, how much he takes, how much he spends. His Holy of Holies is his Income Tax Return. Broken into, thrown open, it would leave him bare to his enemies, and all devils are his enemies. He clutches his take-home pay to his breast and takes it home alone to spend it, to save it, to invest it, to cherish it until death do him part. Communism has a thousand horrors, but only one of them unbearable: his neighbor would know *where he stood;* and capitalism has a thousand blessings, but only one of them indispensable: his neighbor does not know *where he stands.* His reward—remember the director of the Stanford Research Institute?—is his money; his punishment, another man's. He eats his own heart out.

This is the hell beneath all the hells and the ignition of all the fires. This is why wise children would never grow up. This unopenness, this aloneness, this secret sanctimonium that insulates every man from every other, and each from all, this is what drags men deeper and deeper down into hell when they grow up and grow old and find themselves constrained to surrender their every magnanimous impulse to it. This is what the Youth Revolution is about, if it is a revolution; if it is about anything else, it is only a conniption. If it is a revolution, it is a revolution against materialism, all materialism. It is a revolution that only feckless children are capable of making—and they are lost if they do what e.e. cummings calls up-grow and down-forget.

The revolution is overdue—the revolution that Jeremiah and Jefferson evoked when they said that God's justice will not sleep forever. The social evils that were containable under kings are not containable under politicians. A world that spends more on war—in peacetime—than it does on health and education combined is not susceptible of reform. It cries for revolution. But revolution is not the same thing as conniption. The aftermath of the Russian Revolution instructs us that revolution is not a matter of systems but of men: as the men are, so will the revolution be. If the Youth Revolution goes forward, and is not to be a conniption, which would hardly be worth while, the one thing the young must not do is up-grow and down-forget.

The issues are not negotiable. There is no negotiating a little more or less overkill. There is no negotiating a little more or less ghetto or a little more or less nerve-gas research or a little more or less CIA or a little more or less racism. A world which elevates Johnsons and Nixons to power—or Brezhnevs or Dayans or Yahyas—has no intention to negotiate. It will pay lip service to negotiation, provided that the shape of the table is right, as long as it does not have to stop doing the only thing it knows how to do. When it is confronted with stopping doing the only thing it knows how to do, it drops the pretense of negotiation and proceeds to the only thing it knows how to do after that—namely, make its nonnegotiable demands in the form of war. The United States of America had three hundred years to clean house on the basis of negotiable demands by its Negro populace; and so, incidentally, did Harvard University.

The cunning old devil is wretched and lonely, but he has his pristine cunning. If he is persistently, but subserviently, pushed, he will propose gradualism, or gradual withdrawal, by which he means gradually wearing down his victims or, at the very worst, waiting them out until they up-grow and down-forget. He isn't wicked—only unconcerned. And his unconcern is not immoral—only unintelligent. He is possessed by power and, like all its servitors, decorticated by it. He cannot understand that he who takes the sword will perish by it. He cannot understand we are all members of one another. He cannot understand that the greater damnation awaits those who devour widows' houses and make long prayer for a pretense. He didn't mean to be like this—he only wanted the kingdoms of this world. By power possessed, he is by power benighted, and he walks in the noonday as in the night. There is no negotiating with him.

He will come out with his cunning from beneath the false bottom of his bag and observe—he who has torn down the world and put hell in its place—that the revolutionaries want to tear everything down without having anything to put in its place. The blueprint bag.

The revolutionaries do not need to have anything to put in the place of hell, and those who have had (or thought they had) have all lived (if they survived) to learn that the way it turned out was not the way it was blueprinted. It is easy to think up the right thing. What is hard is to stop doing the wrong one. The Lord God Jehovah did not ask his people what they would put in the place of Sidon and Tyre; he asked them to walk in his path and he would show them his way. He did not tell them to do good. He told them, "Cease to do evil—*learn to do good.*"

Rejection, then, would appear to be enough in Sidon and Tyre. When the Viceroy was trying to persuade Mohandas Gandhi to support the British Empire in its war against Japan, he asked the Mahatma what he would do if the British were defeated and the Japanese attacked India. "They," said the Viceroy, "will be much worse than we are, y'know." And the childish Mahatma grinned his childish grin and said, "Yes, of course, you are right, but first we must find out a way to get rid of you and in doing so we may come upon a way to keep the Japanese out."

The revolutionaries need only to say No to be unanswerable; their unanswerable No is Yes enough. They need only say No to the anachronistic idolatry of the state, No to the hard-hatted heartlessness of the police state, No to the killer state which will not let its young live without killing, No to the anti-Communist state whose only admission ticket is anti-Communism. They need only say No to the straight-faced two-faced dumbo dominion of public and private life by secrecy and falsehood and pap, and the contemptuous insult of whiskey-drinking Attorneys General who ask, "Why should we legalize marijuana when it has no redeeming value?" * The revolutionaries need only to be implacable and unappeasable to be unanswerable if, in laying their charges and charging right on, they are right.

And they are right.

They are unappeasable, undisciplinable, unpleasant, unamusing, unwholesome, unmannerly, uninstructable, irreverent, irresponsible, intractable, and inattentive. And right.

They are wrong, too; but their wrongs are all ours. They are wrong to spurn what Spiro Agnew calls the enduring values. Common honesty and industry, rainy-day thrift, the preservation of proper property (I lock up my fiddle and my annotated books against them), the respect for the authority of excellence (and the cultivation of its recognition), self-denial, restraint, reserve (in thought and feeling, and not

* United States Attorney General John Mitchell, quoted in *Newsweek*, September 7, 1970.

just in language), piety, filial piety, solitude, study, sanitation as a bulwark of public no less than private health—these are enduring values, even though Spiro Agnew says they are.

They are wrong to spurn the rituals feebly designed by all experience to strengthen the feeble bonds of feeble creatures. They are wrong—as wrong as Reno—to spurn the romanticism of *einmaliges,* once-only, courtship and compact not simply to sleep together young but to die together old, tottering down the hill t'gither, John Anderson me Joe. They are wrong—as wrong as *Playboy*—to leave nothing of sex to the imagination and thus starve the imagination. They are wrong—as wrong as Peyton Place—to seize the day of tumescence, which is soon over, and spurn the days of diminishment, which are long. Wrong, all wrong; but where they are wrong they are the flowers of our seed; and only where they are right, illegitimate.

But these may be peccadilloes. The pitfall is their adulation of a transient condition—youth—and their self-segregation on the basis of that condition. On the one hand, they represent the arrogance with which twentieth-century man separated himself from his past and thought (with the inexorable disaster that now appears) to go it on his own; the world will end with those who think it began with them. On the other hand, their rejection of their elders *qua* elders represents the infantile anger of the infant denied (and sometimes properly denied) the chocky in front of Let's-Stop-at-Joseph's. There are people under thirty, and under twenty, and under ten, who are not to be trusted to be reflective and to reflect on the whole of human experience; and there is an occasional *ancien* of forty, or fifty, or even of seventy or eighty, who has not sold out and who knows something the young do not of the why, and the wherefore, and the way in which men live.

Separatism is not revolution, and it puts its adherents in a peculiarly exposed position. Their case—like that of the separate sovereign state, and like that of the American black separatist—rests upon their superior capacity to inflict unendurable pain upon not only their oppressors but their nonseparatist sympathizers, a capacity from which so many of the young so admirably shrink—unless they mean only to leave the world behind them and leave the world as it is. Their alternatives are civil war (which, apart from its other inconveniences, they are likely to lose) or emigration.

The resurgence of the communitarian experiment is a form of inner emigration which is peculiarly hard to practice, peculiarly inappropriate to adolescence, and peculiarly unpromising in terms of the record. The communes which flourished in America (and only in

America) from the end of the eighteenth century to the end of the nineteenth were mostly (and of those that survived above a few years, all) established by outward emigrants from central and northern Europe, *come-outers* (or dropouts) from the state-church which punished their deviations much more fiercely than the secular republic punishes its deviants. The New World, which is now the heartland of the Old, offered them (and even it within limits) the liberty not of easy conscience but of the thorny conscience of the Apostolate.

The come-outers of old had known hardship. They had known persecution. They had known (and still knew) commitment. They were phenomenally single-minded, satisfied that they had found themselves and bent only upon finding God's will and doing it. Their communities were "composed of what are customarily called 'common people.' You look in vain for highly educated, refined, cultivated, or elegant men or women. They profess no exalted views of humanity or destiny; they are not enthusiasts; they do not speak much of the Beautiful with a big B. They are utilitarians. Some do not even like flowers; some reject instrumental music. They build solidly, often of stone; but they care nothing for architectural effects. Art is not known among them; mere beauty and grace are undervalued, even despised. Amusements, too, they do not value; only a few communes have general libraries, and even these are of very limited extent. . . . In the beginning, the members of a commune must expect to work hard; and, to be successful, they ought always to retain the frugal habits, the early hours, and the patient industry and contentment with manual labor which belong to what we call the working class. Men cannot play at communism. It is not amateur work. It requires patience, submission; self-sacrifice, often in little matters where self-sacrifice is peculiarly irksome; faith in a leader; pleasure in plain living and healthful hours and occupations." *

Unrelenting pietism was combined with a rigid sexual code, always depreciating sexuality and extending, in some notable instances, to celibacy and an elaborate emphasis on plainness—that is, sexual non-attractiveness—of the women in their dress and their conduct. (In Shakerism and a few of the other societies the prohibition of physical contact extended to the use of separate doorways and staircases for the two sexes.) Fanatical cleanliness and equally fanatical economy, industry, sobriety, and abstemiousness ranging from the mealtime use (and production) of wine and beer among the German immigrants to total abstention from tobacco, even from coffee and tea in some cases—the pattern suggests the antithesis of the youth commune of

* Charles Nordhoff, *The Communistic Societies of the United States,* New York, 1875, pp. 385 ff.

today. But in some respects the two movements are remarkably alike: community of property, including the common obligation to manual labor (nearly all the members of the old communities were manual laborers anyway, either farmers or mechanics); simplicity of living arrangements and furnishings (reducing the chores of the common household to a minimum); production of as many as possible of their necessities, including not only wholesomely grown foods, but clothing, shoes, and even construction materials; disdain not for worship but for its "outward" forms, and emphasis on contemplation and the creation of their own liturgies.

The most notable, and surely the most significant, resemblance of all is in respect to the privacy of personal life. The classic commune was a family—and was often called a family—in which universal openness was insisted upon and separate attachments derogated. The new commune has a much harder time on this head, because of its permissive pairing, but in its claim upon openness and its disparagement of secrecy it is not at all unlike the old. The classic commune did not use terms like *sensitivity session* or *confrontation*, but the practice was as central to the associations as it is to today's. Some of them required full confession—and called it that, though none of the communes of the American past was Roman in derivation—sometimes to the elders, sometimes to the whole community. Even more significant was the common system of mutual criticism. "This system takes the place of backbiting in ordinary society, and is regarded as one of the greatest means of improvement and fellowship. All of the members are accustomed to voluntarily invite the benefit of this ordinance from time to time. Sometimes persons are criticized by the entire family; at other times by a committee of six, eight, twelve, or more, selected by themselves from among those best acquainted with them, and best able to do justice to their character. In these criticisms the most perfect sincerity is expected; and in practical experience it has been found best for the subject to receive his criticism without replying. . . . It is always acceptable to those who wish to see themselves as others see them." *

The communards of a hundred or a hundred and fifty years ago, though they entrusted the whole conduct of their worldly affairs to the founder or his designates as heirs or elders, were accustomed, like those of the new movement, to full discussion of the community's problems in meetings which occurred, again like those of the present, as often as every evening—though their meetings began and ended more sedately than now, and much earlier, since the members of the

* John Humphrey Noyes, founder of the Oneida Communists or "Perfectionists" (as they called themselves), quoted in Nordhoff, *op. cit.*, p. 298.

family rose at dawn and spent the day almost entirely in physical exertion. But their physical exertion, like that of the modern young, was not frenetic. Content to "get ahead slowly" and to get ahead together, they were unconsumed by the competitive maintenance of private establishments and duplicate services. Always industrious (as their modern variants may not be), they nevertheless had (like the modern communes) abundant leisure for their common concerns.

Unlike today's experimenters, they were largely without taste or talent or easy conscience for diversion—unless their singing of hymns, and, in some societies, their formal, and noncontactual, dance patterns may be called diversions; but, like today's communards, they spent much of their leisure time *rapping* (as it wasn't called) and rapping, in their own idiom, about the matters that preoccupy many of the modern communitarians: the conditions of community, of personal (not then known as interpersonal) relationships within it, and the way to salvation here and hereafter. Unlike most of the moderns, they were poorly educated, but, like them, very little given to reading. Their libraries were, on the whole, of no consequence at all, consisting sometimes of very little more than the Bible and Bible tracts.

So self-centered were they in their world that they spurned the specific social issues of their time—the relevant issues, as the young activists would call them now—as irrelevant. They were most of them religious pacifists (as most of the today's communards are irreligious or nonreligious pacifists), but, unlike today's young, they were proud of paying their taxes and of meeting the few obligations the outer world of their time laid upon all its denizens. They opposed slavery— even the hiring of servants, in nearly every case—and some of them (notably the Shakers) were racially integrated, in contrast to the lily-white and, apparently, unconcerned commune today. The charge may be leveled as justly against the old as against the new separatists that they denied the wholeness of humanity and their responsibility for its sorrow and suffering, that they turned away from the needs of the halt, the lame, and the blind, the brutal, the stupid, the unloving, the deteriorated, and the lost of the world. The charge, if it can be made to stand against separatism, perhaps weighs heavier against the old movement than it does against the new, for unconcern is (or should be) characteristic of the very young anywhere, any time. If it is self-love that animates the Youth Movement, in both its activist and retreatist branches, the movement as a whole, like that of the early communes, may stand gently condemned as a violator of its precept of love, stand condemned of being (in the idiom of that older day) respecters of persons.

Men cannot play at communism. However deadly earnest the old come-outers were, they were unflaggingly earnest. But they were not young enthusiasts. They were settled—even in their twenties, and most of them came into the movement in their thirties and forties—in stern middle age. But youth (all the younger for being diapered beyond the age of indiscretion) must be expected to be playful. Whoever has had the opportunity of seeing the youth commune close up, and at its best, cannot escape the conclusion that its members are, appropriately to the special situation of the American adolescent, playing in some measure hooky, in some measure tree-house, and in some measure blind man's buff; and these words, which are, of course, taken for hard, have to be said, and have been, by observers whose only reason for being put on the movement's Ten Most Unwanted Men list is their having lived into their thirty-first year. In some respects the new communes are, at their best, quite literally marvelous; their success in curing hard-drug addiction is commonly attested where the most sophisticated treatment "outside" so characteristically fails. But in others the well-wishing observer's uneasiness persists. A high proportion of their members (if so formal a term may be used) convey the impression of being away from home for a while. They seem to be camping for a season—a summer season—in the woods, living (rather than building) where they are—and the transience of their membership much more often than not reflects an openheartedness to their chronological coevals that must in the nature of the case be disruptive; people who drift casually together drift casually apart.

The traditional commune combined (a combination that works out better in practice than it does in theory) its permanence of commitment and construction, as consciously concerned with continuity as any royal line, with the apocalypticism that engages the Youth Movement today. Christ would come tomorrow, or tonight, or in yet another thousand years; the first order of business, today, tonight, and in yet another thousand years, was to be ready for Him. Meanwhile, in case it should be a thousand years, build the house tight and keep it tight; take that much thought for the morrow. Some seventy of the old experiments survived twenty years or more, all of them millenarian, while some fifty established by secular groups with greater funds and bent on finding the better life were all short-lived. In 1874 some 5,000 persons (including women and children) in the durable communities in thirteen states owned a total of over 150,000 rich acres with a total estimated wealth at that time of twelve million dollars.*

* Nordhoff, *op. cit.,* p. 386.

Still, today's young nay-sayers, in their eyries or out of them, may come closer to universal love than men anywhere have done in this unloving age, perhaps in any age. Their uncritical acceptance of one another—unpropitious as it is for the durability of community—is itself a revolution that appears more clearly all the time to be impossible of subversion by all the powers that power can mount. To love is first of all to accept. Lovelessness is rejection. Who, then, are the rejectors—they, or the rest of us who have grown colder and colder until our gun barrels alone are hot? They want to love. They want not to be predators. They want not to be cold, and secretive, and acquisitive, and alone. Love misbegotten. Love misconceived. Love misdirected to a salvation never to be found anywhere, any time, here below. But love. Love against lovelessness. The childish wish—not the will, only the wish—for innocent openness and open innocence, and I can imagine that only he who is old and still harbors the childish wish can appreciate them and talk to them and be listened to. (*And yet, and yet . . . there was Manson, and more than one Manson.*)

Life is hard, not for lovers, but for those who want to love and not live loveless. Life is hard for the young at the end of the twentieth century. It is arrant nonsense to close the matter by saying that life is always hard for the young; when we were young, we who are old, we knew where we were going and what would become of us. We were wrong, in the event—but then we knew. They don't. They want a world to live in, an acceptable, at least tolerable world; and they have none. They have none because there is none. If what they want is a world that never was and never will be, no matter. If the world has always been the way it is and always will be, still no matter. It shouldn't have been that way, and it shouldn't be.

Will they grow up, and grow old, and grow to be what we have grown to be? I think not: not because they wish (not will) for open innocence and for innocent openness, but because they are the first of all men, of all women, of all children who have reason to believe that they will not live to grow up, and grow old, and grow to be what we have grown to be. We in our time and place (always no worse than other men anywhere any time) find ourselves spending our spiritual substance on the Bomb, and the bigger Bomb, and the still bigger Bomb—not merely buying death wherever we can but selling it to all sides and all comers. (But selling death to all sides makes room for a still bigger Bomb in the Arsenal of Anti-Communism.) They—and I do not much enjoy their mirthless company—are alone realistic enough to face the reality of the end and to see in us the escapists. Their case is poignant, as ours is not; theirs tragic, ours only preposterous. Childish, they, but wrinkled children, the pink-and-blue babes of 1948, aged by the conscious maturity that their elders reject.

If we do not succeed in killing them off, in the pre-eminently American Way, with both guns blazing in the Land of the Free-Fire-Zone, they will win. They do not need God or the big battalions on their side; they need the actuarial table, and they have it. They have already fooled us by reproducing their kind and not their antibodies; for their generations are four or five years, not twenty or thirty, and they are always more and always more redolent of foot and revolutionary of fist. Their mortal errors—of separatism and of violence, *our* mortal errors—are not enough to undo them in the struggle, for their enemies have by those same mortal errors undone themselves, without the ability to surrender a jot or a tittle of their lovelessness. They—the young—will win. If they lose, they will still win; they and we have only to stay the same as they and we are.

They would (as John Sparrow puts it) live hippily ever after, but they do not believe they will; and they are right—deplorable, disgraceful, demerited pink-and-blue Brownies, and right. What matters if it's a put-on, or 90 percent a put-on, their heritage from the hang-dog hippies and their buttons? A man is a human being—do not fold, staple, or mutilate. A woman is a human being, not a Clairol pussy or a *Playboy* foldout or a Jackie Onassis—do not fold, staple, or mutilate. Tell them that they are bad boys and girls. They know whether they are bad boys and girls. Hinder them, hamper them, hamstring them, and harass them, and shoot them down with your Cossacks: They will keep coming.

What to do?

Therapy? Therapists? Look who's therapeutic: the sick physician unto death.

What to do?

Nothing. Out. What are we going to do? Nothing. Where are we going? Out.

Wearing—? *

By now we ought to know—but who are we to know?—that the question is not What ought we to do? but What will we do? Nothing.

Nothing but pray—if only we could remember how to pray or to

---

* "In 1968, the year we went out, Georges Kaplan, "Couturier in Fur," suggested a little something to wear. In the Sunday New York *Times* of December 1, M. Georges took a one-eighth-page ad for "the Georges Kaplan natural Russian crown sable": "It took us four years to gather them, but we now are in the position to offer what we believe to be the most expensive and the most beautiful natural Russian crown sable skins in the world. Just enough skins to make one coat, for only one woman, in time for Christmas." The price: $125,000.

whom or for what. Nothing but pray that they will *do it* and live to do it before we have got them into our sable bag. Nothing but pray that they will live, however deplorably they live, however disgracefully they live, however demeritedly they live, until they have outlived us. It is not that whatever they do they cannot be worse than what we have done, but that they cannot, given the heritage and the opportunity, do as badly.

I love them not. Lovelessly I love them not. I love them not, because their insolent feet are dirty. I love them not, because they love not the loveless. I love them not, because they are right. I love them not, because I forgive them not, and I forgive them not for their reminding me that I was young.

Index

Milton Mayer

Milton Mayer is Professor of English at the University of Massachusetts, in Amherst, and Professor of the Humanities at Windham College, in Putney, Vermont. He is also consultant to the Center for the Study of Democratic Institutions and the Great Books Foundation. Mr. Mayer's journalistic work in America and Europe (he is now roving editor of *The Progressive*) has won him the George Polk Memorial Award, the Benjamin Franklin Citation for Journalism, and other honors. He lives at Woolman Hill, the New England Quaker Center at Deerfield, Massachusetts, where he is John Woolman Resident. A representative of the American Friends Service Committee at home and abroad, he describes himself variously as "a ravening pacifist," "an unemployed newspaperman," and the "man in the Brooks Brothers hair shirt," and continues to resist military service, war taxes, and loyalty oaths.